1 MONTH OF
FREE
READING

at

www.ForgottenBooks.com

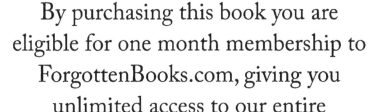

By purchasing this book you are eligible for one month membership to ForgottenBooks.com, giving you unlimited access to our entire collection of over 1,000,000 titles via our web site and mobile apps.

To claim your free month visit:

www.forgottenbooks.com/free1085362

ISBN 978-0-331-85034-5
PIBN 11085362

BIBLIOTHECA INDO-SINICA

ESSAI D'UNE BIBLIOGRAPHIE DES OUVRAGES RELATIFS A LA PRESQU'ÎLE INDO-CHINOISE

PAR

HENRI CORDIER,

Professeur à l'École des Langues Orientales vivantes, Paris.

高

Première Partie: BIRMANIE et ASSAM.

Extrait du *T'oung Pao*, Déc. 1903; Mai, Juillet 1904; Mars 1905; Mars, Mai 1906; Mai 1908.

LIBRAIRIE ET IMPRIMERIE
CI-DEVANT
E. J. BRILL.
LEIDE — 1908.

Vignaud ...ih

....
CENT EXEMPLAIRES SUR PAPIER VAN GELDER.
....

IMPRIMERIE CI-DEVANT E. J. BRILL, LEIDE.

BIBLIOGRAPHIE.

BIBLIOTHECA INDO-SINICA; *Essai d'une Bibliographie des Ouvrages relatifs à la presqu'île indo-chinoise.* — Première Partie: **BIRMANIE** et **ASSAM** [1]).

BIRMANIE.

I. — Ouvrages généraux.

1. — Nerher Dass Gossein, Fukeer, his Account of Meckley, &c. May 25th and 29th. 1763. From Mr. Orme's MSS. Vol. 17. P. 4746. (Dalrymple, *Oriental Repertory*, II, pp. 477—482.)

> The Burmah Country lies between Meckley and China.

2. — A brief Account of the Religion & civil Institutions of the Burmans; and a Description of the Kingdom of Assam, formerly Part of the Empire of Ava, under the King of Pegue, translated from the Alumgeernameh. To which is added, an Account of the Petroleum Wells, in the Burmah Dominions, Extracted from a Journal from Rangoon up the River Eraiwaddy to Amarapoorah, the present Capital of the Burmah Empire. — Calcutta, in-8, pp. 151.

> Voir page 94: Description of the Kingdom of Assam, taken from the Alemgeernameh of Mohammed Cazim, and translated by Henry Vansittart, Esq.

3. — Das Reich der Birmanen. — Ein geographischer Versuch von August Rücker. Berlin, August Rücker, 1824, in-8, pp. 71.

4. — Skizzen über Birma. Von einem englischen Subalternoffizier. [*Asiatic Journal*, Oct.] (*Das Ausland*, 1828, Nos. 309, pp. 1237—8, 310, pp. 1242—4, 311, pp. 1246—8, 360, pp. 1441—3, 363, 1453—4).

---

1) La publication de cette bibliographie ne devait commencer que dans trois ou quatre années, après l'impression de la deuxième édition de la *Bibliotheca Sinica* dont le premier demi-volume doit paraître en Janvier 1904. Si je l'entreprends à présent c'est à la demande d'un certain nombre de savants qui ont besoin d'un guide pour se reconnaître au milieu de la masse de livres et d'articles qui traitent de l'Indo-Chine; il y a donc dans ce travail des lacunes et sans doute des erreurs que je serai reconnaissant à mes lecteurs de vouloir bien me signaler.

5. — A Description of the Burmese Empire, compiled chiefly from native documents by the Rev. Father Sangermano, and translated from his MS. By William Tandy D.D. Member of the Roman subcommittee. Rome: Printed for the Oriental Translation Fund of Great Britain and Ireland. Sold by John Murray... M.DCCC.XXXIII, in-4, pp. vi + 1 f. n. c. p. l'ind. + pp. 224.

> Le ms. italien de cet ouvrage était resté entre les mains des Barnabites après la mort de Sangermano en 1819. L'ouvrage comprend 24 chap. répartis en cinq grandes divisions: Description of the Burmese Empire. Burmese Cosmography. — Constitution of the Burmese Empire. — Religion of the Burmese. — Moral and Physical Constitution of the Burmese Empire. — Burmese Code.

6. — The Burmese Empire a hundred years ago as described by Father Sangermano. With an Introduction and Notes by John Jardine Judge of Her Majesty's High Court of Judicature at Bombay, late judicial Commissioner of British Burma, and President of the Educational Syndicate of British Burma: and sometime Dean of the Faculty of Arts in the University of Bombay. Westminster, Archibald Constable and Co., MDCCCXCIII, in-8, pp. xxxix—311.

> Notice: *Journ. Roy. Asiatic Society*, Oct. 1893, pp. 901—902, by R. F. St. A. St. John.

7. — Burmah: — its Situation, Extent, Population, Productions and Trade: Manners and Customs of the People; their Language, — and those of the Peguans and Karens, Education, Books, &c. By Benevolens. (*Chinese Rep.*, II, 1834, pp. 500—506, 554—563; III, 1835, pp. 89—95.

> By J. T. Jones.

8. — An Account of the Burman Empire, and the Kingdom of Assam; Compiled from the Works and M.S. Documents of the following most eminent Authors and Public Functionaries, viz. Hamilton, Symes, Canning, Cox, Leyden, F. Buchanan, Morgan, Towers, Elmore, Wade, Turner, Sisson, Elliot, &c., &c. Calcutta: Printed for the publisher, 1839. in-8, pp. 155 + 2 ff. prél. p. l. tit. et la tab.

9. — An Account of the Burman Empire compiled from the works of Colonel Symes, Major Canning, Captain Cox, Dr. Leyden, Dr. Buchanan, &c. &c. &c.; a description of different tribes inhabiting in and around that dominion; and a narrative of the late military and political operations in the Burmese empire, with some account of the present condition of the country, its manners, customs and inhabitants. By Henry G. Bell, Esq. With a coloured map. Calcutta: Printed for the publisher by D'Rozario and Co. 1852, in-8, pp. 87 + 3 ff. prél. p. l. tit. &c.

> C'est une nouvelle éd. de l'ouvrage de 1839.

10. — Etat actuel de l'Empire Birman. Par Jos. Smith. (*Asiatic Journal.* — Avril 1841.) (*Nouvelles Annales des Voyages*, II, 1841, pp. 208—235.)
> Signé T. C.

11. — L'Empire Barman d'après les Sources anglaises. Par Léon de Rosny. (*Rev. Or. et Am.*, T. II, 1859, pp. 333—342; III, 1860, pp. 201—211).

12. — L'empire Birman. Par Thomas Anquetil. (*Le Monde*, 15, 20, 21, 23 Août 1867).

13. — Burmah. Aus den nachgelassenen Papieren des in Rangoon verstorbenen Kaiserl. Consul Chr. Deetjen. (*Zeit. d. G. f. Erdk.*, IX, 1874, pp. 133—151).

14. — Upper Burmah. By E. H. Parker. (*China Review*, XV, p. 187.)

15. — Burma Past and Present with Personal Reminiscences of the Country by Lieut.-Gen. Albert Fytche, C. S. I. Late Chief Commissioner of British Burma, and Agent to the Viceroy and Governor-General of India.... With Illustrations. London: C. Kegan Paul, 1878, 2 vol. in-8, pp. xiv + 1 f. n. ch. + 355, viii + 1 f. n. ch. + 348, carte.

16. — British Burma and its People: being Sketches of Native Manners, Customs, and Religion. By Capt. C. J. F. S. Forbes... Officiating Deputy-Commissioner, British Burma. London: John Murray, ... 1878, pet. in-8, pp. ix + 1 f. n. ch. + pp. 364.

Notice: *Nature*, XX, 1879, pp. 3—4. By W. L. D.

17. — La Birmanie Par M. L. Vossion Conférence faite à la Société Académique Indo-Chinoise dans sa séance du 17 Juillet 1879. (*Ann. de l'Ext. Orient*, II, pp. 65—73).

18. — La Birmanie Conférence faite à la Société Académique Indo-Chinoise, dans sa séance du 17 juillet 1879 par M. L. Vossion Ancien Officier, Attaché à la personne du dernier roi de Birmanie, Membre de la Société Académique Indo-Chinoise. — Extrait des *Annales de l'Extrême Orient*. Paris, Challamel ainé, 1879, br. in-8, pp. 15.

Port. de l'auteur et grav. d'un monastère bouddhiste à Mandalay.

19. — La Birmanie. Sa situation actuelle, son industrie et ses relations par M. L. Vossion. (*Bul. Soc. Géog. com.*, II, 1879—80, pp. 42—45).

20. — My Child-Life in Burmah; or, Recollections and Incidents. Olive Jennie Bixby. Boston: Published by W. G. Corthell, Mission rooms. 1880, pet. in-8, pp. xii—172.

21. — La Birmanie anglaise Par M. le Comte Alphonse Dilhan. Communication faite à la Société Académique Indo-Chinoise dans sa séance du 28 février 1880. (*Ann. de l'Ext. Orient*, II, pp. 366—379).

22. — The British Burma Gazetteer in two volumes. Compiled by Authority. Rangoon: Printed at the Government Press. 1880—1879, 2 vol. gr. in-8, pp. x + 2 ff. n. c. + pp. 716 + pp. xxxv p. l'ind., 859 + xviii p. l'app.

La préface est signée par H. R. Spearman, le principal auteur.

«In preparing the chapter on Ethnology I received most willingly-rendered assistance from Dr. Stevens and Messrs. Brayton and Cushing of the American Baptist Mission. That Portion of Chapter II, which relates to Geology is by Mr. Theobald of the Geological Survey of India (who also wrote the chapter on Reptiles) and the second portion was to some extent revised by him. The first part of Chapter III is from the late Mr. Kurz's reports. The first part of Chapter V, is by the Right Reverend Bishop Bigandet, Vicar Apostolic of Pegu, from whose work on Gaudama the second portion is extracted. Chapter XVI is compiled from the works of Blyth (almost entirely) and Jerdon. The Chapter on Ornithology is by Mr. Oates of the Public Works Department. The Chapter on Ichthyology is compiled from Dr. Day's reports and publications, and the last chapter was written by Mr. W. T. Blanford of the Geological Survey of India. Unfortunately in no case except one (Ornithology) has there been time to submit proofs to these authors. [Préface.]

23. — Birmanie — Résumé ethnographique et linguistique Traduit du *British Burmah Gazetteer* avec annotations. Par J. Harmand. Paris, Maisonneuve, 1884, in-8, pp. 81.

24. — Ashé Pyee, the Superior Country; or, The Great Attractions of Burma to British Enterprise and Commerce. By Colonel W. F. B. Laurie, author of «Our Burmese wars and relations with Burma», etc. London: W. H. Allen & Co., 1882, in-8, pp. xv—283.

25. — The Burman His Life and Notions By Shway Yoe Subject of the Great Queen In Two Volumes. London Macmillan and Co. 1882, 2 vol. in-8, pp. ix—370, viii—360.

> «The chapters XVIII. to XX., and XXIII. to XXVII. in the first volume, and chapters V., VIII., X to XIV, XVII, XXIII. and XXIV. in the second, have already appeared, mostly in a shorter form, in the columns of the *St. James's Gazette*. [Préf. p. ix.]

26. — *The Burman, his Life and Notions. By Shway Yoe, Subject of the Great Queen. Second Edition. London, Macmillan & Co., 1896, in-8, pp. xii—603.

27. — Burma as it was, as it is, and as it will be by James George Scott (Shway yoe) author of «the Burman: his life and notions» «France and Tong-King», etc. etc. London George Redway, 1886, in-8, pp. viii—184.

> «In writing this book the author has followed the lines of, and utilized to some extent, a lecture delivered before the Society of Arts in January 1886. The most recent authorities have throughout been consulted, including the Parliamentary Blue-Book of 1886. The author is also particularly indebted for the sketch of the Burmese Constitution to a lecture delivered at Simla, before the United Service Institute, by Mr. R. H. Pilcher, of the Burma Commission». [Preface.]

Notice: *Nature*, XXXIII, 1885—6, pp. 521—2.

28. — *Burma, the Foremost Country. London, 1884, in-8, pp. 146.

29. — Burma and the Burmans; or, «the best unopened market in the World». By Archibald Ross Colquhoun, ... With Map of the Country. London: Field and Tuer the Leadenhall Press, Simpkin, Marshall & Co.; Hamilton, Adams & Co., in-8, pp. xii—58.

30. — Burmah: our gate to China. By Archibald R. Colquhoun. (*As. Quart. Review*, IV, July-Oct. 1887, pp. 256—278).

31. — The Survey of India. By J. T. W. (*Nature*, XXXIII, 1885—86, pp. 441—444; 489—491).

> Mergui, Tenasserim, etc.

32. — Our new eastern province. (*Blackwood's Mag.*, CXXXIX, March 1886, pp. 279—291).

33. — Burma: the Country and People. By J. Annan Bryce. (*Proc. R. Geog. Soc.*, VIII, 1886, Aug., pp. 481—501; carte, pp. 544).

34. — Burma, after the Conquest, viewed in its political, social, and commercial aspects, from Mandalay by Grattan Geary.... London: Sampson Low, 1886, in-8, pp. xvi—345.

35. — La Birmanie et les Birmans. Par M. J.-L. Soubeiran. in-8, pp. 37.

> Ext. du *Bulletin de la Société languedocienne de Géographie*. [Montpellier.]

36. — Cathay and the Golden Chersonese. By A. R. MacMahon, Major-General. (*Blackwood's Mag.*, CXLI, Feb. 1887, pp. 229—246).

37. — Far Cathay and Farther India by Major-General A. Ruxton Mac Mahon, formerly H. M. political Agent at the Court of Ava. London: Hurst and Blackett, 1893, in-8, pp. XII—340.

> Paru en partie dans *Blackwood, Asiatic Quarterly*, etc.
> Notice: *The Athenaeum*, No. 8395, Nov. 19, 1892.

38. — Burma and its people. London: T. Woolmer, ... Price two pence, in-12, pp. 32. s.d. [1888?]

39. — The British Empire in Indo-China. By A. C. Yate. (*As. Quart. Review*, VII, Jan.-April 1889, pp. 343—356).

40. — Note on the State of Burma in March, 1889, by H. T. White. (*Trübner's Record*, Nº 244, pp. 35—41).

41. — Burma and the Burmese. Compiled from Shway Yoe, Hunter, Fytche, Phayre, Smeaton, Grattan Geary and others. Madras: The Christian Literature Society, 1892, br. in-4 à 2 col., pp. 50, grav.

> Sur le titre 1st ed., 2000.

42. — 'Burma and the Burmese. Madras, C. L. Society, in-8, pp. 56.

43. — Birmanie. Par M. L.-B. Rochedragon. (*Bul. Soc. Géog.*, Lyon, XI, 1892, pp. 231—7).

44. — La Birmanie Ce qu'elle a été et ce qu'elle est maintenant. Par le R. P. Wehinger. (*Bul. Soc. Géog. com.*, Paris, XVII, 1895, pp. 440—450).

45. — Notice sur la Basse-Birmanie et les États protégés de la Péninsule malaise (Straits Settlements) — Par le Docteur G. Letellier. (*Bul. Soc. Géog. com. Havre*, 1895, pp. 65—91).

46. — Chez les Birmans. Par H. Charmanne. (*Le Mouv. géog.*, XIII, 1896, col. 580—2, 604—6.)

> Voir VOYAGES.

47. — En Birmanie. (*La Belgique Coloniale*, 29 Nov. 1896, pp. 579—580).

> D'après un rapport de M. Charmanne dans le *Recueil consulaire*.

48. — Birma, Land und Leute. Vortrag von Fritz Noetling. (*Jahresb. Geog. Ges. München*, 1896—7, p. XXXI).

49. — 'Fritz Noetling. — Land und Leute in Birma. (*Jahresbericht Frankfurter Verein für Geographie und Statistik*, LXI—LXIII, pp. 11—13).

50. — 'Picturesque Burma, Past and Present. By Mrs. Ernest Hart, 1897, in-8.

> Notice: *Journ. R. A. S*, July 1897, pp. 656—659, par R. F. St. A. St. John.

51. — The Soul of a People. By H. Fielding. London, Richard Bentley and Son, Publishers in Ordinary to Her Majesty the Queen, 1898, in-8, pp. VIII—363.

52. — Burma, die östlichste Provinz des indischen Kaiserreiches. Nach englischen Quellen und eigenen Beobachtungen Von Dr. H. Schmitz in Hamburg. (*Mitt. k. u. k. geog. Ges. Wien*, 1898, pp. 664—705).

53. — 'Max and Bertha Ferrars. — Burma. London, Sampson Low, 1900, gr. in-8, pp. 250. Illustrations.

> Notices: *Athenaeum*, 9 Juin 1901, pp. 70 et seq.; *Literature*, VII, pp. 13 et seq.

54. — Gazetteer of Upper Burma and the Shan States. — In Five Volumes. — Compiled from Official Papers by J. George Scott, Barrister-at-Law, C.I.E., M.R.A.S., F.R.G.S., Assisted by J. P. Hardiman, I.C.S.

Part I. — Vol. I. Rangoon: Printed by the Superintendent, Government Printing Burma, — 1900, in-8, pp. 2 + 2 + 727 + x.

Chap. I. Physical Geography. — II. History. — The reigns of King Mindôn and King Thibaw from Burmese Sources. — III. History. — The causes which led to the Third Burmese War and the Annexation of Upper Burma. — IV. The first year after the Annexation. — V. Final pacification. — VI. The Shan States and the Tai. — VII. The Kachin Hills and the Chingpaw — VIII. The Chin Hills and the Chin Tribes. — IX. Ethnology with Vocabularies.

Part I. — Vol. II. *Ibid.*, 1900, in-8, pp. 560 + VIII + XI.

Chap. X. Religion and its semblances. — XI. Palace customs and Burma under Native Rule. Archaeology. — XII. Geology and Economic Mineralogy. — XIII. Forest and other vegetation. — XIV. Agriculture and Industrial Arts. — XV. Revenue administration, past and present; Population and Trade. — XVI. Government and Administration under the Burmese Kings. — Glossary.

Part II. — Vol. I. *Ibid.*, 1901, in-8, pp. XI—549.

Contents. — Gazetteer (*A-eng—Kywe-sin.*)

Part II. — Vol. II. *Ibid.*, 1901, in-8, pp. XVI—802.

Contents. — Gazetteer (*Laban—Pyu-yaung.*)

Part II. — Vol. III. *Ibid.*, 1901, in-8, pp. XII—437—VIII.

Contents. — Gazetteer (*Ralang—Zithaung.*) — Glossary to Part II. Cf. *Geographical Journal*, XVII, p. 549; XVIII, p. 636; T. H. Holdich, dans *Man*, 1901, p. 190.

55. — Conférence de M. G. Burghard du 4 mai 1901. — La Birmanie. (*Soc. Géog. Tours, Revue*, 1901, pp. 48—9).

Cte. rendu par J. de V.

56. — *Burma under British Rule — and Before. By John Nisbet. In two Volumes. Westminster: Archibald Constable and Co., Ltd., 1901, 2 vol. in-8, pp. XVII—912.

Notice: *Nature*, lxv, Nov. 1901, to April 1902, pp. 243—244.

57. — *Julius Smith — Ten years in Burma. Cincinnati, 1902, pet. in-8, pp. VI—326.

II. — Géographie.

Ouvrages divers.

58. — Geographical Sketch of the Burmese Empire Compiled in the Surveyor Generals Office Calcutta, July 1824, gr. feuille in plano.

Scale of Bᵗ. Miles 16 to One Inch.

59. — Notes on the Head of Country lying between the Head of the Zimmi River and the source of the Kaundran, adjacent to the Siamese Border Province of Ryout Raung. By E. O'Riley. (*Jour. Ind. Archip.*, IV, 1850, pp. 164—168).

From a Report.

60. — *G. H. Hough. — A general Outline of Geography, in Burmese and English. Maulmain, 1857, in-8, pp. 416.

61. — On the Geography of Burma and its Tributary States, in illustration of a New Map of those Regions. By Captain Henry Yule, F.R.G.S., Bengal Engineers, and Secretary to Major Phayre, late Envoy to the Court of Ava. With Map. Communicated by Sir Roderick I. Murchison. Read, January 26, 1857. (*Journ. Roy. Geog. Soc.*, XXVII, 1857, pp. 54—108).

62. — Notes on the Geography of Burma, in illustration of a Map of that Country. By Capt. Yule, of the Bengal Engineers, F.R.G.S. (*Proc. Roy. Geog. Soc.*, I, 1857, pp. 269—273).

63. — Extracts from a Paper on the Surface Currents of the Bay of Bengal during the S. W. Monsoon. By Lieut. J. A. Heathcote, I.N. (*Proc. Roy. Geog. Soc.*, VI, 1862, pp. 114—117).

64. — Geography in Burmese for the use of schools. Bassein: Catholic Mission Press. 1868, in-8.

65. — A Vocabulary of Proper Names, in Chinese and English, of Places, Persons, Tribes, and Sects, in China, Japan, Corea, Annam, Siam, Burmah, the Straits and adjacent Countries compiled by F. Porter Smith, M.B. Lond. Medic. Miss. in China. Shanghai, 1870, in-8, pp. VI—68—IX.

> Pub. à Dol. 1. 50.
> Notices: *Shanghai Evening Courier*, 10 Jan. 1871; une lettre signée «A Constant Reader» réclamant pour le Dict de Biot la priorité dans ce genre de travail a également paru dans ce journal, 28 feb. 1871 (réimp. dans *The Shanghai Budget*, 1 Mars 1871.) — *Ch. Recorder*, III, p. 228.

66. — An elementary Geography of India, Burma, and Ceylon by Henry F. Blanford, F.R.S. Late meteorological Reporter to the Government of India. London, Macmillan and Co., and New York, 1890, pet. in-8, pp. XII—191.

67. — *Tide-Tables for the Indian Ports for the Year 1894 (also January, 1895). Part I. Western Ports (Aden to Pámban Pass). Part II. Eastern and Burma Ports (Negapatam to Port Blair). By Lieut.-Colonel J. Hill, R.E., and E. Roberts, F.R.A.S., etc. size 6½ × 4½, pp. 1011.

Cartes.

Cartes de l'Amirauté anglaise.

No.	Size	Scale	Title of the Chart	Price s. d.
859	D E	0.2	Mutlah river to Elephant point. *Indian Government surveys to* 1879; *Sept.* 1887, IX. 1900	2 6
82	D E & $\frac{D E}{2}$	1.0	Mutlah river. *Lieut. Ward*, I.N., 1855; *Nov.* 1871, X. 1900	2 6
84	$\frac{D E}{2}$	2.3	Chittagong (Karnafuli) river. *Indian Government Survey*, 1883; XI. 1892	1 6
821	D E	0.21	Elephant point to Cheduba strait. (Plan: Naaf river.) *Indian Gov. Surveys*, 1830—84; *Sept.* 1887, V. 1902	2 0

No.	Size	Scale	Title of the Chart	Price s. d.	
1884	D E	1.0	Arakan river. Akyab. *Indian Gov. Surveys to 1883; July 1884, XII. 1899*	2	6
831	$\frac{DE}{2}$	2.0	Kyauk Pyu harbour. *Indian Gov. Survey, 1885; VII. 1888*	1	6
822	A	0.21	Chedúba strait to Koronge island. *Indian Gov. Surveys, 1826—84; Sept. 1887, IX. 1901*	2	0
832	A	0.5	Chedúba strait and Ramree harbour. *Coms. Dawson and Carpenter,1884; pub. July 1887*	2	0
830	D E	0.05	Bassein river to Pulo Penang, including the Andaman and Nicobar islands and the north coast of Sumatra. *Indian Gov. Surveys to 1898; April 1900, VIII. 1902*	2	6
823	D E & $\frac{DE}{4}$	0.2	Koronge island to White point, including the gulf of Martaban. *Indian Gov. Surveys, 1826—1898; July 1899, VIII. 1902*	3	6
152	Imp.	0.2	Preparis North Channel. *Lieut. Ward*, I.N., 1855; *Jan.* 1880, V. 1902	1	6
834	D E	$\begin{cases}1.0\\0.75\end{cases}$	Bassein river and approaches. *Indian Gov. Survey*, 1889—90, V. 1902	2	6
2135	D E	0.33	Irrawaddy river, Sheet I., from the Sea to Rangoon and Prome. *Lieut. Winsor*, 1825; *Indian Gov. Survey*, 1884; *March* 1886, IV. 1896	2	6
833	D E & $\frac{DE}{2}$	1.35	Rangoon river and approaches. (Plans: — Entrance of China Bakir river. Port of Rangoon.) *Com. Dawson,*1833—4; VII. 1901, *Oct.* 1901	3	6
2136	D E	0.33	Irrawaddy river, Sheet II., from Prome to Yeandabou. *Lieut. Winsor*, 1825; *March* 1881	2	6
1693	$\frac{DE}{2}$	1.0	Salween river. *Lieut. Nolloth*, 1843; *October* 1875	1	6
1845	D E	1.2	Moulmein river and approaches. *Com. Heming*, 1898—99; IX. 1902	2	6
1646	$\frac{DE}{2}$	5.9	Moulmein harbour. *Com. Heming*, 1898; *pub. Jan.* 1901	1	6
835	$\frac{DE}{2}$	1.0	Bentinck sound. Port Owen. *Capt. Laws*, 1830; IX. 1883, *Oct.* 1886	1	6
1272	D E	2.0	Approaches to Yé river. *Indian Gov. Surveys*, 1887; IV. 1898	2	6
824	D E	0.26	White point to Mergui. *Indian Gov. Survey*, 1828—98; V. 1894, *April* 1899	2	6

No.	Size	Scale	Title of the Chart	Price s. d.
924	D E	1.0	Tavoy river. *Com. Carpenter*, 1885; *pub. Sept.* 1886	2
1075	D E	0.97	Approaches to Mergui harbour. *Indian Gov. Survey*, 1885—86; V. 1894	2 6
218	A	4.0	Mergui harbour. *Indian Gov. Surveys*, 1885—6; *July* 1887, V. 1894	2 0
216a	D E	0.3	Mergui archipelago: Lord Loughborough Island to Mergui. *Capt. Ross*, I.N., 1828; *July* 1888, XI. 1899	2
216b	Imp.	0.25	— Sayer islands to Lord Loughborough Island. *Indian Gov. Surveys*, 1828—77; *July* 1880, V. 1893	2 0

Hydrographie française.

3649   Golfe de Martaban: du cap Negrais aux Moscos du Nord, comprenant les rivières de Maulmain et de Rangoon, les bouches de l'Irrawady et la rivière Bassein . . . . . 1 *m* = 4
       Levés anglais. — Edit. de mai 1900.

2333   Rivière Bassein. . . . . 1 *m* = 19
       Levé anglais. 1853. — Corr. en avril 1879.

3793   Bentinck sound. . . . . ¼ *m* = 24
       Levé anglais. 1830.

2626   Côte de Tenasserim et archipel de Mergui; des Moscos du Nord à l'île Sullivan . . . . 1 *m* = 4
       Levés anglais. 1828. — Edit. de fév. 1890.

2962   Port Owen (île Tavoy) . . . . ¼ *m* = 25
       Levé anglais. 1830.

4444   Port de Mergui et ses approches. . . . . ½ *m* = 16
       Levé anglais. 1886.

2628   Côte de Tenasserim et archipel de Mergui: de l'île Domel au détroit de Papura . . . . 1 *m* = 4
       Levés anglais. 1828. — Edit. de fév. 1890.

Maps, Plans, etc., published by the Government of India [1]).

Burma, General Maps.

Ref. No.	Description of Map	Year of Survey	Date of last edition	Scale	Size	Price uncol.
769	Burma and adjacent countries, 2 sheets	—	1890	1″=32 M	40″×34″	6/—
	Burma and the regions adjacent, by Captain H. Yule, Bengal Engineers, 2 sheets	—	1857	1″=32 M	40″×27″	4/—
735	Upper Burma, Preliminary Map	—	1889	1″=16 M	40″×27″	4/—
740	Upper Burma, on 6 sheets. Eastern half on 3 sheets only published	—	1888	1″=8 M	34″×26″	6/—
788	Burma (Burma and Assam Frontier). Skeleton Map of Upper Burma, from Mandalay northward	—	1886	1″=32 M	18″×15″	1/—
780	Part of Karreni	—	1889	1″=4 M	40″×27″	3/—
	Irawaddy River and bordering Country 3 sheets	—	1883	1″=4 M	40″×27″	9/—
660	Mandalay. — Sketch Map of Country round	—	1886	1″=2 M	40″×27″	2/—
859	Upper Burma	—	1894	1″=64 M	14×19	—6 d
769	Burma and adjacent Countries, 2 sheets	—	1898	1″=32 M	40×25	4/6
877	Upper Burma, 2 sheets	—	1890	1″=16 M	40×27	4/6
769	Burma and adjacent Countries, 2 sheets	—	1901	1″=32 M	40×27	4/6

Burma, Frontier Map.

Ref. No.	Description	Year of Survey	Date of last edition	Scale	Size	Price
998	Burma-Siam Boundary, Amherst District and Siam, 6 sheets	1894—96	1897	1″=1 M	30×22	11/3
1029	Burma-Siam Boundary Commission-Shan States and China	1898—99	1900	„	40×27	2/3
1028	Burma-China Boundary Commission, Sheets A, B, C, D, E, 6, 7, 8, 9, 10, 11, 12, 13 13 sheets	1897—99	1899—1900	„	40×27	2/3 each

Burma (India, South-Eastern Trans-Frontier Series), Ref. No. 739.

Ref. No.	Description	Year of Survey	Date of last edition	Scale	Size	Price
1	Lushai and Chin Hills, Upper and Lower Chindwin	—	1890	1″=8 M	40″×27″	3/—
1 S.E.	— Upper and Lower Chindwin	1886—90	1888	1″=4 M	„	„
1 N.E.	— Upper Chindwin, Yeu, &c.	—	1889	„		
2 N.E.	— Lower Chindwin	1886—90	1890	„		
2 S.E.	— Upper Burma	—	1887	„		

---

1) Cette liste a été dressée à l'aide de: A Catalogue of Maps, Plans, &c., of India and Burma and other Parts of Asia. — Published by order of Her Majesty's Secretary of State for India in Council. — London: 1891, in-fol., pp. 154—7. — et les suppl. sous forme d'App. Nos. I—XLIV (May 1908).

Ref. No.	Description of Map	Year of Survey	Date of last edition	Scale	Size	Price
3 Sandoway, Thayetmyo, Prome, &c.		—	1890	$1'' = 8$ M	$40'' \times 27''$	3/
3 N.E. — Upper Burma		—	1888	$1'' = 4$ M	,,	,,
4 N.W. — Myadoung, Bhamo, &c.		1887—89	1889	,,	,,	,,
4 N.E. — Shan States		—	1889	,,	,,	,,
4 S.E. — Shan States		1887—90	1889	,,	,,	,,
4 S.W. — Mandalay, Ruby Mines, &c.		1888—90	1889	,,	,,	,,
5 S.E. — Shan States		1887—90	1889	,,	,,	,,
5 N.W. — Mandalay, Sagain, &c.		1889—90	1889	,,		
5 N.E. — Shan States		1889—90	1889	,,	,,	,,
5 S.W. — Meiktila, &c.		1886—90	1889	,,	,,	,,
6 N.W. — Pyinmana, &c.		1889—90	1889	,,	,,	,,
1 Lushai and Chin Hills, &c.		—	1891	$1'' = 8$ M	,,	,,
3 A Bassein, Thongwa, &c.		—	1890	,,	,,	,,
7 Shwegyin, Amherst, Salween, &c.		—	1890	,,	,,	,,
1 N.W. — Lushai and Chin Hills, &c.		—	1891	$1'' = 4$ M	,,	,,
1 N.E. — Upper Chindwin, Yeu, &c.		1886—91	1891	,,	,,	,,
1 S.E. — Upper and Lower Chindwin, &c.		,,	1891	,,	,,	,,
2 S.E. — Pakokku, Minbu, &c.		1889—91	1892	,,	,,	,,
3 N.E. — Parts of Minbu, Magwe, &c.		1885—91	1892	,,	,,	,,
4 N.W. — Parts of Katha, Ruby Mines, &c.		1886—91	1892	,,	,,	,,
4 N.E. — Parts of Shan States		1887—91	1891	,,	,,	,,
4 S.E. — Part of Shan States		,,	1892	,,	,,	,,
4 S.W. — Ruby Mines, Momeit, &c.		1886—91	1892	,,	,,	,,
5 S.W. — Parts of Meiktilla, &c.		,,	1892	,,	,,	,,
1 N.W. — Lushai and Chin Hills		—	1893	,,		
2 North Arakan, Pakoku, &c.		—	1893	$1'' = 8$ M	,,	,,
3 N.E. Minbu, Magwe, &c.		—	1893	$1'' = 4$ M	,,	,,
4 N.E. North Shan States		—	1892	,,	,,	,,
4 N.W. Ruby Mines and N. Shan States		—	1893	,,	,,	,,
5 N.W. Mandalay, Sagain, &c.		—	,,	,,	,,	,,
5 S.W. Meiktila and S. Shan States		—	,,	,,	,,	,,
5 S.E. Southern Shan States		—	,,	,,	,,	,,
6 N.W. Toungoo, Pyinmana, &c.		—	,,	,,	,,	,,
1 N.E. Upper Chindwin, &c.		1886—92	,,	,,	,,	,,
1 N. Lushai Hills, Chin Hills, &c.		—	1894	$1'' = 8$ M	,,	,,
1 S.W. Chin Hills, Upper Chindwin, &c.		—	1894	$1'' = 4$ M	,,	,,
4 S.E. Northern Shan States		—	1893	,,	,,	,,

Burma (India, North-Eastern Trans-Frontier Series), Ref. No. 766.

| 15 S.E. — Parts of Manipur and Upper Chindwin | | — | 1889 | ,, | ,, | ,, |
| 15 N.E. — Assam and Upper Chindwin | | — | 1886 | ,, | ,, | ,, |

Ref. No.	Description of Map	Year of Survey	Date of last edition	Scale	Size	Price uncol.
22 S.W. — Singpho and Naga Hills		—	1888	1″=4 M	40″×27″	3 /
22 N.W. — Singpho and Naga Hills		—	1888	,,	,,	,,
23 N.W. — Bhamo and Shan States		1888—89	1889	,,		
23 S.W. — Bhamo and Yunan (Chinese)		1887—89	1889	,,		
14 S.E. — Singpho and Naga Hills		1862—88	1890	,,		
15 N.E. — Parts of Assam, &c.		1885—86	1886	,,		
15 S.E. — Part of Manipur, &c.		1881—88	1889	,,		
23 N.W. — Part of Bhamo, &c.		1888—91	1892	,,		
23 S.W. — Part of Bhamo, &c.		1887—90	,,	,,		
22 Part of Assam and Singpho Hills		—	,,	1″=8 M	,,	,,
15 S.E. — Manipur and Upper Chindwin		—	1893	1″=4 M	,,	,,
22 Singpho, Naga Hills, &c.		—	,,	1″=8 M	,,	,,
23 N.W. Katha and Bhamo, &c.		—	,,	1″=4 M	,,	,,
23 S.W. Katha and Bhamo, &c.		—	,,	,,		
22 Lakhimpur, Singpho, Naga Hills, &c.		—	1894	1″=8 M	,,	,,
23 S.W. Bhamo, Khata, &c.		—	,,	1″=4 M	,,	,,

Standard Sheets of the Survey of Upper and Lower Burma.
Ref. No. 669.

						s. d.
140 Bassein	—	1887	1″=1 M		,,	3 0
141 Bassein	—	1887	,,		,,	
142 Bassein. — Bassein Town	—	1890	..			
143 Bassein	—	1888	..			
178 Prome	—	1886	..			
179 Prome	—	1887	..			
180 Prome, Henzada, and Tharrawaddy	—	1887	..			
181 Prome, Henzada, and Tharrawaddy	—	1887	..			
182 Henzada	—	1887	..			
183 Henzada	—	1887	..			
184 Bassein and Henzada	—	1887	.			
185 Bassein and Henzada	—	1887	..			
186 Bassein	—	1887	..			
187 Bassein	—	1890	..			
188 Bassein	—	1889	..			
227 Prome	—	1886	..			
228 Prome and Tharrawaddy	—	1886	..			
231 Henzada, Tharrawaddy, and Hanthawaddy	—	1888	..			
232 Henzada and Hanthawaddy	—	1888	..			
233 Hanthawaddy	—	1888	..			
234 Henzada	—	1890	..			
280 Hanthawaddy and Pegu	—	1889	,,		..	..
— Index Map to Sheets of Survey of Upper and Lower Burma	—	1887	1″=64 M	17″×13″		—6

Ref. No.	Description of Map	Year of Survey	Date of last edition	Scale	Size	Price uncol. s. d.
24	Part of District Akyab	1883—87	1890	1″=1 M	40″×27″	3/
47	Part of District Akyab	1886—87	1890	,,	,,	,,
229	Part of District Tharrawaddy	1880—85	1890	,,		
230	Part of Dist. Tharrawaddy and Henzada	1880—84	1890	,,		
235	Part of District Hanthawaddy	,,	1890	,,		
236	Part of District Hanthawaddy	1881—82	1890	,,		
332	Part of District Shwegyin	—	1890	,,		
225 $\frac{N.W.}{4}$	District Prome	—	1891	4″=1 M	,,	,,
225 $\frac{N.E.}{3}$	Districts Prome, Toungoo, and Thayatmeyo	1891		,,		
225 $\frac{S.E.}{4}$	Districts Prome and Toungoo	—	1891	,,		,,
225 $\frac{S.E.}{1}$	District Prome	—	1891	,,		8 0
226 $\frac{N.E.}{2}$	. . . . . .	—	1891	,,		
226 $\frac{N.E.}{4}$	Districts Prome and Toungoo	—	1891	,,		
7	District Akyab	1885—86	1891	1″=1 M	,,	,,
8	do	1883—87	1891	,,		
9	do	,,	1891	,,		
10	do	,,	1891	,,		
25	do	,,	1891	,,		
26	do	,,	1891	,,		
27	do	,,	1891	,,		
28	do	,,	1890	,,		
43	do	,,	1891	,,		
44	do	,,	1890	,,		
46	Districts Akyab and Kyauk Pyn	,,	,,	,,		
180	Districts Prome, Henzada, and Tharra-waddy	1882—3 & 1885—9		,,	,,	
228	Districts Prome and Tharrawaddy	—	,,	,,		
276	District Tharrawaddy	1883—85	,,	,,		
277	District Tharrawaddy	1882—86	1891	,,		
278	Dist. Hanthawaddy and Tharrawaddy	1880—84	1889	,,		
281	Rangoon	1880—84	1890	,,		
282	Districts Pegu and Hanthawaddy	1881—82	1890	,,		
283	District Hanthawaddy	1881—82	1890	,,		
322	Shwegyin	1884—85	1890	,,		
323	District Shwegyin	1884—85	1890	,,		
324	District Shwegyin	1884—85	1890	,,		
325	Districts Pegu and Shwegyin	1883—85	1891	,,		
326	Pegu	1880—82	1890	,,		

Ref. No.	Description of Map	Year of Survey	Date of last edition	Scale	Size	Price uncol. s. d.
327	District Pegu	1881—83	1891	1″=1 M	40″×27″	3 0
328	do	1880—82	1890	″	″	″
329	do	1880—81	1890	″		
45	District Akyab	1883—87	1891	″		
181	District Henzada	1882—88	1891	″		
227	Prome, Tharrawaddy, etc.	1882—89	1891	″		
569	District Mergui	1890—91	1892	″		
225 $\frac{S.E.}{2}$	Districts Toungoo and Prome	″	″	4″=1 M	″	″
272 $\frac{S.W.}{3}$	District Toungoo	″	″	″		
273 $\frac{N.W.}{1}$	District Toungoo	″	″	″		
273 $\frac{N.W.}{3}$	District Toungoo	″	″	″		
273 $\frac{S.W.}{1}$	District Toungoo	″	″	″		
273 $\frac{S.W.}{3}$	District Toungoo	″	″	″		
226	Prome, Tharrawaddy, &c.	1886—91	1893	1″=1 M	″	″
273 $\frac{N.E.}{3}$	District Toungoo	1891—92	″	4″=1 M	″	″
273 $\frac{S.E.}{1}$	District Toungoo	″	″	″		
273 $\frac{S.E.}{3}$	District Toungoo	″	″	″		
273 $\frac{S.W.}{2}$	District Toungoo	″	″	″		
273 $\frac{S.W.}{3}$	District Toungoo	″	″	″		
186	Districts Bassein and Thongwa	1881—89	″	1″=1 M	″	″
189	do do	1886—91	″	″		
264	District Kyanke	1869—90	″	″		
	Index Map to the Sheets of the Survey of Upper and Lower Burma	—	″	1″=64 M	27×17	— 6
263	Kyaukse District	—	1894	1″=1 M	40×27	3
236	Hanthawaddy and Thongwa District	—	″	″	″	′
237	Thongwa District	—	″	″		
232, 279	Henzada, Hanthawaddy, &c.	—	″	″		
235	Hanthawaddy and Thongwa	—	″	″		
564	Mergui	—	″	″		
572	do	—	″	″		
572 A	do	—	″	″		
271 $\frac{S.W.}{3}$	Toungoo	—	″	4″=1 M	″	″

Ref. No.	Description of Map	Year of Survey	Date of last edition	Scale	Size	Price uncol. s. d.
274	$\frac{N.W.}{2}$ Toungoo	—	1894	4″ = 1 M	40″ × 27	3
„	$\frac{N.W.}{4}$ do	—	-	-		
„	$\frac{N.E.}{1}$ do	—	-	-		
„	$\frac{N.E.}{3}$ do	—	-	-		
„	$\frac{N.E.}{4}$ do	—	-	-		
„	$\frac{S.W.}{2}$ do	—	-	-		
„	$\frac{S.E.}{1}$ do	—	-	-		
„	$\frac{S.E.}{2}$ do	—	-	-		
„	$\frac{S.E.}{3}$ do	—	-	-		
„	$\frac{S.E.}{4}$ do	—	-	„	„	1
234	Hanthawaddy District, &c.	1881—90	„	1″ = 1 M	40 × 25	„
563	Mergui District	1892—93	„	„	„	1
570	do	1892—93	„	„		
571	do	1891—92	„	„		
579	do	1893—93	„	„		
580	do	1889—93	„	„	„	
581	do	1889—90	„	„	„	1
231	Henzada District, &c.	1880—84	„	„	40 × 27	„
258	Mandalay District	1890—91	1895	„	„	·
271	$\frac{N.E.}{2}$ Toungoo District	1893—94	„	4″ = 1 M	„	„
271	$\frac{N.E.}{4}$ do	„	„	„	„	
271	$\frac{S.E.}{4}$ do	„	„	„	„	
272	$\frac{N.E.}{2}$ and $\frac{N.W.}{1}$ do	„	„	„		
319						
273	$\frac{N.W.}{1}$ do	1890—93	„	„		
313	Southern Shan States	1893—94	„	„		
374	Amherst District	1891—94	„	„		
375	do	1891—93	„	„		
376	do	1890—92	„	„		

Ref. No.	Description of Map	Year of Survey	Date of last edition	Scale	Size	Price uncol. s. d.
224 $\frac{N.E.}{1}$	Toungoo District	1893—94	1895	4″=1 M	40×27	3
224 $\frac{N.E.}{2}$	do	″	″	″	″	″
224 $\frac{N.E.}{4}$	do	″	″	″		
224 $\frac{S.E.}{4}$	do	1892—94	″	″		
271 $\frac{N.W.}{1}$	do	1893—94	″	″		
271 $\frac{N.W.}{3}$	do	″	″	″		
271 $\frac{N.E.}{3}$	do	″	″	″		
271 $\frac{S.E.}{2}$ and 318 $\frac{S.E.}{1}$	do	″	″	″		
271 $\frac{S.E.}{3}$	do	″	″	″		
272 $\frac{N.W.}{1}$	do	1892—94	″	″		
272 $\frac{N.W.}{3}$	do	″	″	″		
272 $\frac{N.W.}{4}$	do	″	″	″		
272 $\frac{S.W.}{1}$	do	1892—93	″	″		
318 $\frac{S.W.}{3}$	do	1893—94	″	″		″
224 $\frac{N.E.}{3}$	do	1892—94	″	″		2 3
224 $\frac{S.E.}{2}$	do	″	″	″		
225 $\frac{N.E.}{2}$	do	″	″	″		
225 $\frac{S.E.}{2}$	do	″	″	″		
271 $\frac{N.W.}{2}$	do	″	″	″		
271 $\frac{N.W.}{4}$	do	″	″	″		
271 $\frac{N.E.}{1}$	do	″	″	″		
271 $\frac{S.W.}{2}$	do	″	″	″		
271 $\frac{S.W.}{4}$	do	″	″	″		

Ref. No.	Description of Map	Year of Survey	Date of last edition	Scale	Size	Price uncol. s. d.
271 $\frac{S.E.}{1}$	Toungoo District	1892—94	1895	4"=1 M	40×27	2 3
272 $\frac{N.W.}{2}$	do	"	"	"		
166	Sagaing District	1891—92	"	1"=1 M	"	"
167	do	"	"	"		
168	do	"	"	"		
213	do	"	"	"		
214	do	"	"	"		
215	do	"	"	"		
216	do	"	"	"		
259	Mandalay District, etc.	1890—93	"	"		
260	do	"	"	"		
262	Kyaukse District, etc.	1889—92	"	"		
279 $\frac{N.W.}{4}$	Hanthawaddy District, &c.	1894—95	1896	4"=1 M	"	"
279 $\frac{S.W.}{2}$	do	"	"	"		
306	Northern Shan States	1895—96	1897	1"=1 M	"	"
358	Southern Shan States	1894—95	"	"		
281	Hanthawaddy District, &c.	1881—83	"	"		
477	Amherst District, &c.	1891—96	"	"		
89	Minbu District	1891—92	1898	"		
90	do	"	"	"		
130	do	1892—93	"	"		
314	Southern Shan States	1894—95	"	"		
371	Thaton District	1894—96	"	"		
476	do	"	"	"		
260	Mandalay District	1896—97	"	"		
306	do	1895—97	"	"		
359	Southern Shan States	1894—95	"	"		
232 $\frac{N.E.}{2}$	Hanthawaddy District	"	"	4"=1 M	"	"
279 $\frac{N.W.}{2}$	Pegu District	"	"	"		
282	Hanthawaddy District	1881—82	1897	1"=1 M	"	"
232 $\frac{N.E.}{4}$	do	1894—96	1898	4"=1 M	"	"
278 $\frac{N.W.}{4}$	do	"	"	"		
280 $\frac{N.W.}{1}$	do	"	"	"		
315	Southern Shan States	"	1899	1"=1 M	"	"
352	do	1896—97	1898	"		

Ref. No.	Description of Map	Year of Survey	Date of last edition	Scale	Size	Price uncol. s. d.
353	Southern Shan States	1896—97	1899	1″=1 M	40×27	2 3
362	do	″	1898	″	″	″
374	Thaton District	1891—96	″	″		
273 $\frac{S.W.}{3}$		1890—96	″	4″=1 M	″	″
274 $\frac{N.W.}{1}$		″	″	″		
274 $\frac{N.W.}{2}$		″	″	″		
274 $\frac{N.W.}{3}$		″	″	″		
274 $\frac{N.W.}{4}$		″	″	″		
274 $\frac{S.W.}{1}$		″	″	″		
274 $\frac{S.W.}{2}$		″	″	″		
274 $\frac{S.W.}{3}$		″	″	″		
275 $\frac{N.W.}{1}$		″	″	″		
275 $\frac{N.W.}{2}$		″	″	″		
275 $\frac{N.W.}{3}$		″	″	″		
275 $\frac{N.W.}{4}$		″	″	″		
275 $\frac{S.W.}{1}$		″	″	″		
275 $\frac{S.W.}{2}$		″	″	″		
279 $\frac{S.W.}{4}$		″	″	″		
280 $\frac{N.W.}{2}$		″	″	″		
276 $\frac{N.E.}{1}$	Tharrawaddy District	1896—97	″	″		
305	Northern Shan States	″	1899	1″=1 M	″	″
307	do	1895—97	″	″		
351	do	1896—97	″	″		
358	Southern Shan States	1894—95	″	″		
360	do	1895—96	″	″		
361	do	1895—96	″	″		
398	Northern Shan States	1897—98	″	″		
458	Southern Shan States	″	″	″		
274 $\frac{S.W.}{4}$		1895—97	1898	4″=1 M	″	″

Ref. No.	Description of Map	Year of Survey	Date of last edition	Scale	Size	Price uncol. s. d.
275 $\frac{N.E.}{3}$		1895—97	1898	4″=1 M	40×27	2 3
275 $\frac{N.E.}{4}$		„	„	„		
275 $\frac{S.W.}{3}$		„	„	„		
275 $\frac{S.W.}{4}$		„	„	„		
275 $\frac{S.E.}{1}$		„	„	„		
275 $\frac{S.E.}{2}$		„	„	„		
275 $\frac{S.E.}{3}$		„	„	„		
275 $\frac{S.E.}{4}$		„	„	„		
350	Parts of Mong Mit, &c.	1896—99	1899	1″=1 M	„	„
401	Parts of N. and S. Shan States	„	„	„		
403	Southern Shan States	1897—98	1900	„		
276 $\frac{S.W.}{1}$ Tharrawaddy District		„	„	4″=1 M	„	„
174	Minbu District	1892—93	„	1″=1 M	„	„
260	Mandalay District, &c.	1890—97	„	„		
312	Meiktila District, &c.	1893—99	„	„		
276 $\frac{N.W.}{1}$		1896—98	„	4″=1 M	„	„
276 $\frac{N.E.}{2}$		„	„	„		
276 $\frac{S.W.}{3}$		„	„	„		
276 $\frac{N.W.}{3}$		1897—98	„	„		
89	New No. 72 Minbu District	1891—98	1901	1″=1 M	„	„
130	New No. 113 do	1892—98	„	„		
147	New Series Shwebo District	1892—93	„	„		
194	N. S. do	„	„	„		
313	N. No. 294 Yamethin District, &c.	1893—99	1900	„		
404	N. No. 385 Southern Shan States	1897—98	„	„		
353	N. S. Thaton District	1892—97	1901	„		
145	N. S. Shwebo District	1892—96	„	„		
142	N. S. 125 Bassein District, &c.	1879—80	1890	„		
190	N. S. Shwebo District	1892—96	1901	„		
240	N. S. Mandalay District, &c.	1890—1900	„	„		
262	N. S. 244 Mandalay District, &c.	1889—1900	1902	„		
273	N. S. 255 Toungoo District	1890—92	1896	„		

Ref. No.	Description of Map	Year of Survey	Date of last edition	Scale	Size	Price uncol. s. d.
324 N. S. 305	Toungoo District, &c.	1895—98	1901	1″=1 M	40×27	2 3
326 N. S. 307	Pegu District, &c.	1881—97	″	″	″	″
354 N. S.	Thaton District	1892—95	″	″	″	″
435 N. S.	Manglon District, &c.	1899—1900	″	″	″	″
436 N. S.	N. and S. Shan States	1899—1900	″	″	″	″
71 N. S.	Minbu	1897—98	″	″	″	″
192 N. S.	Shwebo	1892—94	″	″	″	″
261 N. S. 243	Mandalay, &c.	1893—99	1902	″	″	″
291 N. S.	Myelat, &c.	1898—99	1901	″	″	″
292 N. S.	Myelat, &c.	″	″	″	″	″
337 N. S.	South Shan States		″	″	″	″
338 N. S.	do		″	″	″	″
377 N. S.	North Shan States	″	″	″	″	″
378 N. S.	do	″	″	″	″	″
380 N. S.	do	1897—98	1902	″	″	″
381 N. S.	do	″	1901	″	″	″
388 N. S.	South Shan States	″	″	″	″	″
468 N. S.	Tavoy	1891—93	″	″	″	″
247 N. S.	Meiktila District, &c.	1890—1901	1902	″	″	″
307 N. S. 288	Mandalay District, &c.	1895—97	1902	″	″	″
289 N. S.	Mandalay District, &c.	1899—1900	1901	″	″	″
431 N. S.	North Shan States	1900—01	1902	″	″	″
434 N. S.	South Hsenwi State	1899—1900	1901	″	″	″
439 N. S.	South Shan States	1897—1901	1902	″	″	″
507 N. S.	do	1900—01	″	″	″	″
508 N. S.	do	1900—01	″	″	″	″

Burma, Divisional Maps.

252	Pegu. By Captains Fitzroy, R.A., and W. H. Edgecumbe, R.E. Containing parts of Districts Thayetmyo, Prome, Henzada, Tharrawaddy, Bassein, Arakan, Thongwa, &c. 4 sheets	—	1889	1″=4 M	40″×21″	10/—
251	Pegu, Province of. Compiled by Lieutenant C. E. S. Williams and Officers of the Pegu Survey Department from all available information	—	1855	1″=8 M	45″×38″	8/—
	Tenasserim, from the Map of Tenasserim, &c. by Lieutenant A. H. Bagge, R.E.	—	1868	1″=32 M	24″×16″	— 6
254	Tenasserim and the adjacent Province of the Kingdom of Siam, by Lieutenant A. H. Bagge, R.E. 4 sheets	—	1868	1″=8 M	34″×22″	8/col.

Ref. No.	Description of Map	Year of Survey	Date of last edition	Scale	Size	Price uncol. s. d.
253	Tenasserim and the adjacent Province of the Kingdom of Siam, by Lieutenant A. H. Bagge, R.E. 6 sheets	—	1868	1″=4 M	45″×32″	12/— col.
252	Pegu Division. Sheet No. 1	—	1891	„	40×27	2/—
	Pegu Division. Sheet No. 3	—	„	-	„	2/—
253	Tenasserim. 6 sheets	—	1897	„	46×30	9/—
						12/— col.

Burma, Provincial Map.

Ref. No.	Description of Map	Year of Survey	Date of last edition	Scale	Size	Price uncol. s. d.
877	Upper Burma, 2 sheets	—	1895	1″=16 M	40×27 each	6/—
877	do (without hills), 2 sheets	—	1895	1″=16 M	„	6/—
859	Upper Burma	—	1898	1″=64 M	14×14	— 9 d.
877	Upper Burma, 2 sheets	—	1902	1″=16 M	40×27	4/6

Burma, District Maps.

Ref. No.	Description of Map	Year of Survey	Date of last edition	Scale	Size	Price uncol. s. d.
756	Akyab District, Skeleton Map	—	1888	1″=8 M	30″×22″	1/—
778	Port of Bhamo District	—	1889	1″=4 M	40″×27″	3/6
785	Minbu District	—	1889	1″=4 M	40″×27″	3/6
879	Bhamo District	—	1894	1″=8 M	40×24	2/6
908	Katha District	—	1894	1″=4 M	40×27	3/—
879	Bhamo and Myitkyina Districts	—	1896	1″=8 M	40×25	2/—

Burma, Cantonment and City Plans, &c.

Ref. No.	Description of Map	Year of Survey	Date of last edition	Scale	Size	Price uncol. s. d.
406	Kyouk Phyoo Station, 2 sheets	—	1869	12″=1 M	40″×27″	4/6
468	Moulmein Town, 8 sheets	—	1877	1″=400 Feet	„	20/—
469	Moulmein Cantonment	—	1877	1″=200 Feet	„	3/—
462	Rangoon Town and Suburbs, 9 sheets	—	1880	1″=400 Feet	„	22/—
	Tounggyi Civil Station (Southern Shan States)	—	1893	10″=1 M	„	3/—
904	Mandalay and Environs	—	1894	1″=1 M	30×22	1/—
1038	Maymyo and Surrounding Country	—	1902	1″=1 M	34×26	1/6

Burma, Forest Map.

Ref. No.	Description of Map	Year of Survey	Date of last edition	Scale	Size	Price uncol. s. d.
	Pyinma Forest Reserve (Pegu District) 2 sheets	—	1898	4″=1 M	40×25	2/3

Burma, Mining Plans.

Ref. No.	Description of Map	Year of Survey	Date of last edition	Scale	Size	Price uncol. s. d.
	Gold Mining Grants near Kyauk Paya, District Katha, Sheet No. 1	—	1894	8″=1 M	35×25	2/—
	Gold Mining Reserve on Na Maw Chaung, District Katha, Sheet No. 2	—	-		-	

Ref. No.	Description of Map	Year of Survey	Date of last edition	Scale	Size	Price uncol. s. d.
	Gold Mining Grants near Leksawo, District Katha, Sheet No. 3	—	1894	8″=1 M	35×25	2/—
	Kyaukpazat Prospecting Grant near Pa Den Gon, District Katha, Sheet No. 4	—	„	„	„	„
	Mau Daw Prospecting Grant near Pin Lou, District Katha, Sheet No. 5	—	„	„	„	„
	Index Map to the above	—	„	1″=2 M	„	„

Burma, Coal Tract.

	Coal Tract, Letkokbin to Male, Shwebo District, 2 sheets.	1893—94	1894	2″=1 M	40×27	4/—

Burma, Oil-Fields Surveys.

1026	Index to Survey of Yenangyat Oil-Field, Pakoku District	1899—00	1900	1″=1 M	40×27	1/6

Burma, Triangulation Charts.

	Mandalay Meridional Series, No. 5	1893—94	1894	1″=4 M	40×27	2/—
	Five Charts of Triangulation of No. 20 Survey Party, Burma 5 sheets	1882—96	1902	1″=1 M and 1″=2 M	Various	1/6
	Charts of Triangulation, Sheets 254, 256	1890—95	1902	1″=2 M	30×22	1/6 each

68. — Map of the Burman Empire including also Siam, Cochin-China, Ton-king and Malaya. By James Wyld, Geographer to his Majesty.

London, Published by James Wyld, Charing Cross, East, 1882.

69. — *A. Boileau Pemberton. — Map of the Eastern frontier of British India, with the adjacent countries extending to Yunan in China. 4 sections forming together a very large coloured Map, 97 inches × 56, 1838.

Comprenant le Tibet, la Birmanie, le Cambodge, Tenasserim, etc.

70. — Map of the Burman empire. Published by G. & J. Cary, N° 86 St. James's Street London, pièce in-folio.

71. — Map of the Burmese Empire. Thacker, Spink & Co.: Calcutta, 1852.

72. — Stanford's Map of the Empires of China and Japan with the adjacent parts of the Russian Empire, India, Burma, &c. London, Edward Stanford, Oct. 1st., 1875. 10s. 6d.

Il y a une éd. récente.

Fleuves.

Irawadi.

73. — Note on the Discharge of Water, by the Irrawaddy. — By J. McClelland, Esq. F. L. S. Commissioner of Forests, Rangoon. (*Jour. As. Soc. Bengal*, XXII, 1853, pp. 480—484).

74. — Der Irawadi. (*Zeit. f. Allg. Erdk.*, N. F. V, 1858, pp. 359—365.)
D'après Yule's *Narrative.*

75. — The Irawady and its Sources. By Dr. J. Anderson. Read, June 13, 1870. (*Journ. Roy. Geog. Soc.*, XL, 1870, pp. 286—303.)

76. — The Irawady and its Sources. By Dr. J. Anderson. [Extracts.] (*Proc. Roy. Geog. Soc.*, XIV, 1870, pp. 346—356.)

77. — °On the alluvial Deposits of the Irrawadi, more particularly as contrasted with those of the Ganges. (*Records Geolog. Survey India*, III, Pt. 1, 1870.)

78. — °Report on the Irrawaddi River. Part I. Hydrography of the Irrawaddi River. Part II. Hydrology of the Irrawaddi River. Part III. Hydraulics of the Irrawaddi. Part IV. Hydraulic Works connected with the Nawoon River. Parts I. and II. (in one vol.), pp. 195; Part III., pp. 227; Part IV., pp. 151, in-fol. By R. Gordon, Esq., M. I. C. E., &c. Rangoon, 1879—80, 3 vol. in-fol.
Notice: *Nature*, XXVI, 1882, pp. 172—175. By Allan Cunningham.

79. — °R. Gordon. — Hydraulic Work on the Irawadi Delta. (*Min. P. Inst. Civil Engineers*, CXIII, pp. 181—6.)

80. — The Irawadi River. By Robert Gordon. C.E. (*Proc. R. Geog. Soc.*, VII, 1885, May, pp. 292—331; carte, p. 352).

81. — Une monographie du fleuve Iraouaddi. (*Bull. Soc. Géog.*, Avril 1880, p. 373). [R. Gordon].

82. — The River Irawadi and its Sources. By Major J. E. Sandeman, Bengal Staff Corps. (*Proc. R. Geog. Soc.*, Vol. IV, 1882, pp. 257—273).
Avec carte, p. 328.

83. — Remarques sur la source de l'Irrawaddi. (*Ann. de l'Ext. Orient*, 1883—1884, VI, pp. 366—369).
D'après Wilcox.
Traduit de l'anglais par C. H. Desgodins, inspecteur des forêts en retraite.

84. — Note sur l'Iraouady. Par Dutreuil de Rhins. (*Compte rendu, Soc. Géog.*, 1888, No. 1, pp. 12—14).
En réponse au général Walker dans les *Proceedings.*

85. — 'Irrawaddy Flotilla Company. Truth about the Flotilla. Rangoon, 1888, in-8, pp. 74.

   B. M. 08239. f. 30 (8).

86. — 'David Ker. — Burmah's Mighty River. (The Land's numerous Capital cities of the past). (*The New York Times*, 21 June 1888).

87. — Les sources de l'Irrawaddy. Par E. Roux. (*Ann. de Géog.*, V, 1895—6, pp. 483—495.)

   Voir *infra*, Prince Henri d'Orléans.

88. — Notice sur la relation du voyage aux sources de l'Iraouaddi. Par M. Emile Roux. (*Bul. Soc. Géog. Com.*, XX, 1898, pp. 294—296.)

89. — 'G. A. — Irawadis Källor. (*Ymer*, 1896, 2, pp. 125 et seq.).

90. — Les sources de l'Irawádi. (*Bul. Soc. Géog. Est*, 1896, pp. 437—440.)

   D'après l'art. de G. Regelsperger, dans la *Revue de Géographie.*

91. — 'Az Irravadi eredete. (*Földrajzi Közlemények*, XXV, p. 207.)

92. — A Sail down the Irawaddy. By Henry M. Cadell of Grange. (*Scottish Geog. Jour.*, XVII, 1901, pp. 239—265.)

Fleuves divers.

93. — Note sur le Cours inférieur du Dzang bo ou de la grande rivière du Tubet. (*Journ. As.*, VIII, 1826, pp. 302—306).

94. — The Falls of the Tsang-po (San-pu), and identity of that river with the Brahmaputra. By Surgeon-Major L. A. Waddell. (*Geogr. Journal*, V, March 1895, pp. 258—260).

95. — Notes of a trip up the Salween. By Rev. C. Parish. (*Jour. As. Soc. Bengal*, Vol. 34, 1865, Pt. 2, pp. 135—146.)

96. — The Lu River of Tibet; is it the source of the Irawadi or the Salwin? By General J. T. Walker. (*Proc. R. Geog. Soc.*, N. S., Vol. IX, 1887, pp. 352—377.)

   Avec carte, p. 398.

97. — Explorations on the Chindwin River, Upper Burma. By Colonel R. G. Woodthorpe, R. E., C. B. (*Proc. R. Geog. Soc.*, XI, 1889, April, pp. 197—216; carte, p. 260).

Montagnes.

98. — Les chaînes de Birmanie. Par J. G. (*La Géographie*, 15 Avril 1900, pp. 327—328).

A. — La BIRMANIE forme quatre divisions, réparties en districts:

I. *Arakan* Division:
Akyab. — Northern Arakan. — Kyaukpu. — Sandoway.
II. *Pegu* Division:
Ville de Rangoon. — Hanthawadi. — Pegu. — Tharrawadi. — Prome.
III. *Irawadi* Division:
Thayetmyo. — Henzada. — Bassein. — Thongwa.
IV. *Tenasserim* Division:
Ville de Maulmain. — Amherst. — Tavoy. — Mergui. — Shwegyin. — Toung-gu. — Salwen Hill Tracts.

B. — La HAUTE BIRMANIE forme quatre divisions, réparties en districts:

I. *Minbu* Division:
Thayetmyo. — Pakôkku. — Minbu. — Magwe.
II. *Mandalay* Division:
Mandalay. — Bhamo. — Myitkyina. — Katha. — Mines de Rubis.
III. *Sagaing* Division:
Shwebo. — Sagaing. — Lower Chindwin. — Upper Chindwin.
IV. *Meiktila* Division:
Kyauksè. — Meiktila. — Yamèthin. — Myingyan.

Birmanie.

Arakan Division.

99. — An account of Aracan. Written at Islaàmabad (Chittagong.) in June 1777. Communicated by Major R. E. Roberts. Extracted from the Asiatic Miscellany, published at Calcutta. (*Asiatic Annual Register*, 1798—9, pp. 160—166, *Miscel. Tracts.*)

100. — Historical and Statistical Sketch of Arakan. — By Charles Paton, Esq. Sub-Commissioner in Aracan. (*As. Researches*, XVI, 1828, pp. 353—381).

101. — General Remarks on the Coast of Arracan; transmitted by Captain Laws, H. M. S. Satellite; communicated by Captain Beaufort, F. R. S. Read 13th June, 1831. (*Journ. R. Geogr. Soc.*, I, 1831, pp. 175—179).

102. — Geschichte eines Schiffbruchs an der Küste von Arrakan in Ostindien, nach dem Berichte eines jungen Engländers, des Schiffslieutenants W. Mackay, in-12, pp. 1 à 47.

Forme le No. 1 de *Sämmtliche Kinder= und Jugendschriften* von Joachim Heinrich CAMPE. — Vierte Gesammtausgabe der letzten Hand. — Neun und zwanzigstes Bändchen. — Neue Sammlung merkwürdiger Reisebeschreibungen. Erster Theil. — In der Reihe die fünfte Original=Auflage. — Braunschweig, Verlag der Schulbuchhandlung. 1832.

103. — Restoration and Translation of the Inscription on the large Arracan Bell now at Nadrohighát, Zillah Alligarh, described by Captain Wroughton in the Journal of the Asiatic Society, December 1837. (*Journ. As. Soc. Bengal*, VII, April 1838, pp. 287—297.)

104. — Account of Arakan. By Lieut. Phayre, Senior Assistant Commissioner, Arakan. (*Journ. As. Soc. Bengal*, X, Pt. II, 1841, pp. 679—710).

105. — On the History of Arakan. — By Capt. A. P. Phayre, Senior Assistant Commissioner, Arakan. (*Journ. of the As. Soc. of Bengal*, Vol. XIII, Pt. I, No. 145, 1844, pp. 23—52).

106. — The Coins of Arakan: — The Historical Coins, by Capt. A. P. Phayre,

Principal Asst. Commr. Arakan. (*Journ. of the As. Soc. of Bengal*, Vol. XV, No. 171, 1846, pp. 232—237).

[Voir *Int. Numismata Orientalia* by Sir E. C. Bayley, au chap. Numismatique.]

107. — The Coins of Arakan. — The Symbolical Coins. By Lieut. Thos. Latter. (*Journ. of the As. Soc. of Bengal*, Vol. XV, No. 171, 1846, pp. 238—240).

108. — Note on an Arakanese Coin. By Capt. G. E. Fryer... (*Journ. As. Soc. Bengal*, Vol. 41, 1872, Pt. 1, pp. 201—203.)

109. — On a Symbolical Coin of the Wethâli dynasty of Arakan. — By W. Theobald. (*Jour. As. Soc. Bengal*, Vol. 61, 1892, Pt. 1, pp. 102—104.)

110. — Arakan. Past-Present-Future. A Résumé of two Campaigns for its Development by John Ogilvy Hay, J. P. (Old Arakan) Formerly honorary Magistrate of the town of Akyab; author of 'Indo-Burmah-China Railway Connections, a pressing Necessity'. With map. William Blackwood and Sons, Edinburgh and London, MDCCCXCII, in-8, pp. VIII—216 + 2 ff. n. c.

111. — *Report on the Antiquities of Arakan. Rangoon, 1892, in-fol., pp. 67. B. M. 7701. cc. 1. (1).

112. — *C. M. Pleyte Wzn. — Ein arakanesischer Hausgötze. (*Globus*, lxx, pp. 113, 148).

Figure de Bouddha d'après le Journal, 1844.

∴

113. — Folktales of Arakan. By Bernard Houghton. (*Ind. Antiq.*, XXII, 1893, pp. 98—102.)

Translated from a Burmese MS. furnished by Maung Tha Bwin, Myôôk of Sandoway.

114. — The Arakanese Dialect of the Burman Language. By Bernard Houghton. (*Journ. R. As. Soc.*, July 1897, pp. 453—461.)

"It is well known that the people of Arakan are an offshoot of the Burman race, the accepted account being that they first crossed the range of mountains called the Arakan Yoma about B.C. 825 under a Prince Kanruga-gyi. It seems probable that the small portion of the country then inhabited was settled by a few of the advance-guard of the Chin-Lushai or Naga tribesmen, with perhaps some colonies of Indians on the sea-coast. These were expelled or absorbed; and the Arakanese kingdom, having its centre in the flat open plains of the Akyab district, gradually extended south as far as the Mawyon-gyaw Hills, in the Sandoway district, and north to Chittagong (A.D. 1450). It was finally crushed by an invasion of Burmans from the east of the Yoma in 1784".

115. — Arakanese Dialect. By R. F. St. Andrew St. John. (*Ibid.*, Oct. 1897, pp. 940—1).

Remarques sur l'article précédent.

Akyab.

115 bis. — *Arakan Weekly News.*

Northern Arakan ou Arakan Hill Tracts.

116. — Notice of the Khyén Tribe, inhabiting the Yúma mountains, between Ava and Aracan. — By Lieutenant T. A. Trant, His Majesty's 38th Regiment of Foot. (*As. Researches*, XVI, 1828, pp. 261—269).

117. — A Note on some Hill Tribes on the Kuladyne River; — Arracan. By Lieut. T. Latter (67th N.I.), of the Arracan Local Battalion. (*Journ. of the As. Soc. of Bengal*, Vol. XV, N⁰ 169, 1846, pp. 60—78).

118. — Notes on the Heumá or "Shendoos" a tribe inhabiting the hills North of Arracan. By Capt. S. R. Tickell, 31st B. N.I. (*Ibid.*, Vol. XXI, 1852, pp. 207—213).

119. — Extracts from a Journal up the Koladyn River, Aracan, in 1851. By Capt. S. R. Tickell, B. N.I. Communicated through the Secretary. Read April 23, 1853. (*Journ. Roy. Geog. Soc.*, XXIV, 1854, pp. 86—114).

120. — Notes on the Hill Tribes of Arakan. By the Editor. (*The Phoenix*, III, N⁰ 28, October 1872, pp. 61—64).

121. — Affinities of the Dialects of the Chepang and Kusundah Tribes of Nipál with those of the Hill Tribes of Arracan. By Capt. C. J. F. Forbes, F.R.G.S., M.A.S. Bengal, etc. (*Journ. R. As. Soc.*, N. S., Vol. IX, Art. XIII, July 1877, pp. 421—424).

122. — The Hill Tracts of Arakan, by Major W. Gwynne Hughes, F.R.G.S.....
Notice: *Bull. Soc. Acad. Indo-Chinoise*, 2ᵉ sér., III, 1890, pp. 468—486. Par A. M.

123. — Coup-d'oeil sur le District montagneux de l'Arakan et sur les tribus sauvages qui l'habitent, suivi d'un vocabulaire comparatif des langues des *Tchins*, des *Tchandóos* et des *Kamis* d'après le Major Gwynne Hughes, Auteur du livre intitulé: The Hill Tracts of Arakan, par Aristide Marre... — Extrait du *Muséon* — Louvain, Charles Peeters, 1883, br. in-8, pp. 27.

Kyaukpu.

124. — A Three Weeks Sail in search of Health — Province of Arracan — Kyok Phyoo. — Its Harbour, Productions, Capabilities, Geological Features, Visit to an active volcano. By Henry Harpur Spry, M.D., F.G.S., &c., Secretary to the Agricultural and Horticultural Society of India. (*Jour. As. Soc. Bengal*, X, Pt. I., 1841, pp. 138—147).

125. — Journal of a Tour through the Island of Rambree, with a Geological Sketch of the Country, and Brief Account of the Customs, &c., of its Inhabitants. By Lieut. Wm. Foley. (*Ibid.*, IV, Jan. 1835, pp. 20—39; *ibid.*, Feb. 1835, pp. 82—95; *ibid.*, April 1835, pp. 199—207).

Sandoway.

126. — On the Khyeng People of the Sandoway District, Arakan. — By Major G. E. Fryer, Deputy Commissioner, Sandoway. (*Ibid.*, Vol. 44, 1875, Pt. 1, pp. 39—82).
I. Physical and Social Characteristics. — II. Grammatical Notes on the Language. — III. A Vocabulary in Khyeng and English; A Vocabulary in English and Khyeng.

127. — The Khyeng People of the Sandoway District, Arakan. By G. E. Fryer, Major, M. S. C. Deputy Commissioner, Sandoway. — With two plates. —

Calcutta: Printed by C. B. Lewis, at the Baptist Mission Press. 1875, in-8, 2 ff. n. ch. + pp. 44.

> I. 1. — Introductory; 2. — Physical Characteristics; 3. — Individual and Family Life. — II. Grammatical Notes on the Language. — III. Vocabularies a). Khyeng and English; b). English and Khyeng.
> Rep. from *the Journal Asiatic Society of Bengal*, Part I, for 1875.

128. — Folk-Etymology of Place-Names in the Sandoway District of Burma. By B. Houghton. (*Ind. Antiq.*, XXII, 1893, p. 195).

129. — *Note on the Myauktang Teak Plantation in the Arracan District, Burmah, by E. P. Stebbing. (*Indian Forester*, May 1900, Vol. XXVI, No. 5).

Chittagong.

> Quoique Chittagong soit un district du Bengal, nous l'avons rattaché à l'ARAKAN, à cause de sa situation géographique.

130. — Observations of the Tides at Chittagong made in conformity with the Circular of the Asiatic Society. By Lieut. H. Siddons, Engineers. (*Jour. As. Soc. Bengal*, VI, Nov. 1837, p. 949).

131. — Some account of the Hill Tribes in the interior of the District of Chittagong, in a letter to the Secretary of the Asiatic Society. By the Rev. M. Barbe, Missionary. (*Ibid.*, XIV, pt. I, 1845, pp. 380—391).

132. — Diary of a Hill-Trip on the Borders of Arracan. By Lieutenant T. H. Lewin. (*Proc. Roy. Geog. Soc.*, XI, 1867, p. 52).

133. — *Hill Tracts of Chittagong and Dwellers therein. — A Description of the Country, its Rivers, Scenery, Soil, etc. The Rise and Progress of the British Power in the Hill Tracts. Classification of the Hill Tribes — their modes of Life and Habits and Customs. In the Appendices are given a
· Description of the Forest Timber and other Produce of the Hill Tracts and a Comparative Vocabulary of the Hill Dialects. By Captain T. H. Lewin, Deputy Commissioner of the Hill Tracts. 1869, gr. in-8.

134. — Hill Proverbs of the Inhabitants of the Chittagong Hill tracts. By Capt. Thomas Herbert Lewin, Deputy Commissioner of the Chittagong Hill Tracts. Calcutta: printed at the Bengal Secretariat press. 1873, in-fol., pp. ii—30.

> On lit dans le préambule: "The sayings collected here are proverbs of the Khiongtha, the "sons of the river" a wild and simple people of Burmese extraction, speaking a patois of the Burmese language and following Buddhistic tenets who reside in the Hill Tracts of Chittagong".

135. — On a new king of Bengal ('Aláuddín Firúz Sháh), and notes on the Husaini kings of Bengal and their conquest of Chátgáon (Chittagong). By H. Blochmann. (*Jour. As. Soc. Bengal*, Vol. 41, 1872, Pt. 1, pp. 331—340).

136. — Tipera and Chittagong Kukis. (*Indian Antiquary*, I, 1872, pp. 225—6, d'après le *Bengal Times*).

137. — *G. v. d. Gabelentz. — Kuki. (*Allgemeine Encyclopedie* von Ersch und Gruber, Sect. II, Bd. 40, pp. 209 et seq.).

138. — Note on the Chittagong Copper-plate, dated S'aka 1165, or A.D. 1243, presented to the Society by A. L. Clay. — By Pranna'th Pandit. (*Jour. As. Soc. Bengal*, Vol. 43, 1874, Pt. I, pp. 318—324).

139. — *The Chittagong Hill Tribes. Results of a Journey in the year 1882. By Dr. Emil Riebeck. Translated by Prof. A. H. Keane. Asher, 1885.

   Notice: *Nature*, XXXII, 1885, pp. 169—170.
   — The Zoology of Dr. Riebeck's "Chittagong Hill Tribes". — The Gayal and Gaur. By W. T. Blanford. (*Nature*, XXXII, 1885, p. 243).

140. — Notes on the Chittagong Dialect. By F. E. Pargiter. (*Jour. As. Soc. Bengal*, Vol. 55, 1886, Pt. I, pp. 66—80).

141. — Description of a new Species of Phytophagous Coleoptera alleged to be destructive to the Dhan Crops in the Chittagong District. By Joseph S. Baly. (*Ibid.*, Vol. 55, 1886, Pt. 2, p. 412).

142. — Map India Office. — 128 N.E. Chittagong. 1898. — Scale 1"=4 M. — 1 sheet 27 × 20 in. — Price 1/2 uncol.; 1/5 col.

143. — Ansteuerung und Beschreibung des Hafens von Chittagong. Britisch-Indien. Von W. Reising, Kapitän des Dampfers "Steinberger" der Hansa-Linie (Bremen). (*Ann. der Hyd.*, XXVII, 1899, pp. 536—8).

144. — A Chittagong Family. (*Calcutta Review*, CIX, July 1899, pp. 120—122).

145. — Notes on the Maghī dialect of the Chittagong Hill Tracts. By Sten Konow. (*Zeit. D. Morg. Ges.*, Bd. LVII, Hft. 1, 1903, pp. 1—12).

   "Maghī is the local name for Burmese in the Chittagong Hill Tracts. According to the information collected for the Linguistic Survey of India, it is spoken by about 32500 individuals in the Chittagong Hills, and by 16417 in Chittagong. It is, in all essentials, the same dialect as the Burmese of Arakan".

Pegu Division.

Rangoon.

146. — Translation of an Inscription on the Great Bell of Rangoon, with Notes and Illustrations. — By The Rev. G. H. Hough. (*As. Researches*, XVI, 1828, pp. 270—283).

147. — Notes on Rangoon. [Extract of a Letter from Mr. Alexander Brown to Mr. John Fleming, dated Rangoon, 15th Feb., 1867]. (*Proc. Roy. Geog. Soc.*, XI, 1867, pp. 148—149).

148. — Les Cloches de la Pagode de Rangoun. (*Rev. des Trad. populaires*, III, 1888, pp. 123—4).

   Ext. de *Dix mois autour du monde*, par Georges Lieussou.

149. — *E. Maigre. — La pagode de Rangoon (Birmanie). (*Bul. Soc. Géog.*, Marseille, 1888, p. 25).

150. — *David Ker. — Burmah's Golden Pagoda; the famous Shway Dagohu of Rangoon. (*New York Times*, 7 Sept. 1888).

151. — *David Ker. — The Liverpool of Burmah; Rangoon, its Street Scenes and its playhouse. (*Ibid.*, 2 Sept. 1888).

152. — The last Voyage to India and Australia, in the 'Sunbeam'. By the late Lady Brassey. Illustrated by R. T. Pritchett and from Photographs. London: Longmans, 1889, in-8, pp. xxiv—490.

    Rangoon.

153. — A Note on the name Shwe-Dagon. By R. C. Temple. (*Ind. Antiq.*, XXII, 1893, pp. 27—8).

154. — Relics found in Rangoon. By R. F. St. Andrew St. John. (*Journ. R. As. Soc.*, Jan. 1895, pp. 199—201).

155. — *R. D. Oldham. Note on the Alluvial Deposits and Subterranean water-supply of Rangoon. (*Rec. Geolog. Survey India*, XXVI, 1893, II, p. 64).

156. — Einige Bemerkungen über Rangun. Aus dem meteorologischen Journale des Schiffes »Undine", Kapt. H. Otto. (*Ann. der Hyd.*, XXIV, 1896, pp. 58—9).

157. — Bemerkungen über Rangun. Von Kapt. F. Niejahr, Bark »Anna Schwalbe", und Kapt. H. Otto vom Schiff »Undine". (*Ibid.*, XXV, 1897, pp. 228—231).

158. — *Ch. Jambon. — Rangoon. (*Monde moderne*, X, pp. 353—8). Illustrations.

159. — La léproserie de Rangoon. Lettre de M. Freynet, des Missions étrangères de Paris. (*Missions Catholiques*, 11 Sept. 1903, pp. 433—9).

.·.

160. — *Report on the Lunatic Asylum in Rangoon. Management of Lunatics in Burma. Compiled by the Government of Burma. in-fol.

    For the year 1899.

161. — *Statements relating to Rangoon Lunatic Asylum, showing admissions, discharges, etc., of Lunatics. Compiled by the Government of Burma. in-fol.

    For the year 1901.

162. — *Report on the Rangoon Town Police of Burma. Report on the working of Town Police as reorganised by the Rangoon Police Act, 1899. Compiled by the Commissioner of Police. in-fol.

    For the years 1899, 1900, 1901.

163. — *Rangoon Police Manual. Containing Orders and Rules for the Rangoon Police. By R. G. P. P. McDonnell, Commissioner of Police. 1901, gr. in-8.

164. — *Report on the Mayo Sailor's Home Rangoon, for 1901. Working of the Sailor's Home during 1901. 1902, in-fol.

Publications périodiques.

165. — *Anglo-Burman Advocate.*
    Hebdomadaire.

166. — *British Burmah Advertiser.*

167. — *British Burmah Gazette.*
    Hebdomadaire.

168. — *Burmah Herald.* Rangoon, 1872—3, in-fol.

169. — Burma Pocket Almanac and Directory, for 1889. — Printed and Published by G. W. D'Vauz. — D'Vauz Press. — Rangoon, 1889. pet. in-8, pp. 9 + xl + 120 + ff. blancs [Diary] + 180 + 216.

170. — D'Vauz's Burma Pocket Almanac and Directory, for 1890. — Printed and Published by G. W. D'Vauz. — London Agent — W. M. Wills, 151, Canon Street, London. Burma Agent — Messrs. Myles Standish & Co. Barr Street, Rangoon. D'Vauz Press. — Rangoon. 1890. pet. in-8, pp. 9 + lxviii + 128 + Diary + 192 + 255.

    5e année.

171. — *Gazette.*
172. — *Gazette Weekly Budget.*
173. — *Times of Burma.* Rangoon, 1899, etc. in-fol.

Pegu.

174. — A Concise Account of the Kingdom of Pegu; its climate, produce, trade, and government; the manners and customs of its inhabitants. Interspersed with remarks moral and political. With an Appendix, containing an enquiry into the cause of the variety observable in the fleeces of sheep, in different climates, to which is added a description of the caves at Elephanta, Ambola, and Canara, the whole being the result of Observations made on a Voyage, performed by Order of the Hon. East India Company. By W. Hunter, A. M. Surgeon. Calcutta: Printed by John Hay. MDCCLXXXV, in-8, pp. 152.

175. — *A Concise Account ... of the Kingdom of Pegu... by W. Hunter. London, Sewell, 1789, in-12.

    Cat. Langlès, 3518.

176. — Description du Pégu et de l'isle de Céylan. Renfermant des détails exacts et neufs sur le climat, les productions, le commerce, le gouvernement, les moeurs et les usages de ces contrées; par W. Hunter, Chr. Wolf & Eschelskroon; traduite de l'Anglois & de l'Allemand. Par L. L***. [Langlès]. A Paris, chez Maradan... 1793, in-8, pp. 32—354.

177. — The Pegu Pagoda. — By Capt. H. A. Browne, Deputy Commissioner of Rangoon. (*Jour. As. Soc. Bengal*, Vol. 36, 1867, Pt. I, pp. 109—125).

178. — On the History of Pegu. By Major-General Sir Arthur P. Phayre. (*Ibid.*, Vol. 42, 1873, Pt. I, pp. 23—57; 120—159; Vol. 43, 1874, Pt. I, pp. 6—21).

179. — Notes on the early History of Pegu; by the late Sir Arthur Phayre. (*Ind. Antiq.*, XV, 1886, pp. 317—8).

180. — On the Connexion of the Mōns of Pegu with the Koles of Central India. By Capt. C. J. F. S. Forbes, of the Burmese Civil Commission. (*Journ. R. As. Soc.*, N. S., Vol. X, Part II, Art. XI, April 1878, pp. 234—243).

181. — *R. F. St. Andrew St. John. — Notes on some Old Towns in Pegu. (*Trans. Congress Orientalists*, London, 1892, I, pp. 370—375).

182. History of Pegu. By R. F. St. Andrew St. John. (*Jour. R. As. Soc.*, Jan. 1898, pp. 204—7).

> Renferme une lettre du Cap. Gerini, Bangkok, Oct. 21, 1897. Au sujet des Talaings (Môñs), St. John écrit, pp. 204—5:
> "Owing to the great emigration of the Môñs to Siam, when fleeing from the sword of Alompra, most of their histories and works were taken there; but although this is the case, there is still work to be done in Burma. Ancient manuscripts may yet be discovered, old cities overhauled and dug into, and their original names discovered by inquiring into the various Môñ dialects. There can be little doubt that in the earliest years of the christian era the Môñ family extended as far north as the mouths of the Ganges and Brahmaputra, and that the modern Sandoway (Sada?) was one of their trading stations. Somewhere about A.D. 300, people from the east coast of the Bay of Bengal founded colonies on the coasts of the Gulf of Martaban, of which the principal appears to have been Thatôñ, or Saddhammanagara. There was also a city on the Irrawaddy, called Brôm (Prome) or Srikhetra inhabited by a tribe called Pru, who were probably of the Môñ family. In 1050 A.D. Anuruddha the Mrammā (Burman) king of Pagan, is said to have swept down on Thatôñ, and carried away its king and a copy of the Tipiṭakam. After that there was an anarchy, till a Shan(?) of the name of Wareru established a monarchy at Martaban (Muttama) in 1287 A.D, and history thenceforward begins to get clearer. It is however, to the time previous to this to which attention should be turned in order to solve the questions —
>   1. When, whence, and by whom was Buddhism introduced into Pegu?
>   2. Was there ever, prior to 1287 A.D. an important kingdom in South Burma, or were there only a few independent semi-Indian colonies?"

183. — Branginoco. By R. C. Temple. (*Ind. Antiq.*, XXIII, 1893, p. 140).

> King of Pegu, 1551—1581.

184. — Sousa Viterbo. — Um Costume dos habitantes do Pegu. (*Bol. Soc. Geog. Lisboa*, 12ª Serie, 1893, pp. 101—4).

.·.

185. — Notice of Pugan, the Ancient Capital of the Burmese Empire. By Lieut.-Col. H. Burney, H. C.'s Resident in Ava. (*Jour. As. Soc. Bengal*, IV, July, 1835, pp. 400—404).

.·.

186. — Grammatical Notes and Vocabulary of the Peguan Language. To which are added a few pages of Phrases, &c. By Rev. J. M. Haswell. Rangoon: American Mission Press. C. Bennett. 1874, in-8, pp. xvi—160.

187. — — Second Edition. Edited by E. O. Stevens. 1901, gr. in-8, pp. 357.

188. — 'English-Peguan Vocabulary, to which are added a few pages of Geographical Names. By E. O. Stevens. 1896, gr. in-8, pp. 140.

> Les mots pegouans sont imprimés seulement en caractères birmans.

189. — 'E. O. Stevens. — The Peguan Hymnal for Public and Social Worship (in Talaing). Rangoon, American Baptist Mission Press, 1898, pp. 41.

190. — 'A. E. Hudson. — Peguan or Talaing First Standard Reader with Burmese translation. Second Edition. Rangoon, F. D. Phinney, 1898, pp. 38.

Prome.

191. — Birmanie. La ville de Prome. D'après le *Standard*. (*Ann. de l'Extr. Orient*, II, pp. 165—167).

Irawadi Division.

192. — The name "Bassein". By Major R. C. Temple. (*Ind. Antiq.*, XXII, 1893, pp. 18—21).

Tenasserim Division.

193. — 'Tenasserim: or Notes on the Fauna, Flora, Minerals and Nations of British Burmah and Pegu: with systematic Catalogues of the known Minerals, Plants, Mammals, Fishes, Mollusks, Sea Nettles, Corals, Sea Urchins, Worms, Insects, Crabs, Reptiles and Birds; with Vernacular Names. By Rev. F. Mason, F. A. Maulmain. 1831. In-12, pp. 736.

194. — History of Tenasserim, by Captain James Low, Madras Army, M.R.A.S., &c. &c. (*Journ. R. As. Soc.*, II, M.DCCC.XXXV, Art. XIV, pp. 248—275; *ibid.*, III, M.DCCC.XXXVI, Art. II, pp. 25—54; *ibid.*, Art. XIV, pp. 287—336; *ibid.*, IV, M.DCCC.XXXVII, Art. II, pp. 42—108; *ibid.*, Art. XXII, pp. 304—332; *ibid.*, V, M.DCCC.XXXIX, Art. IX, pp. 141—164; *ibid.*, Art. XV, pp. 216—263).

195. — An Account of some of the Petty States lying north of the Tenasserim Provinces; drawn up from the Journals and Reports of D. Richardson, Esq. Surgeon to the Commissioner of the Tenasserim Provinces. By E. A. Blundell, Esq. Commissioner. (*Jour. As. Soc. Bengal*, V, Oct. 1836, pp. 601—625; *ibid.*, Nov. 1836, pp. 688—707).

196. — 'Second Report on the Provinces of Ye, Tavoy, and Mergui on the Tenasserim Coast. By J. W. Helfer, M.D. in-8.

197. — Third Report on Tenasserim — the Surrounding Nations, — Inhabitants, Natives and Foreigners — Character, Morals and Religion — By John William Helfer, M.D. (*Jour. As. Soc. Bengal*, VIII, Dec. 1839, pp. 973—1005).

198. — Report on the Tenasserim Provinces considered as a Resort for Europeans. By John William Helfer, M.D. (*Ibid.*, IX, Pt. I, 1840, pp. 155—189).

199. — Calagouk, or Curlew Island, in the Bay of Bengal, as a Sea-coast Sanitarium. By Duncan Macpherson, M.D., Inspector-General of Hospitals, Madras Establishment. (*Proc. Roy. Geog. Soc.*, VI, 1862, pp. 208—210).

200. — Report on a Route from the Mouth of the Pakchan to Krau, and thence across the Isthmus of Krau to the Gulf of Siam. By Capt. Alexander Fraser, Bengal Engineers, and Capt. J. G. Forlong, Ex. Engineer... (*Miscel. Papers relat. to Indo-China*, I, Lond., Trübner, 1886, pp. 285—297).
 From the *Jour. As. Soc. Bengal*, XXXI, pp. 347—362.

201. — Leonardo Fea nel Tenasserim. (*Bol. Soc. geog. Ital.*, 1888, pp. 627—689).
 Il y a pp. 628—9 une bibliographie des travaux de M. Fea insérée dans les *Annali del Museo Civico di Storia Naturale di Genova*.

202. — The Coast of Tennasserim. By E. H. Parker. (*China Review*, XX, No. 4, pp. 245—263).

Maulmain.

203. — Report of a Trial for Rebellion, held at Moulmein by the Commissioner of Tenasserim. Communicated by the Sudder Dewanny Adawlut. With a plate. (*Jour. As. Soc. Bengal*, XIV, pt. II, 1845, pp. 747—754).

204. — Casting of a Bell in Burmah. (*Jour. Ind. Arch.*, III, 1849, pp. XXVIII—XXIX).

> From the *Maulmain Chronicle*, 17th March 1849.

205. — °David Ker. — Moulmein's Old Caverns, The place itself, its Site, and its great Temple (Correspondence from Moulmein, Lower Burmah). (*The New York Times*, 1 July 1888).

206. — An English Inscription at Maulmain. By R. C. Temple. (*Ind. Antiq.*, XXI, 1892, p. 52).

207. — Notes on an Archaeological Tour through Ramannadesa (the Talaing Country of Burma). By Taw Sein Ko. (*Ibid.*, XXI, 1892, pp. 377—386).

208. — Notes on Antiquities in Ramannadesa (The Talaing Country of Burma). By Major R. C. Temple. (*Ibid.*, XXII, 1893, pp. 327—366, planches).

> Maulmain is "called Maulmain or Moulmein by the English, Mòlâmyaing by the Burmans, Mutmwêlêm by the Talaings, and Râmapura in historical and epigraphic documents". (Note, p. 327.)

Amherst.

209. — Amherst as a Sanatarium; by E. Ryley, Esq. Calcutta; Printed at the Englishman Office. 1850, br. in-8, pp. 21 avec une carte.

Tavoy.

210. — Tavoy, Boardman and Ko thahbyu or Thah-Byoo. (*Siam Repository*, July, 1869, Art. XCVII. and XCVIII, pp. 188—190, 190—191).

> Abstracts from *The Missionary Magazine*.

Mergui.

211. — A Voyage from Calcutta to the Mergui Archipelago, lying on the East Side of the Bay of Bengal; Describing a Chain of Islands, never before surveyed, that form a Strait on that Side of the Bay, 125 Miles in Length, and from 20 to 30 Miles in Breadth; with good Mud Soundings and regular Tides throughout: which Strait lying nearly North and South, any Ship may work up against the South-West Monsoon, and so get out of the Bay of Bengal, when otherwise she might be locked up for the Season. Also, An Account of the Islands Jan Sylan, Pulo Pinang, and the Port of Queda; the present State of Atcheen; and Directions for Sailing thence to Fort Marlbro' down the South-West Coast of Sumatra: to which are added, An Account of the Island Celebes; a Treatise on the Monsoons in India; a Proposal for making Ships and Vessels more convenient for the Accommodation

of Passengers; and Thoughts on a new Mode of preserving Ship Provision: Also, An Idea of making a Map of the World on a large Scale: by Thomas Forrest, Esq. Senior Captain of the Honourable Company's Marine at Fort Marlbro' in 1770, and Author of the Voyage to New Guinea. The whole illustrated with various Maps, and Views of Land; a Print of the Author's Reception by the King of Atcheen; and a View of St. Helena from the Road. Engraved by Mr. Caldwall. — London: Sold by J. Robson, New Bond-Street; I. Owen, No. 168, Piccadilly; and Balfour, Edinburgh. M.DCC.XCII. gr. in-4, 8 ff. n. ch. p. l. tit., tab., etc. + pp. x—141, Port., Pl. cartes.

212. — Extracts from a Journal kept by Mr. J. Emmott, Master Attendant at Mergui, whilst visiting the Sapan Forests. (*Journ. As. Soc. of Bengal*, I, Dec. 1832, pp. 544—549).

213. — A short notice of the Coast-line, Rivers and Islands adjacent, forming a portion of the Mergui Province, from a late survey. By Captain R. Lloyd. (*Ibid.*, VII, Dec. 1838, pp. 1027—1038).

214. — Beschreibung des Mergui-Archipels. Bengalischer Meerbusen. (*Ann. d. Hydrog.*, V, 1877, pp. 165—170).
D'après l'*Hydrographic Notice*, No. 88, du Com*t*. A. D. Taylor.

215. — Gazetteer of the Mergui District, Tenasserim Division, British Burma, by Captain J. Butler, B.S.C., Deputy Commissioner. Rangoon: Printed at the Government Press, 1884, in-8, 2 ff. n. ch. + pp. 84 + pp. x.

216. — The Birds'-Nest or Elephant islands of the Mergui Archipelago. By Alfred Carpenter. (*Nature*, XXXVII, 1887—88, p. 348).

217. — Buddhist Caves in Mergui. By R. C. Temple. (*Ind. Antiq.*, XXIII, 1894, p. 168).

218. — South Tenasserim and the Mergui Archipelago. By Wm. Sutherland. (*Scottish Geog. Mag.*, XIV, 1898, pp. 449—464).
.·.

219. — The Silong Tribe of the Mergui Archipelago. By J. R. Logan. (*Journ. Ind. Archip.*, IV, 1850, pp. 411—412).

220. — 'The Selungs of the Mergui Archipelago, by John Anderson, M.D., F.R.S. London: Trübner, 1890.

221. — Photographies relatives aux habitants des îles Mergui (les Selon). — Quelques observations anthropologiques et ethnographiques sur cette population, par L. Lapicque. (*Bul. Soc. Anth.*, Paris, 1894, pp. 218—230).

222. — Extracts from Official Documents relating to the Selungs of the Mergui Archipelago. By R. C. Temple. (*Ind. Antiq.*, XXVI, 1897, pp. 85—91, 119—126).

Toung-gu.

223. — Toungoo news sheet. *Pro Deo et Ecclesia*. Vol. I. Toungoo, January 1864. No. 1. Pièce in-fol. de 2 ff. à 2 col. imp. sur un seul côté.
On lit à la fin de la pièce:
Printed and published monthly, at the Toungoo Karen Institute Press, for the proprietor F. Mason. Price three rupees per annum payable in advance.
Nous en avons vu 12 nos; le dernier daté *déc.* 1864.

224. — A Karen of Toungoo. Written 1856. Sau quala. By Francis Mason. (*Siam Repository*, July, 1869, Vol. I, Art. XCVI, pp. 186—188).

Karen-ni.
(Pays des Karens rouges.)

225. — Abstract Journal of an Expedition from Moulmien to Ava through the Kareen country, between December 1836 and June 1837. By D. Richardson, Esq. Surgeon to the Commissioner of the Tenasserim Provinces. (*Journ. As. Soc. Bengal*, VI, Dec. 1837, pp. 1005—1022).

226. — The Karean Tribes or Aborigines of Martaban and Tavai, with Notices of the Aborigines in Keddah and Perak. By Lieut.-Col. James Low. (*Journ. Ind. Arch.*, IV, 1850, pp. 413—423).

227. — Notices of the Karens. By D. J. Macgowan, M.D. (*Ibid.*, V, 1851, pp. 345—353).

228. — On the ethnographic Position of the Karens. By J. R. Logan. (*Ibid.*, N. S., Vol. II, 1858, pp. 364—390).

229. — Journal of a Tour to Karen-nee for the purpose of opening a trading Road to the Shan Traders from Mobyay and the adjacent Shan States, through that Territory direct to Toungoo. By Edward O'Riley. (*Ibid.*, N. S., Vol. II, 1858, pp. 391—457).

230. — Notices of Karen Nee, the Country of the Kaya or Red Karens. By E. O'Riley. (*Ibid.*, N. S., Vol. III, Pt. I, 1859, pp. 1—25).

231. — Journal of a Tour to Karen-ni, for the purpose of opening a Trading-Road to the Shan Traders from Mobyay and the adjacent Shan States, through that Territory, direct to Tungu. By Edward O'Riley, Esq., F.G S., &c. With Notes. Read, March 10, 1862. (*Journ. Roy. Geog. Soc.*, XXXII, 1862, pp. 164—216).

232. — Religion, Mythology, and Astronomy among the Karens. — By the Rev. F. Mason... (*Jour. As. Soc. Bengal*, Vol. 34, 1865, Pt. 2, pp. 173—188, 195—250).
      Karen Vocabulary, pp. 239—250.

233. — On Dwellings, Works of Art, Laws, &c. of the Karens. By Rev. F. Mason. (*Ibid.*, Vol. 37, Pt. 2, 1868, pp. 125—169).

234. — Red Karens. By Francis Mason. (*Siam Repository*, April 1869. Vol. I, Art. LXIX, p. 126).

235. — Spatulancy or Augury by Fowls' Bones among the Karens of Burma. By Major McMahon, Deputy-Commissioner of British Burma. (*The Phoenix*, III, N° 25, July, 1872, pp. 9—11).

236. — Etymology of the word Karen. By Major McMahon, Deputy-Commissioner of British Burma. (*Ibid.*, III, N° 28, October 1872, pp. 66—68).

237. — The Karens of the Golden Chersonese. By Lieut.-Col. A. R. McMahon, F.R.G.S., Madras Staff Corps; Deputy Commissioner, British Burma. London: Harrison, 1876, in-8, pp. v + 1 f. n. c. + pp. 423, 1 carte et planches.

238. — Karenni and the Red Karens. By A. R. MacMahon. (*As. Quart. Review*, VIII, July—Oct. 1889, pp. 144—167).

239. — Karens. (*Siam Repository*, Vol. 6, April 1874, p. 303).

240. — On a Karen Inscription. By the Rev. Dr. Nathan Brown. (*Trans. Asiatic Society Japan*, Vol. VII, Pt. II, March 1879, pp. 127—129).
Cf. *Jour. Am. Orient. Soc.*, 1866.

241. — The loyal Karens of Burma. By Donald Mackenzie Smeaton, M.A. Bengal Civil Service. London, Kegan Paul, Trench & Co. 1887, in-8, 2 ff. n. c. p. l. tit. et l. tab. + pp. 264.

242. — Leonardo Fea nei Carin indipendenti. (*Bol. Soc. geog. Ital.*, 1888, pp. 854—868).

243. — 'J. K. Knudsen. — Een Rejse i Rödkarenernes Land. Kolding, Pontoppidan, 1890, pp. 116.

244. — Notes on the National Customs of the Karennis. By T. S. K. (*Ind. Antiq.*, XXI, 1892, pp. 317—318).

245. — Un chapitre de l'Ethnographie des Birmans Karins par M. J.-B. Bringaud, des Missions Étrangères de Paris. (*Miss. Cath.*, XXVIII, 1896, pp. 510, 521, 537, 551).

246. — 'Tod, Begräbnis und Jenseitsvorstellungen bei den Karenen (*Katholische Missionen*, XXVIII, pp. 123—7; 174—6).
D'après J. B. Bringaud.

247. — Die Karenen. Von Ludwig Dürr. (*Deutsche Rundschau f. Geog. u. Stat.*, XX, 1897—1898, pp. 116—122).

248. — '[Die Karenstämme Hinterindiens nach einem Bericht des brittischen Eingeborenen-Superintendenten Hildebrand]. (*Globus*, LXXVIII, p. 396).

248 bis. — Comment on fonde un poste carian en Birmanie. Lettre de M. G. Cance, des Miss. Et. de Paris. (*Miss. Cath.*, XXXIV, 1902, pp. 556—9, 569—73, 579—84).

Langue et Littérature.

(Pwo Karen. — Sgaw Karen. — Bghai Karen.)

249. — 'The Holy Bible. Translated into Sgau Karen. Tavoy, 1833. In-8. 3 vol.

250. — '[J. Wade]. Karen Dictionary. Tavoy, 1842. in-4.
"No title, the work was left unfinished, only 824 pp. published". (Quaritch.)

251. — A Vocabulary of the Sgau Karen Language. By Rev. J. Wade. Tavoy: Karen mission press. C. Bennett. 1849, in-8, pp. 1024.

252. — 'Thesaurus of the Karen knowledge, comprising Traditions, Legends or Fables, Poetry, Customs, Superstitions, Demonology, Therapeutics, etc. Alphabetically arranged, and forming a complete Native Karen Dictionary, with definitions and Examples, illustrating the Usages of every word. Written by San Kau-too, and compiled by J. Wade. Tavoy, 1847—1850. 4 vol. pet. in-8.

253. — 'The Catechism. By J. Wade. Fifth edition. Tavoy (Karen miss. press). 1852. In-16.

254. — Karen Vernacular Grammar, With English interspersed for the benefit of Foreign Students. In four parts. Embracing Termonology, Etymology, Syntax, and Style. By J. Wade. Maulmain: American mission Press. C. Bennett. 1861, in-8.

— — Second Edition. 1888.

255. — *J. Wade. Karen Vernacular Grammar, embracing Termonology, Etymology, Syntax and Style. 3d ed. Rangoon, 1897, in-8.

256. — The Anglo-Karen Dictionary, begun by J. Wade, D.D. revised enlarged and completed by Mrs. J. P. Binney. Published by the Burman Baptist Missionary Convention from "The Wade Printing Fund". Rangoon: American Baptist Mission Press. F. D. Phinney, supt. 1883, in-4, pp. 781.

257. — A Dictionary of the Sgau Karen Language compiled by Rev. J. Wade, D.D. Assisted by Mrs. S. K. Bennett. Recompiled and revised by Rev. E. B. Cross, D.D. Rangoon: American Baptist Mission Press, F. D. Phinney, Supt. 1896, pet. in-8, 2 ff. prél. n. ch. p. l. tit. et la préf. + pp. 1341.

258. — *The House I live in, or the Human Body. Translated into Karen, by Wm. A. Alcott., M.D. Tavoy, 1843. In-12.

259. — *Hymns in Sgau Karen. Maulmain 1845. In-18.

260. — Synopsis of a Grammar of the Karen language, embracing both dialects, Sgau and Pgho, or Sho. By F. Mason. Tavoy: Karen Mission Press, 1846, in-4, pp. VIII—458.

261. — *Primary Geography. By Mr. H. M. Mason. Third edition. Tavoy, Karen Miss. Press. 1848. In-8. (avec figures en bois).

262. — *A Dictionary of the Karen Language; by F. Mason. Tavoy, s. d. In-4, pp. 324.

263. — *The Second Book of Moses, called Exodus. Translated by Rev. F. Mason. Tavoy, Karen Miss. Press. Printed for the American and Foreign Bible Society. 1849. In-8.

264. — Bible: Containing the Old and New Testaments in Sgaw Karen. Translated by Francis Mason. 3rd edition. 1853, gr. in-8, pp. 1250.

265. — An Anglo-Karen Vocabulary. — Monosyllables. — By C. Bennett. For the use of Karen schools. — Tavoy: Karen Mission press. — 1846, in-16, pp. 188.

— — *2nd edition. 1875, in-8, pp. 148.
    C. Bennett = Cephas Bennett.

266. — *Notes on the Epistle to the Hebrews: in Karen. By E. L. Abbot. Tavoy, 1849. In-12.

267. — *Notes on the Acts of the Apostles, in Sgau Karen, by E. L. Abbot. Maulmain, 1853. In-12.

268. — *Notes of a Course of Lectures delivered to the Students of Rev. Mr. Cross' Seminary for native preachers, Tavoy, on various subjects, showing the tendencies of the general Habits, and Customs of the Karens as a People, to the destruction of their physical and mental Constitutions, by W. J. Vansomeren, M.D. Translated into the Karen, by E. R. Cross. Tavoy, Karen Miss. Press, 1850. In-8.

269. — *A Catechism for young Classes in Sabbath Schools (Karen). Tavoy, Karen Mission Press, 1850. In-8.

270. — *Questions on Matthew with explanatory Notes and practical Remarks. In Pwo Karen. By D. L. Brayton. Tavoy, 1852. In-12.

271. — *D. L. Brayton. — The New Testament, translated into Pwo-Karen. 4th Edition. Rangoon, A. B. M. Press, 1891, in-16, pp. 817.

272. — *The Holy Bible translated into Pwo-Karen by D. L. Brayton. Rangoon, Anglo-Burmese Mission Press, 1896, in-8, pp. 1105.

273. — Remarks on the Connection between the Indo-Chinese and the Indo-Germanic Languages, suggested by an Examination of the Sghā and Pghō Dialects of the Karens. By J. W. Laidlay, Esq. (*Journ. Roy. As. Soc.*, XVI, M.DCCC.LVI, art. VI, pp. 59—72).

274. — *C. H. Carpenter. The Anglo-Karen Handbook and Reader. In 3 parts, viz. Part I., Model Sentences; Part II., The Echo; Part III., The Reader. 1875, in-8, pp. 460.

> Tous les mots Karen sont imprimés en caractères birmans.

275. — *T. Thanbya. — Karen School Reader. Rangoon 1887, in-16.

276. — Folk-Lore of the Sgaw-Karens. Translated by B. Houghton, from the Papers of Saya Kiaw zan in the "Sa-tu-waw". (*Ind. Antiq.*, XXII, 1893, pp. 284—8; XXIII, 1894, pp. 26—28.

> The *Sa-tu-waw* is a Sgaw-Karen Periodical published monthly in Rangoon at the American Baptist Mission Press.

277. — Short Vocabulary of Red Karen. By Bernard Houghton. (*Journ. R. As. Soc.*, Jan. 1894, pp. 29—49).

> The Red Karens "(whose English name is a translation of the Burmese *Kayin-ni*- alluding to the colour of their turbans) inhabit the mountains and plateaux east of the British district of Toungoo, their country being bounded on the north by the Shan States and on the east by Siam".   •

278. — *D. A. W. Smith. — The Karen Bible Handbook. Rangoon, Anglo-Burmese Mission Press, 1895, in-8, pp. 610.

279. — *D. A. W. Smith. — The Annotations of the Annotated Paragraph Bible — the New Testament. (In Sgau-Karen). Rangoon, Phinney, 1900, pp. 648.

280. — *D. A. W. Smith. — The Book of Psalms. (In Sgau-Karen). Rangoon, American Baptist Mission Press, 1901, pp. 216.

281. — *E. B. Cross. — A Dictionary of the Sgau-Karen Language. Rangoon, Anglo-Burmese Mission Press, 1896, in-8, pp. 1341.

282. — *E. B. Cross. — A Bible Dictionary (in Sgau-Karen). 3d edition. Rangoon, American Baptist Mission Press, 1898, pp. 540.

283. — *E. B. Cross. — A Commentary on the Epistles to the Hebrews, and on the Epistles of James, Peter, John, and Jude in Sgau-Karen. Rangoon, Phinney, 1900, pp. 326.

284. — E. B. Cross. — A Commentary on Paul's Epistles to the Galatians, Ephesians, ... in Sgau-Karen. Rangoon, Phinney, 1900, pp. 516.

285. — *J. H. Vinton. — Scripture Texts arranged (in Sgau-Karen). Second edition. Rangoon, American Baptist Mission Press, 1898, pp. 516.

286. — *David Gilmore. — A Grammar of the Sgau-Karen Language. Rangoon, F. D. Phinney, 1898, in-8, pp. 51.

287. — *Elementary Hand-book of Red Karen Language. By Captain R. J. R. Brown, I.E.S. 1900, gr. in-8, pp. 84.

Seulement en caractères romains.

Haute Birmanie.

Mandalay Division.

288. — *Marks. — Mandalay revisited. (*Mission Field* 1889, pp. 326—328).

289. — *J. A. Colbeck. — Letters from Mandalay, 1878—79; 1885—88, Edited by G. H. Colbeck. Knaresborough, A. W. Lowe, 1892, in-8, pp. 113.

Notice: *Asiatic Quarterly Review*, II⁰ Serie, IV, in-8, pp. 551 et seq.

Katha.

290. — The Kudos of Katha and their Vocabulary. By Bernard Houghton. (*Ind. Antiq.*, XXII, 1893, pp. 129—136).

Those who speak the Kudô tongue live principally in the Wunthô (Wunbo) sub-division of the Kathâ District. It is clear, however, that they were there before the Shâns appeared in those parts, and that some of them have become absorbed into the Shân race.

Kachin Hill Tracts.

La plus grande partie des quarante villages Kachin se trouvent dans les districts de Bhamo et de Myitkyina; quelques-uns dans le district des Ruby Mines.

Col. Hannay of the Assam Light Infantry, in a work written in 1847, was the first to localize the Chingpaw tribes. (*Gazet.*)

"The name *Kachin* is purely Burmese... The Tai call the Kachins *Kang*; the Chinese call them *Yĕ-jĕn* (wild men) as an ordinary name, but use the term *Shan-teo* (heads of the hills) when they consider it advisable to be civil. In the Burma province the various tribes usually answer to the name of *Chingpaw*, but that of *Khakhu* is also used" (*Gazet*).

291. — *Fritz Noetling. — Note on the Geology of Wuntho. (*Rec. Geolog. Survey India*, XXVII, 1894, IV, pp. 115—124, carte).

292. — *F. A. Steven. — The Kachins of the Chinese borderland. (*China's Millions*, VI, pp. 28 et seq.; 35 et seq.; 50 et seq.; 63 et seq.)

293. — Expeditions among the Kachin Tribes on the North-east Frontier of Upper Burma. Compiled by General J. T. Walker, C.B., F.R.S., from the Reports of Lieutenant Eliott, Assistant Commissioner. (*Proc. R. Geog. Soc.*, XIV, 1892, March, pp. 161—173; carte, p. 204).

294. — Demonolatry among the Kachins. By R. C. Temple. (*Ind. Antiq.*, XXIII, 1894, p. 262).

295. — *M. N. Turner. Report on the Sana Kachin Expedition, 1895—96. Rangoon, 1896, pp. 22—4—8—2—2—4—4—4. Maps.

296. — Note sur les Kachins. (*Rev. coloniale*, II, 1896, pp. 723—728).
Par le Consul de France à Rangoon.

297. — *Les Kachins. (*Bul. Soc. Géog. Est.*, Nancy, 1897, XIX, pp. 84—9).

298. — The Kachin Hills and the Chingpaw. (Scott's *Gazetteer of Upper Burma*, Part I. — Vol. I. 1900, Chap. VII, pp. 331—439).
The basis of this chapter is the *Kachin Gazetteer* drawn up by Captains H. B. Walker and H. R. Davies...

.*.

299. — *A. Symington. Kachin Vocabulary. 1892, in-8, pp. 99.
Privately Printed.

300. — Kachin Spelling Book By Rev. O. Hanson, Bhamo. — Rangoon: American Baptist Mission Press, F. D. Phinney, Supt. 1895. br. in-12, pp. 22.
Essai de transcription du Kachin en lettres romaines.

301. — *O. Hanson. — Kachin spelling book. Second edition. Rangoon, F. D. Phinney, 1898, pp. 24.

302. — *Sacred hymns in Kachin. Translated by O. Hanson. Rangoon, Anglo-Burmese Mission Press, 1896, in-8, pp. 108.

303. — *O. Hanson. — A Grammar of the Kachin language. Rangoon, Anglo-Burmese Mission Press, 1896, in-8, pp. 104.

304. — — With a Vocabulary, 1896, in-8, pp. 231.

305. — *Genesis, Exodus, Obadiah and Jonah (in Kachin). Translated by O. Hanson. Rangoon, F. D. Phinney, 1898—99. 3 vol. pp. 210, 78, 16.

306. — Handbook of the Kachin or Chingpaw Language, containing The Grammatical principles and pecularities of the Language, Colloquial Exercises, and a Vocabulary. By H. F. Hertz, District Superintendent of Police. — Rangoon: Printed by the Superintendent, Government Printing, Burma. 1895, in-8, 2 ff. n. ch. + pp. ii—48.

307. — *A Practical Handbook of the Kachin or Chingpau Language, containing the Grammatical Principles and Peculiarities of the Language, Colloquial Exercises, and a Vocabulary, with an Appendix on Kachin Customs, Laws, and Religion. By H. F. Hertz. Rangoon, 1902, in-8, pp. v—164.

Chin Hills.

308. — The Chins or Hkyens. By R. F. St. Andrew St. John. (*The Phoenix*, III, No. 26, August 1872, pp. 28 —30).
Myanoung, rive ouest de l'Irawadi.

309. — *The Chinbòks. (*Trübner's Record*, II, 3, pp. 73 et seq.).

310. — The Customary Law of the Chin tribe. — Preface by John Jardine, Esq., of H. M.'s Bombay Civil Service, Judicial Commissioner of British Burma, and President of the Educational Syndicate of British Burma, br. in-8, pp. 7.
Rangoon: The 31st March 1884.

311. — Maung tet pyo's Customary Law of the Chin Tribe. Text, translation, and notes, with a preface by John Jardine Esq. H. M.'s Bo. C. S., Judicial Commissioner of British Burma, and President of the Educational Syndicate of British Burma. Rangoon: Printed at the Government Press. 1884, in-8.

312. — Qualche cenno sulle Tribu' seloaggie dei Cin. di G. B. Sacchiero R. Console d'Italia a Rangun. (*Bol. Soc. geog. Ital.*, 1889, pp. 986—992).

313. — Supplement to the "Rangoon Times". — Chinboks, Chinbons, and Yindus. — Notes, dated the 20th April 1890, by Lieutenant R. M. Rainey, Commandant, Chin Frontier Levey, regarding the Chin tribes bordering on the Yaw country in the Pakôkku district. in-fol., pp. 16.

314. — Notes on the Chinboks, Chinbons, and Yindus of the Chin Frontier of Burma. By Lieut. R. M. Rainey. (*Ind. Antiq.*, XXI, 1892, pp. 215—224, 2 pl.).

> Notes, dated 20th April 1890. — Printed originally as a Government Paper.

315. — Chin-Lushai Land including a Description of the various Expeditions into the Chin-Lushai Hills and the final annexation of the country By Surg.-Lieut.-Col. A. S. Reid, M.B. *Indian Medical Service; Medical Officer in charge 2nd Battalion 4th Gurkha Rifles.* With Maps and illustrations. Calcutta Thacker, Spink and Co. 1893, in-8, pp. x + 1 f. n. ch. + pp. 235.

> Notice: *Athenaeum*, March 31, pp. 408 et seq.

316. — Supplement to the "Rangoon Times". — Note on the Tashon and Baungshe Chins, with remarks on their Manners, Customs, Trade, and Agriculture. Pièce in-fol., pp. 4.

> Par D. Ross, Political Officer, Chin Hills.

317. — A Note on the Tashon and Baungshe Chins, with Remarks on their Manners, Customs and Agriculture. (*Ind. Antiq.*, XXI, 1892, pp. 190—3).

> Printed originally as a Government paper, by the chief Commissioner of Burma. The notes were made by Mr. D. Ross, Political Officer in the Chin Hills.

318. — The Chin and the Kachin tribes on the Borderland of Burma. By Taw Sein Ko, Burmese Lecturer, Cambridge University. (*Imp. & As. Quart. Rev.*, N. S., V, 1893, pp. 281—292).

319. — *P. Cushing. — The Great Chin episode. Cheap edition. London, Black, 1894, in-8, pp. 256.

320. — *John Harvey. Report on the Thetta Column and Work in the Southern Chin Hills during the season 1894—95. Maps. Rangoon, 1895, pp. 16—8—6—6, in-8, carte.

321. — The Chin Hills: A History of the People, our dealings with them, their Customs and Manners, and a Gazetteer of their Country, by Bertram S. Carey, C.I.E., Assistant Commissioner, Burma, and Political Officer, Chin Hills, and H. N. Tuck, Extra Assistant Commissioner, Burma, and Assistant Political Officer, Chin Hills. Rangoon: Printed by the Superintendent, Government Printing, Burma. 1896, 2 vol. gr. in-8, pp. iii + 1 f. n. ch. + pp. 236, cclv; 25 photog.

322. — Published by Authority. — Report on the Administration of the Chin Hills For the year 1895—96. — Rangoon: Printed by the Superintendent, Government Printing, Burma. July 1896. (Price, — Re. 0—14—0.] in-fol., pp. 38, 1 carte par H. N. Tuck.

> Date: Falam, the 1st June 1896.

323. — *C. H. Turner. — Report on the Kairuma, Naring, and Daidin Columns, Chin Hills, 1895—96. Rangoon, 1896, in-8, pp. 20, 6, 2, 4, 6, 2, 2. (Illustrations, Carte).

324. — The Southern Chin Hills. (*Geog. Journal*, May 1898, pp. 546—7).

> D'après le rapport du capitaine G. C. Rigby, Rangoon, 1897, sur les opérations militaires de 1896—97 dans le district montagneux entre le Nord de l'Arakan et le district Pakokku de la Haute Birmanie.

325. — *Report on the Administration of the Chin Hills. Administration of the Chin Hills, on the frontier affair of the Upper Chindwin District, the Pakokku Chin Hills and Hill Tracts of Arakan, Compiled by the Government of Burma.

> For the years 1899—1900, 1900—1901.

326. — The Chin Hills and the Chin Tribes. (Scott's *Gazet. of Upper Burma*, Pt. I. — Vol. I, 1900, pp. 441—473).

> Cf. *Chin Gazetteer*, by Carey and Tuck, No. 321.

.*.

327. — *F. M. Rundall — Manual of the Siyin dialect spoken in the Northern Chin Hills. Rangoon, Gov., 1891, in-8, pp. 48.

> Conf. R. N. C.[ust], *J. R. A. S.*, April, pp. 404 et seq.

328. — *Handbook of the Haka or Baungshe Dialect of the Chin Language, by Lieut. D. J. C. Macnabb, B.S.C., Political Officer, Haka. Rangoon, Printed by the Superintendent, Government Printing, Burma, 1891, in-8, pp. 52.

> Notice: *Ind. Antiq.*, XXI, 1892, pp. 128—128, by B. Houghton, C.S.

329. — Essay on the Language of the Southern Chins and its Affinities by Bernard Houghton, C.S., Deputy Commissioner, Sandoway. — Rangoon: Printed by the Superintendent, Government Printing, Burma. — 1892, in-8, pp. 2—131—xx.

> Contient:
> Préface — Preliminary — Grammar — Chin Sentences — Chin-English Vocabulary — English-Chin Vocabulary — Appendix I. — Table of Relationships. — Do. II. — Chin and Ghurka Physical Types — Do. III. — Dravidian Analogies — Do. IV. — Customs and Folklore.

330. — Southern Chin Vocabulary (Minbu District). By Bernard Houghton. (*Jour. Roy. As. Soc*, Oct. 1895, pp. 727—737).

> "The accompanying words and phrases of Southern Chin, as spoken at the foot of the Arakan Yoma Mountains in the Minbu district, were taken down a few years since by Major B. A. N. Parrott, I S C., who later on presented to me the book in which they were written, along with others on Oriental subjects. They are interesting as representing the most Northern dialect of this language, which reaches it most Southern point in the Sandoway district. (I pass by the dialect spoken in Bassein and the South of Henzada as being much corrupted by the extended intercourse which has there taken place between the Chins and the Burmans.)"

331. — Kami Vocabularies. By Bernard Houghton, M.R.A.S. (*Jour. R. As. Soc.*, Jan. 1895, pp. 111—138).

> "From a philological point of view, the Kamis fall under the Chin Lushai group of the Tibeto-Burman family".
> Les quatre vocabulaires ou listes qui accompagnent ce mémoire proviennent: 1) de "Maung Hla Paw Zan, an Extra-Assistant Commissioner in the Akyab district, (under the orders of A. M. B. Irwin, Deputy Commissioner). 2) de Mg. Tha Bwin, Myook of Sandoway. 3 et 4) de "On the Indo-Chinese Borderers" by B. H. Hodgson qui les avait recueillis de Arthur Phayre.

332. — Surg.-Maj. A. G. E. Newland. A practical Handbook of the Language of the Lais, as spoken by the Hakas and other allied tribes of the Chin Hills. Rangoon, 1897, in-8, pp. 6,687.

> En caractères latins seulement.

333. — °The Opening Chapters of John's Gospel (in Chin). Translated by Saya Pyizo. Rangoon, American Baptist Mission Press, 1898, pp. 24.

334. — The Lai Dialect. By H. H. Tilbe. (*Jour. Roy. As. Soc.*, Jan. 1904, pp. 169—171).

335. — Zur Kenntnis der Kuki-Chinsprachen. Von Sten Konow. (*Zeit. d. Morg. Ges.*, Bd. 56, 1902, pp. 486—517).

336. — °Kurt. Klemm. — Sage und Brauch der Chin. (*Beil. Allgem. Zeitung*, cclxxxxv, pp. 1—5; cclxxxxvi, pp. 3—6).

APPENDICE. — *Les routes de la Chine par la Birmanie.*

337. — Abstract Journal of an Expedition to Kiang Hung on the Chinese Frontier, starting from Moulmein on the 13th December 1836. By Lieut. T. E. Mac Leod, Assistant to the Commissioner of the Tenasserim Provinces, with a route map. [Extracted from a Report to E. A. Blundell, Esq. Commissioner, and communicated by the Right Hon. the Governor of Bengal.] (*Jour. As. Soc. of Bengal*, VI, No. 72, Dec. 1837, pp. 989 seq.).

> Voir *infra*, No. 858. — H. Cordier, *Hist. des Relat.*, Vol. I et II.

338. — Short Survey of the Countries between Bengal and China, showing the great commercial and political importance of the Burmese town of Bhanmo, on the Upper Irawady, and the practicability of a direct Trade overland between Calcutta and China. By Baron Otto des Granges. (*Ibid.*, XVII, pt. I, 1848, pp. 132—137).

1° Capt. RICHARD SPRYE.

339. — The British and China Railway, from Rangoon .... to the Yunnan Province of China: with Loop-lines to Siam and Cambogia, Tonquin and Cochin-China... In a series of letters to the Earl of Malmesbury. London, 1858, in-8.

> Privately Printed.

340. — Communication with the South-West Provinces of China from Rangoon in British Pegu. By Capt. R. Sprye, and R. H. Sprye Esq. (*Proc. R. G. S.*, V, 1861, pp. 45—7).

341. — China. No. 2 (1865). — Correspondence respecting direct Commerce with the West of China from Rangoon. — Presented to the House of Lords by Command of Her Majesty. 1865. — London, Harrison, in-fol., pp. 101.

342. — Correspondence between Captain Richard Sprye, and the Rt. Hon. William-Ewart Gladstone, M. P. for South Lancashire, Chancellor of H. M.'s Exchequer, &c., on the Commercial opening of the Shan States, and Western Inland China, by Railway, direct from Rangoon. With a map. London: 1865. Printed for Private Circulation only, gr. in-8, pp. 63.

> La couverture porte la date: London: 1866.

343. — Memorandum on the question of British Trade with Western China via Burmah. By Dr. C. Williams. — 1 carte. (*Jour. As. Soc. of Bengal*, 1864, No. IV, pp. 407—433).

344. — Trade and Telegraph Routes to China, via Burmah. By Dr. Clement Williams, Late H. M. 68th Lt. Inf'y and Agent to the Chief Commissioner, British Burmah, at Mandalay. A Reprint, by permission. [From the *Journal of the Bengal Asiatic Society*.] in-8, s. l. n. d., pp. 37 [1864], 1 carte.

345. — Through Burmah to Western China being Notes of a Journey in 1863 to establish the practicability of a trade-route between the Irawaddi and the Yang-tse-Kiang by Clement Williams formerly Assistant-Surgeon in the 68th light infantry, and first political agent at Mandalay to the Chief Commissioner of British Burmah. William Blackwood and Sons, Edinburgh and London, M DCCC LXVIII, in-8, pp. XIV + 1 f. n. c. + pp. 213.

> 2 cartes et gravures.

346. — Memorandum on Railway Communication with Western China and the intermediate Shan States from the Port of Rangoon in British Burma, with Map, by Captain J. M. Williams, H. M. Indian Army, Assoc. Inst. C. E., and Executive Engineer, Rangoon Division, British Burma. — London, 21 January 1865, in-fol., pp. 21.

> 373. — Ordered, by The House of Commons, to be Printed, 15 June 1865.

347. — East India (Shan States, &c.) — Return to an Address of the Honourable The House of Commons, dated 11 June 1866; — for, "Copy of a Letter from Captain Richard Sprye to the Secretary of State for India, dated the 15th day of January 1866, and of the Maps attached thereto, referring to Commerce with the Shan States and West of China from Rangoon, and Extension of the Indo-European Telegraph by Land from Pegu to Hongkong and the Chinese Open Ports". India Office, 13 June 1866... — Ordered, by the House of Commons, to be Printed, 14 June 1866. [350], in-fol., pp. 40.

⁎

348. — Rangoon and Western China. — Return to an Address of the Honourable The House of Commons, dated 28 March 1867; for, "Copy of further Papers or Correspondence between the Government of India and the Secretary of State, on the proposed Communication between Rangoon and Western China;

with the Dissents, if any, recorded by Members of the Council of India, and
that of Sir Charles Trevelyan (in continuation of Parliamentary Paper, No.
373, of Session 1865)". India Office, 11 April 1867. — Ordered, by the House
of Commons, to be Printed, 12 April 1867 [243]. In-fol., pp. 22.

349. — Rangoon. — Return to an Address of the Honourable The House of
Commons, dated 27 June 1857; — for, "Copies of Letter from Captain
Williams, Public Works Department, Rangoon, to the Commissioner of British
Burmah, dated the 8th day of December 1866, with Map, if any, to be
attached thereto" : "And, of any Correspondence thereon between the Com-
missioner, the Government of India, and the Secretary of State for India
(in continuation of Parliamentary Paper, No. 233, ot the present Session)".
India Office, 28 June 1867. — Ordered, by The House of Commons, to be
Printed, 5 July 1867. [421], in-fol., pp. 7.

350. — Rangoon and Western China. — Return, to an Address of the Honourable The House of Commons, dated 12 August 1867; — for, "Copy of all
Memorials, and of Letters transmitting them, to the First Lord of the
Treasury or other Minister, subsequent to the 7th day of December 1863,
on the subject of opening up a direct Commerce with the Shan States and
West of China, from the Port of Rangoon; and of the Replies thereto (in
continuation of Parliamentary Paper, No. 5, of Session 1864)". India Office,
2 December 1867. [28], in-fol., pp. 32.

351. — Rangoon and Western China. — Return to an Address of the Honourable The House of Commons, dated 28 November 1867; — for, "Copies of
the Survey Report of Captains Williams and Luard, dated the 15th day of
June 1867, and of the Journals, Maps, Sections, &c. attached thereto, respecting Rangoon and Western China" : "Of the Letter forwarding the Report
to the Chief Commissioner, of his Letter forwarding it to the Governor
General of India, and of the Governor General's Despatch transmitting it to
the Secretary of State for India" : "And, of all Correspondence on the Subject,
by Telegram or Letter, between the Governor General and Chief Commissioner
subsequent to the 30th day of June 1867; and between the Governor General
and the Secretary of State for India subsequent to the 15th day of August
1867 (in continuation of Parliamentary Paper, No. 421, of Session 1867, and
not hitherto laid before Parliament)". India Office, 2 December 1867. Ordered,
by the House of Commons, to be Printed, 3 December 1867. [28—I], in-fol.,
pp. 56.

352. — Return to an Address of the Honourable The House of Commons,
dated 23 March 1868; — for, "Copies of the Replies to the several Memorials
contained in the Return to the Address of the House, dated the 12th day
of August 1867, on the subject of Direct Commerce with the Shan States
and West China from the Port of Rangoon" : "And, of all further Memorials

thereon subsequent to those contained in that Return, and of the Replies thereto (in continuation of Parliamentary Paper, No. 28—I., of Session 1867—8)". India Office, 31 March 1868 [192], in-fol., pp. 8.

353. — East India (Rangoon and Western China). — Return to an Address of the Honourable The House of Commons, dated 23rd June 1868; — for, "Copy of the Despatch of the late Governor General of India, Lord Elgin; relative to the proposed construction of a Commercial Way from Rangoon to Kianghung, referred to in the Letter addressed by the Secretary of State for India to the Huddersfield Chamber of Commerce on the 28th day of January 1864; with any Enclosures or Documents referred to in the said Despatch". India Office, 26 June 1868, Ordered, by The House of Commons, to be Printed, 30 June 1868 [367], in-fol., pp. 8.

354. — Rangoon and West of China. — Return to an Order of the Honourable The House of Commons, dated 24 April 1873; — for, Copy "of Memorial of the Association of the Chambers of Commerce of the United Kingdom to the Right Honourable William Ewart Gladstone, M.P., First Lord of Her Majesty's Treasury, dated the 17th day of February 1873; and of the Appendix and Maps attached to the same, the Maps to be in outline only (in continuation of Parliamentary Paper, 'Rangoon and Western China', No. 28—I, of Session 1867—8, and No. 192, of Session 1868". [258], in-fol., pp. 23.

355. — East India (British Burmah). — Return to an Address of the Honourable The House of Commons, dated 26 April 1869; — for, "Copies of all Correspondence by Telegram or Letter, relating to the late Treaty with the Court of Ava, concluded by the Chief Commissioner, British Burmah, on the 26th day of October 1867, between the Governor General of India and Chief Commissioner, and the Governor General and Secretary of State for India, subsequent to the 15th day of January 1867 (in continuation of Parliamentary Paper, No. 193, of Session 1867, and not hitherto laid before Parliament)" : "Of all Correspondence by Telegram or Letter between the Governor General of India and Chief Commissioner, British Burmah, and the Governor General and Secretary of State for India, relative to the Route to Western China via Bhamo, commencing with Letter No. 127 P. — 54 P. S., dated the 21st day of June 1867, from the Chief Commissioner, British Burmah, to the Governor General of India, including the Correspondence regarding the establishment of an Assistant Political Agent at Bhamo, and Captain Sladen's Final Report, with Minute thereon by the Chief Commissioner, British Burmah" + "Of all Papers and Correspondence regarding the further Exploration of the proposed Railway Route from Rangoon to Kyan Hung or Western China (in continuation of Parliamentary Paper, No. 28—I., of Session 1867), and including Letter No. 410—4 R. of the 18th day of July 1868, from Chief

Commissioner, British Burmah, to Government of India, and Reply"; "And, Copies of all Papers and of the Correspondence between the Chief Commissioner, British Burmah, and of the Governor General of India, and the Governor General and Secretary of State for India, relative to the Project for a Railway between Rangoon and Prome, in British Burmah". + [Note. — Captain Sladen's Report has not yet been received, but will, with other Papers, be included in a Supplementary Return.] — India Office, 13 May 1869. — Ordered, by The House of Commons, to be Printed, 8 June 1869. In-fol., pp. 98 [251].

356. — East India (British Burmah). — Further Return to an Address of the Honourable The House of Commons, dated 26 April 1869; — for, Copy of Major Sladen's Report on the Bhamo Route. (In continuation of Parliamentary Paper, No. 251, of Session 1868—9). India Office, May 1871... Ordered, by The House of Commons, to be Printed, 17 April 1871. [165]. in-fol., pp. 161.

357. — East India (British Burmah). — Return to an Address of the Honourable The House of Commons, dated 20 June 1871; — for, "Copies of Captain Richard Sprye's Letters to the Secretary of State for India in Council, dated the 30th day of March and the 31st day of August 1870, and the 21st day of February 1871" : "And, of the several Replies thereto (in continuation of Parliamentary Paper, East India (British Burmah), No. 165, of the present Session"). India Office, 27 June 1871, in-fol., pp. 22, [341].

358. — East India (Mc Leod and Richardson's Journeys). — Return to an Address of the Honourable The House of Commons, dated 6 August 1869; — for, "Copy of Papers relating to the Route of Captain W. C. Mc Leod from Moulmein to the Frontiers of China, and to the Route of Dr. Richardson on his Fourth Mission to the Shan Provinces of Burmah, or Extracts from the Same". India Office, 9 August 1869... Ordered, by The House of Commons, to be Printed, 10 August 1869. [420]., in-fol., pp. 147.

2° EDWARD B. SLADEN.

† 4 janvier 1890. — Voir *supra*, No. 356.

359. — Bhamo Expedition. — Report on the practicability of re-opening the Trade Route, between Burma and Western China. By Captain A. Bowers, R. N. R. Commercial Agent attached to the Expedition under Captain E. B. Sladen, British political Agent at the Court of Mandalay. With an appendix. — Rangoon: American Mission Press. C. Bennett. — 1869, in-8, 3 ff. prél. p. l. tit., déd., etc. + pp. 165. Pl. et cartes.

> L'app. contient "the Preface to the Administration Report of British Burmah for 1867—68, by Major General A. Fytche, C.S.I. Chief Commissioner, and Agent to the Governor General".

360. — Bhamo-Expedition. — Bericht über die Möglichkeit einer Wiedereröffnung der Handelsstrasse zwischen Birma und West-China erstattet vom

Capitain A. Bowers, Handelsagenten der unter Capitain Sladen, britischen Bevollmächtigten am Hofe zu Mandalay, ausgerüsteten Expedition. Ins Deutsche übersetzt von Dr. Merzdorf, grossherzogl. Oldenburg. Oberbibliothekar, Berlin. Carl Heymann's Verlag. 1871. in-8. pp. 180.

361. — Selections from the Records of the Government of India, Foreign Department. — No. LXXIX. — Official Narrative of the Expedition to explore the Trade Routes to China viâ Bhamo, under the guidance of Major E. B. Sladen, Political Agent, Mandalay, with connected Papers. — Published by Authority. — Calcutta: Office of Superintendent of Government Printing. 1870, in-8, pp. VI—187—XCV.

362. — Expedition from Burma, viâ the Irrawaddy and Bhamo, to South-Western China. By Major E. B. Sladen, H. M. Political Resident, Burma. (1 Map.) Read June 26th, 1871. (*Journal Roy. Geog. Soc.*, 1871, pp. 257—281).

> Le Major Sladen quitta la capitale royale de Mandalay le 13 janvier 1868; arriva à Bhamo (900 milles de Rangoon, 300 milles de Mandalay) le 31 Janvier; quitta Bhamo le 26 Fév. 1868; séjourna 7 semaines à Momein; était de retour à Mandalay le 30 Septembre.

363. — Burma: Exploration viâ the Irrawaddy and Bhamo to South-Western China. By Major E. B. Sladen. (*Proc. Roy. Geog. Soc.*, XV, 1871, pp. 343—364).

364. — Journal of a voyage up the Irrawaddy to Mandalay and Bhamo, by J. Talboys Wheeler, Secretary to the Chief Commissioner of British Burma. Rangoon: Printed by J. W. Baynes. London; Trübner and Co. — Calcutta: Newman and Co. Madras: J. Higgenbotham and Co, 1871, in-8, pp. 102—II.

365. — A Report on the Expedition to Western Yunan viâ Bhamô. By John Anderson, M.D., Medical Officer and Naturalist to the Expedition. Calcutta: Office of the Superintendent of Government Printing, 1871, gr. in-8, pp. 3—XII—458, 5 pl. et 1 carte.

366. — The Irawaddy and its Sources. — By Dr. J. Anderson. Read 13 June 1870. (*Jour. R. G. S.*, XL, 1870, pp. 286—303). — Extraits *Proc. R. G. S.*, XIV, 1870, pp. 346—356).

367. — Mandalay to Momien: A Narrative of the Two Expeditions to Western China of 1868 and 1875, under Colonel Edward B. Sladen and Colonel Horace Browne. By John Anderson, M.D. With Maps and Illustrations. London, Macmillan, 1876, in-8, pp. XVI—479.

> Notice: *Nature*, XIII, 1875—6, pp. 422—4.

368. — Anatomical and Zoological Researches: comprising an Account of the Zoological Results of the two Expeditions to Western Yunnan in 1868 and 1875; and a Monograph of the two Cetacean Genera, *Platanista* and *Orcella*. By John Anderson, M.D., Edin., Superintendent Indian Museum, and Professor of Comparative Anatomy, Medical College, Calcutta; Medical Officer to the Expeditions. First Volume — TEXT. London: Bernard Quaritch, 1878,

gr. in-4, pp. xxv—984 + 1 f. n. c. — Second Volume — PLATES (84 Plates).
London: Bernard Quaritch, 1878, gr. in-4, Pl. et pp. xi—29.

> "The First Expedition was despatched in the end of 1867 from Calcutta, and returned in November 1868; and the Second Expedition left Mandalay on the 3rd January 1875, and returned thither on the 10th March of the same year". (Introduction).
> — John Anderson, M.D , F.R S., etc. Nécrologie par H.C.[ordier.] (*T'oung Pao*, 2ᵉ Sér., I, Nᵒ 4, Oct. 1900, p. 346)
> Né à Edimbourg en 1833; † à Buxton, Août 1900.

3ᵉ T. T. COOPER.

369. — Lettre de Ta tsian loo, 26 April 1868. (*N. C. Daily News*, June 15, 1868. — Réimp. *Proc. R. Geog. Soc.* XII, 1868, pp. 336—9).

370. — Lettre de Mgr. Chauveau sur ce voyageur, Ta tsien lou, 21 Sept. 1868; trad. en ang. dans le *N. C. Herald*, 14 Nov. 1868; ce journal, dans le courant de 1868, a publié un grand nombre d'articles sur T. T. C.

371. — Notes on Western China. (*Proc. As. Soc. of Bengal*, 1869, pp. 143—57).

372. — On the course of the Tsan-po and Irrawaddy and on Tibet. (*Proc. R. G. S.*, XIII, 1869, No. 5, pp. 392—5).

> Letter, Calcutta, 8th May 1869.

373. — Travels in Western China and Eastern Thibet. (*Ibid.*, XIV, 1870, pp. 335—346).

> Travels in Western China and Eastern Thibet (*Proc. R. G. S.*, XIV, 1870, pp. 335—356. — Réimp. dans *The Cycle*, 18 fév. 1871).

374. — On the Chinese Province of Yunnan and its Borders. (*Ibid.*, XV, 1871, pp. 163—174).

> Notice: Lettre de l'abbé Desgodins à Francis Garnier, Yerkalo, 15 mars 1872. (*Bull. Soc. Géog.*, Nov. 1872.)

375. — Journal of an overland journey from China towards India. The plains of Hoopeh. By T. J. Cooper, Esq. Calcutta: Office of Superintendent of Government printing. 1869, in-8, pp. vi—193, 2 cartes.

> La préf. est signée *Charles Girdlestone, Officiating Under Secretary* [Foreign Office]. Ce T. J. Cooper est le même que T. T. Cooper.

376. — T. T. Cooper. — Reise zur Auffindung eines Ueberlandweges von China nach Indien. Aus dem Englischen. Mit einem Anhange, die beiden englischen Expeditionen von 1868 und 1875 unter Sladen und Browne, und Margary's Reise betreffend, von H. L. v. Klenze. Illustr. m. Karte. Jena, Costenoble, 1877, gr. in-8, pp. xiii—507.

> Notice: *Mitt. k. u. k. geog. Ges. Wien*, 1878, pp. 337—345, par le Dr. Franz Toula.

377. — T. T. Cooper. (Leslie Stephen's *National Biography*, Vol. XII). Art. de R. K. Douglas.

378. — Travels of a Pioneer of Commerce in Pigtail and Petticoats; or an Overland Journey from China towards India... With map and illustrations. London, John Murray, 1871, in-8.

> *The Phœnix*, No. 11, May 1871. — *Shai. Budget*, July 28 and Aug. 4, 1871.

379. — The Mishmee Hills. An Account of a Journey made in an attempt to penetrate Thibet from Assam to open new routes for Commerce. By T. T. Cooper, ... Henry S. King, London, 1873, pet. in-8, pp. VIII—270.

L'Explorateur, III, 1876; art. de F. Romanet du Caillaud, pp. 496, 519 et 556.

4° Le Colonel HORACE BROWNE. — Assassinat de A. R. MARGARY.

380. — The new Western China Expedition. (*Nature*, XI, 1874—75, p. 209).

381. — Papers connected with the development of trade between British Burmah and Western China and with the Mission to Yunnan of 1874—5. 1876, in-folio, pp. 78. — [C. — 1456.]

382. — *China*. No. 1 (1876). Correspondence respecting the attack on the Indian Expedition to Western China, and the Murder of Mr. Margary. In-folio, pp. 108. — [C. — 1422.]

383. — *China*. No. 4 (1876). Further Correspondence respecting the attack on the Indian Expedition to Western China, and the Murder of Mr. Margary. In-folio, pp. 50. — [C. — 1605.]

384. — *China*. No. 2 (1877). Report by Mr. Davenport upon the trading capabilities of the country traversed by the Yunnan Mission, In-8, pp. 35. — [P. 1712.]

Réimp. dans *The North China Herald*, 30 juin 1877.

385. — *China*. No. 3 (1877). Further Correspondence respecting the attack on the Indian Expedition to Western China, and the Murder of Mr. Margary. (In continuation of Correspondence presented to Parliament August 1867: C. 1605). In-fol., pp. 148. — [P. 1832.]

386. — The Journey of Augustus Raymond Margary, from Shanghae to Bhamo, and back to Manwyne. From his Journals and Letters, with a brief biographical preface: to which is added a concluding chapter. By Sir Rutherford Alcock, K.C.B. With a Portrait engraved by Jeens, and a Route Map. London: Macmillan & Co. 1875. In-8, pp. XXIV—382.

Notices: *Saturday Review*, Vol. 42, Aug. 26, 1876. — *Nature*, XIV, 1876, pp. 229—230.

387. — Notes of a Journey from Hankow to Ta-li-fu, by the late Augustus Raymond Margary, China Consular Service. Shanghai: Printed by F. & C. Walsh... 1875, in-8, pp. VIII—51.

388. — Notes of a Journey from Han-Kow to Ta-li-fu. By the late A. R. Margary. Being Extracts from the Author's Diary. Carte. (*Journ. R. G. Soc.*, Vol. XLVI).

389. — La Chine Méridionale. Journal de M. Margary. (*L'Explorateur*, III, 1876, p. 57; IV, 1876, p. 10).

390. — Margary's Tagebuch auf seiner Reise durch China. Aus der "Bombay Gazette" vom 13 December 1875 in's Deutsche übersetzt von Frl. Josephine v. Hauer. (*Mitt. der K. u. K. Geog. Ges. Wien*, 1876, pp. 253—265).

391. — Extracts of Letters from Mr. Margary. (*Proc. R. Geog. Soc.*, XIX, 1874—75, pp. 288—291).

392. — Extracts from the Diary of the late Mr. Margary, from Hankow to Tali-fu. (*Proc. R. G. Soc.*, XX, 1875—6, pp. 184—215).

393. — Notice sur le Voyage de Margary de Hankow à Ta-li-fu. Par E. Milsom. (*Bull. Soc. Géog.*, Lyon, 1876).

394. — Mr. Margary's Journey from Shanghae to Bhamo. (Chambers' *Journal*, Feb. 1876).

395. — Die Englische Mission nach Junnan. (*Ausland*, No. 39, 1876).

396. — Augustus R. Margary. (*Leisure Hour*, XXVI, 166).

397. — Het Journaal van Margary, door N. W. Posthumus, s. l. n. d., br. in-8, pp. 7.

398. — P. [1994.] *China* (No. 3) 1878. — Report on the Route followed by Mr. Grosvenor's Mission between Tali-fu and Momein (*with Maps*) 4 s. 6 d.

399. — P. [2393.] *China* (No. 2) 1878—1879. — Report by Mr. Baber of his Journey to Ta-Chien-Lu. 1 d.

400. — Journey to Ta-chien-lu, in 1878. — Notes on the Route followed by Mr. Grosvenor's Mission through Western Yünnan, from Tali-fu to Téng-yueh. (Baber, *Travels and Researches in Western China*).

> Compte-rendu du rapport de M. C. E. Baber sur la route entre Tali-fou et Momeia suivie par la mission de M. Grosvenor. Lu à la séance du 16 septembre 1878 par M. le Dr. Louis Delgeur, vice-président de la Société. (*Bull. Soc. roy. Géogr. Anvers*, III, 1878, pp. 75—98).

401. — Monument en l'honneur de Margary, à Chang-hai. (*Miss. Cath.*, XII, 1880, pp. 584—5).

5° Ouvrages divers.

402. — On the Frontiers of China towards Birmah. By Dr. Gützlaff. (*J. R. G. S.*, XIX, 1849, pp. 428).

403. — О торговыхъ путяхъ по Китаю и подвластнымъ ему владѣніямъ. Іеро-монахо Палладія Кафорова. (Записки Импер. Русск. Географическаго Общества Кн. IV, 1850, pp. 224—259).

404. — Memorandum on the Countries between Thibet, Yunân, and Burmah. By the Very Rev. Thomine D'Mazure [sic], Vicar Apostolic of Thibet; communicated by Lieut.-Col. A. P. Phayre, Commissioner of Pegu; (with notes and a comment by Lieut.-Col. H. Yule, Bengal Engineers.) With a Map of the N. E. Frontier prepared in the office of the Surveyor Gen. of India, Calcutta, Aug. 1861. (*Journ. As. Soc. of Bengal*, 1862, Vol. XXX, pp. 367—383).

405. — On the various lines of Overland Communication between India and China. By Dr. M' Cosh, late of the Bengal Medical Staff. (*Proc. R. G. S.*, Vol. V, 1861, pp. 47—54).

406. — On a Communication between India and China by the line of the

Burhampooter and Yang-tsze. By General Sir Arthur Cotton, R.E. Read June 24, 1867. (*J. Roy. G. S.*, XXXVII, pp. 231—9. — *Proc. R. G. Soc.*, XI, 1867, pp. 255—9).

407. — Letter to Major-General Sir Andrew Scott Waugh, on Routes between Upper-Assam and Western China. By F. A. Goodenough, Esq. (Communicated by Sir A. S. Waugh). (*Proc. R. G. S.*, XII, 1868, pp. 334—336).

408. — Letter to the Liverpool Chamber of Commerce on the prospects of a direct Trade Route to China through Moulmein, by John Coryton, esq. Recorder of Moulmein. With an Appendix containing Suggestions for amendments in the Law relating to foreign-grown Salween-borne timber, and a scheme for the prevention of frauds in the Timber trade of Moulmein and the adjustment of disputes between foresters and forest chiefs. — Moulmein: Printed by T. Whittam, at the Advertiser Press. — 1870, in-8, pp. 102—xlvii.

409. — Trade Routes between British Burmah and Western China. By J. Coryton. (*Proc. R. Geog. Soc.*, XIX, 1874—75, pp. 264—288).

410. — 'Trade Routes to Western China, by R. G. — Webb, Hunt & Riding, Liverpool, 1872.

> "A little brochure of eight pages, accompanied by a sketch map. It advocates a route running N.E. from Rangoon to the Lan San River, and will be found of much interest to all who care for the subject it discusses". (*China Review*, I, p. 60).

411. — Trade Routes to Western China. (*Edinburgh Review*, No. 280, April 1873).

412. — Recent Attempts to find a direct Trade-Road to South-Western China. By F. v. Richthofen. (*Ocean Highways*, Jan. 1874, pp. 404—410; — réimp. *Shanghai Budget*, March 26, 1874).

413. — On our Prospects of opening a Route to South-Western China, and Explorations of the French in Tonquin and Cambodia. By Lieut. Col. A. P. Mc Mahon. (*Proc. R. G. Soc.*, XVIII, 1874, pp. 463—7).

414. — Trade Routes to Western China. By Colonel H. Yule, C.B. (*The Geographical Magazine*, April 1875, pp. 97—101).

> Cet article accompagne une carte de E. G. Ravenstein.

415. — A Map shewing the various routes proposed for connecting China with India and Europe through Burmah and developing the Trade of Eastern Bengal, Burmah & China prepared under the direction of John Ogilby Hay, F.R.G.S. 1875. London: Pub. by Edward Stanford, 55 Charing Cross, Aug. 3, 1875.

416. — Overland Route to China viâ Assam, Tenga Pani River, Khamti, and Singphoo Country, across the Irrawaddi river into Yunan. By Henry Cottam. *Proc. R. Geog. Soc.*, XXI, 1876—7, pp. 590—595).

417. — China viâ Tibet. By S. C. Boulger. (*Journ. R. As. Soc.*, N.S., Vol. X, Part I. Art. V. Dec. 1877, pp. 113—130).

418. — 'F. Toula. Von China nach Indien. (*Wien. Abendpost*, 110—121, 1878).

419. — Across China from Chin-kiang to Bhamo, 1877. By J. Mc Carthy. (*Proc. R. Geog. Soc.*, N. S., Vol. I, 1879, pp. 489—509).

> Avec carte, p. 544.

420. — Note on the old Burmese route over Patkai viâ Nongyang (viewed as the most feasible and direct route, from India to China). By S. E. Peal. (*Jour. As. Soc. Bengal*, Vol. 48. Pt. II. 1879, pp. 69—82).

421. — Report on a Visit to the Nongyang Lake, on the Burmese Frontier, Feb. 1879. — By S. E. Peal. (*Ibid.*, Vol. 50, Pt. 2, 1881, pp. 1—30).

422. — Routes to China, viâ Assam. By S. E. Peal. (*Nature*, XX, 1879, pp. 583—5).

423. — Die Ueberlandroute nach China über Assam. (*Ausland*, 1876, 42).

424. — Journey of the Expedition under Colonel Woodthorpe, R.E., from Upper Assam to the Irawadi, and return over the Patkoi Range. By Major C. R. Macgregor, 44th Reg. (Ghurka Light Infantry). (*Proc. R. Geog. Soc.*, N.S., vol. IX, 1887, pp. 19—42).

> Avec carte, p. 68.

425. — Account of the Pundit's Journey in Great Tibet from Leh in Ladákh to Lhása, and of his Return to India viâ Assam. By Captain H. Trotter, R.E. (*Ibid.*, XXI, 1876—7, pp. 325—350).

426. — The Question of an Overland Route to China from Indiâ viâ Assam, with some remarks on the source of the Irawadi River. By Charles H. Lepper. (*Ibid.*, N. S., Vol. IV, 1882, pp. 623—4).

427. — La route de terre de l'Inde à la Chine par l'Assam, par Ch. H. Lepper. (*Ann. de l'Ext. Orient*, 1883—84, VI, pp. 301—308, 330—340).

> Traduction de l'anglais de C. H. Desgodins, Inspecteur des forêts en retraite. — Notice: *Miss. Cath.*, XVIII, 1886, p. 324.

WILLIAM J. GILL.

428. — Szechuen to Burmah (*N. C. Herald*, Dec. 20, 1877, d'après *the Rangoon Daily Review*).

> Lieut. Gill, R.E.; et Mesny, au service de la Chine.

429. — The River of Golden Sand — the Narrative of a Journey through China and Eastern Tibet to Burmah; with illustrations and ten maps from original surveys. By Capt. William Gill, R.E. With an Introductory Essay. By Col. Henry Yule... London, John Murray, 1880, 2 vol. in-8, pp. 95—420, 11—453.

> Notice: *Nature*, XXII, 1880, pp. 26—28.
> Il a été fait un tirage à part du Mémoire et de l'Int. de Yule.

430. — The River of Golden Sand being the narrative of a journey through China and Eastern Tibet to Burmah. By the late Captain William Gill, R.E. Condensed by Edward Colborne Baber, Chinese Secretary to H. M.'s Legation at Peking. Edited with a Memoir and introductory Essay. By Colonel Henry Yule, C.B., R.E. With portrait, Map and Woodcuts. London: John Murray, 1883, in-8, pp. 332.

431. — Travels in Western China and on the Eastern Borders of Tibet. By Capt. W. J. Gill. (*J. Roy. Geog. Soc.*, XLVIII, 1878, pp. 57—172). (Carte). (*Proc. R. Geog. Soc.*, XXII, 1877—8, pp. 255—271 [abrégé]).

432. — Itinéraire de W. Gill en Chine et au Thibet 1877. (*Bull. Soc. Géog.*, Mai 1881, pp. 448—465).

Par Dutreuil de Rhins. — Carte.

ARCHIBALD ROSS COLQUHOUN.

433. — Exploration through the South China Borderlands, from the Mouth of the Si-kiang to the Banks of the Irawadi. By A. R. Colquhoun. (*Proc. Roy. Geog. Soc.*, N. S., Vol. IV, 1882, pp. 713—730).

Avec carte, p. 776.

434. — Special Supplement to the Chamber of Commerce Journal, containing an Original Paper on the Prospects of Trade Extension between Burmah and South-West China (with Explanatory Maps), by Archibald R. Colquhoun. Nov. 15, 1882. Br. in-4 à 2 vol.

Bib. Soc. Géog. Paris, $\frac{E\ 5}{874}$.

435. — The Colquhoun and Wahab Expedition through Southern China into Burmah. — Opinions of the Press on the value of the Expedition. London: Printed by Daniel Greenaway, 1882, br. in-8, pp. 36. Avec une carte.

Bib. Soc. Géog. Paris, $\frac{E\ 5}{865}$.

436. — Across Chrysê, being the narrative of a Journey of exploration through the South China border lands from Canton to Mandalay. By Archibald R. Colquhoun, executive Engineer, Indian Public Works, F. R. G. S., A. M. Inst. C. E. With 3 specially prepared maps, 30 facsimiles of a native drawings and 300 illustrations, Chiefly from Original Photographs and Sketches. In two vol. — London: Sampson Low, Marston, Searle, and Rivington, 1883, 2 vol. in-8, pp. XIV—408, XXX—420.

Notices: *Athenaeum*, 1883, I, 663. — *Saturday Review*, LV, 601. — *Spectator*, LVI, 872. — *Literary World*, Boston, XIV, 206.

437. — 'Quer durch Chryse. Forschungsreise d. d. süd-chinesischen Grenzländer u. Birma von Canton nach Mandalay. Autoris. deutsche Ausgabe von H. Wobeser. M. über 300 Abbildungen u. Karten. 1884, 2 vol. in-8.

438. — Archibald Colquhoun — Autour du Tonkin — La Chine méridionale de Canton à Mandalay. Traduit de l'anglais avec l'autorisation de l'auteur. Par Charles Simond. H. Oudin, lib. éd. Paris — Poitiers. 1884, 2 vol. in-12.

439. — Les Pionniers de l'Europe et le Yunnan. [Par R. Colquhoun.] Par G. d'Orcet. (*Rev. Brit.*, 1883, IV, pp. 461—502; V, 83—124, 369—404; VI, 115—155, 279—318).

440. — Le Tonkín aux points de vue géographique, agricole, administratif, commercial, ethnographique d'après A.-R. Colquhoun. (*Soc. Bretonne Géog.*, IV, 1885, pp. 511—547).

441. — Chine méridionale. Par A. Colquhoun. (*Soc. Bretonne Géog.*, IV, 1885, pp. 492—508, 548—554).

442. — Amongst the Shans, by Archibald Ross Colquhoun, A.M.I.C.E., F.R.G.S. Author of "Across Chrysê", etc. With upwards of Fifty whole-page Illustrations and an historical sketch of the Shans, by Holt S. Hallett, M.T.C.E., F.R.G.S. Preceded by an introduction on the Cradle of the Shan Race, by Terrien de Lacouperie, Professor of Indo-Chinese Philology, University Coll. Lond., ... London: Field & Tuer ..... 1885, in-8, pp. IV—392.

> Notices: *Spectator*, LVIII, 551. — *Athenæum*, 1885, I, 273. — *Literary World*, Boston, XVI, 95. — *Saturday Review*, LIX, 797.

443. — Exploration in Southern and South-Western China. By Archibald R. Colquhoun, C.E. — 1. Wuchau to Pe-sê. — 2. Pe-sê to Ssŭ-mao. — 3. Ssŭ-mao to Tali. (Royal Geog. Society — *Supp. Papers*. Vol. II. Part 1, London, 1887), in-8, pp. 40.

444. — ʻArchibald R. Colquhoun. — Burmah: Our Gate to China. (*Asiatic Quarterly Review*, IV, N° 8, October 1887, pp. 256—278).

445. — Report on the Railway Connexion of Burmah and China, by Archibald R. Colquhoun, ... and Holt S. Hallett, ... with Account of Exploration-Survey, by Holt S. Hallett accompanied by Surveys, Vocabularies and Appendices. — Submitted to Her Majesty's Government and the British Chambers of Commerce. London: Allen, Scott & Co., 30 Bouverie Street, E. C., s. d. [1887], in-fol., pp. 269, avec onze cartes.

446. — The Railway Connection of Burmah and China. By A. R. Colquhoun. (*Jour. Manchester Geog. Soc.*, III, 1887, pp. 141—153).

447. — Exploration Survey for a Railway Connection between India, Siam, and China. By Holt S. Hallett, C.E. (*Proc. R. Geog. Soc.*, VIII, 1886, Jan., pp. 1—20; carte, p. 64).

448. — Address of Mr. Holt S. Hallett, C.E., F.R.G.S., M.R.A.S., upon Burmah: our Gate to the Markets of Western and Central China; treating with the proposed connection of Burmah with China by railway. Delivered before the Birmingham Chamber of Commerce on the 26th May, 1887, Mr. Henry W. Elliott, President of the Chamber, in the Chair. London: P. S. King & Son, Parliamentary Agency. — 1887, in-8, pp. 20.

449. — The Burmah-Siam-China Railway. By Holt S. Hallett. (*Blackwood's Mag.*, CXLVI, Nov. 1889, pp. 647—659).

450. — The Remedy for Lancashire. A Burma-China Railway. By Holt S. Hallett. (*Ibid.*, CLII, Sept. 1892, pp. 348—363).

451. — Les routes commerciales de l'Inde au Thibet et à la Chine. (*Bul. Soc. Géog. de l'Est*, IV, 1882, pp. 505—510).

> Par A. Desgodins, ext. du No. du 13 juin 1882, de l'*Englishman*, de Calcutta, et trad. de l'anglais par Mlle. M. Bourguignon.

452. — La région limitrophe du Thibet, de la Birmanie, de l'Assam et de la Chine. Par A. Desgodins, Provicaire du Thibet. (*Bull. Soc. Géog.*, Paris, VII° Sér., V, 1884, pp. 278—288).

453. — Across China. From Bhamô to Shanghai. By Henry Soltau. (*Scottish Geog. Mag.*, IV, 1888, pp. 83—98).

Henri d'Orléans.

454. — Autour du Tonkin par Henri Ph. d'Orléans. Paris, Calmann Lévy, 1894, in-8, pp. IV—654.

> Notice: *Edinburgh Review*, 183, Jan. 1896, pp. 237—266.

455. — Prince Henri d'Orléans — Du Tonkin aux Indes Janvier 1895—Janvier 1896. Illustrations de G. Vuillier d'après les photographies de l'auteur. Gravure de J. Huyot. Cartes et Appendice géographique par Émile Roux, Enseigne de vaisseau. Paris, Calmann Lévy, 1898, gr. in-8, pp. 442.

456. — Du Tonkin au Yunnan par le Prince Henri d'Orléans. (*Bull. Soc. Géog.*, Paris, 1895, pp. 389—404).

457. — Du Tonkin aux Indes par le Yunnan. — Exploration du prince Henri d'Orléans. (*Rev. française*, XXI, 1896, pp. 129—135, 193—201).

458. — Journey of Prince Henry of Orleans. (*Dublin Review*, CXIX, July 1896, pp. 168—169).

459. — A Journey from Tonkin by Tali-fu to Assam. By Prince Henri d'Orléans. (*Geogr. Journ.*, VIII, Dec. 1896, pp. 566—585).

460. — Aux sources de l'Irraouaddi, d'Hanoï à Calcutta par terre, par M. E. Roux, enseigne de vaisseau. (*Tour du Monde*, 1897, pp. 193—276).

461. — Emile Roux. Enseigne de Vaisseau. — Aux Sources de l'Irraouaddi Voyage de Hanoï à Calcutta par terre, illustré de cent dessins ou gravures directes d'après les photographies rapportées par l'auteur. Hachette & Cie. 1897, gr. in-8, pp. 84 + 1 f. n. ch. p. l. tab.

> Tiré du *Tour du Monde*.

462. — Renseignements géographiques inédits recueillis, en dehors de l'itinéraire suivi, au cours de l'expédition du Prince Henri d'Orléans, de MM. E. Roux et Briffaut du Tonkin aux Indes (Janvier 1895—Janvier 1896) par Emile Roux, Enseigne de vaisseau. (*Bul. Soc. Géog.*, Paris, 1897, pp. 81—95).

463. — Exploration du Tonkin aux Indes. Conférence faite le 12 Mai 1896, par le Prince Henri d'Orléans. (*Soc. Géog. Lille*, Bull., XXV, 1896, 1ᵉʳ sem., pp. 285—309).

464. — Société de géographie de Lille. — Conférence par le Prince Henri d'Orléans 12 mai 1896. Lille, Imprimerie L. Danel, in-16, pp. 63.

> Il y a des ex. sur papier du Japon.

465. — *From Tonkin to India, by the Sources of the Irawadi, 1895—96. By Prince Henri d'Orléans. Translated by Hamley Bent, M.A. Illustrated by C. Vuillier. London, Methuen, 1898, gr. in-8, pp. XII—467.

> Notice: *Nature*, LVII, 1897—8, pp. 557—8.

466. — Voyage du Tonkin aux Indes Anglaises par le Prince Henri d'Orléans Par J. Janssen, de l'Institut. (*Lectures académiques Discours*, pp. 285—288).

.•.

467. — Through Upper Burma and Western China. By John Foster Fraser. (*Trans. As. Soc. Japan*, XXVI, 1898, pp. V—XXVII).

468. — Recent journey from Shanghai to Bhamo through Hunan. By Captain A. M. S. Wingate. (*Geog. Journ.*, XIV, Dec. 1899, pp. 639—646).

469. — *A. M. S. Wingate. — "Things Chinese". With a short account of a journey through the heart of China. (*Jour. United Service Inst. of India*, XXIX, pp. 1—28, carte).

470. — Voyage du capitaine A. Wingate, de Chang-Haï à Bhamo, à travers le Hou-nan. Par J. D.[eniker.] (*La Géographie*, 15 janvier 1900, pp. 61—2).

471. — L'exploration des provinces centrales de la Chine. Par le capitaine Wingate. (*Le Mouv. géog.*, 1900, col. 69, 73).

472. — From Shanghai to Bhamo. By R. Logan Jack, LL.D., F.G.S. (*Geog. Journ.*, XIX, March 1902, pp. 249—277).

473. — *Dr. R. Logan Jack. The Black Blocks of China. London, Arnold, 1904, 10/6d.

> Notice: *Times Weekly Ed. Lit. Sup.*, Feb. 12, 1904.

474. — Du Tonkin en Birmanie. Par M. Jacques Faure. (*Bul. Soc. Géog. com.*, XXIV, 1902, pp. 32—43).

475. — Un voyage du Tonkin en Birmanie. (*Bul. Com. Asie franç.*, Déc. 1901, pp. 378—9).

476. — Un voyage du Tonkin en Birmanie. (*Le Mouv. géog.*, 1902, col. 51—52).

> D'après le *Bul. du Com. de l'Asie française*; Voyage de M. Jacques Faure.

III. — Ethnographie et Anthropologie.

477. — The Ethnology of the British Colonies and Dependencies. By E. G. Latham... London, John van Voorst, MDCCCLI, pet. in-8, pp. vi—264.

478. — Ethnology of India. By E. G. Latham, M.A., M.D., F.R.S. ... London, John van Voorst, MDCCCLIX, in-8, pp. viii—375.

479. — The West Himalaic or Tibetan Tribes of Asam, Burma and Pegu. By J. R. Logan. (*Jour. Ind. Arch.*, N. S., Vol. II, 1858, pp. 68—114, 230—232).

480. — Ethnology of the Indo-Pacific Islands. The Affiliation of the Tibeto-Burman, Mon-Anam, Papuanesian and Malayo-Polynesian Pronouns and Definitives, as varieties of the ancient Himalayo-Polynesian System; and their Relation of that system to the Draviro-Australian. By J. R. Logan. (*Ibid.*, N. S., Vol. III, Pt. I, 1859).

481. — On the History of the Burmah Race. By Lieut. Col. A. P. Phayre, C.B., Chief Commissioner of British Burmah. (*Trans. Ethn. Soc. Lond.*, V, 1867, pp. 13—39).

482. — On the History of the Burma Race. By Col. Sir Arthur Phayre. (*Jour. As. Soc. Bengal*, Vol. 38, 1869, Pt. I, pp. 29—82).

483. — On a Hairy Family in Burmah. By the Rev. W. Houghton. (*Trans. Ethn. Soc.*, VII, 1869, pp. 53—9).

484. — La famille velue de Birmanie; par M. E.-T. Hamy. (*Bull. Soc. Anthrop.*, 1875, pp. 78—9; *La Nature*, IV, 23 janvier 1875, pp. 121—3).
      Cf. Henri Cordier, *Odoric*, pp. 216—7. — Yule, *Ava*, pp. 93—5. — Crawfurd's *Narrative.*

485. — Magitot. — Les hommes velus. (*Gazette médicale de Paris*, 15 nov. 1873).

486. — Bertillon. — Des deux individus exhibés sous le nom d'hommes chiens. (*La Nature*, I, 22 nov. 1873, pp. 185—7).

487. — Krao, the "Human Monkey". By A. H. Keane. (*Nature*, XXVII, 1882—3, pp. 245—6).

488. — Krao. By a Resident. (*Ibid.*, XXVII, 1882—3, pp. 579—80).
      Bangkok, Siam, March 8.

489. — Hr. Bartels. — Krao, ein haariges Mädchen von Laos. (*Verhandl. d. Berliner Ges. f. Anthrop.* ... Jahrg. 1883, p. 118).

490. — Stone implements from Burma. By J. Evans. (*Nature*, II, 1870, pp. 104—5).
      A propos du même sujet traité par M. W. Theobald Junior, dans les *Proceedings Asiat. Soc. Bengal,* July, 1869.

491. — The Celts of Toungoo. By Francis Mason, D.D. (*Indian Antiquary*, I, 1872, pp. 326—8).

492. — Monograph on the Relations of the Indo-Chinese and Inter-Oceanic Races and Languages. By A. H. Keane, M.A.I. — Read before the British Association, Sheffield, August 1879, and reprinted from the Journal of the Anthropological Institute for February, 1880. London: Trübner, 1880, br. in-8, pp. 36.

493. — The Indo-Chinese and Oceanic Races — types and affinities. By A. H. Keane. (*Nature*, XXIII, 1880—81, pp. 199—203; pp. 220—224; pp. 247—251; pp. 271—274).

494. — Classification of the Indo-Chinese and Oceanic Races. By A. H. Keane. (*Ibid.*, XXIII, 1880—81, p. 529).

495. — Notes on Analogies of Manners between the Indo-Chinese Races and the Races of the Indian Archipelago. By Colonel Yule, C.B. (*Journ. Anthrop. Inst. of Great Brit. and Ireland*, Vol. IX, 1880—1881, pp. 290—301).

496. — Ethnology. (*British Burma Gazetteer*, Vol. I, Chap. IV, pp. 141—192).

497. — Histoire anthropologique des peuples de l'Indo-Chine. Par le docteur E. Maurel. (*Bul. Soc. Anthrop.*, Paris, 1886, pp. 287—290).

498. — Notice bibliographique sur l'Anthropologie et l'Ethnographie de l'Indo-Chine. Par le Dr. J. Harmand. (*Arch. Médecine navale*, XXXV, 1881, pp. 153—5).

499. — Anthropologie et Ethnographie de l'Indo-Chine. Lettre du Dr. J. Harmand. (*Ibid.*, XXXV, 1881, pp. 324—330).

500. — Alcuni cenni sulla Tribu' dei Palaung del sig. G. B. Sacchiero vice-console d'Italia a Rangun. (*Bol. Soc. geog. Ital.*, 1890, pp. 920—5).

501. — *Alb. Grünwedel. — Prähistorisches aus Birma. (*Globus*, LXVIII, pp. 14 et seq.).

502. — *Fritz Nötling. — Ueber prähistorische Steinwaffen in Ober-Birma. (*Verh. Berl. Ges. f. Anthr., Eth.*, 1891, pp. 694—5).

503. — *Fritz Noetling. — Ueber das Thanyet, eine merkwürdige Waffe der Birmaner. (*Zeit. für Ethnol.*, XXVIII, pp. 36—40).

504. — *Fritz Noetling. — Ueber Kartenweberei in Birma. (*Ibid.*, XXX, pp. 471).

505. — The Wild Peoples of Farther India. By C. W. Rosset, Freiburg in Baden. (*Bul. Am. Geog. Soc.*, XXV, No. 1, 1893, pp. 289—303).

506. — The gradual extinction of the Burmese race. By G. H. Le Maistre. (*Imp. & As. Quart. Rev.*, N. S., VI, 1893, pp. 321—328).

507. — The Pre-Aryan races of India, Assam, and Burma. By S. E. Peal. (*Jour. As. Soc. Bengal*, Vol. 65, Pt. 3, 1896, pp. 59—63).

508. — *A Lost People in Burmah. By H. Fielding. (*Temple Bar*, CXVIII, Dec. 1899, p. 486).

509. — Ethnology. With Vocabularies. (Scott's *Gaz. of Upper Burma*, Pt. I. — Vol. I, 1900, Chap. IX, pp. 475—727).

510. — A Spear-head and Socketed Celt of Bronze from the Shan States, Burma. Communicated by Henry Balfour, M.A., Curator of the Pitt Rivers Museum, Oxford. (*Journ. Anthrop. Inst. of Gr. Brit. and Ireland*, Vol. XXXI, 1901, *Man*, pp. 97—98).

511. — Contribution à l'étude des caractères céphaliques des Birmans par le Dr. R. Verneau. (*L'Anthropologie*, XV, 1904, Jan.-fév., pp. 1—23).

IV. — Climat et Météorologie.

512. — Table of the Fall of Rain at Tavoy, from 1st May to 31st Oct., in inches and decimals. [Communicated by G. Swinton.] (*Gleanings in Science*, 1831, III, Calcutta, p. 408).

512 *bis.* — Climate of Ava. (*Ibid.*, 1830, II, Calcutta, pp. 199—200).

512 *ter.* — Meteorological Observations kept at the Rangoon Field Hospital, Lat. 16° 47′ N. Long. 96° 13′ 27″ for the Months of May-July 1852. Elevation of the Hospital above the level of the sea about 40 feet; distance from the river about one mile. By J. Fayrer, M.D. Assistant Surgeon, Field Hospital, Rangoon. (*Jour. As. Soc. Bengal*, XXI, 1852, pp. 520—534). — August-Sept., 1852. (*Ibid.*, pp. 621—630). etc.

513. — A Practical Guide to the Climates and Weather of India, Ceylon and Burmah and the Storms of Indian Seas based chiefly on the Publications of the Indian Meteorological Department by Henry F. Blanford, F.R.S., F.R. Met. S. .... London, Macmillan and Co., and New York, 1889, in-8, pp. XIII—369.

> Notice: *Nature*, XL, 1889, p. 221.

514. — *Henry F. Blanford. — On the Variations of the Rainfall at Cherra Poonjee, in the Khasi Hills, Assam. (*Quart. Jour. R. Met. Soc. London*, XVII, pp. 146—154).

515. — The Greatest Rainfall in Twenty-four Hours. By E. Douglas Archibald. (*Nature*, May 25, 1893, p. 77).

> Chirapunji, Khasia Hills, June 24, 1876, 40.8 inches.

516. — *Report on the Rainfall in Burma, for the year ending 31st March 1900. Compiled by the Director, Department of Land Records and Agriculture. 1900, in-fol.

V. — Histoire naturelle.
Divers.

517. — The Natural Productions of Burmah, or Notes on the Fauna, Flora, and Minerals of the Tenasserim Provinces, and the Burman Empire. By Rev. Francis Mason, A.M., ... Maulmain: American Mission Press, Thos. S. Ranney. 1850, in-8, 7 ff. n. c. p. l. tit. et l. préf., + pp. VIII—332.

> Sur un dernier f. n. c. on lit l'annonce de: "In the Press, and shortly will be published, an Appendix to the preceding work...."

518. — Burmah, its People and Natural Productions, or Notes on the Nations, Fauna, Flora, and Minerals of Tenasserim, Pegu and Burmah, with Systematic Catalogues of the known Mammals, Birds, Fish, Reptiles, Insects, Mollusks, Crustaceans, Annalids, Radiates, Plants and Minerals, with Vernacular Names; by Rev. F. Mason, D.D., M.R.A.S. Corresponding Member of the American Oriental Society, of the Boston Society of Natural History, and of the Lyceum of Natural History, New-York. Rangoon : Thos. Stowe Ranney, 1860. — London : Trubner & Co. ..... New-York : Phinney, Blakeman & Mason, in-8, pp. xvii—913.

519. — Burma, its People and Productions; or, Notes on the Fauna, Flora and Minerals of Tenasserim, Pegu and Burma. By Rev. F. Mason, D.D., M.R.A.S., Corresponding member of the American Oriental Society, of the Boston Society of Natural History, and of the Lyceum of Natural History, New York. Published by order of the Chief Commissioner of British Burma, by Stephen Austin & sons, Hertford. 1882—1883, 2 vol. gr. in-8, pp. xxiv—560, xv—787. [Vol. I. Geology, Mineralogy and Zoology. — Vol. II. Botany. Rewritten and enlarged by W. Theobald, late Deputy-Superintendent Geological Survey of India.]

520. — Natural History Notes from Burmah. By R. Romanis. (*Nature*, XX, 1879, p. 362).

> Government High School, Rangoon.

Zoologie.

521. — A letter to Dr. Helfer, on the Zoology of Tenasserim and the neighbouring Provinces. By Assist. Surg. J. T. Pearson. (*Jour. As. Soc. Bengal*, VII, April 1838, pp. 357—363).

522. — Note on a Species of *Arctonix* from Arracan. By Dr. G. Evans, Curator As. Soc. Museum. (*Ibid.*, VII, Aug. 1838, pp. 732—735).

523. — Note on the Animal Productions of the Tenasserim Provinces; read at the meeting of the 10th October, 1838. By J. W. Helfer, Esq. M.D. (*Ibid.*, VII, Oct. 1838, pp. 855—863).

524. — Drafts for a Fauna Indica. (Comprising the Animals of the Himalaya Mountains, those of the Valley of the Indus, of the Provinces of Assam, Sylhet, Tipperah, Arracan, and of Ceylon, with Occasional Notices of Species from the Neighbouring Countries). By Ed. Blyth, Curator of the Asiatic Society's Museum, &c., &c. (*Ibid.*, XIV, Pt. II, 1845, pp. 845—878).

525. — Conspectus of the Ornithology of India, Burma, and the Malayan Peninsula, inclusive of Sindh, Asám, Ceylon and the Nicobar islands. — By E. Blyth, Esq. (*Ibid.*, XIX, 1850, pp. 229—239; *ibid.*, XIX, 1850, pp. 317—342; *ibid.*, XIX, 1850, pp. 501—517).

526. — Journal of the Asiatic Society of Bengal. — Part II. Extra Number. August, 1875. — Catalogue of Mammals and Birds of Burma. By the late

E. Blyth.... With a Memoir, and Portrait of the Author. — Hertford: Stephen Austin, 1875, in-8, pp. xxiv—167.

Edwarth Blyth, né à Londres 23 déc. 1810; † 27 déc. 1874. Notice par A. Grote.

527. — The Mammals and Birds of Burma. (*Nature*, XIV, 1876, p. 153).

A propos de: Catalogue of Mammals and Birds of Burma. By the late E. Blyth, C.M.Z.S. (*Journal of the Asiatic Society of Bengal*, New Series, Vol. XLIII, Part 2.)

528. — Mammals. (*British Burma Gazetteer*, Vol. I, Chap. XVI, pp. 538—568).

Chapter XVI is compiled from the works of Blyth (almost entirely) and Jerdon.

529. — The Land Shells of the Tenasserim Provinces, by Rev. F. Mason, A.M., Corresponding Member of the Boston Society of Natural History, U. S. (*Jour. As. Soc. Bengal*, XVII, Pt. I, 1848, pp. 62—65).

530. — Notes on the Rev. F. Mason's Paper "On the Shells of the Tenasserim Provinces". By W. H. Benson, Esq. (*Ibid.*, XVIII, Pt. I, 1849, pp. 164—166).

531. — Description of a new species of Hornbill, by Capt. S. R. Tickell, Principal Asst. Commr. Tenasserim provinces. (*Ibid.*, XXIV, 1855, pp. 285—287).

532. — On the Hornbills of India and Burmah. By Lieut.-Col. S. R. Tickell. (*Ibis*, VI, 1864, pp. 173—183).

533. — Note on the Gibbon of Tenasserim, *Hylobates Lar*. By Lieut.-Col. S. R. Tickell, in a letter to A. Grote. (*Annals Nat. Hist.*, 3d S., XIV, 1864, pp. 360—3).

534. — Description of a supposed new Genus of the Gadidae Arakan. By Lieut.-Col. S. R. Tickell, Bengal Staff. (*Jour. As. Soc. Bengal*, Vol. 34, 1865, Pt. 2, pp. 32—3).

535. — Characters of seventeen new forms of the *Cyclostomacea* from the British Provinces of Burmah, collected by W. Theobald, jun. By W. H. Benson. (*Annals Nat. Hist.*, 2d Ser., XVII, 1856, pp. 225—233).

536. — Descriptions of three new species of *Paludomus* from Burmah, and of some forms of *Stenothyra* (*Nematura*) from Penang, Mergui, &c. By W. H. Benson. (*Ibid.*, 2d Ser., XVII, 1856, pp. 494—501).

537. — New Species of *Bulimus* from India, Burma, and the Mauritius. Described by W. H. Benson. (*Ibid.*, 2d Ser., XIX, 1857, pp. 327—330).

538. — List of Birds collected at Tavoy, in the Tenasserim Provinces, by Captain Briggs, Deputy Commissioner of Tavoy. By John Gould. (*Proc. Zool. Soc.*, XXVII, 1859, pp. 149—150).

539. — New *Helicidae* collected by W. Theobald, jun., in Burmah and the Khasia Hills, and described by W. H. Benson. (*Annals Nat. Hist.*, 3d Ser., III, 1859, pp. 387—393).

540. — Characters of a new Burmese *Streptaxis* and of two forms belonging to a peculiar section of *Helix* collected by Captain Richard H. Sankey, Madras Engineers. By W. H. Benson. (*Ibid.*, 3d Ser., III, 1859, pp. 471—4).

541. — Observations on the Shell and Animal of *Hybocystis*, a new genus of *Cyclostomidae*, based on *Megalomastoma gravidum* and *Otopoma Blennus*, B.; with Notes on other living Shells from India and Burmah. By W. H. Benson. (*Annals Nat. Hist.*, 3d Ser., IV, 1859, pp. 90—3).

542. — Notes on the Animals of *Rhaphaulus Chrysalis*, *Pupina artata*, *Otopoma clausum*, *Helix Achatina*, and *H. pylaica*. By W. H. Benson. (*Ibid.*, 3d Ser., IV, 1859, pp. 93—6).

543. — Descriptions of Indian and Burmese Species of the Genus *Unio*, Retz. By W. H. Benson. (*Ibid.*, 3d S., X, 1862, pp. 184—195).

544. — Characters of new Land-Shells from Burmah and the Andamans. By W. H. Benson. (*Ibid.*, 3d S., VI, 1860, pp. 190—5).

545. — Contributions to Indian Malacology, No. III. Descriptions of new Operculated Land-Shells from Pegu, Arakan and the Khasi hills. — By William T. Blandford, F.G.S. (*Journ. of the As. Soc. of Bengal*, Vol. XXXI, No. 2, 1862, pp. 135—145).

546. — Contributions to Indian Malacology, No. V, Descriptions of new Land-Shells from Arakan, Pegu, and Ava; with notes on the distribution of described species. By William T. Blandford. (*Ibid.*, Vol. 34, 1865, Pt. 2, pp. 66—105).

547. — Contributions to Indian Malacology, No. VIII. List of Estuary Shells collected in the Delta of the Irawady, in Pegu, with Descriptions of the new species. By William T. Blanford.... (*Ibid.*, Vol. 36, 1867, Pt. 2, pp. 51—72).

548. — Contributions to Indian Malacology, No. XII. Descriptions of new Land and Freshwater Shells from Southern and Western India, Burmah, the Andaman Islands, &c. — By W. T. Blandford. (*Ibid.*, Vol. 49, Pt. 2, 1880, pp. 180—222).

549. — Descriptions of some Indian and Burmese Species of *Assiminea*. By William T. Blanford. (*Annals Nat. Hist.*, 3 S., XIX, 1867, pp. 381—6).

550. — List of Birds obtained in the Irawadi Valley around Ava, Thayet Myo, and Bassein. By W. T. Blanford. (*Ibis*, 2d Ser., VI, 1870, pp. 462—470).

551. — Land, Fresh-water and Estuarine Mollusca. [By W. T. Blanford, of the Geological Survey of India]. (*British Burma Gazetteer*, Vol. I, Chap. XX, pp. 698—716).

552. — The Fauna of British India, including Ceylon and Burma. Published under the Authority of the Secretary of State for India in Council. Edited by W. T. Blanford. — *Mammalia*. By W. T. Blanford, F.R.S. — London: Taylor and Francis... Calcutta and Bombay: Thacker & Co.... Berlin: R. Friedländer & Sohn, 1888. — Part I, 1888, in-8, pp. XII—250; Part II, 1891, in-8, pages 251 à 617 + pp. xx.

     Notices: *Nature*, XXXVIII, 1888, pp. 513—4, par W. H. F. — XLVI, 1892, pp. 5—6, par W. H. F.

— *The Fauna of British India, including Ceylon and Burma. Published under the authority of the Secretary of State for India in Council. Edited by W. T. Blanford. *Birds*. — Vol. I. By Eugene W. Oates. London: Taylor and Francis, 1889, in-8, pp. i—xx, 1—556.

Notice: *Nature*, XLI, 1889—90, pp. 388—390. By R. Bowdler Sharpe.

— *The Fauna of British India, including Ceylon and Burma. Published under the authority of the Secretary of State for India in Council. Edited by W. T. Blanford. *Birds*. — Vol. II. By Eugene W. Oates. London: Taylor and Francis, 1890, in-8, pp. i—x, 1—407.

Notice: *Nature*, XLIII, 1890—91, pp. 266—267. Par R. Bowdler Sharpe.

— The Fauna of British India including Ceylon and Burma. Published under the authority of the Secretary of State for India in Council. Edited by W. T. Blanford. *Birds*. — Vol. III. By W. T. Blanford, F.R.S. London: Taylor and Francis, 1895, in-8, pp. xiv—450.

Notice: *Calcutta Review*, CII, Jan. 1896, pp. vii—viii.

— *Birds*. — Vol. IV. By W. T. Blanford, F.R.S. *Ibid.*, 1898, in-8, pp. xxi—500.

— *The Fauna of British India, including Ceylon and Burma. Edited by W. T. Blanford. Vol. I. *Fishes*. — By Francis Day. London: Taylor and Francis, 1889, in-8, pp. 548; 164 Figs.

Notice: *Nature*, XLI, 1889—90, pp. 101—102. — Il y a deux vol. de Poissons.

— *The Fauna of British India, including Ceylon and Burma.... Edited by W. T. Blanford. *Moths*. — Vol. I. By G. F. Hampson. London, Taylor and Francis, 1892, in-8.

Notice: *Nature*, XLVII, 1892—93, pp. 387—388. Par W. F. K.[irby.]

— *The Fauna of British India, including Ceylon and Burma. Published under the authority of the Secretary of State for India in Council. Edited by W. T. Blanford. *Moths*. — Vol. III. By G. F. Hampson. London: Taylor and Francis, 1895, in-8.

Notice: *Nature*, LI, 1894—95, p. 605. Par W. F. Kirby.

— *The Fauna of British India, including Ceylon and Burma. Published under the authority of the Secretary of State for India. Edited by W. T. Blanford. *Moths*. — Vol. IV. By Sir G. F. Hampson, Bart. London: Taylor and Francis, 1896, in-8, pp. xxviii + 594.

Notice: *Nature*, LV, 1896—97, pp. 245—246.

— *The Fauna of British India, including Ceylon and Burma. Edited by W. T. Blanford, F.R.S. Published under the authority of the Secretary of State for India in Council. *Reptilia and Batrachia*. — By G. A. Boulenger.

Notice: *Nature*, LVI, 1897, pp. 363—364. Par D. S.

— *The Fauna of British India, including Ceylon and Burma. Published under the authority of the Secretary of State for India in Council. Edited by W. T. Blanford. *Rhynchota*, vol. I. (*Heteroptera*). — By W. L. Distant. London: Taylor and Francis, 1902, in-8, pp. xxxviii + 438.

Notice: *Nature*, LXVI, 1902, p. 548.

— *The Fauna of British India, including Ceylon and Burma. Published under

the Auspices of the Secretary of State for India in Council. Edited by W.
T. Blanford. *Hymenoptera.* — Vol. II, Ants and Cuckoo-Wasps. By Lieut.-Col.
C. T. Bingham. London: 1903, in-8, pp. xix + 506.

> Notice: *Nature*, LXVIII, 1903, p. 220. — Le 1er vol. des *Hymenoptera* comprend
> les "Wasps and Bees".

553. — Monograph of Himalayan, Assamese, Barmese and Cingalese Clausiliae.
By William T. Blanford. (*Jour. As. Soc. Bengal*, Vol. 41, Pt. 2, pp. 199—206).

— Postscript to the Monograph of Himalayan and Barmese Clausiliae. By Dr.
F. Stoliczka. (*Ibid.*, pp. 207—210).

554. — Notes on some Reptilia from the Himalayas and Burma. By W. T.
Blanford. (*Ibid.*, Vol. 47, 1878, Pt. 2, pp. 125—131).

555. — On some Mammals from Tenasserim. By W. T. Blanford. (*Ibid.*, Vol.
47, 1878, Pt. 2, pp. 150—167).

556. — Notes on an apparently undescribed *Varanus* from Tenasserim and on
other *Reptilia* and *Amphibia.* — By W. T. Blanford. (*Ibid.*, Vol. 50, Pt. 2,
1881, pp. 239—243).

557. — On some Species of Shells of the Genera *Streptaxis* and *Ennea* from
India, Ceylon, and Burma. By W. T. Blanford. (*Proc. Zool. Soc.*, 1899, pp.
764—770).

558. — *W. T. Blanford. — The Distribution of Vertebrate Animals in India,
Ceylon and Burma. (*Philos. Trans. R. Soc.*, London, Series B, CXCIV, 1901,
pp. 335—436, 1 pl. carte). — Résumé dans *Proc. Roy. Soc.*, London, LXVII,
1901, pp. 484—492).

559. — The Distribution of Vertebrate Animals in India, Ceylon and Burma.
(*Nature*, LXIII, 1900—1901, pp. 287—289).

> Abridged from a paper read at the Royal Society on Dec. 13, 1900, by Dr. W.
> T. Blanford, F.R.S.

560. — Notes on a collection of Land and Freshwater Shells from the Shan
States. — Collected by F. Fedden, Esq., 1864—65. — By W. Theobald, Jun.
(*Jour. As. Soc. Bengal*, Vol. 34, 1865, Pt. 2, pp. 273—279).

561. — Descriptions of some new land shells from the Shan States and Pegu.
By W. Theobald, Jun. (*Ibid.*, Vol. 39, Pt. 2, 1870, pp. 395—402).

562. — Catalogue of the Reptiles of British Birma, embracing the Provinces
of Pegu, Martaban, and Tenasserim; with descriptions of new or little-known
species. By W. Theobald, Jun., Geological Survey of India. (*Jour. Linn. Soc.*,
Zool., X, 1870, pp. 4—67).

563. — Reptilian Fauna. [By W. Theobald, Deputy Superintendent, Geological
Survey of India.] (*British Burma Gazetteer*, Vol. I, Chap. XVIII, pp. 605—640).

564. — Notes on terrestrial Mollusca from the neighbourhood of Moulmein
(Tenasserim Provinces), with Descriptions of New Species. By Dr. F. Stoliczka.
(*Jour. As. Soc. Bengal*, Vol. 40, Pt. 2, 1871, pp. 143—177, 217—259).

565. — Notes on some Indian and Burmese Ophidians. By Dr. F. Stoliczka. (*Jour. As. Soc. Bengal*, Vol. 40, Pt. 2, 1871, pp. 421—445).

566. — Notes on Barmese and Arakanese land shells, with Descriptions of a new species. By W. Theobald and Dr. F. Stoliczka. (*Ibid.*, Vol. 41, Pt. 2, pp. 329—334).

567. — Descriptions of some new Land and Freshwater Shells from India and Burmah. By W. Theobald. (*Ibid.*, Vol. 45, 1876, Pt. 2, pp. 184—189).

568. — Notes on Birds collected in Tenasserim and in the Andaman Islands. By Arthur, Viscount Walden. (*Proc. Zool. Soc.*, 1866, pp. 537—556).

569. — Notes on Birds from Burma. By Arthur, Viscount Walden, F.R.S. (*Ibis*, 3d Ser., V, 1875, pp. 458—463).

570. — Descriptions of some undescribed Species of Birds discovered by Lieut. Wardlaw Ramsay in Burma. By Arthur, Viscount Walden. (*Annals Nat. History*, 4 S., XV, 1875, pp. 400—3).

571. — Description of a new Species of Pigeon from the Karen Hills. By Arthur, Viscount Walden. (*Ibid.*, 4 S., XVI, 1875, p. 228).

572. — On the Freshwater Fishes of Burma. By Francis Day. (*Proc. Zool. Soc.*, 1869, pp. 614—623).

573. — On some Bats collected by Mr. F. Day in Burma. By Prof. W. Peters. (*Ibid.*, 1871, pp. 513—514).

574. — On the Freshwater Siluroids of India and Burmah. By Surgeon Francis Day. (*Ibid.*, 1871, pp. 703—721).

575. — On some new or imperfectly known Fishes of India and Burma. By Surgeon-Major Francis Day. (*Ibid.*, 1873, pp. 107—112).

576. — Report on the Fresh Water Fish and Fisheries of India and Burma, by Surgeon-Major Francis Day, F.L.S. & F.Z.S., Inspector general of Fisheries in India. — Calcutta: Office of the Superintendent of Government Printing. 1873. in-8, pp. 2 + x + 118 + ccovii.

    Notice: *Ocean Highways*, N. S., Vol. I, Oct. 1873, p. 295.

577. — Ichthyology. (*British Burma Gazetteer*, Vol. I, Chap. XIX, pp. 641—697). Compiled from Mr. Day's report and publications.

578. — The Fishes of India; being a Natural History of the Fishes known to inhabit the Seas and fresh Waters of India, Burma, and Ceylon. With Descriptions of the sub-classes, orders, families, genera, and species. By Francis Day, F.L.S., & F.Z.S., &c., Surgeon-major Madras Army, and Inspector-General of Fisheries in India and Burma. — London: Published by Bernard Quaritch, 1875.

    Part I. August 1875, pp. 168 + 40 pl. — Part II. 1876, pages 169 à 368 + pl. 41 à 78. — Part III, August 1877, pages 369 à 552 + pl. 79 à 138. — Part IV, December 1878, pages xx—553 à 778 + pl. 134 à 145.

579. — Description of a new Species of Pheasant of the Genus *Euplocamus* from Burmah, with a List of the known Species by D. G. Elliot. (*Proc. Zool. Soc.*, 1871, pp. 137—8).

580. — Description of a new Cetacean from the Irrawaddy River, Burmah. By John Anderson. (*Proc. Zool. Soc.*, 1871, pp. 142—4).

581. — Notes on *Trionyx Phayrei* of Mr. Theobald and Dr. Anderson. By Dr. J. E. Gray. (*Annals Nat. Hist.*, 4 S., VIII, 1871, pp. 83—9).

582. — On *Scapia Phayrei*. By Dr. J. E. Gray. (*Ibid.*, pp. 320—4).

583. — On *Testudo Phayrei, Theob.* & Dr. *Gray*. By John Anderson. (*Ibid.*, pp. 324—330).

584. — On the Genera *Manouria* and *Scapia*. By Dr. J. E. Gray. (*Ibid.*, X, 1872, pp. 218—9).

585. — On *Trionyx gangeticus*, Cuvier, *Trionyx hurum*, B. H. and Dr. Gray. By Dr. Anderson, Calcutta. (*Ibid.*, pp. 219—222).

586. — Description of some new Asiatic Mammals and Chelonia. By John Anderson, M.D. (*Ibid.*, 4 S., XVI, 1875, pp. 282—5).

587. — Anatomical and Zoological Researches: comprising an Account of the Zoological Results of the two Expeditions to Western Yunnan in 1868 and 1875; and a Monograph of the two Cetacean Genera, *Platanista* and *Orcella*. By John Anderson, M.D., Edin., Superintendent Indian Museum, and Professor of Comparative Anatomy, Medical College, Calcutta; Medical Officer to the Expeditions. First Volume — TEXT. London: Bernard Quaritch, 1878, gr. in-4, pp. xxv—984 + 1 f. n. c. — Second Volume — PLATES (84 Plates). London: Bernard Quaritch, 1878, gr. in-4, Pl. et pp. xi—29.

> "The First Expedition was despatched in the end of 1867 from Calcutta, and returned in November 1868; and the Second Expedition left Mandalay on the 3rd January 1875, and returned thither on the 10th March of the same year". (Introduction.)

588. — On the Madreporaria of the Mergui Archipelago collected for the Trustees of the Indian Museum, Calcutta, by Dr. John Anderson, F.R.S., Superintendent of the Museum. By Prof. P. Martin Duncan. (*Jour. Linn. Soc., Zool.*, XXI, 1889, pp. 1—25).

589. — On the Holothurians of the Mergui Archipelago collected... by Dr. John Anderson. By Professor F. Jeffrey Bell. (*Ibid.*, XXI, 1889, pp. 25—8).

590. — List of the Lepidoptera of Mergui and its Archipelago collected for the Trustees of the Indian Museum, Calcutta, by Dr. John Anderson. By Frederic Moore. (*Ibid.*, XXI, 1889, pp. 29—60).

591. — Report on the Marine Sponges, chiefly from King Island in the Mergui Archipelago, collected... by Dr. John Anderson. By Henry J. Carter. (*Ibid.*, XXI, 1889, pp. 61—84).

592. — On the Ophiuridae of the Mergui Archipelago, collected... by Dr. John Anderson. By Prof. P. Martin Duncan. (*Ibid.*, XXI, 1889, pp. 85—106).

593. — On some Parts of the Anatomy of *Ophiothrix variabilis*, Dunc., and *Ophiocampsis pellicula*, Dunc., based on materials furnished by the Trustees of the Indian Museum, Calcutta. By Prof. P. Martin Duncan. (*Ibid.*, XXI, 1889, pp. 107—120).

594. — On the Polyzoa and Hydroida of the Mergui Archipelago collected... by Dr. J. Anderson. By the Rev. Thomas Hincks. (*Jour. Linn. Soc., Zool.*, XXI, 1889, pp. 121—135).

595. — On a new Species of *Brachyonychus* from the Mergui Archipelago. By Henry Walter Bates. (*Ibid.*, XXI, 1889, p. 135).

596. — List of Birds, chiefly from the Mergui Archipelago, collected for the Trustees of the Indian Museum, Calcutta. By John Anderson, M.D. (*Ibid.*, XXI, 1889, pp. 136—153).

597. — On the *Dichelaspis pellucida*, Darwin, from the scales of an Hydrophid obtained at Mergui. By Dr. P. P. C. Hoek. (*Ibid.*, XXI, 1889, pp. 154—5).

598. — List of the Shells of Mergui and its Archipelago, collected... by John Anderson... By Prof. Eduard von Martens, M.D. (*Ibid.*, XXI, 1889, pp. 155—219).

599. — On the Gephyreans of the Mergui Archipelago, collected... by Dr. John Anderson. By Prof. Emil Selenka, Erlangen. (*Ibid.*, XXI, 1889, pp. 220—2).

600. — Report on the Alcyoniid and Gorgoniid Alcyonaria of the Mergui Archipelago, collected... by Dr. John Anderson. By Stuart O. Ridley, M.A.... (*Ibid.*, XXI, 1889, pp. 223—247).

601. — On two Species of Actiniae from the Mergui Archipelago, collected... by Dr. John Anderson... By Professor Alfred C. Haddon, M.A. (*Ibid.*, XXI, 1889, pp. 247—255).

602. — Report on Annelids from the Mergui Archipelago, collected... by Dr. John Anderson. By Frank E. Beddard. (*Ibid.*, XXI, 1889, pp. 256—266).

603. — Report on the Pennatulida of the Mergui Archipelago, collected... by Dr. John Anderson... By Prof. A. Milnes Marshall, and G. Herbert Fowler. (*Ibid.*, XXI, 1889, pp. 267—286).

604. — Report on the Myriopoda of the Mergui Archipelago, collected... by Dr. John Anderson. By R. I. Pocock. (*Ibid.*, XXI, 1889, pp. 287—303).

605. — Report on the Comatulae of the Mergui Archipelago, collected... by Dr. John Anderson. By P. Herbert Carpenter. (*Ibid.*, XXI, 1889, pp. 304—16).

606. — On the Echinodea of the Mergui Archipelago, collected... by Dr. John Anderson. By Prof. P. Martin Duncan... and W. Percy Sladen. (*Ibid.*, XXI, 1889, pp. 316—319).

607. — On the Asteroidea of the Mergui Archipelago, collected... by Dr. John Anderson... By W. Percy Sladen. (*Ibid.*, XXI, 1889, pp. 319—331).

608. — Report on the Mammals, Reptiles, and Batrachians, chiefly from the Mergui Archipelago, collected for the Trustees of the Indian Museum. By John Anderson, M.D.... (*Ibid.*, XXI, 1889, pp. 331—350).

609. — 'Contributions to the Fauna of Mergui and its Archipelago. London, Taylor and Francis, 1889, 2 vol.

Notice: *Nature*, XLI, 1889—90, pp. 556—557. Par R. M.

610. — Supplementary Notes on the Arachnida and Myriopoda of the Mergui Archipelago: with Descriptions of some New Species from Siam and Malaysia. By R. I. Pocock. ((*Jour. Linn. Soc., Zool.*, XXIV, 1894, pp. 316—326).

611. — Jonas Lamprey. — On the habits of a boring beetle found in British Burma. (*Trans. Entom. Soc.*, 1874, (*Proc.*), p. XII).

612. — Description of a new Species of Woodpecker from British Burmah. By Lieut. R. Wardlaw Ramsay. (*Proc. Zool. Soc.*, 1874, pp. 212—213).

613. — Ornithological Notes from the District of Karen-nee, Burmah. By Robert Wardlaw Ramsay. (*Ibis*, 3d Ser., V, 1875, pp. 348—353).

614. — On an undescribed Species of Nuthatch and another Bird from Karen-nee. [*Orocetes erythrogaster, Sitta magna*]. By Lieutenant R. Wardlaw Ramsay. (*Proc. Zool. Soc.*, 1876, p. 677).

615. — Notes on some Burmese Birds. By Lieut. Wardlaw Ramsay, 67th Reg. (*Ibis*, 4 Ser., I, 1877, pp. 452—473).

616. — Notes on a Collection of Chiroptera from India and Burma, with description of new species. By G. E. Dobson. (*Jour. As. Soc. Bengal*, Vol. 46, 1877, Pt. 2, pp. 310—313).

617. — Sixth List of Birds from the Hill Ranges of the North-East Frontier of India. By Lieut.-Col. H. H. Godwin-Austen. (*Ibid.*, Vol. 47, 1878, Pt. 2, pp. 12—25).

618. — On new species of the Genus *Plectopylis* of the Family *Helicidae*. By Lieut.-Col. Godwin-Austen. (*Ibid.*, Vol. 48, 1879, Pt. 2, pp. 1—4).

619. — On some Land Mollusks from Burmah, with Descriptions of some new Species. By Lieut.-Col. H. H. Godwin-Austen. (*Proc. Zool. Soc.*, 1888, pp. 240—5).

620. — Description of a supposed new Species of *Helix* [*H. (Ægista) mitanensis*, n. sp.] from near Moulmain, Tenasserim. By Lieut.-Col. H. H. Godwin-Austen. (*Annals Nat. Hist.*, 6 S., III, 1889, pp. 107—8).   .

621. — A List of the Lepidopterous Insects collected by Mr. Ossian Limborg in Upper Tenasserim, with Descriptions of new Species. By F. Moore. (*Proc. Zool. Soc.*, 1878, pp. 821—859).

622. — List of the Lepidopterous Insects collected in Tavoy and in Siam during 1884—85 by the Indian Museum Collector under C. E. Pitman, ... Chief Superintendent of Telegraphs. Part I. *Heterocera*. — By Frederick Moore. (*Jour. As. Soc. Bengal*, Vol. 55, 1886, Pt. 2, pp. 97—101). — Part II. *Rhopalocera*. — By H. J. Elwes and Lionel de Nicéville. (*Ibid.*, pp. 413 —442).

623. — List of *Hymenoptera* obtained by Mr. Ossian Limborg east of Maulmain, Tenasserim Provinces, during the months of Dec. 1876, January, March and April 1877, with descriptions of new species. — by Frederick Smith, Biological Department, British Museum. (Communicated by J. Wood-Mason). (*Ibid.*, Vol. 47, 1878, Pt. 2, pp. 167—169).

324. — Description of a new Lepidopterous Insect belonging to the genus *Thaumantis*. By J. Wood-Mason. (*Jour. As. Soc. Bengal*, Vol. 47, 1878, Pt. 2, pp. 175—179).

325. — *Hemiptera* from Upper Tenasserim. By W. L. Distant. Communicated by J. Wood-Mason. (*Ibid.*, Vol. 48, 1879, Pt. 2, pp. 37—41).

626. — List of Diurnal *Lepidoptera* from Port Blair, Andaman Islands, with Descriptions of some new or little-known Species and of a new Species of *Hestia* from Burmah. — By J. Wood-Mason, Deputy Superintendent, Indian Museum, and L. de Nicéville. (*Ibid.*, Vol. 49, Pt. 2, 1880, pp. 223—243).

627. — On some Lepidopterous Insects belonging to the Rhopalocerous Genera *Euripus* and *Penthema* from India and Burmah. — By J. Wood-Mason. (*Ibid.*, Vol. 50, Pt. 2, 1881, pp. 85—87).

628. — "Some Account of the "Palan Byoo", or "Teindoung Bo" (*Paraponyx oryzalis*), a Lepidopterous Insect — pest of the Rice — Plant in Burma. By J. Wood-Mason, Officiating Superintendent, Calcutta Museum. Calcutta, 1885. Notice: *Nature*, XXXIII, 1885—6, p. 6.

629. — Notes on the Visceral Anatomy of the Tupaia of Burmah (*Tupaia belangeri*). By A. H. Garrod. (*Proc. Zool. Soc.*, 1879, pp. 301—5).

630. — The Game Birds of India, Burmah, and Ceylon. Hume and Marshall, [Calcutta, Printed by A. Acton... 1880—1], 3 vol. in-8.

631. — Descriptions of new Species of Lepidoptera from Tenasserim. By Arthur G. Butler. (*Annals Nat. History*, 5 S., X, 1882, pp. 372—6).

632. — On a Collection of Lepidoptera made by Commander Alfred Carpenter, R.N., in Upper Burma, in the Winter of 1885—86. By Arthur G. Butler. (*Ibid.*, 5 S., XVIII, 1886, pp. 182—191).

633. — On Rhyncota from Mergui. By W. L. Distant. (*Ibid.*, 5 S., XI, 1883, pp. 169—172).

634. — *Cicadidae* from the North Chin Hills, Burma. By W. L. Distant. (*Ibid.*, 6 S., XX, 1897, pp. 17—19).

635. — Nesting of Micropternus Phaeoceps. By Charles Bingham, Deputy Conservator of Forests, British Burmah. [Camp Meplay, Thoung-yeen Valley, Tenasserim, April 20, 1882]. (*Nature*, XXXII, 1885, pp. 52—53).
    Hensada, British Burmah, April 13.

636. — Descriptions of four new Species of Butterflies from Burmah. By H. Grose Smith. (*Annals Nat. History*, 5 S., XVIII, 1886, pp. 149—151).

637. — Descriptions of three new Species of Butterflies from Burmah. By H. Grose Smith. (*Ibid.*, 5 S., XIX, 1887, pp. 296—7).

638. — Descriptions of eight new Species of Asiatic Butterflies. By H. Grose Smith. (*Ibid.*, 5 S., XX, 1887, pp. 265—8).

639. — On certain *Lycaenidae* from Lower Tenasserim. By William Doherty, Cincinnati, U.S.A. (*Jour. As. Soc. Bengal*, Vol. 58, 1889, Pt. 2, pp. 409—440).

640. — A List of the Coleoptera, of the Family *Cleridae*, collected by Mr. Doherty in Burmah and Northern India, with Descriptions of new Species; and of some Species from Borneo, Perak, &c., from the Collection of Alexander Fry, Esq. By Rev. H. S. Gorham. (*Proc. Zool. Soc.*, 1893, pp. 566—81).

641. — The Butterflies of India, Burmah and Ceylon. A Descriptive Handbook of all the known species of Rhopalocerous Lepidoptera inhabiting that region, with notices of allied species occurring in the neighbouring countries along the border; with numerous illustrations. — By Major G. F. L. Marshall, Royal Engineers, Fellow of the Zoological Society of London; and Member of the Asiatic Society of Bengal and of the British Ornithologists' Union: and Lionel de Nicéville, Assistant in the Entomological Department, Indian Museum, Calcutta; and Member of the Entomological Society, London, and of the Asiatic Society, Bengal. — The illustrations drawn by Babu Gris Chunder Chuckerbutty and Babu Behari Lall Dass. The wood engravings by George Pearson. The Autotype plates by the Autotype Company of London. The Chromo-lithographs by Messrs. West, Newman & Co. — Calcutta: printed and published by the Calcutta Central Press Co., 1882. Vol. I. — Part I. Danainae. — Part II. Satyrinae, Elymniinae, Morphinae, Acraeinae, in-8, pp. vii—327. — Vol. II. Calcutta.... 1886, pp. viii—332. Nymphalinae, Lemoniidae, Libythaeinae, Nemeobiinae. — Vol. III. Calcutta... 1890, pp. xii—503.

Ces deux derniers vol. ne portent que le nom de Lionel de Nicéville. Notices par H. J. Elwes, *Nature*, XXVII, 1882—3, pp. 50—1; XXXV, 1886—7, p. 486.

642. — Description of a new Nymphaline Butterfly [*Neurosigma nonius*, sp. n.] from Burma. By Lionel de Nicéville. (*Annals Nat. Hist.*, 6 S., XVII, 1896, p. 396). Karenni.

643. — On New or Little-known Butterflies from the Indo- and Austro-Malayan Region. — By Lionel de Nicéville. (*Jour. As. Soc. Bengal*, Vol. 66, 1897, Pt. 2, pp. 543—577).

644. — Descriptions of some new Asiatic *Clausiliae*. By O. F. von Möllendorff. (*Ibid.*, Vol. 51, 1882, Pt. 2, pp. 12—13).

645. — On the Birds of Bhamo, Upper Burmah. By Eugene W. Oates. (*Ibis*, 5 Ser., VI, 1888, pp. 70—3).

646. — On the Species of *Thelyphonus* inhabiting Continental India, Burma, and the Malay Peninsula. By Eugene W. Oates. (*Jour. As. Soc. Bengal*, Vol. 58, 1889, Pt. 2, pp. 4—19).

647. — Descriptive Catalogue of the Spiders of Burma, based upon the Collection made by Eugene W. Oates and preserved in the British Museum. By T. Thorell. London: Printed by Order of the Trustees... 1895, in-8, pp. xxxvi—406.

Notice: *Nature*, LIII, 1895—6, pp. 122—4, by R. I. P.

648. — On a New Species of Pheasant from Burma. By Eugene W. Oates. (*Ibis*, 7 Ser., IV, 1898, pp. 124—5).

649. — On the Silver-Pheasants of Burma. By Eugene W. Oates. (*Ibis*, 8 Ser., Jan. 1903, pp. 93—106).

650. — On a new Silver-Pheasant [*Gennoeus affinis*, n. sp.] from Burma. By Eugene W. Oates. (*Annals Nat. History*, 7 S., XI, 1903, p. 231).

651. — Ornithology. [By Eugene W. Oates, Executive Engineer, D. P. W.]. (*British Burma Gazetteer*, Vol. I, Chap. XVII, pp. 569—604).

652. — Beetles destructive to Rice-Crops in Burma. By Arthur E. Shipley. (*Kew Bull.*, 1889, pp. 13—15).

653. — *Catalogue of the Described Diptera from South Asia. By F. M. Van der Wulp. Published by the Dutch Entomological Society. The Hague, M. Nijhoff, 1896, in-8, pp. 120.
> Notice: *Nature*, LIV, 1896, p. 435. Par W. F. K.

654. — Description of a new Siluroid Fish [*Macrones peguensis*] from Burma. By G. A. Boulenger. (*Annals Nat. History*, 6 S., XIV, 1894, p. 196).
> Sittang River, near Toungoo.

655. — Description of a new Snake of the Genus *Ablabes* [*A. Hamptoni*] from Burma. By G. A. Boulenger. (*Ibid.*, 7 S., VI, 1900, p. 409).

656. — On a new Frog from Upper Burma and Siam. By G. A. Boulenger. (*Ibid.*, 7 S., XII, 1903, p. 219). [*Rana Mortenseni*].

657. — Notes on a Small Collection of Odonata etc. from Upper Burma, with the Description of a new Species. By W. F. Kirby. (*Ibid.*, 6 S., XIV, 1894, pp. 111—113).
> Katha District.

658. — On new Species of Rhopalocera from Toungoo, Burma, and the Battak Mountains in Sumatra. By Major J. M. Fawcett. (*Ibid.*, 6 S., XX, 1897, pp. 111—112).

659. — On the Cteniform Spiders of Ceylon, Burmah, and the Indian Archipelago, West and North of Wallace's Line; with Bibliography and List of those from Australasia, South and East of Wallace's Line. By F. O. Pickard Cambridge. (*Ibid.*, 6 S., XX, 1897, pp. 329—356).

660. — Notes on some Butterflies from Myingyan, Central Burma. By Capt. E. Y. Watson. (*Jour. As. Soc. Bengal*, Vol. 66, 1897, Pt. 2, pp. 606—611).

661. — On the Birds collected and observed in the Southern Shan States of Upper Burma. By Col. C. T. Bingham..., and H. N. Thompson. (*Ibid.*, Vol. 69, 1900, Pt. II, pp. 102—142).

662. — A Treatise on Elephants, their Treatment in Health and Disease. By Vety. Capt. G. H. Evans, A.V.D. Superintendent, Civil Veterinary Department, Burma. Published by Authority. Rangoon: Printed by the Superintendent, Government Printing, Burma. 1901, in-4, pp. 4 + III—262—VII, pl.

662 *bis.* — Report on Burmese Elephants by Vety. Capt. G. H. Evans, A.V.D.; Superintendent, Civil Veterinary Department, Burma. September 1904, in-fol., pp. 11. [Rangoon, 2nd Oct. 1894.]

663. — *Report on the Extermination of Wild Animals Snakes in Burma for the year 1900. Compiled by the Government of Burma. 1901, in-fol.

664. — On the Mode of Copulation of the Indian Elephant. By H. Slade, Conservator of Forests, Maymyo, Burma. (*Proc. Zool. Soc.*, 1903, Vol. I, Pt. I, pp. 111—113).

665. — Liste des espèces de Décapodes Brachyures observés jusqu'à présent dans les eaux douces de l'Inde, de la Birmanie, de la presqu'île de Malacca et de l'Indo-Chine orientale. (*Mission Pavie. — Indo-Chine* 1879—1895 — *Etudes diverses*, III, 1904, pp. 329—330).

Botanique.

666. — Observations on the Burmese and Munipoor Varnish Tree, "Melanorrhoea usitata", which has lately blossomed in the Honorable Company's Botanic Garden. By N. Wallich, M.D. (*Jour. As. Soc. Bengal*, VIII, Jan. 1839, pp. 70—71).

667. — On the Gamboge of the Tenasserim Provinces, by the Rev. F. Mason, A.M. (*Ibid.*, XVI, Pt. II, 1847, pp. 661—663).

668. — The Liquidamber tree of the Tenasserim Provinces, — By the Rev. F. Mason. (*Ibid., Misc.*, XVII, pt. I, 1848, pp. 532—533).

669. — The Gum Kino of the Tenasserim Provinces. — By the Rev. F. Mason. (*Ibid.*, XVII, pt. II, 1848, pp. 223—225).

670. — The Pine tree of the Tenasserim Provinces. By the Rev. F. Mason. (*Ibid.*, XVIII, pt. I, 1849, pp. 73—75).

671. — Flora Burmanica, or a Catalogue of Plants, Indigenous and cultivated, in the Valleys of the Irrawaddy, Salwen, and Tenasserim, from Notes on the Fauna, Flora, and Minerals of the Tenasserim Provinces and the Burman Empire, By Rev. Francis Mason, A.M. Corresponding Member of the American Oriental Society, of the Boston Society of Natural History, and of the Lyceum of Natural History, New York. Tavoy: Karen Mission press. ... C. Bennett. 1851, in-8, pp. chiffrées 545 à 676.

672. — The vegetable Products of the Tenasserim Provinces. By Edward O'Riley. (*Jour. Ind. Archip.*, IV, 1850, pp. 55—65).

673. — Description of a New Genus of *Scrophularineae* from Martaban. By Dr. J. D. Hooker and Dr. T. Thomson. (*Jour. Lin. Soc., Bot.*, VIII, 1865, pp. 11—12).

674. — List of Algae collected by Mr. S. Kurz in Burma and adjacent islands, by Dr. G. v. Martens, in Stuttgardt. Communicated by Mr. S. Kurz. (*Jour. As. Soc. Bengal*, Vol. 40, Pt. 2, 1871, pp. 461—469).

675. — Algae collected by Mr. S. Kurz in Arracan and British Burma, determined and systematically arranged by Dr. G. Zeller, High Councillor of Finance in Stuttgart. (*Ibid.*, Vol. 42, 1873, Pt. 2, pp. 175—193).

676. — New Barmese Plants (Part First). By S. Kurz. (*Ibid.*, Vol. 41, Pt. 2, pp. 291—318).

677. — New Burmese Plants. Part II. By S. Kurz. (*Ibid.*, Vol. 42, 1873, Pt. 2, pp. 59—110). — Part III. (*Ibid.*, pp. 227—254).

678. — Enumeration of Burmese Palms. By S. Kurz. (*Jour. As. Soc. Bengal*, Vol. 43, 1874, Pt. 2, pp. 191—217).

679. — Contributions towards a knowledge of the Burmese Flora. Part I. By S. Kurz. (*Ibid.*, Vol. 43, 1874, Pt. 2, pp. 39—141; Vol. 44, 1875, Pt. 2, pp. 128—190; Vol. 45, 1876, Pt. 2, pp. 204—310; Vol. 46, 1877, Pt. 2, pp. 48—258).

680. — On a new Species of Tupistra from Tenasserim. By S. Kurz. (*Ibid.*, Vol. 44, 1875, Pt. 2, pp. 198—206).

681. — *Preliminary Report on the Forest and other Vegetation of Pegu. By Sulpice Kurz, Curator of the Herbarium, and Librarian, Royal Botanical Gardens, Calcutta. Calcutta, C. B. Lewis, 1875.

> Notice: *Nature*, XVI, 1877, pp. 58—59.

682. — Forest Flora of British Burma. By S. Kurz, Curator of the Herbarium, Royal Botanical Gardens, Calcutta. Published by order of the Government of India. Calcutta: Office of the Superintendent of Government Printing, 1877, 2 vol. in-8, pp. xxx—549, 613.

> Vol. I. Ranunculaceae to Cornaceae. — Vol. II. Caprifoliaceae to Filices.
> Notice: *Nature*, XVIII, 1878, p. 517.

683. — Forest and other Vegetation. (*British Burma Gazetteer*, Vol. I, Chap. III, pp. 68—140).

> The first part of Chapter III is from the late Mr. Kurz's Reports.

684. — Burmese Desmidieae, with Descriptions of new Species occurring in the neighbourhood of Rangoon. By W. Joshua. (*Jour. Linn. Soc., Bot.*, XXI, 1886, pp. 634—655).

685. — On a Collection of Plants from Upper Burma and the Shan States. By Brigadier-General H. Collett, C.B. ..., and W. Botting Hemsley, F.R.S. ... (*Ibid.*, XXVIII, 1891, pp. 1—150).

> Notice: *Nature*, XLIII, 1890—1, pp. 386—7.

686. — The Flora of Diamond Island. By W. Botting Hemsley. (*Nature*, 11 June 1891, p. 138).

> D'après Dr. Prain, who published a Flora in the *Jour. As. Soc. Bengal*.
> Située à l'embouchure de la rivière de Bassein.

687. — The Orchids of Burma (Including the Andaman Islands) described. Compiled from the Works of various Authorities by Captain Bartle Grant, The Border Regiment, Adjutant, Rangoon Volunteer Rifles. Rangoon: Printed at the Hanthawaddy Press, 1895, in-8, 2 ff. n. ch. er. et Pref. + pp. 424 + 8.

688. — *Kew Bulletin*, 1896.

> 3 rapports sur le so-called pickled or *leppett* tea of Burma.

689. — On *Croftia*, a new Indo-Chinese genus of Scitamineae. By G. King and and D. Prain. (*Jour. As. Soc. Bengal*, Vol. 65, 1896, Pt. 2, pp. 297—9).

690. — *On three New Genera of Plants from the Kachin Hills. By Major D. Prain. (*Scientific Memoirs by Medical Officers of the Army in India*, Part XI, 1898).

691. — *P. Hordern. — The bamboo. (*Blackwood's Magazine*, Vol. 148, 1898, pp. 228—232).

692. — *E. Pottinger and D. Prain. — Note on the Botany of the Kachin Hills north-east of Myitkyina. (*Bot. Survey India*, I, No. XI, Calcutta, 1898).

693. — *Doubtful Burmese Bamboos, by Sir Districh Brandis. (*Indian Forester*, March 1900, Vol. XXVI, No. 3).

Géologie et Minéralogie.

694. — On the Fossil Remains of two New Species of Mastodon, and of other vertebrated Animals, found on the left Bank of the Irawadi. By William Clift, Conservator of the Museum of the Royal College of Surgeons. (*Trans. Geolog. Soc.*, London, 2d Ser., II, Pt. III, 1828, pp. 369—375).

695. — Geological Account of a Series of Animal and Vegetable Remains and of Rocks, collected by J. Crawfurd, Esq. on a Voyage up the Irawadi to Ava, in 1826 and 1827. By the Rev. William Buckland, Prof. of Mineralogy and Geology in the University of Oxford. (*Ibid.*, London, 2d Ser., II, Pt. III, 1828, pp. 377—392).

695 *bis*. — Notice of some Tin Ore from the Coast of Tenasserim. By D. Ross. (*Gleanings in Science*, Jan. to Dec. Vol. I. Calcutta, 1829, pp. 143—4).

696. — Examination of a metallic Button, supposed to be Platina from Ava. By J. Prinsep. (*Gleanings in Science*, Calcutta, 1831, III, pp. 39—42).

697. — Note on certain Specimens of Animal Remains from Ava, presented by James Calder, to the Museum of the Asiatic Society. By Hugh Falconer. (*Ibid.*, Calcutta, 1831, III, pp. 167—170).

698. — *Extract from the Journal of Apothecary H. Bedford, deputed to Yenangyoung in Ava in search of Fossil Remains. (*Ibid.*, Calcutta, 1831, III, pp. 168—170).

Noetling.

699. — Examination of Minerals from Ava. By J. Prinsep, Sec. Ph. Cl. (*Jour. As. Soc. of Bengal*, I, Jan. 1832, pp. 14—17).

700. — Note on the Discovery of Platina in Ava. — By James Prinsep, F.R.S., Sec. Ph. Cl. (*As. Researches*, XVIII, 1833, Pt. II, pp. 279—284).

701. — Chemical Analyses. By Jas. Prinsep, Sec., &c. (*Jour. As. Soc. Bengal*, IV, Sept., 1835, pp. 509—514).

702. — Notes on the Geology, &c. of the Country in the Neighbourhood of Maulamyeng (vulg. Moulmein). By Capt. W. Foley. (*Ibid.*, V, May 1836, pp. 269—281).

703. — Examination of the Water of several Hot Springs on the Arracan Coast: from specimens preserved in the Museum of the Asiatic Society. (*Gleanings in Science*, Calcutta, 1831, III, pp. 16—18).

704. — Report of the Tin of the Province of Mergui. By Captain G. B. Tremenheere, Executive Engineer, Tenasserim Division. (*Jour. As. Soc. Bengal*, X, Pt. II, 1841, pp. 845—851).

705. — Some concluding Remarks forwarded for insertion with Capt. Tremenheere's Report on the Tin Ground of Mergui. (*Journ. of the As. Soc. of Bengal*, Vol. XI, Pt. I, n° 124, 1842, pp. 289—290).

706. — Report on the Tin of the Province of Mergui. By Captain G. B. Tremenheere, Executive Engineer, Tenasserim Division. (*Miscel. Papers relat. to Indo-China*, I, Lond., Trübner, 1886, pp. 251—6).

    From the *Jour. As. Soc. Bengal*, X, pp. 845—851.

— Paragraphs to be added to Capt. G. B. Tremenheere's Report on the Tin of Mergui. (*Ibid.*, pp. 258—9).

    Jour. As. Soc. Bengal, XI, pp. 24, 289.

707. — Report on the Manganese of the Mergui Province. By Captain G. B. Tremenheere, Executive Engineer, Tenasserim Division. (*Jour. As. Soc. Bengal*, X, Pt. II, 1841, pp. 852—853).

708. — Report on the Manganese of the Mergui Province. By Captain G. B. Tremenheere. (*Miscel. Papers relat. to Indo-China*, I, Lond., Trübner, 1886, pp. 257—8).

    From the *Jour. As. Soc. Bengal*, X, pp. 852—853.

709. — Second Report on the Tin of Mergui. By Capt. G. B. Tremenheere, F.R.S., Executive Engineer, Tenasserim Division. (*Journ. of the As. Soc. of Bengal*, Vol. XI, Pt. II, N° 129, 1842, pp. 839—852).

710. — Second Report on the Tin of Mergui. By Capt. G. B. Tremenheere, F.R.S., ... (*Miscel. Papers rel. to Indo-China*, I, Lond., 1886, pp. 260—271).

    From the *Jour. As. Soc. Bengal*, XI, pp. 839—852.

711. — Report of a Visit to the Pakchan River, and of some Tin localities in the southern portion of the Tenasserim Provinces. By Captain G. B. Tremenheere, F.G.S. Executive Engineer, Tenasserim Provinces, With a Map and Section of the Peninsula. (*Jour. As. Soc. Bengal*, XII, Pt. II, 1843, pp. 523—534).

712. — Report of a Visit to the Pakchan River, and of some Tin localities in the Southern Portion of the Tenasserim Provinces. By Captain G. B. Tremenheere... With a Map and Section of the Peninsula. (*Miscel. Papers relat. to Indo-China*, I, Lond., Trübner, 1886, pp. 275—284).

    From the *Jour. As. Soc. Bengal*, XII, pp. 523—534.

713. — Report, &c. from Captain G. B. Tremenheere, Executive Engineer, Tenasserim Division, to the Officer in charge of the office of Superintending Engineer, South Eastern Provinces; with information concerning the price of Tin ore of Mergui, in reference to Extract from a Despatch from the Honorable Court of Directors, dated 25th October 1843, No. 20. Communicated by the Government of India. (*Jour. As. Soc. Bengal*, XIV, Pt. I, 1845, pp. 329—332).

714. — Report, &c., from Captain G. B. Tremenheere, Executive Engineer, Tenasserim Division, to the Officer in charge of the Office of Superintending Engineer, South-Eastern Provinces. With information concerning the price of Tin Ore of Mergui, in reference to extract from a despatch from the Hon. Court of Directors, dated 25th October 1843, No. 20. Communicated by the Government of India. (*Miscel. Papers relat. to Indo-China*, I, Lond., Trübner, 1886, pp. 298—301).

     From the *Jour. As. Soc. Bengal*, XIV, pp. 829—883.

715. — °C. B. Tremenheere & Sir Charles Lemon. Report on the Tin of the Province of Mergui in Tenasserim in the Northern Part of the Malayan Peninsula with Introductory Remarks. (*Trans. Geolog. Soc. of Cornwall*, VI, 1846, pp. 68—75).

     Noetling.

716. — Analysis of Iron Ores from Tavoy and Mergui, and of Limestone from Mergui. By Dr. A. Ure, London. Communicated for the Museum Economic Geology of India, by E. A. Blundell, Esq. Commissioner, Tenasserim Provinces. (*Jour. As. Soc. Bengal*, XII, Pt. I, 1843, pp. 236—239).

717. — Analysis of Iron Ores from Tavoy and Mergui, and of Limestone from Mergui. By Dr. A. Ure, London. Communicated for the Museum Economic Geology of India by E. A. Blundell, Esq., Commissioner, Tenasserim Provinces. (*Miscel. Papers relat. to Indo-China*, I, Lond., Trübner, 1886, pp. 272—5).

     From the *Jour. As. Soc. Bengal*, XII, pp. 236—9.

718. — °E. O'Riley. Notes on the Geological Formations of Amherst Beach, Tenasserim Provinces. (Calcutta, *Jour. of Nat. Hist.*, VIII, 1847, pp. 186—9).
     Noetling.

719. — Rough Notes on the Geological and Geographical Characteristics of the Tenasserim Provinces. By Edward Riley. (*Jour. Ind. Archip.*, III, 1849, pp. 387—401).

720. — Remarks on the Metalliferous Deposits and Mineral Productions of the Tenasserim Provinces. By Edward O'Riley. (*Ibid.*, III, 1849, pp. 724—43).

721. — The Origin of Laterite. By Edward O'Riley. (*Ibid.*, IV, 1850, pp. 199—200).

722. — A few Remarks on the subject of the Laterite found near Rangoon. By Capt. C. B. Young. Bengal Engineers. (*Jour. As. Soc. Bengal*, XXII, 1853, pp. 196—201).

723. — Notes on the Geological Features of the Banks of the Irawadi, and of the Country north of Amarapoora. By T. Oldham, Esq. Superintendent of the Geological Survey of India. (Yule's *Narrative of the Mission sent....to the Court of Ava in* 1855.... London, 1858, pp. 309—351).

724. — Dr. Johann Wilhelm Helfer's gedruckte und ungedruckte Schriften über die Tenasserim Provinzen, den Mergui Archipel und die Andamanen-Inseln. (Mitgetheilt in der Versammlung der K. K. geograph. Gesellschaft am 22. März 1859). (*Mitth. k. k. Geog. Ges.*, III, Wien, 1859, pp. 167—390).
Vorwort von F. Foetterle, pp. 167—174.

725. — Note on Specimens of Gold and Gold Dust procured near Shuè-gween, in the Province of Martaban, Burmah, by Thomas Oldham, Superintendent of the Geological Survey of India. (*Mem. Geolog. Survey India*, I, 1859, pp. 94—8).

726. — *T. Ranking. Memorandum on the Geology of Thayetmyo. (*Madras Jour. of Letter and Sciences*, XXI, 1859, (N. S. V), pp. 55—9).
Noetling.

727. — Account of a Visit to Puppa doung, an extinct Volcano in Upper Burma. — By William T. Blanford, F.G.S. (*Jour. of the As. Soc. of Bengal*, Vol. XXXI, N° 3, 1862, pp. 215—226).

728. — On the Beds containing Silicified Wood in Eastern Prome, British Burmah, by Wm. Theobald, Jun., Esq., Geological Survey of India. (*Records Geological Survey of India*, Vol. II, Pt. 4, 1869, pp. 79—86).

729. — On the alluvial Deposits of the Irawadi, more particularly as contrasted with those of the Ganges, — by Wm. Theobald, Jun., Esq., *Geol. Survey of India*. (*Ibid.*, Vol. III, N° 1, 1870, pp. 17—27).
Rangoon, 15th June 1869.

730. — The Axial Group in Western Prome, British Burmah, by W. Theobald, Esq., Geological Survey of India. ((*Ibid.*, Vol. IV, N° 2, 1871, pp. 33—44).

731. — *C. B. Cooke. Tin resources of Tenasserim. (*Indian Economist*, 1872, III, pp. 148—9).

732. — *Mark Fryar. Report on some mineraliferous localities of Tenasserim. (*Ibid.*, IV, 1871, pp. 72, 73).
Noetling.

733. — A few additional Remarks on the Axial Group of Western Prome, by W. Theobald. (*Records Geolog. Survey India*, V, 1872, pp. 79—82).

734. — On the Geology of Pegu, by William Theobald. (*Memoirs Geol. Survey India*, X, 1873, pp. 171).

735. — On the Salt-springs of Pegu, by William Theobald, Geological Survey of India. (*Records Geol. Survey of India*, Vol. VI, Pt. 3, 1873, pp. 67—73).

736. — Stray Notes on the Metalliferous resources of British Burmah, by W. Theobald, Geological Survey of India. (*Ibid.*, Vol. VI, Pt. 4, 1873, pp. 90—95).

737. — *G. A. Strover. Memorandum on the Metals and Minerals of Upper Burma. (*Gazette of India* Supp. 1873. — Rep. *Geolog. Magazine*, 1st decade, Vol. X, pp. 356—361).

738. — On the Building and Ornamental Stones of India, by V. Ball, M.A., Geological Survey of India. (*Records Survey of India*, Vol. VII, Pt. 3, 1874, pp. 98—122).

739. — Notes on the Fossil Mammalian Faunae of India and Burma, by R. Lydekker, B.A., Geological Survey of India. (*Ibid.*, Vol. IX, Pt. 3, 1876, pp. 86—106).

— Addenda and corrigenda. (*Ibid.*, Pt. 4, 1876, p. 154).

740. — Notes on the Osteology of *Merycopotamus dissimilis*, by R. Lydekker, B.A., Geological Survey of India. (*Ibid.*, Vol. IX, Pt. 4, 1876, pp. 144—153).

741. — Teeth of Fossil Fishes from Ramri Island and the Punjab, by R. Lydekker, B.A., Geological Survey of India. (*Ibid.*, Vol. XIII, Pt. 1, 1880, pp. 59—61).

742. — Synopsis of the Fossil Vertebrata of India, by R. Lydekker, B.A., F.G.S., F.Z.S. (*Ibid.*, XVI, Pt. 2, 1883, pp. 61—93).

743. — On the Geographical Distribution of fossil organisms in India, by Dr. W. Waagen. (With a Map). Read at the Meeting of the Mathematical and Natural Science Section of the Imperial Academy of Sciences, Vienna, 1st December 1877. Translated by R. Bruce Foote, F.G.S., Geological Survey of India. (*Ibid.*, Vol. XI, Pt. 4, 1878, pp. 267—301).

744. — The Mud Volcanoes of Rámri and Cheduba, by F. R. Mallet, F.G.S., Geological Survey of India. (*Ibid.*, Vol. XI, Pt. 2, 1878, pp. 188—207).

745. — On the Mineral Resources of Rámri, Cheduba, and the adjacent Islands, by F. R. Mallet, F.G.S., Geological Survey of India. (*Ibid.*, Vol. XI, Pt. 2, 1878, pp. 207—223).

746. — Note on a recent Mud Eruption in Rámri Island (Arakán) by F. R. Mallet, F.G.S., Geological Survey of India. (*Ibid.*, Vol. XII, Pt. 1, 1879, pp. 70—72).

747. — On Corundum from the Khási Hills, by F. R. Mallet, F.G.S., Geological Survey of India. (*Ibid.*, Vol. XII, Pt. 3, 1879, p. 172).

748. — Notice of a Mud Eruption in the Island of Cheduba. By F. R. Mallet. (*Ibid.*, XIV, Pt. 2, 1881, pp. 196—7).

749. — On Native Lead from Maulmain and Chromite from the Andaman Islands; by F. R. Mallet, Deputy Superintendent, Geological Survey of India. (*Ibid.*, XVI, Pt. 4, 1883, pp. 203—204).

750. — Notice of a Fiery Eruption from one of the Mud Volcanoes of Cheduba Island, Arakan. By F. R. Mallet. (*Ibid.*, XVI, Pt. 4, 1883, pp. 204—5).

751. — On the alleged Tendency of the Arakán Mud Volcanoes to burst into eruption most frequently during the rains; by F. R. Mallet, Deputy Superintendent, Geological Survey of India. (*Ibid.*, XVIII, Pt. 2, 1885, pp. 124—5).

752. — Note on Indian Steatite, compiled by F. R. Mallet, Superintendent, Geological Survey of India. (*Ibid.*, XXII, Pt. 2, 1889, pp. 59—67).

753. — *P. Doyle. A Contribution to Burman Mineralogy. Calcutta, 1879.
Noetling.

754. — Record of Gas and Mud Eruptions on the Arakan Coast on 12th March 1879 and in June 1843. (*Records Geol. Survey of India*, Vol. XIII, Pt. 3, 1880, pp. 206—209).

755. — Papers on the Geology and Minerals of British Burma reprinted by order of C. E. Bernard, C.S.I., Chief Commissioner. Calcutta, 1882.

Containing the following:

W. J. Blanford. — Account of visit to Puppa doung, an extinct volcano in Upper Burma.
D'Amato. Short description of the mines of precious stones in the district of Kaytpen in the Kingdom of Ava.
M. Fryar. Report on mineraliferous localities of Tenasserim.
M. Fryar. Coal at Moulmein.
M. Fryar. Correspondence regarding Tenasserim Minerals.
M. Fryar. Report on Minerals in the Amherst District of the Tenasserim Division.
M. Fryar. Report on Minerals at Shwegyeen, Toungoo, and Pahpoon Districts Tenasserim Division.
F. R. Mallet. Mineral Resources of Ramri and Cheduba.
F. R. Mallet. The Mud Volcanoes of Ramri, Cheduba and adjacent Islands.
F. R. Mallet. Note on a recent Mud Eruption in Ramri Island.
F. R. Mallet. Record of Gas and Mud Eruptions on the Arrakan coast on 12 March 1879 and in June 1843.
F. R. Mallet. Notice of a Mud Eruption at Cheduba.
T. Oldham. Remarks and Papers on Reports relative to the discovery of Tin and other ores in the Tenasserim Provinces.
T. Oldham. Geological Report of Ava.
T. Oldham. Notes on the Coal Fields and Tinstone Deposits of the Tenasserim Provinces.
T. Oldham. Memorandum on Coal found near Thayetmyo.
E. O'Riley. Memorandum on Mineral Specimens from Tenasserim.
W. Theobald. On beds containing silicified wood in Eastern Prome, British Burma.
W. Theobald. On the alluvial Deposits of the Irrawadi more particularly as contrasted with those of the Ganges.
W. Theobald. On Petroleum in British Burma.
W. Theobald. The axial group in Western Prome, British Burma.
W. Theobald. A few additional remarks on the axial group of Western Prome.
W. Theobald. A brief Notice of some recently discovered Petroleum Localities in Pegu.
W. Theobald. On the Geology of Pegu.
W. Theobald. On the Salt Springs of Pegu.
W. Theobald. Stray Notes on the metalliferous resources of British Burma.
G. B. Tremenheere. Report on the Tin of the Province of Mergui.
G. B. Tremenheere. Report on the Manganese of the Mergui Province.
I. S. D. White. Letter regarding Coal at Thayetmyo.
(Noetling).

756. — Notice of a recent Eruption from one of the Mud Volcanoes in Cheduba. Letter from Colonel E. B. Sladen, Commissioner of Arakán, to the Secretary to the Chief Commissioner British Burma, Rangoon. Dated Akyab, 4th January 1882. (*Records Geol. Survey of India*, XV, Pt. 2, 1882, pp. 141—2).

757. — Notice of a further Fiery Eruption from the Minbyin Mud Volcano of Cheduba Island, Arakán. From Colonel E. B. Sladen, M.S.C., Commissioner of Arakán, to the Superintendent, Geological Survey of India, dated Akyab, the 27th May 1884. (*Ibid.*, XVII, Pt. 3, 1884, p. 142).

758. — Notice of a fiery Eruption from one of the mud volcanoes of Cheduba Island, Arakan. (*Records Geol. Survey of India*, XIX, Pt. 4, 1886, p. 268).

       [Report from the Deputy Commissioner of Kyauk Pyu, to the Commissioner of Arakan.]

759. — Note on the Earthquake of 31st December 1881, by R. D. Oldham, A.R.S.M., Geological Survey of India. (With a Map). (*Ibid.*, XVII, Pt. 2, 1884, pp. 47—53).

       Affecting the Burmese Coast.

760. — Note on some Antimony Deposits in the Maulmain District, by W. R. Criper, A.R.S.M., F.C.S. (*Ibid.*, XVIII, Pt. 3, 1885, pp. 151—153).

761. — The mineral Resources of Upper Burmah. (*N. C. Herald*, March 24, 1886, pp. 323—4).

       D'après le *Times*.

762. — Analysis of Gold-dust from the Meza Valley, Upper Burma, by R. Romanis, D.Sc., Chemical Examiner to the Government of Burma. (*Records Geol. Survey of India*, XIX, Pt. 4, 1886, pp. 268—270).

763. — Notes on Upper Burma, by E. J. Jones, A.R.S.M., Geological Survey of India (with 2 maps). (*Ibid.*, XX, Pt. 4, 1887, pp. 170—194).

764. — The Birds'-Nest or Elephant Islands, Mergui Archipelago. By Commander Alfred Carpenter, R.N., H.M.I.M.S., S.S. "*Investigator*". (*Ibid.*, XXI, Pt. I, 1888, pp. 29—30).

765. — On certain Features in the Geological Structure of the Myelat District of the Southern Shan States in Upper Burmah as affecting the Drainage of the Country. — By Brigadier-General H, Collett. (*Jour. As. Soc. Bengal*, Vol. 57, 1888, Pt. 2, pp. 384—386).

766. — Tin-mining in Mergui District. By T. W. Hughes Hughes. (With a plan). (*Records Geolog. Survey India*, XXII, 1889, pp. 188—208).

767. — Report on the Prospecting Operations, Mergui District, 1891—92. By T. W. H. Hughes. (*Ibid.*, XXVI, 1893, pp. 40—53).

768. — Geographische Forschungs-Ergebnisse aus Ober-Birma. Von Emil Schlagintweit. (*Globus*, LVIII, 1890, pp. 145—150).

769. — Note on a Salt spring near Bawgyo, Thibaw State, by Fritz Noetling. (*Records Geolog. Survey India*, XXIV, 1891, pp. 129—131).

770. — Preliminary Report on the Economic Resources of the Amber and Jade Mines Area in Upper Burma. By Fritz Noetling. (*Ibid.*, XXV, 1892, pp. 130—5).

771. — Note on the Occurence of Jadeite in Upper Burma, by Dr. Fritz Noetling. (With a Map). (*Ibid.*, XXVI, 1893, pp. 26—31).

772. — On the Occurrence of Burmite, a new Fossil Resin from Upper Burma; by Dr. Fritz Noetling. (*Ibid.*, XXVI, 1893, pp. 31—40).

773. — Carboniferous Fossils from Tenasserim; by Fritz Noetling. (With a plate). (*Records Geolog. Survey India*, XXVI, 1893, pp. 96—100).

774. — Note on the Geology of Wuntho in Upper Burma, by Fritz Noetling. (*Ibid.*, XXVII, 1894, pp. 115—124).

775. — On the Occurrence of Chipped (?) Flints in the Upper Miocene of Burma. By Dr. Fritz Noetling. (*Ibid.*, XXVII, 1894, pp. 101—103).

776. — The Burmese Chipped Flints Pliocene not Miocene. By W. T. Blanford. (*Nature*, LI, 1894—95, p. 608).

777. — On the Discovery of Chipped Flint-flakes in the Pliocene of Burma. By Fritz Noetling. (*Natural Science*, X, 1897, pp. 233—241).
   Cf. *Records Geolog. Survey*, XXVII, 1894, pp. 101—8.

778. — *Noetlings Entdeckung zugeschlagener Feuersteinsplitter im Pliocän von Burma. (*Globus*, LXXII, pp. 15 et seq.).
   Extrait de *Natural Science*, 1897, April, pp. 238—241.

779. — Note on the Occurrence of *Velates schmideliana*, Chemn. and *Provelates grandis*, Sow. sp., in the Tertiary Formation of India and Burma. By Dr. Fritz Noetling. (*Records Geolog. Survey India*, XXVII, 1894, pp. 103—8).

780. — The Development and Sub-division of the Tertiary System in Burma, by Dr. Fritz Noetling. (*Ibid.*, XXVIII, 1895, pp. 59—86).

781. — Note on Dr. Fritz Noetling's Paper on the Tertiary System in Burma in the *Records of the Geological Survey of India* for 1895, Part 2: by Mr. Theobald. (*Ibid.*, XXVIII, 1895, pp. 150—2).

782. — On some Marine Fossils from the Miocene of Upper Burma, by Dr. Fritz Noetling (with 10 plates). (*Memoirs Geolog. Survey India*, XXVII, 1898, pp. 1—45, v, iv).

783. — Fritz Noetling. — Das Vorkommen von Birmit (indischer Bernstein) und dessen Verarbeitung. (*Globus*, Braunschweig, 1896, LXIX, pp. 217—220, 239—242).

784. — *Fritz Noetling. — Über das Vorkommen van Jadeit in Ober-Burma. (*Zeit. fur Ethnologie*, XXVI, p. 246).

785. — *F. Noetling. Ueber das Vorkommen von Jadeit in Ober Birma. (*Neues Jahr. f. Min. Geolog. und Petref.*, 1896, I, pp. 1—17).

786. — Note on a worn femur of *Hippopotamus irravadicus*, Cant. and Falc., from the Lower Pliocene of Burma, by Fritz Noetling. (*Records Geolog. Survey India*, XXX, 1897, pp. 242—249).

787. — The Miocene of Burma by Fritz Noetling, Ph.D., F.G.S. Geological Survey of India. Verhandelingen der Koninklijke Akademie van Wetenschappen te Amsterdam. (Tweede Sectie). Deel VII. N°. 2. (With one Map). Amsterdam, Johannes Müller. 1900, in-8, pp. 131.
   Voir pp. 117—129: Geological Literature on Burma including Arrakan and Tenasserim.
   La carte a été reproduite dans E. Suess, *La Face de la Terre*, trad. franç de E. de Margerie, III, 1° Partie, Paris, 1902, p. 285.

788. — Fauna of the Miocene Beds of Burma. By Fritz Noetling. (*Palaeontologia Indica*, N. S., Vol. I, 1901, gr. in-4, pp. 378).

789. — *Fritz Noetling. — Über prähistorische Funde in Hinterindien. (*Zeit. f. Ethnologie*, XXVI, p. 247).

790. --- *Fritz Noetling. — Werkzeuge der Steinperiode in Birma. (*Ibid.*, XXVI, pp. 588—593).

791. — *Tom D. La Touche. — Note on the Geology of the Lushai Hills. (*Rec. Geolog. Survey of India*, XXIV, pp. 98—9).

792. — Geological Sketch of the Country north of Bhamo, by C. L. Griesbach. (*Ibid.*, XXV, 1892, pp. 127—130).

793. — On a New Fossil, Amber-like Resin occuring in Burma, by Dr. Otto Helm, of Danzig. (Translated by Thomas H. Holland). (*Ibid.*, XXV, 1892, pp. 180—1).

794. — Further Note on Burmite, a new amber-like fossil resin from Upper Burma. By Dr. Otto Helm of Danzig. (Translated from the German by Professor Bruhl). (*Ibid.*, XXVI, 1893, pp. 61—4).

795. — Note on the Alluvial Deposits and Subterranean water-supply of Rangoon, by R. D. Oldham. (With a Map). (*Ibid.*, XXVI, 1893, pp. 64—70).

796. — *R. D. Oldham. The Alleged Miocene Man in Burma. (*Natural Science*, 1895, VII, pp. 201—2).

797. — Note on Granite in the Districts of Tavoy and Mergui, by P. N. Bose. (With a plate). (*Records Geolog. Survey India*, XXVI, 1893, pp. 102—3).

798. — Notes on the Geology of a part of the Tenasserim Valley with special reference to the Tendau-Kamapying Coal-field; by P. N. Bose. (With 2 Maps). (*Ibid.*, XXVI, 1893, pp. 148—164).

799. — On the Jadeite and other rocks, from Tammaw in Upper Burma: by Prof. Max Bauer, Marburg University: (translated by Dr. F. Noetling and H. H. Hayden). (*Ibid.*, XXVIII, 1895, pp. 91—105).

800. — *M. Bauer. Der Jadeit und die andern Gesteine der Jadeit Min. Geol. von Tammaw in Ober-Birma. (*Neues Jahr. f. lagerstätte und Petref.*, 1896, Vol. I, pp. 18—51).

801. — *Jadeït aus Birma. Von O. L. (*Prometheus*, Berlin, 1896, VII, pp. 410—11).

802. — Report on the Steatite Mines, Minbu District, Burma, by H. H. Hayden. (*Records Geolog. Survey India*, XXIX, 1896, pp. 71—6).

803. — *A. H. Bromly. Note on Gold-mining in Burma. (*Transact. Federat. Instit. of Mining Engineers*, 1896).
       Noetling.

804. — Caves of the Amherst District, Burma. By R. C. Temple. (*Ind. Antiq.*, XXVI, 1897, p. 336).

805. — Geology of parts of the Myingyan, Magwe and Pakoku Districts, Burma, by G. E. Grimes. (*Mem. Geol. Survey India*, XXVIII, Pt. I, 1898, pp. 30—71).

806. — Geology and Economic Mineralogy. (*British Burma Gazetteer*, Vol. I, Chap. II, pp. 32—67).

> That Portion of Chapter II which relates to Geology is by Mr. Theobald of the Geological Survey of India and the second portion was to some extent revised by him.

807. — *R. — Wurle Bernstein von Hinterindien nach dem Western exportirt? (*Natur*, I, p. 10).

808. — *Der barmanische Bernstein. (*Ibid.*, XXVII, p. 323).

> D'après Noetling.

809. — *Hinterindischer Bernstein. (*Ausland*, XL, p. 638).

> D'après A. B. Meyer, *Abhandlungen der Gesellschaft Isis* in Dresden 1893, pp. 63 et seq. — Comparer également *Globus*, LXIV, p. 236.

Pétrole.

810. — An Account of the Petroleum Wells in the Burmha Dominions, extracted from the Journal of a Voyage from Ranghong up the river Erai-Wuddey to Amarapoorah, the present Capital of the Burmha Empire. — By Captain Hiram Cox, Resident at Ranghong. (*Asiatick Researches*, VI, pp. 127—136).

> Réimp. dans *The Asiatic Annual Register*, 1800, *Miscel. Tracts*, pp 815—820.

811. — Chemical Examination of the Petroleum of Rangoon. By Robert Christison, M.D. F.R.S.E. Professor of Materia Medica in the University of Edinburgh, &c. (*Trans. Royal Soc. Edinb.*, XIII, 1836, pp. 118—123).

812. — On the Composition of the Petroleum of Rangoon, with Remarks on Petroleum and Naphtha in general. By William Gregory, M.D., F.R.S.E., Lecturer on Chemistry. (*Ibid.*, XIII, 1836, pp. 124—130).

813. — Chemical Examination of Burmese Naphtha, or Rangoon Tar. By Warren De La Rue, Ph.D., F.R.S., and Hugo Müller, Ph.D. (*Proc. Royal Soc. Lond.*, VIII, 1857, pp. 221—8).

> Réimp. *Philosophical Mag.*, 4th Ser., XIII, 1857, pp. 512—517.

814. — *Warren & Storer. Examination of Naphta obtained from Rangoon Petroleum. (*Memoirs American Acad. of Arts and Science*, Cambridge and Boston, 1867, N. S., IX, p. 208).

> Noetling.

815. — Note on Petroleum in Burmah, &c., by William Theobald, Esq., Geological Survey of India. (*Records Geological Survey of India*, Vol. III, N° 3, 1870, pp. 72—73).

816. — A brief notice of some recently discovered Petroleum localities in Pegu, by W. Theobald, Geological Survey of India. (*Ibid.*, Vol. V, Pt. 4, 1872, pp. 120—122).

817. — *Dr. H. Friedländer. The Country of the Earth-oil in Upper Burma. Rangoon, Suppl. to the *British Burma Gazette*, Feb. 14, 1874.
     Noetling.

818. — The Petroleum Question. — England as a Petroleum Power, or the Petroleum fields of the British Empire. By Charles Marvin... — London: R. Anderson & Co., br. in-4, pp. 32.
     Pétrole en Birmanie.

819. — *Charles Marvin. — The oil wells of Burma. (*National Review*, London, November).

820. — Report on the Oil-Wells and Coal in the Thayetmyo District, British Burma, by R. Romanis, D.Sc. (*Records Geol. Survey of India*, XVIII, Pt. 3, 1885, pp. 149—151).

821. — Note on the Occurrence of Petroleum in India, by H. B. Medlicott, Geological Survey of India. (With two plates). (*Ibid.*, XIX, Pt. 4, 1886, pp. 185—204).
     Assam, Arakan, Burma.

822. — Report on the Oil-Fields of Twingoung and Beme, Burma; by Fritz Noetling, Ph.D. (With 1 plate and a Map). (*Ibid.*, XXII, 1889, pp. 75—136).

823. — Note on the Chemical qualities of Petroleum from Burma; by Professor Dr. Engler (Karlsruhe). (Translated by Dr. Fritz Noetling, G.S.I.). (*Ibid.*, XXVII, 1894, pp. 49—54).

824. — The occurrence of Petroleum in Burma, and its technical exploitation, by Dr. Fritz Noetling. (*Memoirs Geolog. Survey India*, XXVII, 1898, pp. 47—272, pl.).

824 bis. — *David Ker. — Petroleum in Burmah; primitive and expensive methods in use, etc. (*New York Times*, 14 Oct. 1888).

825. — *Th. Holland. — Crude Mineral Oil from Burma. (*Records Geolog. Survey India*, XXIV, 1894, pp. 251—7).

826. — Petroliferous Sands and Mud Volcanoes in Burma. By H. B. W. (*Nature*, LVIII, 1898, pp. 20—21).
     Cf. F. Noetling, *Mem. Geolog. Survey India*, XXVII, Part 2.

Mines de rubis.

827. — Short Description of the Mines of Precious Stones, in the District of Kyat-pyen, in the Kingdom of Ava. [Translated from the original of Père Giuseppe d'Amato]. (*Jour. As. Soc. of Bengal*, II, feb. 1833, pp. 75—76).

828. — Birmanie. (*Ann. de l'Ext. Orient*, 1885—86, VIII, pp. 377—8).
     Mines de rubis.

829. — Les mines de rubis en Birmanie. (*Ibid.*, 1886—87, IX, pp. 254—6).

830. — The Ruby Mines of Burma. By Mr. G. Skelton Streeter. (*Jour. Manchester Geog. Soc.*, III, 1887, pp. 216—20).

831. — On the Ruby Mines near Mogok, Burma. By Robert Gordon, C.E. (*Proc. R. Geog. Soc.*, X, 1888, May, pp. 261—75; carte, p. 324).

832. — The Ruby Mines of Burma. By Robert Gordon. (*As. Quart. Review*, VII, Jan.—April 1889, pp. 410—23).

833. — Note on the reported Namseka Ruby-mine in the Mainglòn State, by Fritz Noetling. (*Records Geol. Survey India*, XXIV, 1891, pp. 119—25).

834. — *M. Bauer. Ueber das Vorkommen der Rubine in Burma. (*Neues Jahrb. f. Min. Geol. & Petrefact.*, 1896, II, pp. 197—238).
      Noetling.

835. — *Brown & Judd. The Rubies of Burma and associated Minerals, their mode of Occurence Origin and Metamorphosis. A contribution to the History of Corundum. (*Philos. Transact. Roy. Soc.*, London, Vol. 187, pp. 151—228)

Charbon.

836. — *H. Walters. — Coal from Sandoway District. (*Jour. As. Soc. Bengal*, II, 1833, pp. 263—4).

837. — Note on the Coal discovered at Khyùk Phyú, in the Arracan District. By J. P. (*Ibid.*, II, Nov. 1833, pp. 595—7).

838. — Report on the Coal discovered in the Tenasserim provinces, by Dr. Helfer, dated Mergui, 23rd May, 1838. (*Ibid.*, VII, Aug. 1838, pp. 701—6).

839. — Papers relative to the New Coal Field of Tenasserim. Nº 1. Report on the Coal Field at Ta-thay-yna, on the Tenasserim river, in Mergui province. By J. W. Helfer, M.D. (*Ibid.*, VIII, May, 1839, pp. 385—9; Nº 2. Report on the new Tenasserim Coal Field. By Lieut. Hutchinson, Madras Artillery; (*ibid.*, pp. 390—3).

840. — Report of the Coal Committee. By M. J. M. M'Clelland, Secretary Coal Committee. (*Ibid.*, IX, Pt. I, 1840, pp. 198—214).

841. — Note on the Map attached to the Report of the Coal Committee in the 98th Number of the Journal of the Asiatic Society. — By Capt. Macleod, M.N.I. late in charge of Ava Residency. (*Ibid.*, IX, Pt. I, 1840, pp. 582—94).

842. — Notice of Tremenheerite, a new carbonaceous mineral, by Henry Piddington, Curator Museum of Economic Geology. (*Ibid.*, XVI, pt. I, 1847, pp. 369—71).

843. — On a new Kind of Coal, being Volcanic Coal, from Arracan, by Henry Piddington, Curator Museum of Economic Geology. (*Ibid.*, XVI, pt. I, 1847, pp. 371—73).

844. — Examination and Analysis of two specimens of Coal from Ava, by H. Piddington, Curator Museum Economic Geology. (*Ibid.*, XXIII, 1854, pp. 714—17).

845. — 'Papers on the Coal of the Nerbudda Valley, Tenasserim Provinces, and Thyetmyo, 1854 and 1855. No. X.

846. — *T. Oldham. Memorandum on Coal found near Thayetmyo on the Irrawaddi River. (*Selections from the Records of the Gov. of India*, X, 1856, pp. 99—107).

847. — H. B. Medlicott. — On the prospects of useful Coal being found in the Garrow Hills, Bengal. (*Records Geological Survey of India*, Vol. I, Pt. I, 1868, pp. 11—16).

848. — Coal in India, by Theo. W. H. Hughes, C.E., F.G.S., Associate, Royal School of Mines. (*Ibid.*, Vol. VI, Pt. 3, 1873, pp. 64—66).

849. — Coal in the Garo Hills, by Mr. H. B. Medlicott. (*Ibid.*, Vol. VII, Pt. 2, 1874, pp. 58—62).

850. — Note on Coals recently found near Moflong, Khasi Hills, by F. R. Mallet, Esq., Geological Survey of India. (*Ibid.*, VIII, Pt. 3, 1875, p. 86).

851. — Analysis of Coal and Fire-clay from the Makum Coal-field, Upper Assam. By F. R. Mallet. (*Ibid.*, XV, Pt. 1, 1882, pp. 58—63).

852. — Note on Borings for Coal at Engsein, British Burma. By R. Romanis, D.Sc., F.G.S.E. (*Ibid.*, XV, Pt. 2, 1882, p. 138).

853. — The Daranggiri Coalfield, Garo Hills, Assam. — By Tom D. La Touche, B.A., Geological Survey of India. (*Ibid.*, XV, Pt. 3, 1882, pp. 175—178).

854. — On the Outcrops of Coal in the Myanoung Division of the Henzada District. — By R. Romanis, D.Sc., Chemical Examiner, British Burma (with a plan). (*Ibid.*, XV, Pt. 3, 1882, pp. 178—181).

855. — Note on the Cretaceous Coal-measures at Borsora in the Khasia Hills, near Laour in Sylhet, by Tom D. La Touche, B.A., Geological Survey of India. (*Ibid*, XVI, Pt. 3, 1883, pp. 164—166).

856. — Report on the Langrin Coal Field, South-West Khasia Hills, by Tom D. La Touche, B.A., Geological Survey of India. (With a map). (*Ibid.*, XVII, Pt. 3, 1884, pp. 143—146).

857. — Note on Coal and Limestone in the Doigrung River, near Golaghat, Assam, by Tom D. La Touche, B.A., Geological Survey of India. (*Ibid.*, XVIII, Pt. 1, 1885, pp. 31—32).

858. — *F. Noetling. Report on the Upper Chindwin Coal-fields. Calcutta, 1890. Only 100 copies published. (Noetling).

859. — Coal on the Great Tenasserim River, Mergui District, Lower Burma, by T. W. H. Hughes. (*Records Geol. Survey India*, XXV, 1892, pp. 161—3).

VI. — Population.

860. — *Report on the Census of British Burma taken in August 1872. Rangoon, 1875. In-fol.

861. — *The Burma Census Report, 1892; Chapter VIII "Languages".
Notice: *Ind. Antiq.*, XXIII, 1894, pp. 194—6, by Bernard Houghton.

862. — *Census of India, 1901. Vol. XII*a*. Burma. Part II. Imperial Tables. By C. C. Lowis. Rangoon, 1902, in-8, pp. 432.

863. — Die Bevölkerung der Erde. — Periodische Übersicht über neue Areal-berechnungen, Gebietsveränderungen, Zählungen und Schätzungen der Bevölk-erung auf der gesamten Erdoberfläche (begründet von Ernst Behm und Hermann Wagner). Herausgegeben von Alexander Supan. XI. Asien und Australien samt den Südsee-Inseln. (Ergänzungsheft N°. 135 zu "Peternianns Mitteilungen"). Gotha: Justus Perthes. 1901. in-4, 1 f. n. ch. + pp. 107.
Japan, p. 36. — Korea, p. 39. — Chinesisches Reich, p. 41. — Französische Indo-China, p. 52. — Siam, p. 55. — Straits Settlements und Dependensen, p. 57. — British-India, p. 58.

VII. — Gouvernement [1]).

864. — *Selections from the Records of the Hlutdaw, compiled by Taw Sein Ko, Government Translator, and published by Authority. Rangoon, 1889.
Notice by R. C. Temple, *Ind. Antiq.*, XIX, 1890, pp. 75—6.

865. — *Catalogue of the Hlutdaw Records. Volume I. Compiled by the Govern-ment of Burma. 1901, gr. in-8.

VIII. — Jurisprudence.

866. — *The Damathat, or the Laws of Menoo, translated from the Burmese. By D. Richardson Esq. Principal Assistant to the Commissioner Tenasserim Provinces.· Maulmain, 1847. In-8, pp. 752.

867. — *The Damathat or the Laws of Menoo, in Burmese, with an English translation by D. Richardson. Rangoon, 1874, 14 vol. en 1, in-8, pp. 776.

---

1) Voir le chap. consacré à l'Administration anglaise.

868. — 'King Wagaru's Manu Dhammasattham. Text, Translation, and Notes. Rangoon, Government Printing office, 1892, in-8, pp. 7, 71, 39.

Préface par J. Jardine. — Editeur: E. Forchhammer.

869. — Notes on the Tenure and Distribution of Landed Property in Burmah. Contributed by Colonel Phayre, Chief Commissioner of British Burmah. (*Trans. Ethn. Soc.*, N. S., VI, 1868, pp. 227—232).

870. — Notes on Buddhist Law by the Judicial Commissioner British Burma. I. — Marriage. 1. — How contracted. 2. — Its Incidents. — Rangoon: printed at the Government Press, 1882, in-8, pp. II—9—12.

Judicial Commissioner, British Burma: JOHN JARDINE.

II. — Marriage. 1. — How dissolved: The right to divorce and the rights flowing from Divorce. Rangoon: 1882, in-8, pp. 16—33.

III. — Marriage.

— Preface including introductory remarks by Dr. E. Forchhammer, Professor of Pali.
1. Translation of the Wonnana Dhammathat on Marriage: with a Commentary.
2. Translation of the Wonnana Dhammathat on Divorce: with a Commentary.
— Appendices.
A. Translation of the Wini Tsaya Paka Thani Dhammathat on Marriage and Divorce.
B. Cases illustrative of the Buddhist Law as now administered in the Court of the Judicial Commissioner of British Burma and the Subordinate Courts. Rangoon... 1883. br. in-8, pp. XX—32—XXIX.

IV. — Marriage and Divorce.

1. On the Hindu Origin of the Burmese Law by John Jardine, Judicial Commissioner of British Burma.
2. Introductory Preface by Dr. E. Forchhammer, Professor of Pali.
3. Translation of the Wagara Dhammathat on Marriage and Divorce from a Pali Manuscript on Palm Leaves by Dr. E. Forchhammer, Professor of Pali.
4. Translation of the Manoo Reng Dhammathat on Marriage and Divorce from the printed Edition of Moung Tet Too with notes by Dr. E. Forchhammer, Professor of Pali.
5. Appendix of cases illustrating the Burmese Law of Marriage and Divorce as now administered. Rangoon... 1883, br. in-8, pp. 26—10—7—XVII.

V. — Inheritance and Partition.

— Preface.
1. Translation by Mr. S Minus of the Chapter on Inheritance and some miscellaneous sections of the Manoo Wonnana Dhammathat as edited in Burmese by Moung Tet Too, with Notes by J. Jardine, Esq., Judicial Commissioner of British Burma.
2. Translation of the Law of Inheritance according to the Wagaru Dhammathat by Dr. E. Forchhammer, Professor of Pali, from a Pali Manuscript on Palm Leaves in his possession. Rangoon... 1883, br. in-8, pp. V—3—35—4.

VI. — Inheritance and Partition.

— Preface.
— Translation by Moung Theka Phyoo of the Law of Inheritance according to the Mohavicchedani Dhammathat from a Burmese Manuscript. Edited by Dr. E. Forchhammer, Professor of Pali. Rangoon... 1883, br. in-8, pp. 9.

VII. — Inheritance and Partition.

— Preface.
— Translation by Moung Theka Phyoo and Mr. S. Minus, from a Burmese manuscript on palm leaves, of the Law of Inheritance in the Dhammavilasa. Revised and edited by Dr. E. Forchhammer, Professor of Pali. Rangoon... 1883, br. in-8, pp. 19.

VIII. — Marriage and Divorce.

— Preface.
— Translation by Mr. S. Minus of the Law of Marriage and Divorce according
to the Mohavicchedani Dhammathat from a Burmese manuscript on palm-leaves.
Edited by Dr. E. Forchhammer, Professor of Pali. Rangoon... 1883, br. in-8,
pp. 5—6.

* .

871. — The Jardine Prize An Essay on the sources and development of Burmese
Law from the era of the first introduction of the Indian Law to the time
of the British occupation of Pegu. By Dr. E. Forchhammer, Ph. D., Professor
of Pali at the Government High School, Rangoon. Rangoon: Printed at the
Government Press, 1885, in-4, pp. iii—109.

En tête rapport de Mgr. Bigandet sur le Prix Jardine.

872. — Burma Code. Edition 1899. gr. in-8.

873. — *Heiraten in Birma. (Aus allen Welttheilen, XXV, pp. 50 et seq.).

IX. — Histoire.
Divers.

874. — The Elements of General History in two volumes. — Translated from
the seventh volume of the "Instructor", by E. A. Stevens. Published with
the sanction of Government, for the use of Schools. — Maulmain: American
Mission Press, Thos. S. Ranney. 1853, 2 vol. in-8.

En Birman.

874 bis. — Summary of Burmese history. Compiled by the Editor. (The Phoenix,
N°. 12, June 1871, pp. 205—207; ibid., II, N°. 13, July, 1871, pp. 26—28).

875. — General Summary of the History of Burma. — Part I. Introduction
(Siam Repository, July 1871, Vol. 3, art. 115, pp. 329—333). — Part II.
Portuguese Annals. (ibid., July 1871, Vol. 3, art. 121, pp. 345—347, art. 124,
pp. 352—354, art. 127, pp. 360—362, art. 130, pp. 367—372. Oct. 1871,
art. 134, pp. 377—378, art. 137, p. 383, art. 140, pp. 391—393, art. 146,
pp. 409—412, art. 153, pp. 433—435). — Part III, Modern Annals (ibid.,
Oct. 1871, Vol. 3, art. 161, pp. 462—465, art. 166, pp. 485—488, art. 169,
pp. 497—500).

876. — Notizie intorno alla Storia Birmana, di C. A. Racchia, Comandante
della R. Corvetta Principessa Clotilde. (Bol. Soc. Geog. ital., VII, 1872,
pp. 35—94).

D'après un ouvrage anglais imprimé à Rangoon.

877. — Burman History. By R. T. (Siam Repository, Vol. 5, July 1873,
pp. 391—392).

878. — A Short History of India and of the Frontier States of Afghanistan,
Nipal, and Burma. By J. Talboys Wheeler, late assistant-secretary to the
Government of India, Foreign Department, and late Secretary to the government of British Burma. With maps and tables. London: Macmillan and Co.
1880, in-8, pp. xiv + 1 f. n. c. pour la liste des cartes + pp. 744.

879. — Legendary History of Burma and Arakan by Captain C. J. F. S. Forbes, late Deputy Commissioner, British Burma. [Published by Authority of Government]. Rangoon: Printed at the Government Press. — 1882, in-8, pp. II—34.

880. — Notes on the Early History and Geography of British Burma. — I. — *The Shwe Dagon Pagoda.* in-8, pp. 17.

— Notes on the Early History and Geography of British Burma by Em. Forchhammer, Ph. D., Government Archaeologist and Professor of Pali at the Rangoon High School. — II. — *The First Buddhist Mission to Suvannabhumi.* Rangoon: Printed at the Government Press, 1884, in-8, pp. 15.

881. — Mandalay Massacres. — Upper Burma during the Reign of King Theebaw. — Rangoon Gazette Press. 1884, in-8, pp. 44.

    By David M. Gray, Editor, *Rangoon Gazette.* — Rangoon, 24th October, 1884.

882. — The Alaung pra Dynasty comprising the Period of Burmese History prescribed for the middle School Examination. By James Gray, Author of "Elements of Pali Grammar", &c. — 1885. "Burma Herald" Steam Press. Rangoon. in-12, 4 ff. n. c. + pp. 182.

883. — A Catechism of the History of Burma for upper primary schools; by L. A. Stapley, Educational Department, British Burma. — Second Edition. — Revised and enlarged. — Rangoon: American Baptist Mission Press, F. D. Phinney, Supt. 1886, pet. in-8, pp. 26.

884. — Outlines of the Modern History of Burma with a General Summary of Burmese History for Primary Schools. — Ninth Edition. Akyab, Akyab Press, 1888, pet. in-12, pp. 26.

    By J. Simeon.

885. — Extrait d'un ouvrage sous presse: La France et l'Angleterre dans l'Indo-Chine. — La Chute des Allompra ou la fin du royaume d'Ava. — Résumé de l'histoire diplomatique de l'annexion de la Haute-Birmanie (1884—1886). Par ***. Paris, Challamel, s. d., in-8, pp. XVII—277, 3 cartes.

    Par Philippe Lehault = Frédéric Haas, Consul de France.

886. — La France et l'Angleterre en Asie par Philippe Lehault Membre de la Société de Géographie, explorateur en Asie. — Tome premier. INDO-CHINE. Les derniers jours de la dynastie des Rois d'Ava. Berger-Levrault, Paris [et] Nancy, 1892, in-8, pp. XXXII—XVII—772, 6 cartes.

887. — Origin of Alompra. By Taw Sein Ko. (*Ind. Antiq.*, XXI, 1892, p. 259)

888. — The Order of Succession in the Alompra Dynasty of Burma. By Major R. C. Temple. (*Ind. Antiq.*, XXI, 1892, pp. 287—293).

889. — *The Kani Sitkè. — Mandalay yadanabònmahayazawindaw. Mandalay, Maung In, 1892. In-8, pp. 210.

    Histoire des règnes de Mindon et Thibau.

890. — *Monchoisy. — Myn-Goou-Min, un Prétendant au trône de Birmanie. (*Revue politique et littéraire*, T. 43, 25, pp. 785—91).

891. — Some dates of the Burmese Common Era. By F. Kielhorn. (*Ind. Antiq.*, XXIII, 1894, pp. 139—140).

892. — A Sketch of Burmese History. By E. H. Parker. (*China Review*, XXI, Nº 1, pp. 40—53).

893. — An Almanac or Corresponding English and Burmese Dates from A. D. 1822 to 1896 compiled and edited by J. Copley Moyle of Lincoln's Inn, Esquire, Barrister-at-Law. An Advocate of the High Court of Calcutta and of the Courts in Burma. Fifth Edition. (Third New and Revised Edition). Rangoon Myles Standish and Co., Moulmein at the Bulletin Press MDCCCXCV, in-8, 3 ff. n. ch. + pp. XLIII—296.

894. — 'Maung Kyaw Yan. — An Almanac of corresponding English and Burmese dates from A. D. 1899 to 1908. Rangoon, Jenkins, 1899, pp. 26.

895. — 'A. M. B. Irwin. — Burmese Calendar. London, Sampson Low, 1901. In-4.

896. — Thibaw's Queen by H. Fielding. Illustrated. London and New York, Harper & Brothers, 1899, in-8, pp. VII—294.

  Notice: *Literature*, V, pp. 165 seq.

897. — History of Burma including Burma proper, Pegu, Taungu, Tenasserim, and Arakan. From the Earliest Time to the End of the First War with British India. By Lieut.-General Sir Arthur P. Phayre.... London: Trübner, 1883, in-8, pp. XII—311. Carte.

  Fait partie de *Trübner's Oriental Series.*

Antiquités.

898. — 'A Burmese Inscription (*Buddhist*, (Colombo), X, pp. 174 seq).

  Extrait de J. Crawford: *Journal of an Embassy to the Court of Ava* (1827).

899. — Translation of an Inscription in the Burmese Language, discovered at Buddha Gaya, in 1833. — By Lieutenant-Colonel H. Burney, British Resident in Ava. (*As. Researches*, XX, 1830, Part I, pp. 161—189).

900. — 'R. C. Temple. — Old Burmese inscription at Buddha Gayâ. (*Academy*, XLII, p. 366).

901. — Account and Drawing of two Burmese Bells now placed in a Hindu Temple in Upper India. By Capt. R. Wroughton, Revenue Surveyor, Agra Division. (*Journ. As. Soc. of Bengal*, VI, Dec. 1837, pp. 1064—1072).

902. — An Account of the Ancient Buddhist Remains at Pagán on the Iráwádi. By Captain Henry Yule, Bengal Engineers. (*Journ. of the As. Soc. of Bengal*, vol. XXVI, Nº 1, 1857, pp. 1—52).

903. — The Remains of Pagan. By H. Yule. (*Trübner's Record*, 3rd. ser., Vol. I, Pt. I, 1889, p. 2).

  To introduce notes by Dr. E. Forchhammer.

904. — Limestone Caves in Burmah. (*The Phoenix*, III, Nº 25, July, 1872, p. 19).

905. — List of Objects of Antiquarian Interest in Lower Burma. I. Arakan. br. in fol., pp. 9.

— Arakan.

    I. — Mahamuni Pagoda, gr. in-4, pp. 1—14, 8 pl. phot. 1 à 8.

    II. — Mrohaung, pp. 15—43, 1 carte formant la pl. 9, pl. phot. 10 à 31.

    III. — Launggyet, Minbya, Urritaung, Akyab, and Sandoway, pp. 45—67. pl. phot. 32 à 44.

— Pagan. I. — The Kyaukku Temple, gr. in-4, pp. 9, 8 pl. photog.

906. — *E. Forchhammer. — Inscriptions of Pagan, Pinya and Ava. Rangoon, 1892. In-fol.

907. — List of Objects of Antiquarian and Archaeological Interest in British Burma. Rangoon: Printed at the Government Press. 1884, br. in-8, pp. 39.

908. — *List of Objects of Antiquarian and Archaeological Interest in British Burma. Rangoon, Government Press, 1892, in-8, pp. 45.

909. — *List of Objects of Antiquarian and Archaeological Interest in Upper Burma. Compiled by the Government of Burma. 1901, in-fol.

910. — Notes on an Archaeological Tour through Ramannadesa (the Talaing Country of Burma). By Taw Sein-Ko. — Reprinted from the Indian Antiquary. Bombay: Printed at the Education Society's Steam Press, 1893, br. in-4, pp. 10.

911. — A Preliminary Study of the Poôuôdaung Inscription of S'inbyuyin, 1774 A. D. By Taw Sein Ko. (*Ind. Antiq.*, XXII, 1893, pp. 1—11).

    Près de Prome, sur la rive droite de l'Irawadi.

912. — Archaeology in Burma. By Taw Sein Ko. (*Ind. Antiq.*, XXIX, 1900, pp. 363—4).

913. — *R. C. Temple. — Notes on antiquities in Ramannadesa (the Talaing Country of Burma). London: Luzac, 1894, in-4, pp. 40, 24 dessins et une carte.

914. — Correspondence. By R. F. St. Andrew St. John (*Journ. Roy. As. Soc.*, Jan. 1894, pp. 149—151).

    Sur Mr. F. O. Oertel et les Antiquités de Birmanie.

915. — Inscriptions copied from the Stones collected by King Bodawpaya, and placed near the Arakan Pagoda, Mandalay. (Rangoon, 1897). By R. F. St. Andrew St. John. (*Jour. Roy. As. Soc.*, July 1898, pp. 648—651).

    D'après les 2 vol. imprimés en birman à la Government Press; il y a des exemplaires à l'Indian Institute, Oxford; et à la R. A. S.

916. — *Maung Tun Nyein. — Maung gun gold plates. (*Epigraphia Indica*, V, pp. 101 et seq.).

    Inscriptions pâli du District de Prome.

917. — *Fritz Noetling. Ueber die Pagoden von Pagan in Ober-Birma. (*Zeit. für Ethnol.*, XXVIII, pp. 226—235).

918. — *[Ber. über Vort. v. Noetling und Ehrenreich über die Pagoden von Pagan]. (*Beil. Allgemeine Zeitung*, LXXI, pp. 7 et seq.).

919. — *[Ueber F. Noetling's Geschenke an das Kgl. Museum für Völkerkunde in Berlin]. (Beilage *Allgemeiner Zeitung*, CLI, pp. 7 et seq.).

Figures bouddhiques de Birmanie.

920. — *H. Thomann-Gillis. — Ueber eine birmanische Sammlung. (*Zeitschrift für Ethnologie*, XXXII, pp. 383 et seq.).

Trouvée dans les fouilles de Pagan.

921. — *A. Grünwedel. — Notizen über Indisches. (*Ethnol. Notizbl.*, I, Heft 2, pp. 6—11).

1. Pasten aus Pagan, Oberbirma. 2. Parnaka; Kapardin [= Mann mit Blätter-schürze; mit Kauri-Muscheln geschmückt]. 3. Padmasambhava-Legenden in Lepcha-Sprache.

922. — *Albert Grünwedel. — Temples and archaeological Treasures of Burma. (*Open Court*, XV, pp. 464—479).

923. — *Die Skulpturenhöhlen bei Maulmein: (*Globus* LXV, p. 263).

924. — *Henry Balfour. — A Spear-Head and Socketed Celt of Bronze from the Shan States, Burma. (*Man*, 1901, p. 97).

925. — *Publications of the Archaelogical Department, Burma, N° 2. — *List of Pagodas at Pagan under the custody of Government.* In English and Burmese. Compiled by the Government of Burma. 1901, in-fol.

926. — *Reports on Archaeological Work in Burma, etc. Rangoon, 1889—91, in-fol.

British Museum, 7701. c. 1 (4).

927. — *Report on Archaeological Work in Burma for the year 1901—1902. — Rangoon, 1902, in-fol.

Notice: *Bull. Ecole française Ext. Orient*, III, Oct.—Déc. 1903, pp. 676—7. Par L. F[inot].

928. — *Report on Archaeological Work in Burma for the year 1902—1903. — Rangoon, 1903, in-fol.

Notice: *Bull. Ecole française Ext. Orient*, III, Oct.—Déc. 1903, pp. 676—677. Par L. F[inot].

Numismatique.

929. — The International Numismata Orientalia. Supported by Sir E. C. Bayley, General A. Cunningham,..... Mr. Edward Thomas. Volume III. Part I. Coins of Arakan, of Pegu, and of Burma. By Lieutenant-General Sir Arthur P. Phayre..... London: Trübner, 1882, in-4, 4 ff. n. c. p. l. tit. etc. + pp. 47 et 5 pl.

Notice: *Bull. Soc. Ac. Indo-Chinoise*, 2° Sér., III, 1890, pp. 438—445, par A. R. Havet.
Voir Nos. 106, 107, 108, 109.

930. — Burmese Coinage and Currency. By R. C. Temple. (*The Academy*: I, Oct. 11, 1890: II, Oct. 18, 1890; III, 1 Nov.).

931. — Burmese Leaden Coins. By Edward Nicholson. (*The Academy*, Oct. 25, 1890, p. 371).

Rép. au Capt. Temple.

932. — Currency and Coinage among the Burmese. By R. C. Temple. (*Ind. Antiq.*, XXVI, 1897, pp. 154, 197, 232, 253, 281; XXVII, 1898, 1, 29, 57, 85, 113, 141, 169, 197, 253).

933. — Notes on the Development of Currency in the Far East. By R. C. Temple. (*Ind. Antiq.*, XXVIII, 1899, pp. 102—110).

934. — Beginnings of Currency. By R. C. Temple. (*Ind. Antiq.*, XXIX, 1900, pp. 29, 61).

X. Religion.
Bouddhisme.

935. — An Account of the Religion and Civil Institutions of the Birmans. (From Lieut. Colonel Symes's *Embassy to Ava*). (*Asiatic An. Reg.*, 1800, *Miscel. Tracts*, pp. 79—89).

936. — An Account of the Andaman Islands (From Lieut. Colonel Symes's *Embassy to Ava*). (*Ibid.*, pp. 89—95).

937. — On the Religion and Literature of the Burmas. By Francis Buchanan, M. D. (*Asiatick Researches*, VI, pp. 163—308).

938. — The Ceremonial of the Ordination of a Burmese Priest of Buddha, with Notes, communicated by George Knox, Esq., of the Hon. East-India Company's Medical Establishment, Madras. Read 18th of June 1831 (pp. 271—284).

939. — Discovery of Buddhist Images with Deva-nágari Inscriptions at Tagoung, the Ancient Capital of the Burmese Empire. By Colonel H. Burney, Resident at Ava. (*Jour. As. Soc. Bengal*, V, March 1836, pp. 157—164).

940. — Selections from the Vernacular Boodhist Literature of Burmah. By Lieut. T. Latter, 67th Regiment Bengal Native Infantry. Maulmain: American Baptist Mission Press. Thos. S. Ranney. 1850, in-4.

.*.

941. — Legend of the Burmese Buddha, called Gaudama. By the Revd. P. Bigandet.

> C'est une série d'articles qui a été commencée dans «The Journal of the Indian Archipelago and Eastern Asia», VI, May 1852, pp. 278—289.

942. — The Life, or Legend of Gaudama, the Buddha of the Burmese, with Annotations. The Ways to Neibban, and Notice on the Phongyies, or Burmese Monks. By the Rt. Rev. P. Bigandet, Bp. of Ramatha, Vicar ap. of Ava and Pegu. Rangoon: American Mission Press, C. Bennett, 1866, in-8, pp. xi—538—v.

> C'est la seconde édition de l'ouvrage; la première est de 1858.
> Notice: *The Phoenix*, III, Feb. 1873, pp. 185—6.

943. — The Life or Legend of Gaudama the Buddha of the Burmese. With Annotations. The Ways to Neibban, and Notice on the Phongyes or Burmese Monks. By the Right Reverend P. Bigandet, Bishop of Ramatha, Vicar Apostolic of Ava and Pegu. In two volumes. Third edition. London: Trübner & Co. 1880, 2 vol. in-8, pp. xx—267, viii—326.

> Fait partie de *Trübner's Oriental Series*.

944. — Vie ou légende de Gaudama, le Bouddha des Birmans, et Notice sur les Phongyies ou Moines Birmans, par Monseigneur P. Bigandet, Evêque de Ramatha, vic. apostolique d'Ava et Pégou, traduit en français par Victor Gauvain, lieutenant de vaisseau. Paris, Ernest Leroux, 1878, in-8, pp. 540.

945. — Some Account of the Order of Buddhist Monks or Talapoins. By P. Bigandet. (*Jour. of the Indian Archipelago*, IV, Singapore, 1850).

946. — Mémoire sur les Phongies ou religieux Bouddhistes, appelés aussi Talapoins. Par Mgr. Paul Bigandet. (*Revue de l'Orient*, Sér. IV, 1865).

947. — "In Memoriam". Right Reverend Dr. P. A. Bigandet, K. C. C. I., F. C. U. Bishop of Ramatha and Vicar Apostolic of Southern Burma. Bassein: Printed at St. Peter's Institute Press. 1894, in-8, pp. 75.

Extraits de Journaux.

948. — Religion. (*British Burma Gazetteer*, Vol. I, Chap. V, pp. 193—234.)

The first part of Chapter V is by the Right Reverend Bishop Bigandet, Vicar Apostolic of Pegu, from whose work on Gaudama the second portion is extracted.

∴

949. — *Life of Gaudama: A Translation from the Burmese Book entitled *Ma-la-len-ga-ra Wottoo*. By Rev. Chester Bennet. New York, 1853.

950. — Mulamuli, or the Buddhist Genesis of Eastern India, from the Shan, through the Talaing and Burman. By Rev. Francis Mason, M.D. (*Jour. American Orient. Soc.*, IV, 1854, pp. 103—116).

951. — Original Text and Translation of a Scroll of Silver in the Burmese Language, found in a Buddhist Pagoda at Prome. — By Major Phayre, Commissioner of Pegu. (*Jour. As. Soc. Bengal*, XXV, 1856, pp. 173—178).

952. — Buddhaghosha's Parables: Translated from Burmese By Captain T. Rogers, R. E. With an Introduction, containing Buddha's Dhammapada, Or "Path of Virtue", Translated from Pâli By F. Max Müller, M. A., ... London: Trübner, 1870, in-8, pp. clxxii—206.

953. — Some Account of the Senbyú Pagoda at Mengún, near the Burmese Capital, in a Memorandum by Capt. E. H. Sladen, Political Agent at Mandalé; with Remarks on the Subject, by Col. Henry Yule, C. B. (*Journ. Roy. As. Soc.*, N. S., IV, 1870, Art. X, pp. 406—429).

∴

954. — Buddhist Countries according to Burmese Books. By R. F. St Andrew St. John. (*The Phoenix*, II, Nº 23, May, 1872, pp. 189—190).

955. — Thatone, the Cradle of Buddhism in Burma. By R. F. St. Andrew St. John, Esq., of the British Burmah Commission. (*The Phoenix*, II, Nº 23, May, 1872, pp. 180—182; Nº 24, June, 1872, pp. 204—206; III, Nº 26, August, 1872, pp. 35—36).

956. — The Burmese "Hitopadesa" translated by R. F. St. Andrew St. John. — Reprinted from "The Indian Magazine", in-8, s. l. n. d., pp. 42, [London, 1887]

957. — The Burmese Hitopadesa. By R. F. St. Andrew St. John. (*Jour. Roy. As. Soc.*, April 1895, pp. 431—2).

958. — Kumbha Jātaka or the Hermit Varuṇa Sūra and the Hunter. Translated from the Burmese by R. F. St. Andrew St. John. (*Jour. Roy. As. Soc.*, July 1893, pp. 567—570).

959. — The Story of Thuwannashan, or Suvaṇṇa Sāma Jātaka, according to the Burmese Version, published at the Hanthawati Press, Rangoon. By R. F. St. Andrew St. John, M. R. A. S. (*Journ. Roy. As. Soc.*, April 1894, pp. 211—229).

960. — 'R. F. St. Andrew St. John. — Ari. (*Journ. Roy. As. Soc.*, 1899, pp. 139—141).

∴

961. — The Lokaniti translated from the Burmese Paraphrase. By Lieut. R. C. Temple. (*Jour. As. Soc. Bengal*, Vol. 47, 1878, Pt. 1, pp. 239—257).

962. — The Mengla Thut. (*Ind. Antiq.*, VIII, 1879, p. 82, d'après l'*Arakan News*). — Note on the *Mengala Thok*. By Lieut. R. C. Temple. (*Ibid.*, pp. 329—330).

963. — A Preliminary Study of Kalyani Inscriptions. By Major R. C. Temple. (*Ind. Antiq.*, XXII, 1893, pp. 274—5). — Voir No. 992.

964. — Talapay-Talapoin. By R. C. Temple. (*Ind. Antiq.*, XXII, 1893, p. 326).

965. — A Burmese Saint. By R. F. St. Andrew St. John. — Pir Badar in Burma. By R. C. Temple. (*Journ. Roy. As. Soc.*, July 1894, pp. 565—576).

Le mémoire du Major Temple avait paru dans la *Rangoon Gazette*, Oct. 1893.

966. — Bao. By R. C. Temple. (*Ind. Antiq.*, XXVII, 1898, p. 196; p. 280).

967. — The Thirty-seven Nats (Spirits) of the Burmese. By R. C. Temple. (*Ind. Antiq.*, XXIX, 1900, pp. 117, 190, 256, 289, 350, 387).

Cf. *Journal of Indian Art*, 1900.
Cf. *British Association Advancement of Science*, Report, lxix, pp. 878 seq.

∴

968. — The Namakkára, with Translation and Commentary. By H. L. St. Barbe, B. C. S. (*Journ. R. As. Soc.*, N. S., Vol. XV, Art. VII, April, 1883, pp. 213—220.

969. — Notes on the early History and Geography of British Burma by Em. Forchhammer, Ph. D., Government Archaeologist and Professor of Pali at the Rangoon High School. Rangoon: Printed at the Government Press.

— I. — *The Shwe Dagon Pagoda.* 1883. br. in-8, pp. 17.

— II. — *The First Buddhist Mission to Suvannabhumi.* 1884, br. in-8, pp. 16.

970. — Brahmans and Sanskrit Literature in British Burma. Rangoon: Printed at the Government Press, 1885, br. in-8, pp. 8.

Par le Dr. Em. Forchhammer.

971. — Geschied- en Oudheidkundige Nasporingen in Britisch Burma. Door H. Kern. (*Bijd. Taal-, L. Volk. Ned. Ind.*, X., 4e Sér., 1885, pp. 532—557).

972. — The Story of We-than-da-ya A Buddhist Legend Sketched from the Burmese Version of the Pali Text By L. Allan Goss Inspector of Schools,

Burma Illustrated by a native Artist All rights reserved. Rangoon, Printed at the American Baptist Mission Press F. D. Phinney, Supt. 1886, pet. in-4, pp. III—80.

973. — The Story of We-than-da-ya A Buddhist Legend Sketched from the Burmese Version of the Pali Text By L. Allan Goss Inspector of Schools, Burma — All rights Reserved — Rangoon Printed at the American Baptist Mission Press F. D. Phinney, Supt. 1895. (Second Edition). Pet. in-8, 2 ff. n. ch. + pp. III—95.

974. — On Buddhism in its Relation to Brāhmanism. By Professor Sir Monier Monier-Williams C. I. E., D. C. L., M. R. A. S. (*Journal Roy. As. Soc.*, N. S., Vol. XVIII, Art. VIII, April 1886, pp. 127—156).

975. — °Mahâthera Anurudha, Abhidhammattha Sangaha. Buddhist Metaphysics. Pali Text. Rangoon, 1887, in-8.

976. — °Thinkârabâzani Kyan. Notes on Buddhist Karma. Rangoon, 1887, in-8, pp. 106.

977. — °Sayadaw U Kin. — Zinatta Pakathani Kyan. Rangoon, Maung Po O, 1887, in-8, pp. 781.

    En birman. — Vie de Bouddha.

978. — °U. Awbatha. — Temi Jâtaka Vatthu. Rangoon, Ripley, 1888, in-8, pp. 218.

979. — °U Awbatha. — Mahosadha Jâtaka Vatthu. Rangoon, Ripley, 1888. 2 Vol. in-8, pp. 492.

980. — °U Thumana. — Vandanadi Vinicchaya Kyan. Rangoon, Maung O, 1888, in-8, pp. 38.

    En birman. — Les dogmes de la secte Culaganthi.

981. — °J. A. Colbeck. — Buddhism in Upper Burmah. (*Indian Church Quarterly*, 1888, N° 1).

982. — °G. D'Cruz. — Letter to a Pòngyi. Bassein, P. R. Lucas, 1888, in-8, pp. 142.

    Exposition birmane de la religion bouddhiste au point de vue chrétien.

983. — Catéchisme bouddhique ou introduction à la doctrine du Bouddha Gotama-Extrait, à l'usage des Européens, des livres saints des Bouddhistes du Sud et annoté par Soubhadra Bhikshou. Paris, Ernest Leroux, 1889, in-12, pp. 120.

    Forme le Vol. LXI de la *Bibliothèque orientale elzévirienne*.

984. — Nat-Worship among the Burmese by Louis Vossion F. P. G. S. — Reprinted from the Journal of American Folk-Lore, April—June, 1891. The Riverside Press Cambridge Massachusetts 1891, br. in-8, pp. 8.

    Read at the Annual Meeting of the American Folk-Lore Society at New York, November 28, 1890.

985. — Indo-Burmese Mythology — The Nats or Spirit-Worship among the Burmese and the Wild Tribes of the Iraouddy Valley by Louis Vossion Consul

de France F. P. G. S. Member of the American Philosophical Society —
Reprinted from the Journal of American Folk-Lore (April-June 1891) —
First Edition — The Riverside Press Cambridge Massachussets U. S. 1891 —
Second Edition — Blais, Roy et Cie... Poitiers ... 1895 — Paris, Ernest Leroux,
br. in-8, pp. 18.

986. — Die Wanderungen der indischen Buddhisten nach Birma und nach den
Sunda-Inseln. Vortrag von Professor Dr. E. Müller-Hess in Bern. (*Cte. rendu
V° Cong. inter. Sc. géog.*, Berne — 1891, pp. 693—701).

987. — *The Burmans and Buddhism. (*Catholic World*, 1891, November).

988. — The 'Tam-chhò-dŭng' (*rtsa-mchhog-grong*) of the Lamas, and their
very erroneous identification of the site of Buddha's death. By L. A. Waddell.
(*Jour. As. Soc. Bengal*, Vol. 61, 1892, Pt. 1, pp. 33—42).

989. — *L. A. Waddell. — Burmese Buddhist Rosaries. (*Proc. Asiat. Soc. Bengal*,
1892, pp. 189—191).

*   *
*

990. — *Taw Sein Ko. — The Spiritual World of the Burmese. (*Trans. Congress Orientalists*, London 1892, I, pp. 174—185).

991. — The Kalyānī Inscriptions erected by King Dhammaceti at Pegu in
1476. A. D. Text and Translation. Rangoon: Printed by the Superintendent,
Government Printing, Burma, 1892, in-4, pp. II—VI + 1 f. n. ch. er. +
pp. 105, 2 photog.
    By Taw Sein Ko.

992. — A Preliminary Study of the Kalyani Inscriptions of Dhammacheti 1476
A. D. By Taw Sein Ko. (*Ind. Antiq.*, XXII, 1893, pp. 11, 29, 85, 150, 206, 236).
Voir No. 963.

993. — Some Remarks on the Kalyani Inscriptions. By Taw Sein Ko. (*Ind.
Antiq.*, XXIII, 1894, pp. 100, 222, 255).

994. — The Mahājanaka Jātaka being the Story of one of the Anterior Births
of Gotama Buddha. — Translated into English, with Notes by Taw Sein Ko,
Government Translator, Burma. Rangoon: American Baptist Mission Press,
1896, pet. in-8, pp. 110.

995. — The Sasanavamsa. By Taw Sein Ko. (*Ind. Antiq.*, XXIX, 1900, p. 308).
    A propos de Mrs. Bode's ed. of the Sâsanavaṁsa.

*   *
*

996. — *Htsing-tè thing-gyo a-kank. Commentary in burmese of Abhidham-
mattha-Sangaha. Rangoon, 1893, in-8, pp. 202.

997. — *Henry M. Lütter. — A Manual of Buddhist Law. Mandalay, Star of
Burma Press, 1894, in-8, pp. 108.

998. — *Maung Chan Tun Aung and Maung Kyaw Zan U. — Buddhist Law
of Inheritance. (En birman) Akyab, Kaung Chan Rhi, 1894, in-8, pp. 12.

999. — *The Great Temples of India, Ceylon and Burma. Madras, C. L. Society,
1894, in-8, pp. 104, illustrations.

1000. — Jinâlaṅkâra or « Embellishments of Buddha » by Buddharakkhita Edited, which Introduction, Notes, and Translation by James Gray, Professor of Pali, Rangoon College.... London, Luzac, 1894, in-8, pp. 110.

1001. — Preti Eremiti e Monache in Birmania. Par Magg. Tarsillo Barberis. (*Geogr. per tutti*, IV, 1894, pp. 100—103).

1002. — A Buddhist illustrated Manuscript in Burmese. By Herbert Baynes. (*Actes Congr. Orient.* Genève, II⁰ Partie, pp. 129—136).

1003. — *Herbert Baynes. — An ancient Baudd'a tile. (*Academy*, XLIX, pp. 99 et seq.).

1004. — Hpongyis und Hpongyi-Kyaung's. Birmanische Mönche und Mönchsklöster. Von J. A. E. Gehring. (*Deutsche Rund. f. Geog. u. Stat.*, XVII, 1894—1895, pp. 101—107).

1005. — The Kutho-daw. By F. Max Müller. (*Nineteenth Century*, XXXVIII, Sept. 1895, pp. 494—505).

1006. — *[Abstract of a Lecture delivered by Max Müller upon « The Kutho-Daw»]. (*Academy*, XLVII, pp. 505 et seq.).

A Buddhist Monument in Burma, consisting of about 700 Temples, each one containing a slab of white marble on which the entire Buddhist Bible has been engraved.

1007. — *F. Max Müller. [The Kutho-Daw]; (*Academy*, XLIX, p. 388).

1008. — *Mahâjanaka Jâtaka Vatthu. Edited by the Vernacular Text Books Committee. Rangoon, Anglo-Burmese Mission Press, 1895, in-8, pp. 256.

1009. — *Alb. Grünwedel. — Buddhistische Studien. (Publications du K. Museum f. Völkerkunde, V Band). Berlin, Dietrich Reimer (E. Vohsen), 1897, in-4, pp. III — 136, 97 Abb.

1010. — Buddhist Law. By Sir John Jardine. (*Asiatic Quart. Rev.*, 3d Ser., Oct. 1897, IV, pp. 367—375).

1011. — *Mabel Haynes Bode. — A Burmese Historian of Buddhism. Woking & London, Printed by Unwin brothers, [La préface date du 1ᵉʳ Juillet 1898], pp. 68.

1012. — *H. Fielding. — The Soul of a People; a Study of Buddhism. London, Bentley, New York, Macmillan, 1898. In-8, pp. VIII—363.

Traite de la Birmanie, spécialement du bouddhisme du pays. (Notices: *Acad.*, LIV, pp. 215 et seq., *Athenaeum*, 27 Août, pp. 281 et seq., *Literature*, III, p. 5.)

1013. — *H. Fielding. — The Soul of a People, 3rd edition. London and New York. Macmillan, 1899, pp. XII—350.

La seconde édition parut en 1898.

1014. — *H. Fielding. — De Ziel van een Volk. Het Boeddhisme als volksgeloof in Burma. Vertaald door F. Ortt. 'sGravenhage, Drukkerij Vrede, 1900, pp. VIII—367.

1015. — *Buddhism in Burma. By Henry Ellis (*Positivist Review*, VII, Feb. 1899, p. 24).

1016. — 'Buddhist Temples of the Law at Mandalay; the Most Curious Temple in the East (*Ill.*) (*Sunday Strand*, I, Feb. 1900, p. 238).

1017. — A Religious Fair in Burma. By M. C. Conway-Poole. (*The Wide World Mag.*, V, Oct. 1900—March 1901, pp. 171—176).

1018. — 'U. Dhammaloka's Buddhistischer Aufruf gegen die Christliche Mission in Burma. (*Das freie Wort*, 1901, p. 191).

1019. — 'O· Hanson. — Religions in Upper Burma. (*Independent*, New York, XLIX, p. 1082).

1020. — 'Içvar Chandra Gupta. — Explanation of Shan-Burmese Picture. The Titans fighting with the Gods. (*Journ. Buddh. Text Soc.*, III, II, p. II.

Avec remarques de Çarat Chandra Das, pp. II et seq.

1021. — 'W. A. P. — Burma. Pegu then and Pegu now. (*Buddhist*, (Colombo), X, pp. 66—68; 82—85).

Sur les sanctuaires bouddhistes.

1022. — The Thathanabaing, Head of the Buddhist Monks of Burma. By D. H. R. Twomey. (*Imp. & Asiat. Quart. Rev.*, April 1904, pp. 326—335).

Missions Catholiques.

Le vicariat apostolique d'Ava et Pegou fut détaché en 1722 du diocèse de St. Thomas de Méliapour; en 1866, il fut divisé en trois vicariats: Birmanie centrale, Birmanie orientale, Birmanie occidentale et méridionale.
En 1870, la division fut ainsi modifiée:
1° *Birmanie septentrionale*, Mandalay, Missions étrangères de Paris.
2° *Birmanie orientale*, Toungou, Miss. ét. de Milan.
3° *Birmanie méridionale*, Rangoon, Miss. ét. de Paris.

1023. — De la Mission del Pegu; para la qual fueron señalados los Padres Baltasar de Siquera, y Iuan de Acosta. (L. de Guzman, *Historia de las Misiones... de la Compañia de Iesus*, Alcala, 1601, in-fol., Vol. I, pp. 171—173. Cap. XLIIII).

1024. — Itinerario de las Missiones que hizo el Padre F. Sebastian Manriqve Religioso Eremita de S. Agustin Missionario Apostolico treze años en varias Missiones del India Oriental, Y al presente Procurador, y Diffinidor General de su Prouincia de Portugal en esta Corte de Roma. Con una Summaria Relacion del Grande, y opulento Imperio del Imperator Xa-zia-han Corrombo Gran Mogol, y de otros Reys Infieles, en cuios Reynos assisten los Religiosos de S. Agustin. Al Eminentiss. Señor, el Señor Cardenal Pallotto Protector de la Religion Agustiniana. Con privilegio. En Roma, Por Francisco Caballo, M DC XLIX. Con licencia de los Superiores. in-4, pp. 476 à 2 col. + 6 ff. prél.

1025. — Relazione o sia lettera Scritta da un Missionario abitante in Macao nella Cina, in cui si danno recenti Notizie dell' accaduto ne i Regni di Siam, del Pegu, di Bracma, o sia di Bengala, di Concinkina, di Tunkin, e l'Impero stesso della Cina. Pekino nella Cina 24. Decembre 1767. Pièce in-4, 2 ff. n. c.

A la fin: In Roma MDCCLXVIII. Nella Stamperia Chracas, presso S. Marco al Corso.

1026. — Compendium // Doctrinae // Christianae // idiomate // Barmano sive Bomano. // Romae Anno a Nativitate Christi // MDCCLXXVI. // Praesidum facultate. in-8.

En Birman.

1027. — Preces // Christianae // Barmanorum lingua // atque litteris editae // Romae MDCCLXXXV // Typis Sac. Congreg. de Propaganda Fide // Praesidum Adprobatione. // in-8.

En Birman.

1028. — Catechismus // pro Barmanis // eorum lingua primisque nunc litterarum // typis excusus // aldita etiam // latina interpretatione // Opera // Clericorum Regularium S. Paulli // in regno Avae Missionariorum // adprobante // Sac. Congreg. de Propaganda Fide // Romae MDCCLXXXV. // Typis ejusdem Sac. Congregationis // Praesdum [sic] facultate.

Le texte birman est suivi du texte latin:

1029. — Interpretatio // Catechismi // pro Barmanis // Cui Barmana lingua titulus est // Liber, quo modus traditur cuilibet nationi // servandus, tum in credendo, tum in agendo, // iuxta Dei revelationem, ac legem. // Romae MDCCLXXXVI. // Typis Sac. Congreg. de Propaganda Fide // Praesidum Facultate. in-8, pp. 76.

1030. — 'Luigi Gallo. — Storia del Cristianesimo nell' Impero Birmano. Milano, tip. Boniardi Pogliardo, 1862, 3 vol. in-16.

1031. — Missions de la Birmanie. (*Annales Prop. Foi*, XXXVI, 1864, pp. 47—53).

«Le premier apôtre de la Birmanie fut un Franciscain, né en France et appelé Bonfer. En 1554, deux années seulement après la mort de St. François-Xavier, il aborda dans un port du Pégu, et y trouva déjà établie une forte colonie de Portugais. Son zèle parait avoir été plus utile à ces Européens qu'aux indigènes, car il repartit au bout de trois ans, rebuté par l'indifférence d'un peuple qui ne répondait à ses prédications que par des menaces de mort. Deux pères jésuites, qui le remplacèrent en 1604, furent plus heureux, et par leurs soins on vit bientôt s'élever dans Syriam la première église catholique du pays.

«En 1722, les Pères barnabites succédèrent aux religieux de la Cie. de Jésus dans la direction de l'apostolat birman..... Le R. P. Sigismond Calchi en fut le premier vicaire apostolique.....» Le P. d'Amato le dernier, † 1831.

En 1831, arrivée de la Congrégation italienne des Oblats de Marie..... Mgr. Balma, vicaire apostolique de 1849 à 1854, donne sa démission. Transfert aux Missions étrangères de Paris et nomination de Mgr. Bigandet.

1032. — Vicariat apostolique de la Birmanie. (*Ann. Prop. Foi*, XXXVIII, 1866, pp. 5—16.

1033. — A Compendious History of the New Testament, with Moral Reflections. By the Rev. N. Polignani, Cath. Miss. Second Edition. Bassein Catholic Mission Press, 1867, in-8.

En Birman.

1034. — History of the Churches of India, Burma, Siam, the Malay Peninsula, Cambodia, Annam, China, Tibet, Corea, and Japan, entrusted to the Society of the « Missions Etrangères ». By E. H. Parker. (*China Review*, XVIII, N°. 1, pp. 1—33).

D'après un travail latin du P. Wallys. [lire Edmond Wallays.]

1035. — Histoire générale de la Société des Missions Etrangères par Adrien Launay de la même Société. Paris, Téqui, 1894, 3 vol. in-8, pp. IX—595, 594, 646.

1036. — Le Séminaire Saint-Louis de Gonzague à Mandalay. Lettre de Mgr. Usse, vicaire apostolique. Mandalay, 21 oct. 1896. (*Miss. Cath.*, XXVIII, 1896, pp. 589—590).

1037. — Prayer Book in Burmese by a Catholic Missionary. — 3rd. Edition. — Bassein: Catholic Mission Press. 1868, in-8.

1038. — 'G. Kern. — Catholic Hymn book in Burmese. Rangoon, British Burma Press, 1900, pp. 260.

Vie des Missionnaires catholiques.

Amato, *Giuseppe*, né à Naples; † à Moun-lha, avril 1832.

1039. — Memoir of Giuseppe d'Amato. [Extract of a private letter from Major H. Burney, Resident at the Burmese Court, dated Ava, 9th April 1832]. (*Journ. As. Soc. of Bengal*, I, Aug. 1832, pp. 349—353).

Ambiehl, *René,* né à Rüstenhart (Strasbourg, Alsace) 29 juin 1867; parti 13 sept. 1893 pour la Birmanie mérid.; † 19 juillet 1903.

1040. — Notice. (*Cte. rendu des Miss. étrangères*, de Paris, 1903, pp. 393—397).

Bérard, *Joachim Pierre Antoine*, né à Valbonnais, Isère, 15 fév. 1863; parti 11 nov. 1891; † 5 juin 1895, Birmanie sept.

1041. — Notice. (*Cte. rendu* 1895, pp. 399—402).

Bernard, *Louis Noël*, né à Saint-Étienne-de-Mont-Luc (Loire-Inférieure), 25 déc. 1822; parti 23 déc. 1849 pour la Birmanie mérid.; † 30 mai 1888.

1042. — Notice. (*Cte. rendu* 1888, pp. 248—250).

Bertrand, *Pierre*, né à Plaisance, dioc. de Rodez, 24 oct. 1832; parti pour la Birmanie mérid., 19 juillet 1857; † 15 juillet 1899.

1043. — Notice par E. Luce. (*Cte. rendu* 1899, pp. 358—366).

Biet, *Louis Marie*, né à Langres, 27 avril 1845; parti pour la Birmanie mérid., 15 mars 1868; † 4 sept. 1886.

1044. — Notice. (*Cte. rendu* 1886, pp. 223—228).

Biffi, *Eugène*, du Séminaire des Missions ét. de Milan; ancien préfet apostolique de la Birmanie orient.; né à Milan 22 déc. 1829; évêque de Carthagène (États-Unis de Colombie) 7 fév. 1882; † 1896.

1045. — Nécrologie. (*Miss. Cath.*, XXVIII, 11 déc. 1896, p. 599).

1046. — Ext. d'une let. de M. Eugène Biffi aux Membres des Conseils centraux de l'oeuvre de la Prop. de la Foi. Tounghoo, 30 déc. 1870. (*Annales Prop. Foi*, XL, 1872, pp. 15—19).

> La Propagande, en novembre 1866, érigea en préfecture apostolique la Birmanie orientale entre la Salouen et le Mekong qu'elle confia aux Missions ét. de Milan. Les quatre premiers missionnaires, Eugène Biffi, préfet apostolique, Tancrède Conti, Sébastien Corbone et Roch Tornatore, partirent le 9 déc. 1867 de Milan; ils furent rejoints en sept. 1869 par Godefroy Conti.

1047. — Ext. d'une let. de M. Eugène Biffi à Mgr. Marinoni, supérieur du Séminaire des Miss. ét. à Milan. Toungoo, 1er juillet 1873. (*Ann. Prop. Foi*, XLVI, 1874, pp. 14—22).

Bigandet, *Paul-Ambroise*, né à Malans, canton d'Amancey (Doubs) 13 août 1813; parti 13 juin 1837; † 19 mars 1894 à Rangoon; évêque de Ramatha et coadj. du vic. ap. de Malaisie (1856); vic. ap. de la Birmanie méridionale (1870).

1048. — Notice. (*Cte. rendu* 1894, pp. 314—325). — (*Miss. Cath.*, XXVI, 30 mars 1894, p. 160; 18 mai 1894, pp. 243—244).

1049.* — Let. de Mgr. Bigandet à MM. les Directeurs de l'Oeuvre de la Prop. de la Foi. Rangoun, 18 janvier 1863. (*Annales Prop. Foi*, XXXVI, 1864, pp. 53—59).

L. (*Ibid.*, pp. 59—66).

L. à M. Albrand, Sup. du Sém. des Miss. ét. de Paris. Nabeck, 25 mai 1864. (*Ibid.*, XXXVIII, 1866, pp. 17—31).

L. aux Membres ... de la Prop. de la Foi. Rangoon, 1er oct. 1876. (*Ibid.*, XLIX, 1877, pp. 434—439).

1050. — 'Mgr. Bigandet. — La mission de Birmanie, trad. de l'anglais par A. Launay. Paris, Téqui, 1890, in-8, pp. 166, illustrations.

Conférer : de Bizemont, *Polybiblion, partie littéraire*, Mars, p: 197.

1051. — « In Memorian ». Right Reverend Dr. P. A. Bigandet, K. C. C. I., F. C. U. Bishop of Ramatha and Vicar Apostolic of Southern Burma. Bassein : Printed at St. Peter's Institute Press. 1894, in-8, pp. 75.

Extraits des journaux. — Voir No. 947.

Bohn, *Xavier*, né le 25 avril 1867 à Bleinschwiller, dioc. de Strasbourg; parti 19 juillet 1893 pour la Birmanie mérid.; † 10 déc. 1901.

1052. — Notice par E. Luce. (*Cte. rendu* 1901, pp, 383—389).

Bourdon, *Charles Arsène*, du dioc. de Sées; parti 16 août 1863; évêque de Dardanie; vic. ap. de la Birmanie sept. en 1872; démissionnaire en 1887.

1053. — Let. de Mgr. Bourdon, vic. ap. de la Birmanie sept. à MM. les Membres ... de la Prop. de la Foi. Mandalay, 8 nov. 1873. (*Ann. Prop. Foi*, XLVI, 1874, pp. 97—103).

Bringaud, *Jean-Baptiste*, né 1837, dioc. de Tulle; parti pour la Birmanie 16 août 1863.

1054. — Let. de M. Bringaud. (*Ann. Prop. Foi*, nov. 1902, pp. 442—450).

Cadoux, *Claude*, né à Bissy-sous-Uxelles (Saône-et-Loire) 8 oct. 1850; parti 16 déc. 1874 pour la Birmanie sept.; † 28 mai 1893.

1055. — Notice. (*Cte. rendu* 1893, pp. 346—350).

Cance, *Georges-Jean*, né en 1873, dioc. de Montpellier; parti 1896.

1056. — Comment on fonde un poste carian en Birmanie. Lettre de M. G. Cance, des Missions Etrangères de Paris, missionnaire en Birmanie méridionale. (*Miss. Cath.*, XXXIV, 21 nov. 1902, pp. 556—559; 28 nov., pp. 569—573; 5 déc., pp. 579—584).

Carbone, *Sébastien*, des Miss. ét. de Milan.

1057. — Sa vie a été publiée à Milan par un de ses confrères, M. Scurati, vers 1873.

Cardot, *Alexandre*, né 10 janvier 1857, à Fresse, Hte. Saône, dioc. de Besançon; parti 29 oct. 1879; sacré à Rangoon, 24 juin 1893, évêque de Limyre et coadj. de Mgr. Bigandet; vic. ap. de Birmanie mérid., 1894.

1058. — *Missions Cath.*, XXV, 1893, p. 328.

Cherbonnier, *François-Marie-Thérèse*, né à Champtoceaux, dioc. d'Angers, 15 oct. 1848; parti pour la Birmanie mérid., 29 janvier 1873; † 12 janvier 1886.

1059. — Notice. (*Cte. rendu* 1886, pp. 168—170).

Chirac, *Pierre Marie Richard Henri de*, né 1863, dioc. de Mende; parti pour la Birmanie mérid. 5 mai 1886.

1060. — Lettre [Incendie de l'église Saint-Joseph à Moulmein]. (*Miss. Cath.*, XXVII, 1895, p. 520).

Devos, *Benoit Louis*, né à Seroux, dioc. de Cambrai, 21 oct. 1833; parti pour la Birmanie 5 mars 1861; † 6 janvier 1878 à la procure de Singapore.

1061. — Notice. (*Cte. rendu* 1878, p. 71).

Ellerbach, *Léon*, né 27 fév. 1860, à Gevenatten, village annexe de la paroisse de Tranbach-le-Haut, dép. du Haut-Rhin; parti pour la Birmanie sept. 21 nov. 1883; † 16 janvier 1885.

1062. — Notice. (*Cte. rendu* 1885, pp. 164—165).

Fercot, *Jules Emile*, né le 1er Mai 1851, dioc. de Nancy; parti pour la Birmanie sept. 27 janvier 1875; † 23 mars 1892.

1063. — Notice. (*Compte rendu* 1892, pp. 332—334).

Freynet, *Etienne*, né 1853, dioc. de Lyon; parti pour la Birmanie mérid. 29 oct. 1879.

1064. — Lettre de Birmanie. La léproserie de Rangoon. (*Miss. Cath.*, XXXV, 1903, pp, 433—438).

Guérin, *Félix-Alphonse*, né 1er avril 1832, à Morelmaison, village de l'arrondissement de Neufchâteau, dép. des Vosges; parti pour la Birmanie mérid., 1er juin 1856; † 7 mai 1896.

1065. — Notice. (*Cte. rendu* 1896, pp. 383—390).

Hailles, *Pierre Frédéric*, né 23 août 1846, à Nederbrakel, dioc. de Gand; parti 30 nov. 1873 pour la Birmanie sept.; † 17 août 1881.

1066. — Notice. (*Cte. rendu* 1881, p. 131).

Lafon, *Louis*, né 1873, dioc. de Rodes; parti 1895.

1067. — Lettre de Pyinmana (Birmanie sept.) (*Miss. Cath.*, XXXI, 22 sept. 1899, p. 448).

Lecomte, *Auguste*, né le 16 nov. 1832; parti pour la Birmanie sept. 1er juin 1856; † 21 fév. 1892.

1068. — Notice. (*Compte rendu* 1892, pp. 329—332).

Legendre, *Louis Magloire*, né à Paris 22 sept. 1863; parti 4 avril 1888 pour la Birmanie sept.; † 4 sept. 1895.

1069. — Notice. (*Cte. rendu* 1895, pp. 360—362).

Luce, *Eugène Jean Baptiste Ferdinand*, né 1863, dioc. de Rouen; parti 5 mai 1886; provicaire de la Birmanie méridionale.

1070. — Lettre de Gyobingank (Birmanie méridionale), 10 octobre 1895. (*Miss. Cath.*, XXVII, 20 déc. 1895, p. 605).

Lettre de Rangoon, 19 Mai. (*Miss. Cath.*, XXXIV, 20 juin 1902, p. 292).

Lyet, *Marie Jean Joseph*, né 24 nov. 1846, à Auxelles, dioc. de Besançon; parti 2 juillet 1873 pour la Birmanie sept.; † 9 déc. 1878.

1071. — Notice. (*Cte. rendu* 1879, p. 81).

Maria, des Miss. Etr. de Milan.

1072. — Lettre de Toungoo (Birmanie orient.) (*Miss. Cath.*, 13 juin 1902, p. 280).

ourlanne, *Jean-Baptiste*, né 1866, dioc. de Bayonne; parti 1890 pour la Birmanie méridionale.

73. — Lettre de Rangoon (Birmanie). (*Miss. Cath.*, XXXV, 6 mars 1903, p. 110).

oysan, *Yves-Marie*, né 11 mai 1869 à Plougonver (Côtes-du-Nord); parti 29 août 1894 pour la Birmanie sept.; † 16 avril 1901 en France.

74. — Notice par F. Delort. (*Cte. rendu* 1901, pp. 335—338).

aude-Theil, *Jean Roch*, né à Peyrouse (Htes. Pyrénées) 16 août 1822; parti pour a Birmanie mérid., 21 juillet 1847; † 2 juin 1900.

75. — Notice par E. Luce (*Cte. rendu* 1900, pp. 349—354).

ercoto, *Gio. Maria*, † 1776.

76. — *Padre D. M. Griffini, Della Vita di Monsignor Gio. Maria Percoto. Udine, 1781.

77. — *[Griffini, Michel Angelo]. Kurze Nachrichten von den Reichen Pegu und Ava. Aus der italienischen Lebensbeschreibung des Missionarius Johann Maria Percoto gezogen. (*Beiträge zur Völker- und Landeskunde.* Th. 11, pp. 3—26, Leipzig, 1793, in-8).

78. — *E. Teza. — Voci birmane nella vita del padre G. M. Percoto, scritta dal padre M. A. Griffini. Nota. Venezia, tip. Ferrari, 1896, in-8, pp. 7.

   Ext. des *Atti del R. Istituto Veneto di Sc., Let. ed Arti*, Ser. VII, T. VII, 1895—6.

ermandet, *Jean-Baptiste*, né 1867, dioc. d'Autun; parti 1893 pour la Birmanie sept.; missionaire à Yna-Dan (district de Shwebo).

79. — Lettre. (*Miss. Cath.*, 5 fév. 1897, pp. 63—64).

angermano, *Vincent*, né à Arpinum, en Italie; envoyé comme missionnaire en 1782 arrivé à Rangoon en juillet 1783; † à Arpinum, 1819.

ir Nos. 5 et 6.

mon, *Pierre Ferdinand*, né le 2 mars 1855 à Chaillé-les-Marais, dioc. de Luçon; parti le 4 sept. 1878; évêque de Domitiopolis; vic. ap. de la Birmanie sept.; † 20 juillet 1893.

80. — Notice. (*Cte. rendu* 1894, pp. 307—313). — (*Miss. Cath.*, XXV, 4 août 1893, p. 372.)

see, *Antoine*, né 1860; dioc. de St. Flour; parti 3 déc. 1884 pour la Birmanie sept.; évêque de Selge, 1893; vic. ap. de la Birmanie sept.; démissionnaire.

81 — Lettre de Mandalay, 29 oct. 1894. (*Miss. Cath.*, XXVIII, 5 avril 1895, p. 160).

L. de Mandalay, 21 oct. 1896, sur le Séminaire de Saint-Louis de Gonzague de Mandalay. (*Ibid.*, 11 déc. 1896).

L. de Mandalay, 1ᵉʳ avril 1897. (*Ibid.*, XXIX, 1ᵉʳ oct. 1897, pp. 472—473).

L. de Mandalay. (*Ibid.*, XXX, 23 sept. 1898, pp. 447—448).

82. — Let. de Mgr. Usse. (*Ann. Prop. Foi*, LXIX, 1897, pp. 250—258).

erstraeten, né 2 déc. 1854; parti le 27 nov. 1889 pour la Birmanie sept.; † 18 juin 1892.

83. — Notice. (*Compte rendu* 1892, pp. 350 –351).

ullies, *Clément*, né 1873, dioc. d'Annecy; parti 1897 pour la Birmanie sept.

84. — Ext. de lettre de Mandalay. (Birmanie) (*Miss. Cath.*, XXXV, 3 avril 1903, p. 159).

Ext. de let. de Birmanie. (*Ibid.*, 19 juin 1903, p. 291).

Wehinger, *Jean*, des Miss. ét. de Paris; † 6 sept. 1903. (*Miss. Cath.*, XXXV, 30 oct. 1903, p. 527.)

1085. — Let. à Mgr. Simon. (*Miss. Cath.*, XXV, 7 avril 1893, pp. 158—159).

1086. — Der Aussatz in Birma. (*Oesterreichische Monatsschrift für den Orient*, XXII, 1893, pp. 23—26).

> D'après: *Drei Jahre unter den Aussätzigen, Mandalay in Birma* de J. Wehinger. (Vienne, 4 Postgasse) in-8, pp. 72.

Missions protestantes.

1087. — The recent Sufferings of the American Missionaries in the Burman Empire, during the late war: with their signal deliverance, by being conveyed to the British Camp. From authentic documents. Edinburgh: Printed for Waugh and Innes; M. Ogle, Glasgow; R. M. Tims, Dublin; James Duncan, J. Nisbet and F. Westley, London. MDCCCXXVII, pet. in-8, p. 129.

1088. — *A Digest of Scripture, consisting of Extracts from the Old and New Testament, on the plan of Brown's «Selection of Scripture Passages». In the Burmese Language. Maulmain 1838. In-8.

1089. — The Gospel in Burmah. By Mrs. Macleod Wylie. — Calcutta: G. C. Hay and Co., Cossitollah. London: W. H. Dalton, 1859, in-12, pp. 519, carte.

1090. — Personal Recollections of British Burma And its Church Mission Work In 1878—79. By the Right Rev. J. H. Titcomb, DD., First Bishop of Rangoon. London: Published for the Society for the Propagation of the Gospel in Foreign Parts, by Wells Gardner, Darton and Co. 1880, in-8, pp. VIII—103.

> Carte et gravures.
> L'Evêché protestant de Rangoun fut créé aux dépens de celui de Calcutta en 1877, grâce à la munificence du diocèse de Winchester.

1091. — *O· Flex. — Die S. P. G. in Barma. (*Allgemeine Missionen-Zeitung*, pp. 13—26, 62—74, 107—117, 193—222).

> Society of the Propagation of the Gospel in Foreign Parts.

1092. — *A. Mayr. — Die S. P. G. in Barma. Berichtigung (*Allgemeine Missionen-Zeitung*, XX, pp. 378 et seq.).

1093. — Preaching the Gospel to the Laos in Burmah. By Rev. W. C. Dodd (*ill.*) (*Mission-Rev.*, XII, May 1899, p. 337).

1094. — *Sister Katherine. — Towards the Land of the Rising Sun; or Four Years in Burma. London, Society for Promoting Christian Knowledge, 1900, pp. 162.

> Notice: *Athenæum*, 16 juin 1901, p. 745.

1095. — *F. D. Phinney. — The American Baptist Mission Press, Rangoon. Rangoon, American Baptist Mission Press, 1901, pp. 48.

1096. — *The Christian Tower:* set for the Defence of Truth and Remedy of Error. Rangoon, 1877—78, in-8.

Rapports.

1097. — Seventh Annual Report of the Burmah Baptist Missionary Convention. Including Reports of the Stations and Statistics for the year 1871—2, with the Minutes of the Seventh Annual Meeting, Held in Rangoon Nov. 9th to 13th 1872. Rangoon: American Mission Press. C. Bennett...... 1873, br. in-8, pp. 87 + 1 tab.

1098. — Eighth Annual Report of the Burmah Baptist Missionary Convention. Including Reports of the Stations and Statistics For the year 1872—3, with the minutes of the Eighth Annual Meeting, held in Shway-Gyeen, Nov. 1st to 5th 1873. Rangoon: American Mission Press. C. Bennett...., 1873, in-8, pp. 76 + 1 tab.

1099. — The Seventeenth Annual Report of the Burmah Bible and Tract Society. For the year 1878. With the Treasurer's Report, &c. — Instituted 1861. — Rangoon: C. Bennett...... American Mission Press. 1878, br. pet. in-8, pp. 32.

1100. — The Twelfth Annual Report of the Burmah Bible and Tract Society, for the year 1873. With the Treasurer's Report, &c. Instituted, 1861. Rangoon: American Mission Press. C. Bennett..... 1873, br. in-8, pp. 24 + 1 tab.

1101. — The Third Annual Report of the Eurasian Ladies' Society, 1877—78. — With a List of Contributors and Donors, Treasurer's Report, etc. — Organized 1874. — Rangoon: C. Bennett: — American Mission Press. 1878, br. in-8, pp. 20 + 1 f. n. c.

1102. — Proceedings of the first Diocesan Church Conference held in Rangoon, December 4th and 5th 1878. — Times press, br. in-8, pp. 42.

1103. — Annual Congregational Report submitted to a Meeting of the Congregation held on Wednesday 9th April 1879. — Rangoon: C. Bennett... American Mission Press. 1879, br. in-12, pp. 11.

Vies des Missionnaires protestants.

Judson, *Adoniram*, né à Malden, Massachussets, 9 août 1788; † 12 avril 1850 en mer en route pour l'île de France; il s'était embarqué à Salem sur le brick *Caravan* le 19 fév. 1812 pour Calcutta où il arriva le 17 juin 1812.

1104. — Christian Baptism. A Sermon, preached in the Lal Bazar Chapel, Calcutta: On Lord's-Day, September 27, 1812: previous to the Administration of the Ordinance of Baptism. With many Quotations from Pedobaptist Authors. By Adoniram Judson, A. M. Printed in the year, 1813, in-8, pp. 88

1105. — Christian Baptism. — A Sermon, preached in the Lal Bazar Chapel, Calcutta, on Lord's-Day, September 27, 1812, previous to the Administration of the Ordinance of Baptism, With many Quotations from Pedobaptist Authors. By Adoniram Judson, A. M. Third American edition. Boston: printed and published by Lincoln & Edmands, N°. 53, Cornhill. 1818, in-8, pp. 40.

1106. — A Sermon on the Nature and subjects of Christian Baptism. By
Adoniram Judson, D.D. Burmah. — Glasgow; Published by Peter Sinclair and
sold by Waugh & Innes, and Oliphant & son, Edinburgh: Robertson & Co.,
Dublin: George Wightman, and Simpkin & Marshall, London. MDCCCXXXIV,
in-8, pp. 84.

1107. A Letter to Christian Women, on Ornamental Dress, by Adoniram Judson,
Baptist Missionary in Burmah, originally addressed to the Female Members
of Christian Churches in the United States, pièce pet. in-8, pp. 8.

> La lettre est datée: Maulmain, 1831. — On lit à la fin: London: Printed by
> Edward Couchman.... for the *Tract Association of Friends*. Sold at the De-
> pository, 84 Houndsditch, 1860.

1108. — A Correction of Erroneous Statements concerning the Embarkation of
the Rev. Messrs. Judson and Newell, at Salem, February 18, 1812. Reprinted
from the *Christian Review*, N°. LIV. Boston: Press of T. R. Marvin, March,
1849, in-8, pp. 24.

1109. — The Life and Character of Adoniram Judson, late Missionary to Burmah:
a Commemorative Discourse delivered before the American Baptist Missionary
Union, in Boston, May 15, 1851. By William Hague. Published by request
of the Union. Boston: Gould and Lincoln. 1851, in-8, pp. 38.

1110. — Memoir of Adoniram Judson: being a Sketch of his Life and Missionary Labors. By J. Clement, Auburn: Derby and Miller. 1851, in-12, pp. 336.

1111. — A Sketch of the Labors, Sufferings and Death of the Rev. Adoniram
Judson, D. D. by A. D. Gillette, A. M. pastor of the Eleventh Baptist Church,
Philadelphia. — Philadelphia: published by Daniels & Smith, 1851, in-16, pp.160.

1112. — A Memoir of the Life and Labors of the Rev. Adoniram Judson, D. D.
by Francis Wayland, President of Brown University. In two volumes. Boston:
Phillips, Sampson, and Company. London: Nisbet and Company. 1853, 2 vol.
in-12, pp. 544, 522, Portrait.

1113. — A Memoir of the Life and Labours of the Rev. Adoniram Judson, D. D.
By Francis Wayland, D. D. President of Brown University, Rhode Island, U.S.
and Professor of Moral Philosophy. In two volumes. London: James Nisbet & Co.
MDCCCLIII, 2 vol. in-8, pp. VIII—440, IV—418 + 1 f. n. c.

1114. — The Earnest Man. A Sketch of the Character and Labors of Adoniram
Judson First Missionary to Burmah. By Mrs. H. C. Conant. Boston: Phillips,
Sampson, and Company. New York: Sheldon, Blakeman & Co. 1856, pet. in-8,
pp. 498. Portrait.

1115. — A Missionary of the Apostolic School: Being the Life of Dr. A. Judson,
of Burmah. Revised and edited by Horatius Bonar, D. D. London: James Nisbet
& Co. 1871, pet. in-8, p. VII—374.

> Condensé de l'ouvrage de Wayland avec quelques nouveaux renseignements.

1116. — The Life of Adoniram Judson by his Son Edward Judson. New York,
Anson D. F. Randolph & Co, in-8, pp. XII—601. Port. Cartes et ill. [1883].

1117. — Adoniram Judson, D. D. his Life and Labours. By his Son Edward Judson. London: Hodder and Stoughton, M DCCC LXXXIII, in-8, pp. VIII—601.

MÊme éd. que celle de New York, s. d., sans la déd. et la courte préface.

1118. — The Apostle of Burma. A Memoir of Adoniram Judson, D. D. By the Rev. Jabez Marrat..... London: Charles H. Kelly, 1890, pet. in-8, pp. 128.

1119. — *Eine Barmanen-Familie. Aus Missionar Judsons Arbeit. 4te Auflage. (*Kleine Missionstraktate* N°. 56). Basel, Missionsbuchhandlung, 1894, in-8, pp. 16, illustr.

1120. — *Edward Judson. — Adoniram Judson. Ein Apostel unter den Birmanen. Eine Biographie von seinem Sohne. Hamburg, Oncken Nachf., 1896, in-8, pp. 166, mit Abbild. und Bildnis.

Judson, *Ann Hasseltine*, née à Bradford, Mass., 22 déc. 1789; ép. le Rev. Ad. Judson à Bradford, 5 fév. 1812; † à Amherst, oct. 24, 1826.

1121. — An Account of the American Baptist Mission to the Burman Empire. In a Series of Letters addressed to a Gentleman in London. By Ann H. Judson. Second Edition. London: Joseph Butterworth and Son, M DCCC XXVII, in-12, pp. VIII—316. Carte.

1122. — An Account of the American Baptist Mission to the Burman Empire: in a Series of Letters, addressed to a Gentleman in London. By Ann H. Judson. London: Printed for J. Butterworth & Son and T. Clark, Edinburgh. M D CCC XXXIII, in-8, pp. XV—326. Carte.

1123. — Early Life of Mrs. Judson. Pièce pet. in-8, pp. 8.

Forme le n° 363 de «The First Series Tracts of the Religious Tract Society. Instituted 1799. London: Printed for the Religious Tract Society, Vol. X».

1124. — Life of Mrs Ann H. Judson, late Missionary to Burmah; with an Account of the American Baptist Mission to that Empire. Prepared for the American Sunday School Union; by James D. Knowles. Pastor of the Second Baptist Church in Boston. Revised by the Committee of Publication. American Sunday School Union, Philadelphia: 1830, in-12, pp. 263 + 3 pp. n. c. p. l'app.

1125. — Memoir of Mrs. Ann H. Judson, Wife of the Rev. Adoniram Judson, Missionary to Burmah. Including a History of the American Baptist Mission, in the Burman Empire. — By James D. Knowles, Pastor of the Second Baptist Church in Boston. — Second edition. London: Printed for the Proprietor, in-8, pp. 324. Port. et carte.

1126. — Memoir of Mrs. Ann. H. Judson, Wife of the Rev. Adoniram Judson, Missionary to Burmah. Including a History of the American Baptist Mission, in the Burman Empire. By James D. Knowles, Pastor of the Second Baptist Church in Boston. Third edition. London: Printed for Wightman and Co., Waugh and Innes, Edinburgh: and W. Curry, Jun. and Co., Dublin. 1830, in-8, pp. 324. Port. et carte.

1127. — *Memoiren d. Mrs. Anna H. Judson, Missionarin iu Burmah. Herausgegeben von J. D. Knowles, in-12, Port. et carte.

1128. — American Biography; or Memoirs of Mrs. Ann Judson, and Mrs. Martha Laurens Ramsay. Abridged for the use of Village Libraries. By the Author of Lily Douglas. Edinburgh: published by William Oliphant, and sold by W. Collins, Glasgow; Hamilton, Adams and Co. and J. Nisbet, London; W. M'Comb, Belfast; and W. Curry, Jun. and Co. Dublin. M.DCCC.XXXI, in-12, pp. 372.

> Par Miss Grierson.

1129. — Fourth thousand. — The Lives of Mrs. Ann H. Judson and Mrs. Sarah B. Judson, with a biographical sketch of Mrs. Emily C. Judson, missionaries to Burmah. In three parts. By Arabella W. Stuart. Auburn: Derby and Miller. 1852, in-8, pp. 356.

1130. — Twenty-second thousand. — The Lives of Mrs. Ann H. Judson, Mrs. Sarah B. Judson, and Mrs. Emily C. Judson, Missionaries to Burmah. In three Parts. By Mrs. Arabella M. Willson. New York and Auburn: Miller, Orton & Mulligan, 1856, in-8, pp. 371.

> Même ouvrage augmenté que celui de 1852 signé: Arabella W. Stuart.

1131. — A Sketch of Mrs. Ann H. Judson. By Mrs. Clara Lucas Balfour. London: W. & F. G. Cash, 1854, in-12, pp. 51.

> Comprend aussi des essais biographiques sur les deux autres femmes du Dr. Judson.

1132. — Anna Judson. Ein christliches Lebensbild aus der Mission, gezeichnet von W. Ziethe, Prediger an der Parochialkirche zu Berlin. Berlin, 1868, Verlag von Wiegandt und Grieben, in-8, 4 ff. prél. n. c. + pp. 150.

> Forme la IVe partie de «Frauenspiegel. Lebensbilder Christlicher Frauen und Jungfrauen. Im Verein mit gleichgesinnten Freunden herausgegeben von W. Ziethe, Prediger an der Parochial-Kirche zu Berlin. Berlin, 1868. Verlag von Wiegandt und Grieben.

Judson, *Sarah Boardman Hall,* née à Alstead, N. H., Nov. 4, 1803; seconde femme du Rev. Ad. Judson, qu'elle ép. 10 avril, 1834; † 1 sept. 1845 à Ste Hélène.

1133. — Missionary Biography. The Memoir of Sarah B. Judson, Member of the American mission to Burmah. By Fanny Forester. With an Introductory Notice, by Edward Bean Underhill. London: Aylott & Jones, 1848, pet. in-8, pp. XII—180.

> Fanny Forrester = Miss E. C. Chubbuck depuis Mrs Judson.

1134. — Sarah B. Judson. Born 1803. Died 1845.

> Dans le vol. intitulé: Faithful Service: Sketches of Christian Women. By Mary Pryor Hack. London: Hodder and Stoughton, MDCCCLXXXV, Chapter V, pp. 151—196, in-8.

Judson, *Emily Chubbuck,* née à Eaton, Etat de New York, 22 août 1817, troisième femme du Rev. Ad. Judson, qu'elle ép. 2 juin 1846; † 1 juin 1854.
Elle a écrit sous le pseud. de Fanny Forrester.

1135. — The Kathayan Slave, and other Papers connected with Missionary Life. By Emily Judson. Boston: Ticknor, Reed, and Fields. M DCCC LIII, in-8, ff. prél. n. c. 3 + pp. 186.

> The *Kathayan Slave* a été réimp., pp. 580 et seq. de *The Life of Ad. Judson by his son Edward Judson,* 1883. — Voir No. 1117.

1136. — The Life and Letters of Mrs. Emily C. Judson. By A. C. Kendrick, Professor of Greek Literature in the University of Rochester. London: T. Nelson and sons, Edinburgh; and New York. MDCCCLXI, in-8, pp. 400.

Lambert, *C. W.*

1137. — *Brief record of the life and missionary labours of C. W. Lambert in Upper Burma, Missionary martyr of Thibaw. London, Partridge, 1896, in-8, pp. 144, 1 portrait, illustrations.

Mason, *Francis,* né à Walmgate, York, Angleterre, 2 avril 1799.

1138. — The Karens: or Memoir of Ko Thah-Byu, the first Karen Convert. By a Karen Missionary. Tavoy: Karen Mission Press, 1842, in-12, pp. IX—202.
Par Francis Mason.

1139. — The Karens: or Memoir of Ko Thah-Byu: the first Karen Convert. By a Karen Missionary. Second edition: with a new introduction. Tavoy: Karen Mission Press. 1843, pet. in-8, pp. 221.

1140. — The Karen Apostle: or, Memoir of Ko Thah-Byu, the first Karen Convert, with Notices concerning his Nation. By the Rev. Francis Mason, Missionary to the Karens. London: The Religious Tract Society, in-12, pp. IV—120, s. d.

1141. — The Karen Apostle; or, Memoir of Ko Thah-Byu, the first Karen Convert: with an Historical and Geographical Account of the Nation, its Traditions, Precepts, Rites, &c., by Rev. Francis Mason, missionary to the Karens. Revised by H. J. Ripley, Professor in Newton Theological Seminary. Fourth thousand. Boston: Gould, Kendall, and Lincoln, 1847, in-12, pp. 108.

1142. — A Cenotaph To a Woman of the Burman Mission; or, Views in the Missionary Path of Helen M. Mason. By Francis Mason. New York: published by Lewis Colby, 1851, in-12, pp. 187, grav.

1143. — Civilizing Mountain Men or Sketches of Mission work among the Karens. By Mrs. Mason of Burmah. Edited by L. N. R... London: James Nisbet & Co., 1862, in-8, pp. X—384.

1144. — The story of a Working man's life: With Sketches of Travel in Europe, Asia, Africa, and America, as related by himself. By Francis Mason, D.D. With an introduction. By William R. Williams, D.D. New York: Oakley, Mason & Co., 1870, in-12, pp. XXVII—462.

1145. — Dr. and Mrs. Mason's Land Leases in Toungoo by Mrs. Eleanor Mason. «Whittam» Press, — Rangoon 1874, in-8, pp. 13—10—10.
Sur la couv. ext. Land Leases in 1873. Toungoo British Burma. Mrs Mason's d'Oyly School Place. By Mrs Eleanor Mason. — Whittam Press, — Rangoon 1874.

1146. — Last Days of the Rev. Francis Mason, D.D. By Mrs. Eleanor Mason. «Whittam» Press, — Rangoon 1874, br. in-8, pp. 2—2—61.

Wade, *Jonathan.*

1147. — *Maung San Lòn. — Sketch of the Life of Rev. Jonathan Wade, D.D. (In Sgau-Karen.) Rangoon, F. D. Phinney, 1899, pp. 57.

XI. — Sciences et Arts.

Sciences morales et philosophiques.

Education.

1148. — Vernacular Education in British Burmah. (*Siam Repository*, Jan. 1870, Vol. 2, art. 66, pp. 138—140.)

Extrait du *Rangoon Times*.

1149. — A Glance at Education in British Burma. By H. A. (*The Phoenix*, III, N° 31, January, 1873, pp. 112—113).

1150. — Burmese Girl's Boarding-School. Maulmain. (*Siam Repository*, Vol. 6, Oct. 1874, pp. 565—566).

Extrait de *«the Helping Hand»*.

1151. — Burma. Schools. (*Siam Repository*, Vol. 6, April 1874, art. 52, pp. 211—212).

1152. — Minute by Mr. J. Jardine, Bo. C. S. Judicial Commissioner of British Burma, on the necessity of incorporating the Educational Syndicate, British Burma, by an Act of the Governor-General in Council. Dated the 13th March 1884. — Rangoon: printed at the Government Press. br. in-8, pp. 11.

1153. — 'Education Department Series. — Burmese Reader No. 1. Printed at the Hanthawaddy Press, 1887, in-16, pp. 64.

La seconde partie avait paru en 1886.

1154. — 'Reports on Public Instruction in Lower Burma for the years 1888—89 and 1889—90. Rangoon, 1889—90, in-folio.

1155. — An Episode in Burmese History. (Being a Contribution to the History of Indigenous Oriental Education. By P. Hordern, Late Director of Public Instruction in Burma). (*Imp. & As. Quart. Rev.*, N. S., IV, 1892, pp. 29—42).

1156. — 'Educational Code, Burma, 5th Edition. A guide to Civil Officers, Municipal Committees, Managers of Government and Aided Schools and others interested in Education in the Province of Burma. Compiled by the Director of Public Instruction, Burma. gr. in-8.

En anglais et en birman.

1157. — Education Department, Burma. Elementary Science Text Books Series. Prepared by the Text Book Committee No. III, Standard V. Adapted from Murchè's Science Readers. London: Macmillan. Rangoon: The American Baptist Mission Press, 1898, br. in-8.

En birman.

1158. — The Educational Problems of Burma. By H. C. Richards. (*Calcutta Review*, Jan. 1903, pp. 1—5.)

Sciences Mathématiques.

1159. — Lessons in Arithmetic. Bassein, 1866, in-8.
En birman.

1160. — Abridgment of Arithmetic. Bassein, 1867. br. in-8.
En birman.

1161. — The approaching Eclipse of the Sun. By Editor. (*Nature*, XI, 1874—75, pp. 201—3).

1162. — Notes on the Burmese System of Arithmetic. By Major R. C. Temple. (*Ind. Antiq.*, XX, 1891, pp. 53—69.)

Sciences Médicales.

1163. — A Medical School in Burmah. (*Siam Repository*, Vol. 5, Oct. 1873, pp. 459—460).
Extrait du *Rangoon Times*.

1164. — La Medecina in Birmania. Por Dott. Barbieri de Introini. (*Geografia per tutti*, I, 1891, pp. 67—69).

1165. — [Leprosy in Burmah]. By E. H. Parker. (*China Review*, XX, No. 5, pp. 330—1).

1166. — Der Aussatz in Birma. (*Oest. Monats. f. d. Orient*, 1896, pp. 23—6.)
Voir Wehinger, N°. 1086.

Economie rurale.

1167. — °D. Brandis. — Report on the Teak Forests of Pegu, 1856. London, 1860, in-fol.

— — Report... Teak Forests in Pegu, 1860—1. [Calcutta], 1862, in-8.

— — Progress Report of Forest Administration in British Burmah. [Calcutta], 1863, in-8.

— — Progress Report... Forests... Tenasserim Martaban Provinces, 1858—9 and 1859—60. Calcutta, 1861, in-8.

— — List... of some of the Woods of British Burmah... Rangoon, 1862, in-4.

1168. — H. Leeds. Progress Report... Forest Adm. in British Burmah. [Calcutta], 1864, in-8.

— — Progress Report... British Burmah, 1863—4. Calcutta, 1865, in-fol.

— — Id. 1864—65. Calcutta, 1865, in-fol.

— — Id. 1865—66. Calcutta, 1867, in-fol.

— — Id. 1866—67. Calcutta, 1868, in-fol.

— W. J. Seaton. Progress Report, Forest Adm. British Burmah 1867—68. Calcutta, 1870, in-fol.

— — Id. 1868—69 and 1869—70. Calcutta, 1870, in-fol.

— B. Ribbentrop. Report, Forest Adm. British Burma, 1875—76. Rangoon, 1876, in-fol.

— — 1876—77. Rangoon, 1877, in-fol.

— W. J. Seaton & B. Ribbentrop. Id. 1877—78. Rangoon, 1878, in-fol.

1169. —· *W. Schlich. Report... Pyinkadoh Forests of Arakan. Rangoon, 1873, in-4.
On the Ironwood of Burmah (*Xylia dolabriformis*, Benth.).

1170. — *Report on Forest Administration of Burma. Resolution of the Government of Burma on the Forest Administration of Burma with a review of the various Circle Reports and accompanying statements, subjoined in detail. Compiled by the Government of Burma.
For the years 1598—99, 1899—1900, 1900—1901.

1171. — Extracts from P. G. India. — The Forests of Burmah. (*Siam Repository*, Jan. 1870, Vol. 2, Art. 9, p. 27).

1172. — *S. Kurz. — Preliminary Report on the Forest and other Vegetation of Pegu. Calcutta, 1875, in-fol.

1173. — Etude sur la végétation, l'administration et les produits des forêts de la Birmanie anglaise. (*Excursions et Reconnaissances*, N° 15, 1883, pp. 491—579).
Rapport de M. Kurz.

1174. — Indian Building Timber. By R. Benson. (*Nature*, XVIII, 1878, p. 569).
Pyenkadoo, genre de bois, *nan-ma*, vient de Birmanie.

1175. — Cochinchine française — Étude sur la végétation, l'administration et les produits des Forêts de la Birmanie anglaise par M. Harmand. — Saigon, Imprimerie du Gouvernement, 1883, in-8, pp. 91.

1176. — *For the Pyu-Kun Working Circle of the Toungoo Forest Division to be known as Pyu-Chaungand and Pyu-Kun Reserves. Published 1902. Compiled by the Conservator of Forests, Tenasserim Circle, Burma. in-fol.

1177. — Les forêts de la haute Birmanie. Par M. Hardy (Montpellier). (*La Géographie*, 15 nov. 1902, p. 334).
Upper Burmah Gazetteer.

1178. — Le foreste dell' alta Birmania. (*Soc. Geog. Ital., Boll.*, Gennaio 1903, pp. 54—55.)
D'après *La Géographie*, nov. 1902.

1179. — La culture du riz en Birmania. Par C. G. (*Ann. de l'Ext. Orient*, 1882—1883, V, pp. 289—298).
C. G. = Ch. Grémiaux.

1180. — Le riz dans la Birmanie anglaise. (*Ibid.*, 1885—6, VIII, pp. 254—5).
D'après une brochure de L. Vossion intitulée: Le marché du riz à Rangoon et dans la Birmanie anglaise en 1883—84.

1181. — Le Riz noir de Birmanie. (*Bull. Soc. Accl.*, 1893, 1ᵉʳ Sem., p. 190).

1182. — La production et le commerce du riz en Birmanie. (*Rev. coloniale*, II, pp. 231—243.)
Rangoon, 28 sept. 1895.

1183. — Notice sur la culture du ver à soie et la production de la soie en Birmanie. Par L. Vossion Ancien Consul de France à Rangoon. Paris, Challamel aîné, 1893, br. in-8, pp. 8.

1184. — *Memorandum on Crop-Measurement Statistics in Burma. By the Director of the Department of Land Records and Agriculture, Burma. in-fol. Collected during the years 1898—1899, 1899—1900.

1185. — Reports on the Department of Land Records and Agriculture, Burma, for the years 1888—89 and 1889—90. Rangoon, 1889—90, in-folio. Maps.

1186. — *Report on the Department of Land Records and Agriculture, Burma. Compiled by the Director, Department of Land Records and Agriculture. in-fol. For the years 1899—1900, 1900—1901.

Arts et Industries.

1187. — On the Manufacture of the Sylhet Lime. (*Gleanings in Science*, 1830, II, Calcutta, 1830, pp. 64—3.)

1188. — Pernambuco Cotton in Ava. [Letter from Major Burney] (*Ibid.*, 1831, III, Calcutta, pp. 334—5.)

1189. — Some Account of the Lacquered or Japanned Ware of Ava. By Major H. Burney, Resident at the Burmese Court. (*Journ. As. Soc. of Bengal*, I, May 1832, pp. 169—182).

1190. — *Madras and Burmese Art-Ware, permanent Photographs of 50 *plates of various objects of Eastern Art*. London, Autotype Co., 1886, oblong folio. Only a small edition has been printed for the India Office.

1191. — *Birmanisches Kunstgewerbe. (*Globus*, LXIII, pp. 270—3).

1192. — Monograph on the Brass and Copper Wares of Burma, by Harry L. Tilly. — Rangoon: Printed by the Supdt., Govt. Printing, Burma. April 1894, br. in-8, pp. 12.

1193. — Monograph of the Pottery and Glassware of Burma, 1894—95, by Taw Sein-ko, M. R. A. S., F. A. I., Govt. Translator and Hony. Archaeological Officer, Burma. — Rangoon: Printed by the Supdt., Govt. Printing, Burma. Sept. 1895. [Price,—Re.0—8—0.] br. in-8, 1 f. n. ch. p. l. tab., pp. 13 + 11 pl.

1194. — Account of Dyes and Dyeing in Burma. — Rangoon: Printed by the Supdt., Govt. Printing, Burma. May 1896. [Price,—Re.0.6.0.]. br. in-8, pp. 17 + pp. IV et 3 pl.
Signé: J. D. Fraser.

1195. — Note on Dyes and Dyeing in the Southern Shan States. — Rangoon: Printed by the Supdt., Govt. Printing, Burma. July 1896. [Price,—Re.0—2—0.] br. in-8, pp. 8.
Signé: H. G. A. Leveson, Assistant Superintendent, Southern Shan States.

1196. — Note on the Dyes and Process of Dyeing in Karenni. — Rangoon: Printed by the Supdt., Govt. Printing, Burma. July 1896. [Price,—Re.0—2—0.]. Br. in-8, pp. 7.

> Daté: Loikaw: The 28th April 1896; et signé: F. H. Giles, Assistant Political Officer, Karenni.

1197. — *Haraprasād Çāstri. — Burmese inscribed Pottery. (*Proceed. As. Soc. Bengal*, 1897, pp. 164 et seq.).

1198. — *Monograph on Ivory-Carving in Burma. By H. S. Pratt, Esq., I. C. S. 1901, gr. in-8.

1199. — *Monograph on Silk in Burma with lithoplates. By J. P. Hardiman, I. C. S. 1901, gr. in-8.

1200. — *Glass Mosaics of Burmah with Photographs. By Harry C. Tilly. Rangoon, 1901, in-fol., pp. 12 + 13 photog.

XII. — Langue.

Etudes Comparées.

1201. — On the Languages and Literature of the Indo-Chinese Nations. By J. Leyden, M.D. (*Miscel. Papers relat. to Indo-China*, Lond., Trübner, 1886, I, pp. 84—171.)

> From the *Asiatic Researches*, X, 1808, pp. 158—289.

1202. — A Comparative Vocabulary of the Barma, Maláyu and Thái Languages. Serampore: Printed at the Mission Press. 1810, in-8, pp. LV—II—239.

> By J. Leyden.

1203. — *De l'influence de l'écriture sur le language.... suivi de grammaire Barmane et Malaie, etc., par A. A. E. Schleiermacher. Darmstadt, 1835. In-8.

1204. — Comparison of Indo-Chinese Languages, by the Rev. N. Brown, American Missionary stationed at Sadiyá at the north-eastern extremity of Assám. (*Jour. As. Soc. Bengal*, VI, Dec. 1837, pp. 1023—1038).

1205. — Remarks on «a Comparison of Indo-Chinese Languages», &c. By the Rev. W. Morton. (*Ibid.*, VII, Jan. 1838, pp. 56—64).

1206. — Comparison of Asiatic Languages. (*Ibid.*, VII, Aug. 1838, pp. 707—10).

1207. — Remarks on the Indo-Chinese Alphabets. By Dr. A. Bastian. (*Journ. Roy. As. Soc.*, N. S., Vol. III, MDCCCLXVIII, Art. II, pp. 65—80).

1208. — Sprachvergleichende Studien mit besonderer berücksichtigung der Indochinesischen Sprachen von Dr. Adolf Bastian. Leipzig: F. A. Brockhaus, in-8, pp. XXXVIII + 1 f. n. ch. + pp. 344.

1209. — Burmese Transliteration. By H. L. St. Barbe, Esq. Resident at Mandelay. (*Journ. R. As Soc.*, N. S., Vol. X, Part II, Art. X, April, 1878, pp. 228—33).

1210. — On Tibeto-Burman Languages. By Capt. C. J. F. S. Forbes, of the Burmese Civil Commission. (*Ibid.*, N. S. Vol. X. Part II, art. IX, April, 1878, pp. 210—227.)

1211. — Comparative Grammar of the Languages of further India: A Fragment. And other essays. The literary remains of the late Capt. C. J. F. S. Forbes, of the British Burma Commission, Author of «British Burma and its people; Sketches of Native Manners, Customs and Religion». London: W. H. Allen & Co. 1881, in-8, pp. VIII—192.

1212. — On the Relations of the Indo-Chinese and Inter-Oceanic Races and Languages. By A. H. Keane, Esq., M. A. I. (*Journ. Anthrop. Inst. of Great Britain and Ireland*, Vol. IX, 1880—1881, pp. 254—289).

1213. — On the Relations of the Indo-Chinese and Inter-Oceanic Races and Languages. By A. H. Keane. br. in-8, pp. 36.

> Reprinted from the *Journal of the Anthropological Institute*, Feb. 1880.

1214. — Indo-Chinese Languages. By Prof. Em. Forchhammer. (*Ind. Antiq.*, XI, 1882, pp. 177—189.)

1215. — Indo-Chinese Languages. By Prof. Em. Forchhammer [Reprinted from the «Indian Antiquary»]. br. in-4, pp. 13.

1216. — Notes on the Languages and Dialects spoken in British Burma. — Rangoon: Printed at the Government Press, 1884, br. in-8, pp. 20.

> Lettres du Dr. Forchhammer, du Dr. Bennett, de Mr. P. H. Martyr, et note de Mr G. D. Burgess.

1217. — Ueber Herkunft und Sprache der transgangetischen Völker. — Festrede zur Vorfeier des Allerhöchsten Geburts- und Namensfestes Seiner Majestät des Königs Ludwig II. gehalten in der öffentlichen Sitzung der k. Akademie der Wissenschaften zu München am 25. Juli 1881 von Ernst Kuhn a. o. Mitglied der philos.-philol. Classe. München 1883. Im Verlage der k. b. Akademie. Pièce in-4, pp. 22.

1218. — E. Kuhn. — Beiträge zur Sprachenkunde Hinterindiens. (*Sitz. philos.-philol. Cl. k. Bayer. Ak. Wiss.*, 1889, pp. 189—236.)

1219. — Corruptions of English in Burma. By R. C. Temple. (*Ind. Antiq.*, XX, 1891, p. 89.)

1220. — Der Einfluss des Arischen Indiens auf die Nachbarländer im Süden und Osten — Rede beim Antritt des Rectorats der Ludwig-Maximilians-Universität gehalten am 21. November 1903 von Dr. Ernst Kuhn — München 1903, C. Wolf & Sohn, in-4, pp. 28.

1221. — A Comparison of the Japanese and Burmese Languages. By Percival Lowell. (*Trans. As. Soc. Japan*, XIX, 1891, pp. 583—597.)

1222. — Touching Burmese, Japanese, Chinese, and Korean. — By E. H. Parker. (*Ibid.*, XXI, Nov. 1893, pp. 136—151.)

1223. — Les langues monosyllabiques. Par C. de Harlez. (*Actes du Cong. Orient. Genève*, V° Sect., pp. 67—88).

> Le Birman, p. 88.

1224. — Sanskrit Words in the Burmese Language. By Taw Sein-ko. (*Ind. Antiq.*, XXI, pp. 94—5).

1225. — Sanskrit words in the Burmese Language. By Bernard Houghton. (*Ibid.*, XXII, 1893, pp. 24—7).

1226. — Sanskrit words in Burmese. By R. C. Temple. (*Ibid.*, XXI, 1892, pp. 193—4).

1227. — Sanskrit Words in the Burmese Language. By Taw Sein-ko. (*Ibid.*, XXII, 1893, pp. 162—5).

Rép. à Houghton, *Ibid.*, p. 24.

— Sanskrit Words in the Burmese Language. A Rejoinder. By Bernard Houghton. (*Ibid.*, XXIII, 1894. pp. 165—7).

1228. — Sanskrit Words in the Burmese Language. By R. C. Temple. (*Ibid.*, XXIII, 1894, p. 168).

1229. — Contributions towards the History of Anglo-Burmese Words. By R. C. T. (*Journal Roy. Asiatic Society*, Oct. 1893, pp. 878—885; January 1894, pp. 152—164).

1230. — Early Indo-Chinese Influence in the Malay Peninsula. As Illustrated by some of the Dialects of the Aboriginal Tribes. By C. Otto Blagden. (*Jour. Straits Br. R. As. Soc.*, N°. 27, Oct. 1894, pp. 21—56).

1231. — Outlines of Tibeto-Burman Linguistic Palaeontology. By Bernard Houghton, B. A., M. R. A. S. (*Journ. R. A. S.*, Jan. 1896, pp. 23—55).

1232. — Eine indochinesische Causativ-denominativ-bildung und ihr Zusammenhang mit den Tonaccenten. — Ein Beitrag zur vergleichenden Grammatik der indochinesischen .Sprachen, insonderheit des Tibetischen, Barmanischen und Chinesischen, vom Dr. August Conrady. Leipzig, Otto Harrassöwitz, 1896, pp. XIX—208.

Notices: *Jour. R. As. Soc.*, Jan. 1897, pp. 144—5. — *Toung Pao*, VIII, Mars 1897, pp. 117—8, par G. Schlegel.

1233. — 'R. C. Temple. — Some Burmese expressions at Port Blair. (*Indian Antiquary*, XXX, p. 551).

1234. — Linguistic Survey of India. — Vol. V. Indo-Aryan Family. Eastern Group. Part I. Specimens of the Bengali and Assamese Languages. Compiled and edited by G. A. Grierson, C. I. E., Ph. D., etc. Calcutta: Office of the Superintendent, Government Printing, India. 1903, gr. in-4, pp. IV—446.

Standard List of Words and Sentences in Assamese and Mayãng, pp. 437—446.

1235. — The Languages of India, and the Census of 1901. By G. A. Grierson. (*Imp. & Asiat. Quart Rev.*, April 1904, pp. 267—286).

Langue Birmane.

Lexicographie: Dictionnaires.

1236. — An English and Burman Vocabulary, preceded by a Concise Grammar, in which the Burman Definitions and Words are accompanied with a Pronunciation in the English Character; designed to extend the Colloquial Use of the Burman Language. — By G. H. Hough, of Rangoon. Serampore: 1825, in-8 oblong, pp. 37 + 424.

1237. — *G. H. Hough. — English and Burmese Vocabulary. Maulmain, 1852, in-12.

1238. — An Anglo-Burmese Dictionary, Part I. Cconsisting of Monosyllables. By the Rev. G. H. Hough, Superintendent of Government Schools, Tenasserim Provinces. — Published for the use of Schools, Under the Sanction of the local committee of public instruction. Maulmain: printed at the American mission press. 1845, 2 ff. n. c. p. l. tit. et la préf. + pp. 147.

> Les pp. 137—147 comprennant *Short sentences for reading*.

— Part II — Dis-syllables, pp. 363.

— Part III — Three Syllables, pp. 346.

1239. — An Anglo Burmese Dictionary of the monosyllabic words in the english language. — By G. H. Hough, Head Master of the Government School, Maulmain: a second edition, with many corrections and improvements. Rangoon: Printed and published by Thos. S. Ranney. 1861, in-8, pp. 177 + 1 f. d'errata.

1240. — A Dictionary of the Burman Language, with Explanations in English. — Compiled from the Manuscripts of A. Judson, D. D. and of other missionaries in Burmah. — Profits devoted to the support of the Burman Mission. — Calcutta: Printed at the Baptist Mission Press, Circular Road; and sold by Messrs. W. Thacker and Co. St. Andrew's library, Calcutta; and by the American Missionaries in Burmah. 1826, in-8, pp. IV pour la préf. sig. J. Wade + 4 ff. chiffrés pp. 9 à 15 + pp. 411.

1241. — *A. Judson. — English-Burmese Dictionary. Maulmain, 1849, in-4, pp. 589.

1242. — A Dictionary, English and Burmese. By A. Judson. Second edition. Rangoon: American Baptist Mission Press, C. Bennett. 1866, in-8, pp. IV—968.

1243. — English and Burmese Dictionary. By A. Judson. Third edition. Rangoon. W. H. Sloan: American Mission Press. 1877, in-8, pp. 862.

> On lit dans la préf. signée C. B., Rangoon, Aug. 1877: «The first edition of the English and Burmese Dictionary was published in 1849. A second edition was printed in 1866, being a copy of the first, only the form was changed from a quarto to an octavo, as more handy for use in Schools, where the demand was considerable, and the edition exhausted.
> «The present work has, in addition to all of the above, as left by Mr. Judson, more than five hundred additional definitions that are Mr. Judson's, but not in the former editions of his Dictionary. There are also a few additional words and definitions, prepared by the Rev. E. O. Stevens, and some few by Dr. Mason; all of these words are marked with an s, or an m, after the definition, to show the source whence they came».

1244. — English and Burmese Dictionary. — By A. Judson. — Fourth edition. — Rangoon: American Baptist Mission Press, E. B. Roach, Supt. 1894, in-8, 3 ff. n. ch. + pp. 930.

1245. — *Judson's English and Burmese Dictionary. Edited by Miss Phinney. Fifth Edition. Rangoon, 1901, gr. in-8, p. 928.

1246. — Judson's English and Burmese Dictionary, abridged. First edition. Rangoon: W. H. Sloan: American mission press. 1877, pet. in-8, 2 ff. prél. n. c. p. l. tit. et l. préf. signée C. B. + pp. 544.

1247. — Judson's English and Burmese Dictionary, abridged. Second edition. — Rangoon: American Baptist Mission Press. F. D. Phinney, Supt. 1889. in-8, pp. v—544.
— Third Edition. Rangoon .... 1891, in-8, pp. 544.

1248. — Judson's English and Burmese Dictionary, Abridged. Fourth edition. — Rangoon: American Baptist Mission Press, E. B. Roach, Supt. 1893, pet. in-8, pp. IV + 1 f. n. ch. + pp. 544.

1249. — A Dictionary, Burmese and English. By A. Judson. Maulmain: American Mission Press, Thos. S. Ranney, 1852, in-8, pp. VII—780.
> Ed. orig. — La préf. est signée par l'*editor*, E. A. Stevens.

1250. — A Dictionary Burmese and English, by A. Judson. Rangoon: American Baptist Mission Press, F. D. Phinney, Supt. 1883, in-8, pp. VIII—782 + 1 f. n. c. p. l. corrigenda.
> La préf. de cette 2° éd. est signée par Edward O. Stevens, (Prome, Aug. 1883) fils du Rev. E. A. Stevens.

1251. — Judson's Burmese-English Dictionary. — Revised and enlarged by Robert C. Stevenson, Burma Commission. — Rangoon: Printed by the Superintendent, Government Printing Burma. — 1893, in-8, pp. VII—1188—6.
> Ces dernières pages contiennent: Burmese Proverbs, Aphorisms and quaint Sayings. .

1252. — The New Burmese Dictionary. By R. F. St. Andrew St. John. (*Journ. Roy. As. Soc.*, July 1894, pp. 556—8).

1253. — Burmese Pocket Dictionary compiled from Dr. Judson's Dictionaries. — English and Burmese, By F. D. Phinney, M.A. — Burmese and English, By Rev. F. H. Eveleth. — With an abridgement of Dr. Judson's Burmese Grammar. — Rangoon: American Baptist Mission Press, F. D. Phinney, Supt. 1887. haut in-12, 2 ff. prél. n. c. + pp. 382.
> On lit au commencement de la préface:
> «The first Edition of Dr. Judson's English and Burmese Dictionary was published in 1849, and was soon followed by two editions of an abridgement by G H. Hough, called «An English and Burmese Vocabulary», and giving an Anglicized pronunciation with the Burmese definitions. This was in turn followed in 1858 by «The Pocket Companion» by T. S. Ranney, the vocabulary being enlarged about two-fifths, with the Anglicized pronunciation altered to a different system. In 1876 appeared «A Practical Method with the Burmese Language», by Rev. W. H. Sloan, M.A., in which, as the compiler says in his preface, the vocabulary portion is «substantially Mr. Ranney's». The Anglicized spellings are, however, again entirely altered».

1254. — A Dictionary, English and Burmese. — By Charles Lane, Esq., F.A.S. for many years a Resident of Ava. The whole of the Burmese portion carefully revised by His Highness the Prince of Mekhara, uncle to the then reigning king of Burmah. Calcutta: Published by Ostell and Lepage, british library, Tank Square. 1841, in-4, 3 ff. n. c. p. l. tit., etc. + pp. 468 à 2 col.

1255. — 'C. Bennett. — Vocabulary and Phrase Book, in English and Burmese. Maulmain, 1857, in-12.

1256. — *Rev. C. Bennett. Vocabulary and Phrase Book in English and Burmese. Rangoon, 1866, in-8.

1257. — Vocabulary and Phrase Book in English and Burmese: by Rev. C. Bennett. Third edition, Revised by M. H. Eveleth. — Rangoon: American Baptist Mission Press. F. D. Phinney, supt. 1886, in-8, 2 ff. n. ch. p. l. tit. et l. tab. + pp. 155 + 1 f. n. ch.

    Pub. à Rs. 1—8.

1258. — *Jamál Abu. — Burmese and Gujaráti Vocabulary, termed as «Myama Saga Arthávali» in Gujaráti Characters. Surat, 1892. In-8, pp. 53.

1259. — A Vocabulary English and Peguan, to which are added a few pages of geographical names: compiled by Rev. Edward O. Stevens, M.A. — Rangoon: American Baptist Mission Press, F. D. Phinney. Supt. 1896, in-8, pp. VII—140.

    La préface est datée de «Moulmein, September 1896». — Les «geographical names» occupent les pp. 131—139. — Les «corrigenda» la dernière page.

Manuels de Conversation.

1260. — Technical Dialogues in English and Roman Burmese for The Use of Public Works Department Students and Others connected with Engineering, Arranged and compiled by J. Watson, Shwaygyin Division, Public Works Department, Translated by A. G. Mackertoom, Head Master, Shwagyin, Government School. Rangoon. Printed at the Albion Press, 1883, in-8, pp. 43 + 3 ff. prél.

1261. — Technical Dialogues in English and Burmese With the Burmese text carefully printed in the Roman character for The Use of Public Works Department Students and others in Birma connected with Engineering compiled by J. Watson Shwe-gyin Division, P. W. D. Translated by A. G. Mackertoom, Head Master, Shwe-gyin Government School. — Second Edition — Rangoon: Myles Standish & Co., 1885. in-16, 3 ff. n. ch. p. l. t. etc., + pp. 76.

Grammaires.

1262. — *A Grammar of the Burman Language, to which is added a list of the simple roots from which the language is derived, by F. Carey. Serampore, Mission Press, 1814, in-8.

    Cat. Langlès, 1049 bis.

1263. — Grammatical Notices of the Burmese language: by A. Judson. Maulmain: American Baptist mission press. 1842, in-8, pp. 76.

1264. — A Grammar of the Burmese Language, By Rev. A. Judson, D. D. — Rangoon: American Baptist Mission Press. F. D. Phinney, Supt. 1888, in-8, pp. 61.

1265. — Grammaire birmane. Par A. Judson, traduite de l'anglais, et augmen-
tée de quelques exemples, et de la prononciation figurée des mots birmans.
Par Louis Vossion, Membre de la Société d'ethnographie de Paris et de la
Société de Géographie de Masseille [sic]. Rangoon, Imprimerie de la Mission
Américaine 1878, in-8, pp. 76 + 2 ff. prél. p. le tit. et la préf.

   Tiré à 200 exemplaires numérotés.
   Notice: *Ann. de l'Est. Orient*, II, pp. 121—2.

1266. — Grammaire franco-birmane d'après A. Judson augmentée d'un grand
nombre d'exemples inédits, d'un appendice relatif aux livres sacrés et à la
littérature des Birmans et de la prononciation en français de tous les mots
birmans qui paraissent dans le texte par Louis Vossion, ancien consul de
France à Rangoon. Précédée d'une préface par Léon Feer, conservateur des
manuscrits orientaux à la Bibliothèque nationale. Ornée d'un portrait d'Adoniram Judson. Paris, Imprimerie nationale —, Ernest Leroux, éditeur, —
MDCCCLXXXIX. pet. in-8, pp. xx—111 + 1 f. n. c.

1267. — *The Oxford Oriental Series*. A Burmese Reader being an easy In-
troduction to the written Language and Companion to Judson's Grammar
For the Use of Civil Service Students and others who wish to acquire the
Language quickly and thoroughly by R. F. St. Andrew St. John, Hon. M. A.
Member of the Royal Asiatic Society, Teacher of Burmese in the University
of Oxford and University College, London and Late Deputy Commissioner in
Burma. Oxford, at the Clarendon Press, 1894, in-8, pp. xxxii, 4 pl. de texte,
pp. 256, 10s. 6d.

   Notices: *Journ. Roy. As. Soc.*, April 1894, pp. 409—413. Par B. H. — *Athenaeum*,
   24 Feb. 1894, p. 243. — *Bul. Soc. Ethnog.*, XXXVI, pp. 202 et seq.

1268. — A Grammar of the language of Burmah, by Thomas Latter, Lieute-
nant, Bengal Army. Calcutta: sold by Messrs. Thacker and Co. and Messrs.
Ostell, Lepage and Co. London: Messrs. Smith, Elder and Co. and Ostell,
Lepage and Co., in-4, pp. lvi—203 [1845].

1269. — An Anglo-Burmese Grammatical Reader for Beginners, containing Words
of one syllable. Revised. Rangoon: American Baptist Mission Press, F. D.
Phinney, Supt. 1889, pet. in-8, pp. 79.

1270. — Burmese Grammar and Grammatical Analysis. By A. W. Lonsdale
Education Department, Burma. Rangoon, British Burma Press — 1899,
pet. in-8, pp. xi—461, 1 tableau.

1271. — 'Sam Chin Htin. — The Junior Burmese Grammar. Rangoon, British
Burma Press, 1899, pp. 118.

Chrestomathies. Manuels.

1272. — Anglo-Burmese Hand-book, or Guide to a practical knowledge of the
Burmese language, compiled by Dormer Augustus Chase, Lieut. 64th Regiment
Bengal N. 1. and officiating Assistant Commissioner T. P. Maulmain: American
Mission Press, Thos. S. Ranney. 1852, in-12 obl., pp. xii—142—ii.

1273. — *Anglo-Burmese Hand-book... by Dorner Augustus Chase... Revised by F. D. Phinney. Rangoon, 1890, in-8, pp. 209.

1274. — Burmese Spelling Book. Bassein: St. Peter's Institute Press. 1875. in-8.
En Birman.

1275. — A Practical Method with the Burmese Language, by W. H. Sloan, M.A. — Copyrighted. — Rangoon: American Mission Press. C. Bennett. 1876, in-8, pp. 232.

1276. — *A Practical Method with the Burmese Language, by W. H. Sloan... Second Edition, revised. Rangoon, 1887, in-8, pp. 209.
Vocabulary, pp. 169. — Spelling Lessons and Phrases, pp. 40.

1277. — The Burmah School Series. — The first step in Burmese. Being an easy introduction to the language. — For the use of schools, and for private instruction. By A. W. Lonsdale. Rangoon: C. Bennett... American Press. 1878, in-8, pp. 66.

1278. — *A. W. Lonsdale. — Analysis of Burmese sentences, Book I and II. Rangoon, V. J. Mariano, 1898, pp. 80, 128.

1279. — Anglo-Vernacular Readers. Book I. Second Edition. Revised and Enlarged. Bassein, St. Peter's Institute Press, 1880, pet in-8, pp. 40.

— Anglo-Vernacular Readers. Book II. Rangoon: C. Bennett... American Mission Press. 1879, in-8, pp. 84.

— Anglo-Vernacular Readers. Book II. Second edition. — Revised. Rangoon: C. Bennett... American Mission Press. 1881, in-8, pp. 84.

— Anglo-Vernacular Readers. Book III. Rangoon: C. Bennett... American Mission Press. 1880, in-8, pp. 120.

— Anglo-Vernacular Readers. — Book VI. Bassein: P. P. Lucas, at St. Peter's Press. 1881, in-8, pp. III—232.

1280. — *Anglo-Burmese Primer. Bassein, 1882, in-8, pp. 33.
British Museum 13902. aaa. 23 (6).

1281. — Anglicized Colloquial Assistant, Based upon the principle of a «Sign for a Sound»; A trustworthy *Key* to the pronunciation of the Burman Language. By R. B. Hancock. Printed for the Publisher at the American Baptist Mission Press... Rangoon. F. D. Phinney Superintendent. pet. in-8, pp. 128—8, s. d.
A la fin: Rangoon, November 15, 1883.

1282. — Phonetic Transliteration; For the Writing of English Names in Burman Signs, and Burman Names in English Signs. By R B. Hancock. Printed at the American Baptist Mission Press, Rangoon, in-8, pp. 44 [1883].

1283. — A Hand-Book to Colloquial Burmese in the Roman Character. — By H. K. Gordon. — Second edition, revised and enlarged. Rangoon: Printed at the American Baptist Mission Press. F. D. Phinney, Supt. 1886, in-4, p. 63.

1284. — Companion to a Hand-Book to Colloquial Burmese in the Roman
Character, By H. K. Gordon. — In the Burmese character. — Rangoon:
American Baptist Mission Press. F. D. Phinney, Supt. 1886, in-12 carré, pp. 106.

1285. — Manual of Burmese; also of Pronunciation, Grammar, Money, Towns,
&c. For the use of Travellers, Students, Merchants, and Military. By Capt.
Chas. Slack, ... London: Simpkin, Marshall, & Co., 1888, pet. in-8, pp. 39, Carte.

1286. — Anglicised Colloquial Burmese. Or, How to speak the Language in
three months. By Lieut. F. A. L. Davidson, Royal Scots Fusiliers. London:
W. H. Allen & Co., 1889, pet. in-8, pp. VIII + 1 f. n. ch. + 103 + 1 f. n. ch. +
4 ff. pliés.

1287. — *Fourth Standard Burmese Reader. Edited by the Text-Book Committee. Rangoon, A. B. M. Press, 1891, in-16, pp. 148.

1288. — *J. G. Adam. The Griffin's Guide to Burmese. Rangoon, 1892, in-8.
British Museum 12906. df. 45.

1289. — *James Gray. — Burmese grammatical primer. Rangoon, Anglo-Burmese
Mission Press, 1894, in-8, pp. 41.

1290. — Elementary Hand-Book of the Burmese Language by Taw Sein-Ko,
M. R. A. S., ... Government Translator and Honorary Archaeological Officer,
Burma. Rangoon: Printed by the Superintendent, Government Printing,
Burma. 1898, gr. in-8, pp. II—VI—121.

1291. — *A. Raphael. — Short lessons in colloquial English and Burmese.
Bassein, St. Peter's Press, 1901, pp. 63.

Divers.

1292. — Alphabetum // Barmanorum // seu // Regni Avensis // — Editio // altera
emendatior // Romae M D CC LXXXVII // Typis Sac. Congregationis de Propaganda Fide // Praesidum Adprobatione // in-8, pp. XVI—64.
La première éd. est de Rome, 1776, in-8. — Cf. De Gubernatis, *Viaggiatori Italiani*,
1875, pp. 66—71.

1293. — Note on the Burmese language. By the Editor. (*The Phoenix*, III, n° 31,
January, 1873, pp. 118—119).

1294. — *S. M. Mackertich. Anglo-Burmese Letter Writer. Maulmain, 1881,
in-8, pp. 93.
British Museum 14302. h. 1.

1295. — The Anglo-Burmese Ninety-nine Stories being a Collection of Instructive
and Entertaining Tales from Chambers' and other Works. Compiled and
Translated by Stephen M. McKertich. Rangoon: Printed at the Hanthawaddy
Press. 1887. pet. in-8, pp. 191.

1296. — *Anglo-Vernacular Student's Speller. An aid to Burmese Spelling.
Rangoon, 1892, in-8, pp. 174.
B. M. 12907. bb. 45.

1297. — Ratanasingha-Shwebo-Moutshobo-Kòngbaung. By R. C. Temple. (*Ind. Antiq.*, XXII, 1893, p. 28).

1298. — Moutshòbò. By Taw Sein-Ko. (*Ibid.*, XXII, 1893, p. 28).

1299. — Interchange of initial K and P in Burmese Place-Names. By R. C. Temple. (*Ibid.*, XXII, 1893, p. 326).

1300. — *Maung Maung. — Hints in the Burmese language. Part I. Rangoon, G. W. D'Vauz, 1894, in-8, pp. 204.

1301. — List of geographical names of which the Burmese orthography has been authorized by the Text-book Committee. Rangoon: Printed by the Supdt., Govt. Printing, Burma. Feby. 1895. [Price, — Re. 0—4—0] br. in-8, pp. 50.

1302. — List of Terms used in Arithmetic, Algebra and Geometry of which the Burmese Equivalents have been authorized by the Text-Book Committee. — Rangoon: Printed by the Supdt., Govt. Printing, Burma. June 1895. [Price, — Re. 0—4—0]. br. in-8, pp. 20.

.∗.

1303. — The New Testament of our Lord and Saviour Jesus Christ. 2d Burmese Edition. — 10.000. — Maulmein: American Baptist Mission Press. 1837, in-8.

1304. — *The Old Testament in Burmese. Translated by Dr. Judson. Maulmain, 1835. 3 vol. in-8.

1305. — Remarks on Passages in the Rev. Dr. Judson's Burmese Version of the Four Gospels. By the Rev. G. H. Hough. — Rangoon. Printed at the Pegu Press. Thos. S. Ranney, 1856, in-4, pp. III—19.

1306. — *Judson's Burmese Bible edited by J. N. Cushing. Rangoon, Phinney, 1900, pp. 40.

1307. — *J. A. Colbeck. — An explanation of the Apostles Creed. Transl. (in Burmese). London, Society Promot. Christian Knowledge, 1888. In-8.

1308. — *The Gospel by John (in Talaing). Translated by J. M. Haswell. Rangoon, F. D. Phinney, 1899, pp. 108.

.∗.

1309. — *Tables for the Transliteration of Burmese into English, with Lists showing the names in English and Burmese of the Divisions, Districts, Sub-divisions, Townships, and Circles of Burma; also of the Post Offices, Railway Stations, Police Offices, and other places of interest. Rangoon, 1896, pp. XVIII—202.
— Rangoon, 1898, in-8, pp. 202.
  B. M. 14302. k. 4 (2).

1310. — *Burmese Translation Book. English and Burmese on opposite columns. s. d., in-8, pp. 146.

1311. — *Memorandum on the Transliteration of Burmese Words into English, in-folio, s. d.

1312. — *The Leepeedeepeeká or Telegraph Code, for Upper Burma. Compiled by the Kyee Atwen Won Yaw Myoza Men Mengyee Menhla Maha Tseethoo, Minister of the Interior. Translated by Major A. R. McMahon. Rangoon: Secretariat Press. 1871.
  Notice: *The Phoenix*, III, n° 25, July, 1872, p. 20.

Pali.

1313. — Translation of an Inscription in the Pali and Burma Languages on a stone slab from Ramávati, (Ramree Island,) in Arracan, presented to the Asiatic Society by H. Walter, Esq. C. S. as explained by Ratna Paula. (*Jour. As. Soc. of Bengal*, III, May, 1834, pp. 209—215).

1314. — A Pali Grammar On the basis of Kachchayano... With Chrestomaty & Vocabulary. By Francis Mason, D. D. Member of the Royal Asiatic Society, and American Oriental Society. Toungoo: Institute Press, Printed by Sau Kada, 1868, in-8, 2 ff. n. c. p. l. tit. et les noms des souscrip. + pp. IV p. l. préf. + pp. IV p. l. tab. + pp. VIII p. l'int. + pp. 214.

1315. — The Pāli Text of the Ajjhatta-Jaya-Maṅgalaṁ with Vocabulary, Grammatical Notes, Translation, and Examination Questions. Edited by James Gray, Government School, Maulmain. — Maulmain, Advertiser Press, 1878, pet. in-8, pp. 35.

1316. — Pāli Primer. Adapted for Schools in Burma. By James Gray, Government School, Maulmain. Maulmain. — 1879, in-8, pp. 64.

1317. — Elements of Pali Grammar adapted for schools and private Study, by James Gray, author of The Translation of the Dhammapada, &c. — Published under the Patronage of the Education Department, British Burma. — Rangoon: printed at the American Baptist Mission Press, and sold by the Curator, Government Book Depot. — 1883, in-8, 3 ff. n. c. + pp. 126.

1318. — *Chanksaungdwé. — Six Pali Texts on Religion, with Burmese Translation. Rangoon, 1887, in-8.

1319. — *Kozaungdwé. — Nine Pali Texts on Religion, with Burmese Translation. Rangoon, 1887, in-8.

1320. — Pali Derivations in Burmese. By H. L. St. Barbe. (*Jour. As. Soc. Bengal*, Vol. 48, 1879, Pt. 1, pp. 253—257).

1321. — Temiyajātakaṁ. Translation. [By James Gray]. Calcutta: Printed at the Baptist Mission Press. 1900, in-8, pp. 43.

1322. — Report by Dr. E. Forchhammer, Professor of Pali, Rangoon High School for the year 1879—80. br. in-fol., pp. 8—xx.

    Les dernières pp. renferment la liste des mss. palis de la bibliothèque de cette Ecole qui a pour origine la collection du prof. Childers.

1323. — *Tha Do Oung. — A Grammar of the Pāli Language. Akyab, Vols. I, II and III, 1900. Vol. IV, 1902, gr. in-8, pp. IV—40.

XIII. — Littérature.

Divers.

1324. — Specimen of the Burmese Drama, translated by J. Smith, Esq., communicated by C. A. Blundell, Esq. Commissioner, &c., Moulmein. (*Jour. As. Soc. Bengal*, VIII, July 1839, pp. 535—551).

1325. — Æsop's Fables Burmese Illustrated. in-8.

En Birman.

1326. — *Contes birmans, d'après le *Thoudamma Sari Dammazat*, par Loui Vossion, ancien consul à Rangoon. in-18.

Forme le vol. XXIV de la *Collection de Contes et de Chansons populaires*, publiée par Ernest Leroux.

1327. — Ancient Proverbs and Maxims From Burmese Sources; or, the Nîti Literature of Burma. By James Gray, ...London: Trübner & Co. 1886, in-8, pp. xii—179.

Fait partie de Trübner's *Oriental Series*.

1328. — *Sadaing Hmut U Ku, Okkalaba Pyazat. Two Parts. Burmese Drama. Rangoon, 1887, in-8.

1329. — *Sadaing Hmut U Ku, Tabin Shweti Pyazat. Burmese Drama. Rangoon, 1887, in-8.

1330. — *Saya Pe, Maung Pu Nyo Teiktin. Burmese Poetry. Rangoon, 1887, in-8.

1331. — *Saya Thin, Alaungdan Shwe Yòu Mia Pyazat. Burmese Drama. Rangoon, 1887, in-8, pp. 94.

1332. — *Saya Thin, Bandula and Malika Pyazat. Burmese Drama. Rangoon, 1887, in-8.

1333. — *Saya Thin, Law kadat Maung So and Kyankkathu Mè Mo Pyazat. Burmese Drama. Rangoon, 1887, in-8.

1334. — *Saya Thin, Maung Pu Nyo Gusothi Thigyin. Burmese Poetry. Rangoon, 1887, in-8.

1335. — *Saya Thin, Maung Thogi Pyazat. Burmese Drama. Rangoon, 1887, in-8.

1336. — *Saya Thin, Shweyyobyu Mulagè Pyazat. Burmese Drama. Rangoon, 1887, in-8.

1337. — *Saya Thin, Tasegale Maung Pe Ba Pyazat. Burmese Drama. 3rd Edition. Rangoon, 1887, in-8, pp. 100.

1338. — *Saya Thin, Thudamasari Miuthami Hawza. Metrical Version of the Life of Princess Thudamasari. Rangoon, 1887, in-8.

1339. — *Saya Thin, Wunthudan Pyazat. Burmese Drama. Rangoon, 1887, in-8, pp. 111.

1340. — *Saya Pye. — Lokapaññati. Rangoon, Maung O, 1888, in-8, pp. 100.

En birman. — Proverbes.

1341. — Counting-out Rhymes in Burma. By R. C. Temple. (*Ind. Antiq.*, XXIII, 1894, p. 84.)

1342. — A Burmese Love-Song. (*Ibid.*, XXIII, 1894, pp. 262—3.)

1343. — *A Legend of Old Burma. Mahaw the Wise. (*Calcutta Review*, CVII, pp. 294—306).

1344. — *The Arabian Nights translated into Burmese by Abdool Rahman. Rangoon, «Friend of Burma» Press, 1896, in-8, pp. 414.

Bibliographie.

1345. — Antonio de Leon Pinelo. Epitome de la Bibliotheca Oriental, y Occidental, nautica y geografica, de Don Antonio de Leon Pinelo... añadido y enmendado nuevamente, en que se contienen los escritores de las Indias Orientales, y occidentales, y reinos, convecinos China, Tartaria, Japon, Persia, Armenia, Etiopia, y otras partes. Madrid. En la officina de Francisco Martinez Abad, Año de 1737—38. 3 vols. folio.

1346. — Bibliotheca Orientalis. Manuel de bibliographie orientale. II. Par J. Th. Zenker, Dr. — Leipzig, Guillaume Engelmann. 1861. in-8.

   Littérature de l'Indo-Chine et de la Malaisie, pp. 483—497.

1347. — Trübner's Catalogue of Dictionaries and Grammars of the principal languages and dialects of the World. Second Edition considerably enlarged and revised, with an alphabetical index. A guide for students and booksellers. London, Trübner, 1882, in-8, pp. VIII—170.

XIV. — Moeurs et Coutumes.

Ouvrages divers.

1348. — On the Burmha Game of Chess: compared with the Indian, Chinese, and Persian Game of the same denomination. By the late Captain Hiram Cox. Communicated in a letter from him to J. H. Harington, Esq. (*As. Researches*, VII, 1801, pp. 486—511).

1349. — «Invenire». — The Indian Game of Chess; by Sir William Jones, President of the Asiatic Society of Bengal. And the Burmha Game of Chess compared with The Indian, Chinese, & Persian Games. By Captain Hiram Cox. (Reprinted from «Asiatick researches».) — Privately printed for the Aungervyle Society, Edinburgh. — 1883. in-8, pp. 30.

   Tiré à 150 exemplaires. — Fait partie de la seconde série des *Aungervyle Society Reprints*.

1350. — An Account of the Funeral Ceremonies of a Burman Priest. — Communicated By Wm. Carey, D.D. (*As. Researches*, XII, 1816, pp. 186—91).

1351. — 'Florence Layard. — Burma and the Burmese. (*Fortnightly Review*, 1887, July, pp. 152—155).

1352. — 'The Burman at Home. (*Cornhill Magazine*, février 1887).

1353. — Le carnaval en Birmanie. Par A. Certeux. (*Revue des Traditions populaires*, III, 1888, pp. 300—1).

   Extrait du *Journal des Voyages*, No. 558, 18 Mars 1888, p. 178; art. de Mahé de la Bourdonnais.

1354. — 'G. Th. Reichelt. — Volksfeste in Birma. (*Ausland*, LXIV, pp. 506—10).

1355. — Sette anni in Birmania (Note etniche e di costumi) Par Dr. Barbieri de Introini. (*Geografia per tutti*, I, 1891, pp. 81—84).

1356. — *T. Barberis. — In Birmania. (*Ibid.*, 1894, No. 6).

1357. — *Barbieri de Introini. — Brevi cenni sulla Birmania. (*Ist. Lomb. di sc. e lett., Rendc.* Ser. II, XXIV, 13, pp. 850—865).

1358. — Women and Worship in Burmah. By Violet Greville. (*Nineteenth Century*, XXXI, 1892, pp. 1001—1007).

1359. — *H. D. Keary. — Dacoity in Upper Burma. (*National Review*, London, July. [1890].

1360. — Burman Dacoity and Patriotism. By General Sir H. N. D. Prendergast, V.C., K.C.B. (*Imp. & As. Quart. Rev.*, N. S., V, 1893, pp. 271—280).

1361. — *H. C. Moore. — The Dacoits treasure, or in the days of Po Thaw: a story of adventure in Burma. Illustrated by Harold Piffurd. London, Addison, 1897, pp. 432. In-8.

1362. — In the Shadow of the Pagoda. Sketches of Burmese Life and Character. By E. D. Cuming. London: W. H. Allen & Co., ... 1893, in-8, 3 ff. n. ch. + pp. 362.

> La seconde partie du volume porte le titre: *Passages in the Life of a Dacoit.* Notice: *Asiat. Quart. Review*, II° Sér., VIII, 13, pp. 218 et seq.

1363. — *E. D. Cuming. — With the jungle folk: a sketch of Burmese Village Life. Illustr. by a Burmese Artist. London, Osgood, 1896, in-8, pp. 408.

> Notice: *Athenæum*, Dec. 19, p. 868.

1364. — Burmese Women. By H. Fielding. (*Blackwood's Mag.*, CLVII, 1895, May, pp. 776—788).

1365. — How the famine came to Burma. By H. Fielding. (*Ibid.*, CLXI, 1897, April, pp. 536—544).

1366. — On a famine-camp in Burmah. By H. Fielding. (*Macmillan's Mag.*, LXXVI, Aug. 1897, pp. 242—247).

> Myingyan, April 22nd, 1897.

1367. — Dedicated to the Young Folks of the Anglo-East Indian Community of Burma. A Song of the Famine By Mrs. Eleanor Mason. Rangoon — Printed at the «Albion» Press, Soolay Pagoda Road, No. 16, in-8, pp. 32 [1874].

1368. — *Paula Karsten. — Notes sur la vie birmane. (*A travers le monde*, 1898, pp. 409—412; 417—420).

1369. — *[Bericht über einen Vortrag von Hahn: Die Stellung der Frauen bei den Hindu und bei den Burmanen] (*Jahresbericht Gesellschaft für Erdkunde*, Köln, 1898—99, pp. 17—19).

1370. — *A Burmese Maid. By the Author of 'Reginald Vernon'. Rangoon, the Hanthawaddy Press.

1371. — *How Elephants are captured and trained in Burmah. By C. J. S. Makin (*ill.*) (*English Illustrated Mag.*, XXIII, June 1900, p. 273).

1372. — *Umes Chandra Nág. — Brahmadesa. Burma. Dacca, Published by the Author, 1900, pp. 23.

> Un court résumé de la Birmanie et de son peuple en vers bengali.

Folk-Lore, Légendes, etc.

1373. — Translated from the Burmese. I. The two Wild Dogs and the Tiger. (*Siam Repository*, April 1870, Vol. 2, p. 184).

1374. — Burmese Astrology. By R. F. St. Andrew St. John. (*The Phoenix*, III, N° 25, July, 1872, p. 19).

1375. — 'H. Ling Roth. — Notes on a Hkoung beht set. (*Journ. Anthrop. Institute of Great Brit.*, XXX, pp. 66. Illustrations.
　　　Talisman birman.

1376. — 'Some Burmese Superstitions. (*Chambers' Journal*, 24 March 1888, p. 189).

1877. — Folklore in Burma. By Taw Sein Ko. (*Ind. Antiq.*, XVIII, 1889, pp. 275—7; XIX, 1890, pp. 437—9: XXII, 1893, pp. 159—61).

1378. — Thwe-thank. By Taw Sein Ko. (*Ibid.*, XX, 1891, pp. 423—4).
　　　Thwe-thank in Burmese means 'one who has drunk blood'.

1379. — The Evil Eye. By Bernard Houghton. (*Ibid.*, XXII, 1893, p. 56).

1380. — An unlucky flaw-Burmese Superstition. By B. Houghton. (*Ibid.*, XXV, 1896, p. 112).

1381. — Notes on Burmese Folk-lore. By Bernard Houghton. (*Ibid.*, XXV, 1896, pp. 142—3).

1382. — Wishing Stones in Burma. By R. C. Temple. (*Ibid.*, XXII, 1893, p. 165).

1383. — The «Bloody Hand» at Mandalay — The Rise of a Myth. By R. C. Temple. (*Ibid.*, XXIX, 1900, p. 199).

1384. — 'R. C. Temple. — The «bloody hand» at Mandalay — the rise of a myth. (*Academy*, XLVIII, pp. 363 et seq.).

1385. — '«Mimosa» — Told on the Pagoda. Tales of Burmah. London, Unwin, 1895.
　　　Notices: *Athenæum*, Aug. 24, p. 256; *Folk-Lore*, VI, p. 287; *As. Quart. Review*, N. S., X, pp. 480 et seq.

1386. — 'H. Calthrop. — Burmese Tales and Sketches. N°. 1. Calcutta, Thacker, Spink & Co., 1895, in-8, pp. 54.

1387. — A legend of old Burma. Mahaw the Wise. (*Calcutta Review*, CVII, Oct. 1898, pp. 294—306).

Monnaies, Poids & Mesures.

1388. — A Short Treatise on Mensuration in English and Burmese. Part I. 1877. Bassein: St. Peter's Institute Press, in-8, pp. 40.
　　　Sur la couverture: An easy Anglo-Vernacular Practical Course of Land Measuring for use in Burma. Part I. 1877. Bassein: St. Peter's Institute Press.

1389. — A Short Treatise on Mensuration in English and Burmese. Part II. Second Edition. Bassein, St. Peter's Institute Press, 1879, in-8, pp. 49 + 1 f. n. ch.
　　　Sur la couverture extérieure: An easy Anglo-Vernacular practical Course of Land-measuring for use in Burma. Part II. Second Edition. — Bassein: P.P. Lucas at St. Peter's Institute Press. 1879.
　　　La première édition est de 1877.

1390. — A short Treatise on Mensuration in English and Burmese. Part III. Bassein: St. Peter's Institute Press, 1877, in-8, pp. 95.

    Une quatrième partie était en préparation, mais je ne l'ai pas vue.
    Sur la couverture: An easy Anglo-Vernacular Practical Course, etc. 1878.

1391. — Currency and Coinage among the Burmese. By R. C. Temple. Voir No. 932.

1392. — Derivation of Sateleer. By R. C. Temple. (*Ind. Antiq.*, XXVI, 1897, p. 280).

1393. — *Fritz Noetling. — Ueber birmanisches Maass und Gewicht. (*Zeit. für Ethnol.*, XXVIII, pp. 40—46).

XV. — Voyages.

Nicolò de' CONTI.

1394. — Deux Voyageurs dans l'Extrême-Orient au XVe et au XVIe siècles. Essai bibliographique Nicolò de' Conti — Lodovico de Varthema par Henri Cordier, Socio della R. Deputazione Veneta di Storia Patria. (*T'oung Pao*, X, No. 4, Oct. 1899, pp. 380—404).

    Tirage à part: E. J. Brill, Leide, 1899, in-8, pp. 25. — Cent ex. sur Papier Van Gelder.

Girolamo di SANTO STEFANO.

1395. — Lettera (Dans l'édition portugaise de *Marco Polo*, Lisbonne, Val. Fernandez, 1502).

    — Ramusio, I.
    — En hollandais; Amsterdam, Abraham Wolfgang, 1664 (*Markus Paulus Venetus*).

1396. — Account of the Journey of Hieronimo di Santo Stefano, a Genovese, addressed to Messer Giovan Jacobo Mainer. Translated by R. H. Major. (R. H. Major, *India in the Fifteenth Century*, 1857, pp. 10.)

    Cf. Amat di S. Filippo, pp. 206—9.

1397. — *Prospero Peragallo. Viaggio di Geronimo da Santo Stefano e di Geronimo Adorno in India nel 1494—99. (Testo portogh. e ital°). (*Bol. Soc. Geog. Ital.*, I, 1901, pp. 24—40.)

1398. — The Travels of Athanasius Nikitin, of Twer. Translated from the Russian, with Notes, by Count Wielhorsky, late Secretary of the Russian Legation at the Court of St. James's. (R. H. Major, *India in the Fifteenth Century*, 1857, pp. 32.)

Lodovico de VARTHEMA.

1399. — Deux Voyageurs dans l'Extrême-Orient au XVe et au XVIe siècles. Essai bibliographique Nicolò de' Conti — Lodovico de Varthema par Henri Cordier, Socio della R. Deputazione Veneta di Storia Patria. (*T'oung Pao*, X, No. 4, Oct. 1899, pp. 380—404.)

    Tirage à part: E. J. Brill, Leide, 1899, in-8, pp. 25. — Cent ex. sur Papier Van Gelder.

Fernão Mendes Pinto.

1400. — Peregrinacam de Fernam Mendez Pinto. Em qve da conta de mvytas e mvyto estranhas cousas que vio & ouuio no reyno da China, no da Tartaria, no do Sornau, que vulgarmente se chama Sião, no do Calaminhan, no de Pegù, no de Martanão, & em outros muytos reynos & senhorios das partes Orientais, de que nestas nossas do Occidente ha muyto pouca o nenhũa noticia. E tambem da conta de mvytos casos particulares que acontecerão assi a elle como a outras muytas pessoas. E no fim della trata breuemente de algũas cousas, & da morte do Santo Padre mestre Francisco Xauier, vnica luz & resplandor daquellas partes do Oriente, & Reytor nellas vniuersal da Companhia de Iesus. Escrita pelo mesmo Fernão Mendez Pinto. Dirigido à Catholica Real Magestade del Rey dom Felippe o III. deste nome nosso Senhor. Com licença do Santo Officio, Ordinario, & Paço. Em Lisboa. Por Pedro Crasbeeck. Anno 1614. A custa de Belchior de Faria Caualeyro da casa del Rey nosso Senhor, & seu Liureyro. Com priuilegio Real. Està taixado este liuro a 600 reis em papel... in-folio, 303 feuillets, sans le titre, priv. et déd. 2 feuillets au commenc., et la table, 5 feuillets à la fin.

Ouvrage fort rare dont Silva, Vol. II, pp. 285—289, écrit:
«D'esta primeira edição existem hoje na Bibl. Nacional não menos de tres exemplares: um pertencente ao antigo fundo do estabelecimento, e os dous provindos das livrarias n'elle incorporadas de Cypriano Ribeiro Freire, e D. Francisco de Mello Manuel. Os poucos exemplares que d'ella apparecem rarissimas vezes à venda, tem corrido pelos preços de 2:400 até 3:600 réis».
Nous avons examiné l'ex. de la Bib. Greaville, Fo. 6580.
Voir *Bibliotheca Sinica*.

Gasparo Balbi.

1401. — Viaggio dell' Indie orientali, di Gasparo Balbi, Gioiellerio Venetiano. Nelquale si contiene quanto egli in detto viaggio hà veduto per lo spatio di 9. Anni consumati in esso dal 1579. fino al 1588. Con la relatione de i datij, pesi, & misure di tutte le Città di tal viaggio, & del gouerno del Rè del Pegù, & delle guerre fatte da lui con altri Rè d'Auuà & di Sion. Con la Tauola delle cose più notabili. Con Privilegi. In Venetia, MDXC. — Appresso Camillo Borgominieri. pet. in-8, 16 ff. n. ch. p. l. tit. et l. tab. + ff. 149 (ch. 159 par erreur) + 23 ff. n. ch.

— — Venezia, 1600, in-8.

— De Bry, Francofurti, 1606, in-4.

— Voyages... Faits de Perse aux Indes Orientales... par le Sr. Jean Albert de Mandelslo... Amsterdam, MDCCXXVII, 2 vol. in-fol.

Voir *Bib. Sinica*. — Renferme un abrégé du voyage de Balbi.
Cf. P. Amat di S. Filippo, *Studi biog. e bibliog.*, pp. 324—336.

1402. — Gasparo Balbi his Voyage to Pegu, and Observations there; gather'd out of his Italian Relation. (*Collection of Voyages and Travels*, by John Harris, London, MDCCV, I, p. 279).

1403. — Gasparo Balbi's Voyage to Pegu, and Observations there gathered from his own Italian Relation. (*General Collection of Voyages and Travels*, by John Pinkerton, London, 1811, IX, pp. 395—405).

Ralph FITCH.

1404. — The long, dangerous, and memorable Voyage of Ralph Fitch, by the way of Tripolis in Syria, to Ormuz, Goa in the East Indies, Cambaia, the River Ganges, Bengala, Bacola, Chonderi, Pegu, Siam, &c., begunne in 1583 and ended in 1591. (Hakluyt, *Principal Navigations*, 1889, Vol. 2.)

1405. — Ralph Fitch. Voyage to Ormus, and so to Goa, in the East Indies, to Cambaia, Ganges, Bengala; to Bacola, and Chonderi to Pegu, to Jamahay in the Kingdom of Siam, and backe to Pegu, and from thence to Malacca, Zeilan, Cochin, and all the Coast of the East Indias, 1583—91. (Purchas, *his Pilgrimes*, Vol. 2, Book 10.)

1406. — A Voyage perform'd by Mr. Ralph Fitch, Merchant of London, to Ormus, and from thence through the whole East-Indies. Written by himself. (*Collection of Voyages and Travels*, by John Harris, London, M.DCCV, I, pp. 206—214).

1407. — The Voyage Of Mr. Ralph Fitch, Merchant of London, To Ormus, and so to Goa in the East India; to Cambaia, Ganges, Bengala; to Bacola and Chonderi, to Pegu, to Jamahay in the Kingdom of Siam, and back to Pegu, And from thence to Malacca, Zeilan, Cochin, and all the Coast of the East India. Begun in the Year of our Lord 1583, and ended 1591. (*General Collection of Voyages and Travels*, by John Pinkerton, London, 1811, IX, pp. 406—425).

1408. — Ralph Fitch England's Pioneer to India and Burma His Companions and Contemporaries with his remarkable Narrative told in his own words. By J. Horton Ryley Member of the Hakluyt Society. London, T. Fisher Unwin, 1899, in-8, pp. xvi—264.

1409. — Aanmerklyke // Reys // van // Ralph Fitch, // Koopman te Londen, // Gedaan van Anno 1583 tot 1591. // Na Ormus, Goa, Cambaya, Bacola, Chonderi, Pegu, // Jamahay in Siam, en weer na Pegu: van daar na // Malacca, Ceylon, Cochin, en de geheele // Kust van Oost-Indien. // Nu aldereerst uyt het Engelsch vertaald. // Met schoone Figueren, en een volkomen Register. // Te Leyden, // By Pieter Vander Aa, Boekverkooper // 1706. — Met Privilegie. in-8. — (*Naaukeurige Versameling der gedenk-waardigste Reysen Na Oost en West-Indiën*, Vol. 66, pp. 43 + 3 ff. n. c.

1410. — Aanmerklyke // Reys // van // Ralph Fitch, // Koopman te Londen, // Gedaan van Anno 1583 tot 1591. // Na Ormus, Goa, Cambaya, Bacola, Chonderi, Pegu, Ja- // mahay in Siam, en weer na Pegu: van daar na Malacca, // Ceylon, Cochin, en de geheele Kust van // Oost-Indien. // Nu aldereerst uyt het Engelsch vertaald. // Met schoone Figueren, en een volkomen Register. // Te Leyden, // By Pieter vander Aa, Boekverkoper, 1706. // — Met Privilegie. (*De aanmerkenswaardigste Zee- en Landreizen*, deel 5, col. 31.) 1 f. n. c. p. l. t.

1411. — Naauw-keurige Aanteekeningen // Van // William Methold, // President van de Engelsse Maatschappy, // Gehouden op sijn // Voyagie, // In het Jaar 1619. — Aangaande de Koningrijken van Golconda, Tanassary, Pegu, Arecan // en meer andere Landen, geleegen langs de Kust van den Zeeboesem // van Bengale; als mede den Koop-handel, die door de Engelsse // in die Land-streeken gedreeven word. // Beneffens den Gods-dienst, Aart, Zeeden en Gewoontens ontrent de Stammen deser // Volkeren, Huuwelijken, Verbranding der Vrouwen met hare Mannen; ook // op wat wijse de Diamanten uyt des selfs Mijn aldaar gehaalt wor- // den; door den Schrijver selfs ondersogt en besien; // Van hem in het Engels beschreeven, en nu alder-eerst uyt // die Spraak vertaalt. // Met noodig Register en Konst-Printen verrijkt. // Te Leyden, // By Pieter Vander Aa, Boekverkoper. // — Met Privilegie. // In fol. — (*De aanmerkenswaardigste Zee- en Landreizen*, deel 6, col. 22).

1412 — Sevende Reys // Na // Oost-Indien, // Op kosten van de Engelse Maatschappy; // Door Kapiteyn // Antony Hippon, // Waar in naauw-keurig worden aangeweesen de Hoogtens // van de Son en Sterren, gelegenheyd der Dieptens, en // forgelijke Ondieptens, van verscheyde Zee-Havenen // in Indiën, op wat wijse de Klippen, Stranden, // Banken en andere Gevaarlijkheeden, omtrent // dese Kusten, zijn te mijden, en de Baayen en // Ree's, veylig konnen werden aangedaan // En om dat de bysondere voorvallen aan Land in de voorsz. // Reys zijn overgeslagen, so is hier bygevoegt het Dag-Register // Van // Pieter Williamson Floris, // Na // Patane en Siam; // Die voor Koópman op dit selfde Schip gevaren, en dit alles // met een bysondere naarstigheyd heeft opgeteekend; // ook een kort verhaal van de Op- en Ondergang // van Siam, en een voorval des Schrijvers met // den Gouverneur van Masulipatan. // Gedaan in het Jaar 1611 en vervolgens. // Nu aldereerst uyt het Engels vertaald. // Met noodig Register en Konst-Printen verrijkt. // Te Leyden, // By Pieter Vander Aa, Boekverkooper 1707. // Met Privilegie. // In-8. (*Naaukeurige Versameling der Gedenk-waardigste Reysen Na Oost en West-Indiën*, Vol. 96, pp. 42 + 2 ff. n. c. p. l. t.

1413. — Sevende Reys // Na // Oost-Indien, // Op Kosten van de Engelse Maatschappy; // Door Kapiteyn // Antony Hippen, // Waar in naauw-keurig worden aangeweesen de Hoogtens van de Son en // Sterren, gelegenheyd der Dieptens, en sorgelijke Ondieptens, van // verscheyde Zee-Havenen in Indiën, op wat wijse de Klippen, // Stranden, Banken en andere Gevaarlijkheeden, omtrent // dese Kusten, zijn te mijden, en de Baayen en // Ree's, veylig konnen werden aangedaan. // En om dat de bysondere voorvallen aan Land in de voorsz. Reys zijn overgeslagen, // so is hier by gevoegt het // Dag-Register // Van // Pieter Williamson Floris, // Na // Patane en Siam; // Die voor Koopman op dit selfde Schip gevaren, en dit alles met een bysondere naarstig- // heyd heeft opgeteekend; ook een kort verhaal van de Op- en Ondergang van Siam, // en een voorval des Schrijvers met den Gouverneur van Masulipatan. // Gedaan in het Jaar 1611. en vervolgens. // Nu alder-eerst uyt het Engels vertaald. // Met noodig Register en Konst-Printen verrijkt. // Te Leyden, // By Pieter Vander Aa, Boekverkoper. // — Met Privilegie. // In-fol. (*De aanmerkenswaardigste Zee- en Landreizen*, Deel 6, col. 24). 1 f. n. c.

1414. — Journal of a March from Ava to Kendat, on the Khyendwen River, performed in 1831, by D. Richardson, Esq. Assistant Surgeon of the Madras Establishment, under the orders of Major H. Burney, the Resident at Ava. (*Jour. As. Soc. of Bengal*, II, Feb. 1833, pp. 59—70).

1415. — Abstract of the Journal of a Route travelled by Capt. S. F. Hannay, of the 40th Regiment Native Infantry, from the Capital of Ava to the Amber Mines of the Húkong valley on the South-east frontier of Assam. By Capt. R. Boileau Pemberton, 44th Regt. N. I. (*Ibid.*, VI, April, 1837, pp. 245—278).

1416. — Travels in South-Eastern Asia, embracing Hindustan, Malaya, Siam, and China; with notices of Numerous Missionary Stations, and a full account of the Burman Empire, by the Rev. Howard Malcom, of Boston, U. S. *London, Charles Tilt*, MDCCCXXXIX, 2 vol. in-12, pp. xi—324, viii—364.

Cet ouvrage a eu de nombreuses éditions. La première est de Boston, 1839, 2 vol. in-12; — 1839, in-8; Edin., «People's Edition»; 10th amer. ed., Phil., 1857.

1417. — Travels in the Burman Empire. By Howard Malcom. Illustrated with a Map of South-Eastern Asia, and Wood Engravings. Edinburgh: William and Robert Chambers. 1840, in-8, pp. 82 à 2 col.

People's Edition.

1418. — Report on a Route from Pakung Yeh in Ava, to Aeng in Arracan. By Lieut. Trant, of the Q. M. G. Dept. (*Journ. of the As. Soc. of Bengal*, Vol. XI, Pt. II, No. 132, 1842, pp. 1136—1157).

1419. — Posthumous Papers bequeathed to the Honorable the East India Company, and Printed by Order of the Government of Bengal. — Journals of Travels in Assam, Burma, Bootan, Affghanistan and the Neighbouring Countries. — By the late William Griffith, Esq., F.L.S., ... — Arranged by John M° Clelland, F.L.S., Surgeon, Bengal Service — Calcutta: Bishop's College Press, 1847, in-8, 3 ff. n. ch. + pp. xxxii—529.

Né à Ham Common, près de Kingston-upon Thames, 4 mars 1810; † 9 fév. 1845.

— Posthumous Papers.... Vol. II. — Itinerary Notes of Plants collected in the Khasyah and Bootan Mountains, 1837—38, in Affghanisthan and neighbouring countries, 1839 to 1841. — By the late William Griffith...... Calcutta: J. F. Bellamy, 1848, in-8, pp. lxiv—435 + pp. lxv—lxix pour l'er.

1420. — Six months in British Burmah: or, India beyond the Ganges in 1857. By Christopher T. Winter. Richard Bentley, 1858, pet. in-8, pp. XII—282 + 3 ff. n. c.

1421. — Yule, voir *Relations de l'Angleterre*.

1422. — Up and Down the Irrawaddi; or The Golden Dagon: being Passages of Adventure in the Burman Empire. By J. W. Palmer, M.D., ... New and Revised Edition. New York: Rudd & Carleton, ... MDCCCLIX, pet. in-8, pp. x—311.

1423. — Four Years in Burmah. By W. H. Marshall, Esq., late Editor of the «Rangoon Chronicle». London: Charles J. Skeet, 1860, 2 vol. in-8, pp. VIII— 322, IV—307.

1424. — Die Geschichte der Indochinesen. — Aus einheimischen Quellen von Dr. Adolf Bastian. Leipzig 1866, Otto Wigand, in-8, pp. XVI—576.

> Birma — Pegu — Siam — Kambodia.

— Reisen in Birma in den Jahren 1861—1862. Von Dr. Adolf Bastian. Leipzig 1866, Otto Wigand, in-8, pp. XIII—521.

> Forment les Vol. I & II de *Die Voelker des Oestlichen Asien. — Studien und Reisen von* Dr. Adolf Bastian.

1425. — Notes on the Burmese Route from Assam to the Hookoong Valley. By Henry Lionel Jenkins, Esq. (Communicated by F. A. Goodenough, Esq., F.R.G.S.) (*Proc. Roy. Geog. Soc.*, XIII, 1869, pp. 244—248).

1426. — An Abstract of a Trip in Burmah. From Mr. Cushing. (*Siam Repository*, Oct. 1869, Vol. I, Art. CXXIV, pp. 244—247).

1427. — Maulmain to Bangkok Overland. By C. H. Carpenter. (*The Phoenix*, III, No 25, July, 1872, pp. 3—5).

> Du *Siamese Weekly News*.

1428. — The Land of the White Elephant. Travels, Adventures, and Discoveries in Burma, Siam, Cambodia, and Cochin-China By Frank Vincent, Jr., M.A. .... Illustrated with Maps, Plans, and Engravings. Third Edition. New York, Harper & Brothers, 1882, in-8, pp. XXIII—383.

> 1st ed., 1873; 2d. ed., 1881. — Notice: *Ocean Highways*, N. S., Vol. I, Jan. 1874, p. 427.

1429. — Two months in Burmah. By Frank Vincent, Jr. (*J. Am. Geog. Soc.*, VIII, 1876, pp. 162—187).

1430. — The Land of the White Elephant by Frank Vincent, Jr., M.A. New York, 1882. Notice par M. E.-A. Grattan, vice-président de la Société. (*Bull. Soc. roy. Géogr. Anvers*, VIII, 1883—1884, pp. 172—185).

1431. — A Narrative of Travel and Sport in Burmah, Siam, and the Malay Peninsula. By John Bradley. London: Samuel Tinsley, 1876, in-8, pp. VI—338.

1432. — Our Trip to Burmah. With Notes on that Country. By Surgeon-General Charles Alexander Gordon, M.D., C.B., ... London: Baillière, Tindall, and Cox, in-8, s. d. [1877], pp. XII—265.

> 1874—1875.

1433. — Excursions autour du monde. Les Indes, la Birmanie, la Malaisie, le Japon et les Etats-Unis par le Cte Julien de Rochechouart, Ministre plénipotentiaire. Ouvrage orné de gravures. Paris, E. Plon, 1879, in-18, pp. III—282 et 1 f. table.

1434. — Sport in British Burmah, Assam, and the Cassyah and Jyntiah Hills. With notes of sport in the Hilly Districts of the Northern Division, Madras Presidency, indicating the best localities in those countries for sport, with Natural History Notes, Illustrations of the People, Scenery, and Game, together with Maps to guide the traveller or sportsman, and hints on weapons, fishing tackle, etc., best suited for killing game met with in those provinces. By Lieut.-Colonel Pollok, Madras Staff Corps. With Illustrations. London: Chapman and Hall, 1879, 2 vol. in-8, pp. XIII + 1 f. n. ch. + pp. 253, VI + 1 f. n. ch. + pp. 230.

1435. — Wild Sports in Burma and Assam. By Colonel Pollok, late Staff Corps, and W. S. Thom, Assistant District Superintendent of Police, Burma: With Illustrations and Maps. London: Hurst and Blackett, 1900, in-8, pp. xx—507.

1436. — Im fernen Osten. Reisen des Grafen Bela Széchenyi in Indien, Japan, China, Tibet und Birma in den Jahren 1877—1880. Von Gustav Kreitner, k. k. Oberlieutenant und Mitglied der Expedition. Mit zweihundert Original-Holzschnitten und drei Karten. Wien, 1881. Alfred Hölder, k. k. Hof- und Universitäts-Buchhändler, in-8, pp. VIII—1013.

> Gustav Kreitner, né à Odrau (Silésie autrichienne) 2 août 1848; † 21 nov. 1893; consul d'Autriche à Chang hai, 1888; consul à Yokohama, 1884. — Notice, *T'oung Pao*, No. 1, 1894, par G. S.[chlegel].

1437. — Langt Mod Ost. Rejseskildringer fra Indien, Kina, Japan, Tibet og Birma, af G. Kreitner. Deltager i Grev Béla Széchenyis Expedition i Aarene 1877—80. Med 194 Illustrationer og i Kort. Forlagsbureauet i Kjøbenhavn. (O. H. Delbanco. G. E. C. Gad. F. Hegel. C. C. Lose.) 1882, in-8, pp. 851.

1438. — A Winter Tour through India, Burmah and the Straits by H. E. Falk. London, Longmans & Co., 1880, pet. in-8, pp. VII—90.

1439. — Hinterindische Länder und Völker. — Reisen in den Fluszgebieten des Irrawaddy und Mekong; in Birma, Annam, Kambodscha und Siam. — Unter besonderer Berücksichtigung der neuesten Zustände in Birma bearbeitet von Friedrich von Hellwald. Zweite vermehrte Auflage. Mit 70 in den Text gedruckten Abbildungen und 4 Tonbildern. — Leipzig. Otto Spamer. 1880, in-8, pp. VIII—376.

> Fait partie de la collection: *Das Neue Buch der Reisen und Entdeckungen.* — *Otto Spamer's Illustrirte Bibliothek der Länder- & Völkerkunde zur Erweiterung der Kenntnisz der Fremde.* Unter Redaktion von Friedrich von Hellwald und Richard Oberländer.

1440. — Ein Besuch beim Könige von Birma. — Von Wilhelm Joest. Besonderer Abdruck aus der Kölnischen Zeitung. 1880. Köln, 1882, M. Du Mont-Schauberg, in-8, pp. 46.

1441. — Un Français en Birmanie ouvrage rédigé Sur ses Notes de Voyage par Le Cte A. Mahé de La Bourdonnais Ingénieur, Explorateur en Birmanie et Siam Membre de la Société Indo-Chinoise; et complété Par M. Gabriel Marcel Attaché à la Section géographique de la Bibliothèque Nationale. — Paris, Paul Ollendorff, [1883], in-12, pp. IV—244.

1442. — Un Français en Birmanie Ouvrage rédigé sur ses Notes de Voyage par le Cte A. Mahé de La Bourdonnais, Ingénieur, Explorateur en Birmanie et Siam, Membre de la Société Indo-Chinoise; et complété Par M. Gabriel Marcel Attaché à la Section géographique de la Bibliothèque nationale, in-12, pp. IV—244.

> Sur la couverture extérieure: 2e édition, Paul Ollendorff, s. d. — Avant-Propos, 1er sept. 1883.

1443. — Un Français en Birmanie — Notes de voyage rédigées par le Comte A. Mahé de la Bourdonnais Ingénieur Explorateur en Birmanie et Siam.... Troisième édition revue et augmentée. — Paris, F. Fetscherin et Chuit, 1886, in-12, pp. IV—288.

> — 4e édition. Paris, Jeandé, in-12, pp. IV—324.
> — Paris, Delagrave, 1896, pp. 190. Illustrations d'A. Duplais-Destouches.

1444. — Journal of a Lady's Travels round the World. By F. D. Bridges.... With Illustrations from Sketches by the Author. London, John Murray, 1883, in-8, pp. XI + 1 f. n. c. + pp. 413.

> Burmah — Rangoon — Canton — Japon — Pekin, etc.

1445. — *Mme L. Jacolliot. — Trois mois sur le Gange et le Brahmapoutre. Paris, Clavel, in-18 jésus, pp. 208 et grav., 3 fr.

1446. — Lettere del sig. Fea dalla Birmania. (*Bol. Soc. geog. Ital.*, 1885, pp. 589—594, 751—762, 855—856, 942—953) etc.

1447. — Leonardo Fea in Birmania. Par A. Brunialti. (*Geogr. per tutti*, V, 1895, pp. 337—8).

1448. — Quattro Anni fra i Birmani e le Tribù limitrofe — Viaggio di Leonardo Fea illustrato da 195 figure e da 3 tavole topografiche Pubblicato col concorso della Società Geografica Italiana. Ulrico Hoepli, Milano, 1896, in-8, pp. XVII—565 + 1 f. n. ch.

1449. — *Cosimo Bertacchi. La Birmania e il viaggio di Leonardo Fea. (*Mem. Soc. Geog. Ital.*, Roma, 1897, VI, pp. 241—285.)

1450. — Leonardo Fea ed i suoi Viaggi — Cenni biografici di R. Gestro. Genova, Tip. R. Istituto Sordomuti, 1904, in-8, pp. 60, carte et portrait.

> Est. dagli *Annali del Museo Civico di Storia Naturale di Genova*, Serie 3^a, Vol. I (XLI), 1904.
> Pubblicazioni di Leonardo Fea, pp. 23—4.
> Elenco delle memorie scientifiche in cui sono illustrate collezioni zoologiche fatte da Leonardo Fea in Birmania e nelle regioni vicine, pp. 25—34.

1451. — A Parson's Holiday; being an Account of a Tour in India, Burma, and Ceylon, in the Winter of 1882—83. By W. Osborn B. Allen, Vicar of Shirburn, Oxon. — Tenby: F. B. Mason, 1885, in-8, pp. VIII—228.

1452. — In Birmania — Note di Viaggio illustrate di Aristide Perucca Ex-Colonnello Birmano. 1886, G. B. Paravia, Roma—Torino—Milano—Firenze, in-8, pp. VII—110.

1453. — *Viaggio di Aristide Perucca nella Birmania centrale (1883—84). — I. Da Mandalè a Gnung-iuè. II. Da Gnung-iuè a Monè. (*Cosmos*, IX, 1886—88, Torino, pp. 78—88, 119—122).

1454. — Quinze jours en Birmanie, par M. E. Cavaglion. 1886. (*Tour du Monde*, 1892, II, pp. 385—400).

1455. — Verslag Eener zending naar Opper-Burma van J. F. Breijer, Kapitein van het Ned. Ind. Leger. (Met bijlagen en schetsen). — Uitgegeven met machtiging van Zijne Excellentie den Commandant van het Leger en Chef van het Department van Oorlog in Nederlandsch-Indie. in-8, pp. VII—IV—219. Batavia, October 1887.

1456. — *J. F. Breijer. — Verslag eener zending naar Opper-Burma. (Met bijlagen en schetsen). (*Ind. militair Tijdschr.*, 1888 (19 Jahrg.) Nr. 1.)

1457. — Eighteen hundred miles on a Burmese Tat through Burmah, Siam, and the Eastern Shan States. By an ordinary British Subaltern, to wit Lieutenant G. J. Younghusband, Queen's own Corps of Guides. London: W. H. Allen, 1888, in-8, pp. 162, carte.

1458. — Overland from India to Upper Burma. By Major General J. J. H. Gordon, C.B. (*Ill. Naval & Milit. Mag.*, Feb. 1889, pp. 187—200.)

1459. — A Burmese Boat-Journey. By P. Hordern. (*Blackwood's Mag.*, CXLV, April 1889, pp. 557—560).

1460. — J. K. Knudsen: En Rejse i Rødkarenernes Land. — Med et forord af H. Nutzhorn samt billeder, kort og et facsimile. Kjøbenhavn, V. Pontoppidan, 1889, in-8, pp. XIV—98 + 1 f. n. ch.

1461. — Cinque anni in Birmania — Note del Maggiore Tarsillo Barberis Già nel Corpo degl'irregolari d'Africa, Membro della Società Teosofica di Madras (Adjar) India. — Antica casa editrice Dott. Francesco Vallardi, Milano, &c., s. d. [1889], in-4, pp. 201 + 1 f. n. c. p. l'ind. + ff. prél. n. c.

1462. — Tarsillo Barberis e le sue note sulla Birmania. (*Geogr. per tutti*, V 1895, p. 338).

Voir No. 1356.

1463. — Tarsillo Barberis. Par Dott. Lodovico Corio. (*L'Universo*, VI, 1896, pp. 257—258).

† 13 sept. 1896, à San Martino della Battaglia (Brescia).

1464. — *M. Barbaran-Tessari. Impressioni e memorie del mio viaggio nell' India e Birmania. Padova, Sacchetto, 1890, in-8.

1465. — På Budda's Veje Oplevelser og Meddelelser fra Burma ved Jens Kr. Knudsen — Med et forord af L. Schroder samt ti autotypier, tegninger af V. Jastrau (tildels efter fotografier) — Tre kort et facsimile udgivet af den Danske Mission i Bagindien — Kjøbenhavn, V. Pontoppidan, 1891, in-8, pp. X + 1 f. n. ch. + pp. 177.

Voir No. 243.

1466. — *B. F. — A Tour in Burma. (*Murray's Mag.*, Jan. 1891.)

1467. — Life and Travel in Lower Burmah A Retrospect by Deputy-Surgeon-General C. T. Paske late of the Bengal Army Edited by F. G. Aflalo.... London, W. H. Allen & Co., s. d., in-8, [1892], pp. VIII—265.

　　　　Notice: *Athenaeum*, 21 jan. 1893, p. 81.

1468. — Memorandum of a Tour in parts of the Amherst, Shwegyin, and Pegu districts by Taw Sein Ko, Government Translator, on special duty. — Rangoon: printed by the Supdt. Govt. Printing, Burma, Feby. 1892, br. in-8, pp. 14.

　　　　Voir sur la langue des Taungthus ou Pha-o qui parait se rapprocher davantage de la langue des Talaing ou des Birmans plutôt que de celle des Shans.

1469. — Four years in Upper Burma. By W. R. Winston. London: C. H. Kelly, 1892, in-8, pp. XII—266.

1470. — De Rangoon a Mandalay. (*Geog. per tutti*, IV, 1894, pp. 91—93.)

1471. — Im Sattel durch Indo-China. — Von Otto E. Ehlers. Mit Illustrationen. Berlin. Allgemeiner Verein für Deutsche Litteratur. 1894. 2 vol. in-8, pp. 332, 301.

　　　　De la Serie XIX de l'*Allgemeiner Verein für Deutsche Litteratur*.

1472. — When we were Strolling Players in the East by Louise Jordan Miln. With Illustrations. London, Osgood, M° Ilvaine and Co., 1894, in-8, pp. XIV—354.

　　　　Quelques articles avaient paru dans la *Pall Mall Gazette* et le *Pall Mall Budget*.

1473. — An Australian in China, being the Narrative of a Quiet Journey across China to British Burma. By G. E. Morrison...... London, Horace Cox, 1895, in-8.

　　　　Third Edition, 1902.

1474. — *H. Charmanne. Exploration commerciale en Birmanie. (*Recueil consulaire* [*belge*], XCII, 1896, pp. 286—328).

　　　　Tirage à part, 1896, pp. 45 — Voir nos. 46—47.

1475. — Among Pagodas and Fair Ladies An Account of a Tour through Burma by Gwendolen Trench Gascoigne. With numerous Illustrations. London, A. D. Innes & Co., 1896, in-8, pp. 312.

　　　　A small portion of this little book first made its appearance in the pages of *The Sporting and Dramatic News*.
　　　　Notice: *Athenaeum*, Dec. 19, 1896, p. 869.

1476. — Six Years in Burma by Kamakhya Nath Gupta. Published by the Author. Calcutta: K. B. Das, 1896, in-12, pp. 136 + 1 f. n. ch. er.

1477. — *T. Cook. Guide to Burma. London, 1896, pp. 56, obl. 8vo.
　　　　B. M. 10055. de. 8.

1478. — *Von der Forschungsexpedition Pottinger in Birma. (*Osterreichische Monatschrift* XXIII, p. 108).

1479. — En Birmanie — Lettre de M. E. Gallois. (*Soc. Géog. Lille, Bull.*, XXVII, 1897, 1er sem., pp. 115—120.)

1480. — *Eug. Gallois. En Birmanie. (*Rev. géog. intern.*, 1897, IV, pp. 395—410). — (*Bull. Soc. Géog. Lille*, 1897, XXVII, pp. 115—120.)

1481. — La Birmanie. — Les pagodes et les monastères. — Le cours de l'Irraouaddy. (*Comptes Rendus Soc. de Géogr.*, 1898, pp. 5—10).

1482. — Au Pays des Pagodes et des Monastères — En Birmanie par M. Eugène Gallois, Membre de la Société de Géographie — Ouvrage Orné de nombreuses cartes, photographies et dessins inédits de l'auteur. Paris, Ch. Delagrave, 1899, gr. in-8, pp. 118.

1483. — Au pays des Pagodes et des Monastères. Par Eugène Gallois. (*Rev. de Géog.*, XLIII, 1898, pp. 457—467).

1484. — Au pays des Pagodes et des Monastères. Par C. R. (*Rev.´ française*, XXIV, 1899, pp. 36—46).
> Sur Eug. Gallois.

1485. — Wanderings in Burma by George W. Bird (Educational Department, Burma). — With Illustrations and Maps — First Edition — Bournemouth: F. J. Bright & Son, ... London: Simpkin, Marshall, Hamilton, Kent & Co., ... 1897, gr. in-8, 4 ff. n. ch. + pp. 410—IV.

1486. — Ein Zug nach Osten. — Reisebilder aus Indien, Birma, Ceylon, Straits Settlements, Java, Siam, China, Korea, Ostsibirien, Japan, Alaska und Canada von Moritz Schanz. Hamburg. W. Mauke Söhne, 1897, 2 vol. in-8, 1897.
> Erster Band. — Reisebilder aus Indien, Birma, Ceylon, Straits Settlements, Java, Siam, pp. VIII—423.
> Zweiter Band. — Reisebilder aus China, Korea, Ostsibirien, Japan, Alaska und Canada, pp. VI—424 + 1 f. n. ch.

1487. — Emile Roux Enseigne de Vaisseau — Aux Sources de l'Irraouaddi Voyage de Hanoï à Calcutta par terre, illustré de cent dessins ou gravures directes d'après les photographies rapportées par l'auteur. Hachette & Cie. 1897, gr. in-8, pp. 84 + 1 f. n. ch. p. l. tab.
> Tiré du *Tour du Monde*. — Voir Henri d'Orléans au chap. *Les Routes de la Chine par la Birmanie*, No. 337 et seq.

1488. — Girolamo Civati. Par Dott. L. Corio. (*L'Universo*, VII, 1897, pp. 219—21).

1489. — With the Jungle Folk A Sketch of Brumese [sic] Village Life by E. D. Cuming. Illustrated by a Burmese Artist. London, Osgood, Mc Ilvaine & Co., 1897, in-8, pp. 400.
> Voir nos. 362—363.

1490. — Picturesque Burma Past & Present by Mrs. Ernest Hart. London, J. M. Dent, 1897, in-8, pp. XIV—400.
> Notices: *Academy*, LI, p. 471. — *Athenæum*, 22d May, p. 673.

1491. — A Handbook for Travellers in India Burma and Ceylon including the Provinces of Bengal, Bombay, and Madras the Punjab, North-West Provinces, Rajputana, Central Provinces, Mysore, etc. The Native States, Assam, and Cashmere. Third edition With seventy-four Maps and Plans. London: John Murray, 1898, pet. in-8, pp. lxxxix—484.
> First edition, 1892. — Second edition, 1894.
> Burma, pp. 413—489.
> Notice: *Jour. Roy. Asiat. Soc.*, Oct. 1908, pp. 903—4.

1492. — Quaint Corners of Ancient Empires Southern India, Burma and Manila by Michael Meyers Shoemaker... Illustrated. G. P. Putnam's Sons, New York and London, The Knickerbocker Press, 1899, in-8, pp. xix—212.

1493. — An English Girl's First Impressions of Burmah. — By Beth Ellis. — Wigan: R. Platt; London: Simpkin, 1899, pet. in-8, 4 ff. n. ch. + pp. 248.

1494. — Towards the Land of the Rising Sun Or, Four Years in Burma by Sister Katherine Published under the Direction of the Tract Committee. Society for Promoting Christian Knowledge, London, 1900, pet. in-8, pp. 160.

1495. — Comment j'ai parcouru l'Indo-Chine par Isabelle Massieu — Birmanie, États Shans, Siam, Tonkin, Laos — Préface de M. F. Brunetière, de l'Académie française — Ouvrage accompagné de 65 gravures et d'une carte. Paris, Plon, 1901, pet. in-8, pp. xii—404.

> Notices: *La Géographie*, 15 juillet 1901, p. 80, par Charles Rabot. — *Bul. Comité Asie française*, juillet 1901, p. 179. — Voyage d'une Française dans l'Indo-Chine par Jules Leclercq Ancien Président de la Société royale belge de Géographie (Extrait de *La Revue Générale*, nov. 1901). Bruxelles, Oscar Schepens, 1901, in-8, pp. 13.

1496. — Mme Isabelle Massieu. — Une Française au Ladak. — Une colonie anglaise. Birmanie et Etats shans. (*Revue des Deux Mondes*, 1ᵉʳ juil. 1897, 15 sept. 1899, pp. 397—416).

1497. — De Mandalay à Hué. Par Mme I. Massieu. (*Bul. Soc. Géog. com.*, XX, 1898, pp. 530—534).

1498. — Burma by Max and Bertha Ferrars. London, Sampson Low, 1900, in-4, pp. xii—237. Ill.-Carte.

> Notes on Burmese Music; by Mr. P. A. Mariano, pp. 210—1.

1499. — Burma by Max. and Bertha Ferrars. Second Edition. London, Sampson Low, 1901, in-4, pp. xii—237.

> Voir no. 53.

1500. — 'O· von der Heyde. — Forstliche Reisebilder aus Burma (Hinterindien). (*Zeitschft. f. Forst- und Jagdwesen*, Berlin, XXXIII, 1901, pp. 339—365).

1501. — 'Ten Thousand Miles through India and Burma. By Cecil Headlam. London, Dent, 1903, in-8.

1502. — Further India being the Story of Exploration from the earliest Times in Burma, Malaya, Siam, and Indo-China. By Hugh Clifford, C.M.G. ... With Illustrations from Drawings, Photographs, and Maps. And Maps by J. G. Bartholomew. London, Lawrence and Bullen, 1904, in-8, pp. xi—378.

> Fait partie de la collection: *The Story of Exploration edited by J. Scott Keltie*,... Notice: *Geographical Journal*, XXV, April 1905, pp. 445—6. — *Lond. & China Telegraph*, Oct. 10, 1904.

1503. — En Birmanie. Par Lucien Bourgogne. (*Autour du Monde par les Boursiers de Voyage de l'Université de Paris*, 1904, pp. 27—71).

1504.' — A Yankee on the Yangtze being a Narrative of a Journey from Shanghai through the Central Kingdom to Burma by William Edgar Geil.... With one hundred full-page illustrations. London, Hodder and Stoughton, MCMIV, in-8, pp. xv—312.

1505. — The Silken East A Record of Life and Travel in Burma. By V. C. Scott O'Connor Comptroller of Assam With 400 Illustrations including 20 coloured Plates by J. R. Middleton, Mrs. Otway Wheeler Cuffe and Saya Chone. London: Hutchinson & Co., 1904, 2 vol. in-8.

1506. — °Une croisière en Extrême-Orient, par le Comte de Marsay. Paris, Delagrave, 1904, in-16, pp. 272.

1507. — °The Burma Route Book. Part I. Routes in Northern Burma. Compiled by Captain M. C. Nangle, for the Intelligence Branch, Quarter-Master General's Department, Simla. 1903. Calcutta, 1904, ... pp. 206. Index Map.

1508. — Among the Burmans A record of fifteen years of work and its fruitage By Henry Park Cochrane. Illustrated. New York, Chicago, ... Fleming H. Revell Co., in-8, pp. 281.

1509. — André Chevrillon — Sanctuaires et Paysages d'Asie — Ceylan bouddhique — Le matin à Bénarès — La Sagesse d'un Brahme — La mort à Bénarès — Le Bouddha birman. Paris, Hachette, 1905, in-16, pp. 361.

XVI. — Commerce et Navigation.

1510. — Calculations for Burmah Produce. London: Carter and Bromley, 1858, in-4, pp. 110.

1511. — Report on the Trade and Customs of British Burma 1872—1873. — Chapter I. General Review of Trade by Sea and Land. (*Siam Repository*, Vol. 6, April 1874, pp. 194—195).

1512. — Burma. (*Ibid.*, Vol. 6, April 1874, art. 46, pp. 193—194).

1513. — Burmah-Rangoon Customs Department. (*Ibid.*, Vol. 6, Jan. 1874, art. 18, pp. 64—65).

> Extrait du *«Friend of Burmah»*.

1514. — °Papers connected with the Development of Trade between British Burmah and Western China, and with the Mission to Yunnan of 1874—75. 1876, in-folio.

> Voir nos. 380—401.

1515. — In the Privy Council on Appeal from the Court of the Recorder of Rangoon. — Between The Bombay Burmah Trading Corporation «limited», (Defendants). Appellants. And Mirza Mahomed Ally Sherazee, (Plaintiff) The Burmah Company «limited», (Co-Plaintiffs).... Respondents. — Date of Judgment of the Recorder of Rangoon.... 4th November 1876. — Date of Application by Appellants for leave to Appeal to Her Majesty in Council, ... 19th March 1877. — Rangoon: British Burmah Press. — 1877, 2 vol. in-4, pp. 232 + lxxxv, 28.

1516. — Le commerce extérieur de la Birmanie indépendante. (*Ann. de l'Ext. Orient*, 1885—1886, VIII, pp. 172—176).

1517. — La Birmanie. (*Ibid.*, 1885—1886, VIII, p. 283).

1518. — *Report on the Trade between Burma and the adjoining Foreign Countries for the Three Years ending the 31st March 1890. Rangoon, 1890, in-folio. Map.

1519. — *L. Vossion. — Études statistiques. La Birmanie... Paris, Challamel aîné, 1895, in-8, pp. 30. — Voir no. 1542.

1520. — *Victor Zollikofer. — Handel und Industrie von Burma. (*Export*, Berlin, 1896, XVIII, pp. 637—8, 691—4).

1521. — *The Trade of Burmah, 1897—1898. (*Board of Trade Journal*, XXVI, June 1899, p. 668).

1522. — *Memorandum on the Trade between Burma and adjoining Foreign Countries, for the year ending 31st March 1900. Containing the exports and imports of Trade between Burma and adjoining Foreign Countries for the year 1899—1900. Compiled by the Government of Burma. 1900, in-fol.

1523. — *Note on the Transfrontier Trade of Burma for the year 1900—1901. Compiled by the Financial Commissioner, Burma. 1901, in-fol.

1524. — *Report (or Memorandum) on the Internal Trade of Burma for the years 1889—90, 1891—92, 1892—93, and 1893—94. Rangoon, 1890—94, in-folio.

1525. — *Memorandum on the Internal Trade of Burma for the year ending March 31, 1897. Rangoon, 1897. — Carte.

1526. — *Report on the Trade and Navigation of Burma for the year 1888—89, with Memorandum on the Inland Trade. Rangoon, 1889, in-folio.

1527. — *Report on the Trade and Navigation of Burma for the year 1889—90. Rangoon, 1890, in-folio.

1528. — Rules, Notifications, and Orders under the Sea Customs Act, VIII of 1878. — Rangoon: Printed by the Supdt., Govt. Printing, Burma. February 1894, in-8, pp. 21.

1529. — Rules for the Port of Akyab. — Rangoon: Printed by the Supdt., Govt. Printing, Burma, Jany. 1896, in-8, pp. 11.

1530. — Rules for regulating Passenger Boats and other Boats plying in the Port of Akyab. Rangoon: Printed by the Supdt., Govt. Printing, Burma. Jany. 1896, in-8, pp. 3.

1531. — The Moulmein Port Manual. — A Collection of Rules and Orders specially concerning the Port of Moulmein. First Edition. — Rangoon: Printed by the Supdt., Govt. Printing, Burma. 1898, in-8, pp. III—59.

1532. — *Report on the Trade and Navigation of Burma. Annual Review on the Trade of Burma. Compiled by the Government of Burma. in-fol.
　　　　　For the years 1899—1900, 1900—1901.

1533. — *Report on the Government Steamers, Vessels and Launches in Burma. Compiled by the Government of Burma. in-fol.
　　　　　For the years 1899—1900, 1900—1901.

1534. — *Thirty-fourth Annual Report on the Light-houses and Light Vessels off the coast of Burma for the year 1900—1901. Compiled by the Government of Burma. 1901, in-fol.

1535. — *Annual Statement of the Sea-borne Trade and Navigation of Burma for the year ending 31st March 1900. By the Chief Collector of Customs, Burma. 1901. in-fol. — Vol. II. — Coasting, in-fol.

1536. — Le commerce de la Birmanie par terre. (*Bull. Com. Asie française*, Mai 1901, pp. 81—82).

> D'après le rapport de M. R. Monnet, vice-consul de France à Rangoun.

1537. — *Annual Statement of the Sea-borne Trade and Navigation of Burma for the year 1900—1901. Part I — Foreign. — Part II — Coasting. By the Chief Collector of Customs, Burma. 1902, in-fol.

1538. — La Birmanie, sa situation économique. Le Commerce français. Par J. Claine. (*Bul. Soc. Géog. com.*, XXIII, 1901, pp. 673—4).

1539. — Le Commerce de la Birmanie en 1901—1902. (*Bull. Com. Asie française*, Juin 1903, p. 273).

> D'après un Rapport de M. Claine, consul français à Rangoon.

1540. — Le Commerce de la Birmanie par terre en 1902—1903. (*Ibid.*, Nov. 1903, p. 514).

XVII. — Relations étrangères.

1) Divers.

1541. — Burmans in Siam. (*Siam Repository*, Vol. 4, July 1872, pp. 362—3).

1542. — Etudes sur l'Indo-Chine — Birmanie et Tong-Kin Par Louis Vossion Ancien Officier Chargé de mission scientifique en Birmanie par le Ministère de l'Instruction publique et des Beaux-Arts Officier d'Académie. — Extrait de la *Nouvelle Revue* du 15 janvier 1880 — Paris Challamel Ainé, Editeur — 1880, in-8, pp. 32. — Voir no. 1519.

1543. — Kula. By R. C. Temple. (*Ind. Antiq.*, XXVII, 1898, pp. 27—8).

2) Chine.

1544. — Voir *Marco Polo*.

1545. — Mémoires très intéressantes (*sic*) sur le Royaume de Mien de Mgr. Claude de Visdelou, évêque de (Claudiopolis). Traduction du Chinois. (*Revue de l'Extrême Orient*, T. II, Nos. 1 & 2, 1883, pp. 72—88).

> Ces mémoires sur le Pegou ont été publiés par M. Henri Cordier d'après le recueil ms *Add.* 16915 du British Museum.

1546. — Description du royaume de Laos et des pays voisins, présentée au roi de Siam en 1687, par des ambassadeurs du roi de Laos. (*Nouv. Jour. As.*, X, 1832, pp. 414—421).

— Extrait d'une Relation de quatre Chinois transalpins qui, avec vingt ou trente mille individus de la province de Yun nan, s'étaient réfugiés dans l'Ava et dans le Pégu, et ensuite dans le Siam, pour ne pas être forcés à se raser les cheveux, selon l'usage des Tatares. An 1687. (*Nouv. Jour. As.*, pp. 421—438).

> Ces deux mémoires envoyés par le P. de Visdelou et publiés par Klaproth sont, ainsi que les notes qui les accompagnent, fort intéressants à cause des renseignements qu'ils renferment sur les fleuves du Yun nan et de la péninsule indochinoise.

1547. — Wars between Burmah and China, described by Marco Polo, and by Burmese historians. By E. C. Bridgman. (*Chin. Rep.*, IX, 1840, pp. 134—42).

— Narrative of a four years' war between Burmah and China: translated from the Burmese Chronicles by Colonel Burney. (*Ibid.*, pp. 169—90).

— Embassies between the Court of Ava and Peking: translated from Burmese Chronicles, by lieut.-col. H. Burney, late resident in Ava. (*Ibid.*, pp. 437—83).

1548. — 乾隆征緬甸記. — Histoire de la Conquête de la Birmanie par les Chinois, sous le règne de Tçienn Loñg (Khien long), traduite du chinois par M. Camille Imbault-Huart. (*Jour. As.*, sér. VII, XI, Fév.-Mars 1878, pp. 135—178).

Ext. du *Cheng Wou ki* 聖武記. — Voir *Bib. Sinica*, col. 632—633.

1549. — Burmah, or Mien. By Bonnet-Rouge. (*N. C. Herald*, Dec. 12, 1886, pp. 678—679).

1550. — La Birmanie et la Chine. Par M. d'E.[strey] (*Ann. de l'Ext. Orient*, 1886—1887, IX, pp. 169—174).

1551. — China and Burmah. By Professor Robert K. Douglas. (*The As. Quart. Review*, January, 1886. Vol. I, No. 1, pp. 141—164).

1552. — China and Burmah. By E. H. Parker. (*China Review*, XVI, pp. 122—23).

1553. — Burmah v. China. By E. H. Parker. (*Ibid.*, XVIII, No. 4, p. 264).

1554. — Burma with special Reference to her Relations with China by Edward Harper Parker, H. M. Consul, Kiung chow, officiating Adviser on Chinese Affairs in Burma. — Printed and published at the «Rangoon Gazette» Press. — 1893, in-12, pp. 3, 103.

1555. — Digest of the Yung-ch'ang Annals on Burma. By E. H. Parker, Esq., Late Adviser on Chinese Affairs in Burma. Simla: Printed at the Government Central Printing Office. 1894, in-fol., pp. 7 + 2 ff. de chinois.

1556. — E. H. Parker. — Burma's supposed «Tribute» to China. (*As. Quart. Review*, VI, 1898, pp. 152—173).

1557. — Une ambassade chinoise en Birmanie en 1406. Par Ed. Huber. (*Bull. Ecole française Extrême Orient*, IV, Nos. 1 et 2, Janvier-Juin 1904, pp. 429—32).

3) Angleterre.

Généralités.

1558. — Historical Review of the Political Relations between the British Government in India and the Empire of Ava; from the earliest date on record to the end of the year 1834: compiled by G. T. Bayfield, Esq., Acting Assistant to the Resident in Ava, and revised by Lieutenant-Colonel Burney, British Resident. — Calcutta: Samuel Smith and Co., 1835, in-4, pp. 75.

1559. — Burmah: British relations with that Country; Travels in the interior among the Singphos near Ásám and towards the Chinese frontier; Revolution in the Government. By E. C. Bridgman. (*Chin. Rep.*, VI, 1837, pp. 250—3).

1560. — Burmah and the Burmese. In Two Books. By Kenneth R. H. Mackenzie,... London: George Routledge and Co., 1853, pet. in-8, pp. xi—212.

1561. — Our Burmese Wars and Relations with Burma: being an abstract of military and political operations 1824—25—26, and 1852—53. With various local, statistical, and commercial information, and a summary of events from 1826 to 1879, including a sketch of King Theebau's progress. By Colonel W. F. B. Laurie, author of «Rangoon» and «Pegu» narratives of the second Burmese War. London, W. H. Allen & Co., Publishers to the India Office, 1880, in-8, pp. xx—487.

1562. — Joseph Chailley-Bert. Les Anglais en Birmanie. (*Rev. des Deux Mondes*, CVIII, Dec. 15, 1891, pp. 842—881; CIX, 1ᵉʳ janv. 1892, pp. 43—85; CX, 15 avril 1892, pp. 877—921).

1563. — *Joseph Chailley-Bert. La colonisation de l'Indo-Chine. Paris, Colin, pp. 398.

1564. — *A Collection of Treaties, Engagements, and Sanads relating to India and neighbouring Countries. Compiled by C. U. Aitchinson, B.C.S., Under-Secretary to the Government of India in the Foreign Department. Third Edition, 1892, gr. in-8.

Vol. I. — The Bengal Presidency, Assam, Burma, and the Eastern Archipelago.

1565. — Historique abrégé des relations de la Grande-Bretagne avec la Birmanie par Henri Cordier. Paris, Ernest Leroux, 1894, br. in-8, pp. 28.

On lit au verso du titre: «Tiré à 100 exemplaires sur papier glacé, et 100 exemplaires Van Gelder».
Avait paru dans la *Revue d'histoire diplomatique*.... Huitième année. — No. 1, Paris, E. Leroux, 1894, pp. 28—55.
Notice: *China Review*, XXI, No. 4, pp. 378—380, by E. H. Parker.

1566. — The Story of Burma by Ernest George Harmer. London, Horace Marshall & Son, s. d. [1902], in-16, pp. 211.

Collection *The Story of the Empire* edited by Howard Angus Kennedy.

Mission d'Edward Fleetwood (1695).

1567. — Embassy of Mr. Edward Fleetwood to Ava, 1695. (Dalrymple, *Orient. Repertory*, II, pp. 5—404).

Suivi des Instructions données par Nath. Higginson, Lieut.-général de l'Inde, à Thomas Bowyear, pp. 396—404.

George Baker (1755).

1568. — Capt. George Baker's Account of the City of Pegu. (*Ibid.*, I, Int. Second number, pp. I—II).

— Captain George Baker's Observations at Persaim and in the Journey to Ava and Back, 1755. (*Ibid.*, I, pp. 133—142).

— Captain George Baker's Journal of a Joint Embassy to the King of the Bûraghmahns. (*Ibid.*, pp. 143—162).

— A Short Character of the King of the Bûraghmahns. (*Ibid.*, pp. 163—8).

— Short Account of the Buraghmah Country, by Captain George Baker. (*Ibid.*, pp. 169—176).

— Account of the English Proceedings at Dagoon. (*Ibid.*, pp. 177—200).

Mission de l'Enseigne Lester (1757).

1569. — Ensign Lester's Embassy to the King of Ava, 1757. (*Ibid.*, pp. 201—22).

— Treaty concluded with the King of Ava, 28th July 1757. (*Ibid.*, pp. 223—6).

Affaire de Negrais (1759).

1570. — Letter concerning the Negrais Expedition; and concerning the adjacent Countries. By A. Dalrymple. (*Ibid.*, pp. 97—128).

— The Consequence of Settling an European Colony on the Island Negrais. (*Ibid.*, pp. 129—132).

— Account of the Loss of Negrais, 1759. (*Ibid.*, pp. 343—350).

Mission du Cap. Alves (1760).

1571. — Capt. Walter Alves's Proceedings in Ava, on an Embassy, 1760. (*Ibid.*, pp. 351—393).

Divers.

1572. — Brief Account of the Trade of Arracan, 1761, by Mr. William Turner. (*Ibid.*, pp. 227—8).

Nagore, 7th July, 1761.

1573. — Translation of a Letter, from the King of the Bûraghmahns, to the Governor of Madrass. October 1760. (*Ibid.*, pp. 394—5).

1574. — Antonio the Linguist, To the Honourable George Piggot, Esq. Governor of Fort St. George. Persaim, 24th Nov. 1760. (*Ibid.*, p. 396).

1575. — Translation of a Letter from Maugee Norata, Prince of Persaim, &c. To the Honourable George Pigot, Esq. President and Governor of Fort St. George. (Dalrymple, *Oriental Repertory*, I, pp. 397—8).

Mission du Cap. Michael Symes (1795).

1576. — An Account of an Embassy to the Kingdom of Ava, sent by the Governor-General of India, in the year 1795. — By Michael Symes, Esq. Major in His Majesty's 76th Regiment. — London: Printed by W. Bulmer and Co., ... and sold by Messrs. G. and W. Nicol...; and J. Wright, ... 1800, in-4, pp. xxiii—504. Cartes et gravures.

1577. — An Account of an Embassy to the Kingdom of Ava, in the year 1795. By Lieut.-Colonel Michael Symes; to which is now added, a narrative of the late military and political operations in the Birmese Empire. With some account of the present condition of the country, its Manners, Customs and Inhabitants. In two volumes. Edinburgh: Printed for Constable and Co. 1827, 2 vol. in-12, pp. xviii—312, vii—233—87. Les 87 dernières pages sont occupées par: A Narrative of the late military and political operations in the Birmese empire, with some account of the present condition of the country, its Manners, Customs and Inhabitants. By Henry G. Bell, Esq. Edinburgh: Printed for Constable and Co. 1827.

> Ces ouvrages forment les vol. VIII et IX de *Constable's Miscellany*.

1578. — Embassy to Ava; sent by the Governor general of India in the year 1795. By Michael Symes, Esq. Lieutenant Colonel in His Majesty's 76th Regiment. (*General Collection of Voyages and Travels*, by John Pinkerton, London, 1811, IX, pp. 426—572).

1579. — Relation de l'ambassade anglaise, envoyée en 1795 dans le royaume d'Ava, ou l'empire des Birmans; par le major Michel Symes, chargé de cette ambassade. Suivie d'un Voyage fait, en 1798, à Colombo, dans l'Ile de Ceylan, et à la Baie de Da Lagoa, sur la côte orientale de l'Afrique; — de la Description de l'Ile de Carmcobar et des Ruines de Mavalipouram; traduits de l'anglais avec des notes, par J. Castéra. Avec une Collection de 30 Planches in-4°, gravées en taille-douce par J. B. P. Tardieu, dessinées sur les lieux sous les yeux de l'Ambassadeur. A Paris, chez F. Buisson. An IX (1800), 3 vol. in-8, pp. vii—380, 396, 318.

> L'Atlas contient 2 cartes et 28 grav. gravées par J. B. Tardieu, Delignon, Niquet et Delvaux.

1580. — Gesandschaftsreise nach dem Königreiche Ava im Jahre 1795 auf Befehl des General-Gouverneurs von Ostindien unternommen vom Major M. Symes. Nebst Einleitung in die Geschichte von Ava, Pegu, Arracan, Beschreibung des Landes und Bemerkungen über Verfassung, Sitten und Sprache der Birmanen. — Aus dem Englischen mit Vorrede und Anmerkungen von Dr. Hager. — Nebst einer Karte und neun Kupfern. — Hamburg, 1800, bei B. G. Hoffmann. in-8, pp. xvi—479, carte.

1581. — Gesandtschaftsreise nach dem Königreiche Ava, im Jahre 1795 auf Befehl des General-Gouverneurs von Ostindien unternommen vom Major M. Symes. Nebst einer Einleitung in die Geschichte von Ava, Pegu, Arracan, Beschreibung des Landes und Bemerkungen über die Verfassung, Sitten und Sprache der Birmanen. — Aus dem Englischen mit Vorrede und Anmerkungen von Dr. Hager. — Mit 1 Karte und 6 Kupfern. — Berlin und Hamburg. 1801, in-8, pp. 434 + 1 f. n. c.

1582. — 'M. Symes. — Relazione dell' Ambasciata inglese, spedita nel 1795 nel Regno d'Ava o nell' Impero dei Birmani. Tradotto dal francese da Giuseppe Carozzi con una carta geografica e rami colorati. Milano, Raccolta di viaggi Sonzogno, 1813, 4 vol. in-16.

Mission de Hiram Cox (1796—1798).

1583. — Journal of a Residence in the Burmhan Empire, and more particularly at the Court of Amarapoorah. — By Capt. Hiram Cox, of the Honourable East India Company's Bengal native infantry. London: John Warren and G. and W. B. Whittaker, MDCCCXXI, in-8, pp. VIII—431. Planches color.

1584. — Voyage du Capitaine Hiram Cox dans l'empire des Birmans, avec des notes et un essai historique sur cet empire, les peuples qui occupent la presqu'ile au-dela du Gange, et sur la Compagnie anglaise des Indes orientales. Par A.-P. Chaalons d'Argé, Attaché à la Bibliothèque du Depôt de la guerre. Orné de figures, de costumes coloriés, et de la carte du théâtre de la guerre entre ce peuple et les Anglais. Paris, Arthus Bertrand, 1825, 2 vol. in-8, pp. CLVI—202, 420.

1585. — Voyage du Capitaine Hiram Cox dans l'Empire des Birmans, avec des notes et un essai historique sur cet Empire les peuples qui occupent la presqu'ile au-dela du Gange, et sur la Compagnie anglaise des Indes orientales par A.-P. Chalons d'Argé. Deuxième édition, ornée de cartes, figures et costumes coloriés. Paris, Arthus Bertrand, 1841, in-8, pp. XI—CLVI—210, 402.

1586. — Viaje al imperio de los Birmanes, por el capitan Hiran Cox. (N. Fernandez Cuesta, *Nuevo Viajero Universal*, II, Madrid, 1860, pp. 290—313).

.·.

1587. — Memorandum on the subject of an Embassy to Ava. (*Asiatic Annual Register*, 1807, *Miscel.*, pp. 146—150).

Première guerre birmane.

Déclarée 5 mai 1824. — Traité de Yandabou, 21 février 1826.

1588. — 'Coloured Illustrations of the War in Rangoon in 1824, a series of 24 large and finely coloured plates, illustrating Storming of Stockades, Naval Engagements, Landing of the Forces, Indian Pagodas, Temples, etc., 1826.

1589. — Two Years in Ava. From May 1824, to May 1826. By an Officer on the Staff of the Quartermaster-General's Department. London: John Murray, MDCCCXXVII, in-8, pp. xvi—455. Maps and plate.

By Capt. Thomas Abercrombie Trant.

1590. — Narrative of the Captivity of an Officer, who fell into the hands of the Burmāhs during the late war. Madras: Printed at the Asylum Press, 1827, in-8, pp. ii—145.

By Captⁿ Bennett, 1st or Royal Regᵗ of Infⁿʸ.

1591. — Narrative of the Burmese War, detailing the Operations of Major-general Sir Archibald Campbell's Army, from its Landing at Rangoon in May 1824, to the conclusion of a Treaty of Peace at Yandaboo, in February 1826. By Major Snodgrass, Military Secretary to the Commander of the Expedition, and Assistant Political Agent in Ava. — London: John Murray, MDCCCXXVII, in-8, pp. xii—319.

1592. — Medical Sketch of the Topography of the South-Eastern Part of the Chittagong District, and of the Sickness which has lately prevailed to a serious extent among the troops serving therein. By A. Macdougall, M.D. — Presented March 6, 1824. (*Trans. Medical and Phys. Soc. Calcutta*, I, 1825, pp. 190—8).

1593. — On the Endemic Fever of Arracan, with a Sketch of the Medical Topography of that Country. By. J. Grierson, Esq. — Presented Sept. 3, 1825. (*Ibid.*, II, 1826, pp. 201—219).

1594. — Sketch of the Medical Topography of Arracan, and Observations on the Diseases prevalent there, embracing a Period from the 1st of April 1825, to 20th January 1826. By R. N. Burnard, Esq. — Presented June 3, 1826. (*Ibid.*, III, 1827, pp. 25—85).

1595. — Remarks on the Sickness which prevailed among the European Troops in Arracan, in 1825, and on the Medical Topography of that Country. By W. Stevenson, Esq. Jun. — Presented Aug. 5, 1826. (*Ibid.*, pp. 86—127).

1596. — On the Diseases which prevailed among the British Troops at Rangoon. By G. Waddell, M.D. — Presented July 1, 1826. (*Ibid.*, III, 1827, pp. 240—80).

1597. — Documents illustrative of the Burmese War. With an Introductory Sketch of the Events of the War, and an Appendix. — Compiled and edited by Horace Hayman Wilson, Esq. — Calcutta: From the Government Gazette Press, by G. H. Huttmann, 1827, in-4, 4 ff. n. ch. + pp. 96 + 248 + lxxxxiii, carte.

1598. — Vergrosserung der brittischen Macht in Indien auf Kosten der birmanischen Reichs. (Mit einer Charte). (*Das Ausland*, 1828, Nos. 72, pp. 285—7, 73, pp. 291—92, 74, pp. 294—5).

1599. — Reminiscences of the Burmese War, in 1824—5—6. (Originally published in the Asiatic Journal.) By Capt. F. B. Doveton, late First Madras European Fusiliers, an Eye-Witness. With Illustrations, from Original Sketches

by the Author. London: Allen and Co., Taunton: Printed by W. A. Woodley.
— 1852, pet. in-8, pp. VIII—375.

1600. — Reminiscences of the Burmese War, In 1824—5—6. (Originally published in the Asiatic Journal.) By Capt. F. B. Doveton, late First Madras European Fusiliers, an Eye-Witness. With Illustrations, from Original Sketches by the Author. London: Allen and Co., 1852, pet. in-8, pp. VIII—375.

Même éd. avec des titres différents.

1601. — Political Incidents of the First Burmese War. By Thomas Campbell Robertson, late of the Bengal Civil Service. London: Richard Bentley, 1853, in-12, pp. VII—252, carte.

1602. — A Personal Narrative of Two Years' Imprisonment in Burmah, 1824—26. By Henry Gouger. With Illustrations. London: John Murray, 1860. in-12, pp. XII—327.

1603. — A Personal Narrative of Two Years' Imprisonment in Burmah. By Henry Gouger. With Illustrations. — Second edition. — London: John Murray, 1862. in-12, pp. XII—345.

Avec l'addition d'un nouveau chapitre.

1604. — An unpublished Document relating to the first Burmese War. Préface by R. C. Temple. (*Ind. Antiq.*, XXVI, 1897, pp. 40—7).

1605. — "The Arracan Expedition, 1825: From the Diary of an Artillery Officer. First Burmese War, 1824—6. (*Proc. of the R. Artillery Inst.*, 1900, Vol. XXVII, pp. 65—74, carte).

1606. — Marching to Ava, a Story of the First Burmese War by Henry Charles Moore — Illustrated — London, Gall and Inglis, s.d. [1904], pet. in-8, pp. 318.

Mission de John Crawfurd (1826).

1607. — Brief Narrative of an Embassy from the Governor-General of India to the King of Ava, In 1826—27; with Commercial Notices of our new Provinces on the Eastern coast of the Bay of Bengal. And an Appendix, giving an Account of the new Settlement of Amherst. By a member of the Embassy. London: Smith Elder, and Co., 1827, in-8, pp. 35.

1608. — Journal of an Embassy from the Governor General of India to the Court of Ava. By John Crawfurd... late Envoy. With an Appendix containing a Description of fossil Remains by Professor Buckland and Mr. Clift. London, 1829, in-4.

1609. — Journal of an Embassy from the Governor General of India to the Court of Ava. By John Crawfurd, Esq. F.R.S. F.L.S. F.G.S. &c. late Envoy. With an Appendix, containing a Description of fossil Remains by Professor Buckland and Mr. Clift. Second edition. In two volumes. London: published for Henry Colburn, by R. Bentley; Bell and Bradfute, Edinburgh; and John Cumming, Dublin. 1834, 2 vol. in-8, pp. X—541, 319—163, Carte et pl.

Deuxième guerre birmane (1852).

1610. — The recent Operations of the British Forces at Rangoon and Martaban. By the late Rev. Thomas Turner Baker, B.A. Chaplain and Naval Instructor of H. M. S. «Fox». London, Thomas Hatchard, 1852, in-8, pp. VII—78.

1611. — Six Months at Martaban during the Burmese War; and an Essay on the Political Causes which led to the Establishment of British Power in India. By an Officer in active Service on the spot. London: Partridge, Oakey & Co., s. d., in-12, pp. 131.

1612. — The Second Burmese War. A Narrative of the Operations at Rangoon. in 1852. By William F. B. Laurie, Lieut., Madras Artillery, Author of «Orissa and the temple of Jagannath», etc. With Illustrations, by Officers of the Force serving in Burmah. London: Smith, Elder & Co., Bombay: Smith, Taylor & Co. 1853, in-8, pp. XII—280.

1613. — Pegu, being a Narrative of Events during the Second Burmese War, from August 1852 to its conclusion in June 1853. With a Succinct Continuation down to February 1854. By William F. B. Laurie, Lieut., Madras Artillery, Author of «a Narrative of the operations at Rangoon in 1852», etc. etc. With Plans and Sketches, by Officers of the Force serving in Burmah. London: Smith, Elder & Co., Calcutta: Thacker, Spink and Co., Madras: Bainbridge and Co., Bombay: Smith, Taylor and Co. MD.CCC.LIV, in-8, pp. XI—535.

Mission de Arthur Phayre (1855).

1614. — Narrative of Major Phayre's Mission to the Court of Ava, with Notices on the Country, Government, and People. Compiled by Capt. H. Yule. Printed for submission to the Government of India. Calcutta, J. Thomas..... 1856, in-4, pp. XXIX + 1 f. n. ch. p. l. er. + pp. 315 + pp. CXIV + pp. IV and pp. 70.

> Les dernières pp. IV—70 renferment: Notes on the Geological features of the banks of the River Irawadee and on the Country north of the Amarapoora, by Thomas Oldham.... Calcutta, 1856.

1615. — A Narrative of the Mission sent by the Governor-general of India to the Court of Ava in 1855, with Notices of the Country, Government, and People. By Captain Henry Yule, Bengal Engineers, F.R.G.S., late Secretary to the Envoy (Major Phayre), and Under-Secretary (D.P.W.) to the Government of India. With Numerous Illustrations. London: Smith, Elder, and Co. 1858, gr. in-8, pp. VI—391, carte.

— Arthur Purves Phayre, Lieut. General Sir, C.B., K.C.S.I., G.C.M.G. (*Proc. R. Geog. Soc.*, VIII, 1886, pp. 103—112).

> Born at Shrewsbury 7th of May 1812; † 20th of Dec. 1885.

Troisième guerre birmane.

Les troupes anglaises entrèrent à Mandalay, le 28 nov. 1885. — Annexion de la Birmanie, 1er janvier 1886.

1616. — The Burmese War. By Sir Henry Durand. (*Calcutta Review*, No. 22, Nov. 1882).

1617. — Burma, The Foremost Country, A Timely Discourse. To which is added John Bull's Neighbour Squaring up; or, How the Frenchman sought to win an Empire in the East. With Notes on the Probable Effects of French success in Tonquin on British Interests in Burma. By the author of «Our Burmese Wars and Relations with Burma», «Ashé Pyee», &c. London: W. H. Allen, 1884, in-8, pp. xxviii—146.

1618. — Memorial on the Conquest of Burma. (*North-China Herald*, March 24, 1886, p. 317).

By Ts'ên Yü-ying, Vice-roy of Yun-nan.

1619. — La Birmanie et la politique coloniale de l'Angleterre. Par Octave Sachot. [*Quart. Rev.*, *Asiatic Q. R.*, etc.] (*Rev. Brit.*, 1886, I, pp. 369—404).

1620. — The Subjugation of Burmah. (*The Mail*, London, Friday, October 22, 1886).

1621. — Les Anglais en Birmanie. Par J. Raubert. (*Ann. de l'Ext. Orient*, 1885—1886, VIII, pp. 335—337).

1622. — Gli Inglesi in Barmania. Conferenza del Prof. A. Brunialti. (*Bol. Soc. geog. Ital.*, 1886, pp. 218—236).

1623. — *A. Keene. — The Third Burmese War, 1885—1887. (*Journal United Service Institute India*, XXVIII, pp. 34—55).

1624. — *W. W. Hooper. Lantern Readings illustrative of the Burmah Expeditionary Force. London, 1887, in-8, pp. 39.

B. M. 010057. e. 2. (4).

1625. — *Charles Bernard. — Burma. The new British Province. (*Scottish geogr. Mag*, IV, 1888, N° 2, pp. 66—83).

1626. — The Coming of the Great Queen, A Narrative of the Acquisition of Burma. By Major Edmond Charles Browne, Royal Scots Fusiliers.... London: Harrison, 1888, in-8, pp. 451.

Ouvrage divisé en deux livres: Book I. History of Burma from the Earliest Times to the Outbreak of the late War. — Narrative of Expedition, 1885 (Third War). — Events subsequent to the Fall of Mandalay. — History, Fluctuations, and future Prospects of Trade. — Dacoits and Dacoity. — The Burmese Women. Book II. Our Neighbours in the Far East (Karens, Shans, China or Khyins, Kayens or Kachins, Yunanese, Siamese, Annamese and Tonkingese). — The Indo-Chinese Question. 8 cartes et grav.
Notices: *Athenaeum*, 17 mars 1888, pp. 855 seq.; *Proc. R. Geog. Soc.*, April 1888, p. 251; *Saturday Review*, 28 April 1888, pp. 505 seq.

1627. — Edmond Plauchut. — Un royaume disparu. (La Birmanie). (*Revue des Deux Mondes*, 1er juillet, 1889, pp. 160—185).

1628. — Letters from Mandalay A Series of Letters For the most part written from the Royal City of Mandalay during the Troublous Years of 1878—79; together with Letters written during the last Burmese Campaign of 1885—88, By the late James Alfred Colbeck S.P.G. Mission Priest, and Acting Chaplain to the Forces. Edited by George H. Colbeck Formerly Mission Priest of Mandalay. Knaresborough: Printed and published by Alfred W. Lowe, 1892, pet. in-8, pp. v—113 + ii.

1629. — The last Days of an Empire. (*Blackwood's Mag.*, CLIII, May 1893, pp. 658—669).

1630. — The Life of the Marquis of Dufferin and Ava by Sir Alfred Lyall, P.C. With Portraits and Illustrations. London, John Murray, 1905, 2 vol. in-8, pp. xii + 1 f. n. ch. + pp. 328, viii + 1 f. n. ch. + pp. 339.
    Notice: *Times Weekly Ed. Lit. Sup.*, 10 Feb. 1905.

Divers.

1631. — The Burmese Embassy in Birmingham. (*Siam Repository*, Vol. V, Jan. 1873, pp. 84—86).

1632. — La Birmanie et la Chine méridionale D'après les Documents anglais par A.-R. Havet Secrétaire de la Société Académique Indo-Chinoise, ... Avec deux notices générales sur le commerce de la Birmanie anglaise par L. Vossion, Vice-Consul de France à Rangoon, ... Paris, au Siége de la Société, 1885, in-8, pp. 59.
    Ext. du *Bull. Soc. Ac. Indo-chinoise*, 2ᵉ série, t. 1ᵉʳ, 1881, pp. 284—291.

1633. — Cosmopolitan Essays by Sir Richard Temple, Bart. M.P. G.C.S.I. C.I.E. D.C.L. LLd. ... With Maps. London: Chapman and Hall, Limited. 1886, in-8, pp. xvi—508.
    Voir: Chap. X. The Politics of Burmah, pp. 202—259.

1634. — Conventions anglo-chinoises relatives à la Birmanie. (*Ann. de l'Ext. Orient*, 1886—1887, IX, pp. 65—69).

1635. — Ober-Birma unter Englischer Verwaltung von Emil Schlagintweit. (*Oest. Monats. f. d. Orient*, 1887, pp. 42—44).

1636. — France and England in Eastern Asia. By Holt S. Hallett. (*As. Quart. Review*, V, Jan.-April 1888, pp. 336—361).

1637. — Ce qu'est devenue la Birmanie — Ce que peut devenir l'Indo-Chine française. Par Paul Macey. (*Bul. Soc. Géog. Est*, 1896, pp. 349—354).

1638. — The Burma-China Trade Convention. By E. H. Parker. (*Imp. & As. Quart. Review*, July 1897, pp. 27—34).

1639. — Les Anglais en Birmanie. Conférence par Mme Isabelle Massieu. (*Bul. Soc. normande Géog.*, XXI, 1899, pp. 29—40).

1640. — Burma under British Rule — and Before by John Nisbet D. Œc Late Conservator of Forests, Burma.... Westminster, Archibald Constable, 1901, 2 vol. in-8, pp. viii + 1 f. n. ch. + pp. 459, viii + 452, Cartes.
    Voir No. 56. — Notice: *Imp. & Asiat. Quart. Rev.*, July-Oct. 1902, pp. 421—2.

1641. — Englands Grenzen in Birma. Von Dr. Emil Schlagintweit (Zweibrücken). (*Petermanns Mitt.*, 49. Bd. 1903, XII, pp. 267—8, carte).

1642. — L'Indo-Chine Anglaise et l'Autonomie birmane. (*Bull. Com. Asie française*, Janvier 1905, pp. 24—29).

Blue Books.

1643. — BURMAH (1883). — Papers relating to recent Negotiations between the Governments of India and Burmah. — Presented to both Houses of Parliament by Command of Her Majesty. — London, 1883, [C. — 3501], 10*d.*, in-fol., pp. 77.

1644. — BURMAH (1886). — Correspondence relating to Burmah since the Accession of King Theebaw in October, 1878. — Presented.... — London, 1886, [C. — 4614], 2*s.* 11*d.*, in-fol., pp. XI—266.

1645. — BURMAH, No. 2 (1886). — Telegraphic Correspondence relating to Military Executions and Dacoity in Burmah. — Presented.... — London, 1886, [C. — 4690], 1½*d.*, in-fol., pp. 12.

1646. — BURMAH, No. 3 (1886). — Further Correspondence relating to Burmah. — Presented.... — London, 1886, [C. — 4887], 3*s.* 4*d.*, in-fol., pp. IV—120, carte.

1647. — BURMAH, No. 1 (1887). — Further Correspondence relating to Burmah. (In continuation of No. 3 of 1886.) — Presented.... — London, 1887, [C. — 4962], 2*s.* 8*d.*, in-fol., pp. V—248.

1648. — East India (Upper Burma, Licences). Return of Licences for the Sale of Intoxicating Liquors.... 2 August 1888. London, [319], 1½*d.*, in-fol., pp. 11.

1649. — — Return of Licenses for the Sale of Opium, 2 August 1888. London, [320], ½*d.*, 1 f. in-fol.

1650. — — Copies of Correspondence..... relating to the issuing of Licences..... 9 August 1888. London, [338], 2½*d.*, in-fol., pp. 18.

1651. — — Returns of Licences for the Sale of Intoxicating Liquors and Opium, 9 February 1892. London, [22], 6*d.*, in-fol., pp. 59.

1652. — — Further Returns of Licenses for the Sale of Opium and Intoxicating Liquors, 27 March 1893. London, [149], 6*d.*, in-fol., pp. 59.

1653. — BURMAH, No. 2 (1887). — Correspondence respecting the Ruby Mines of Upper Burmah. — Presented.... — London, 1887, [C. — 5140], 6*d.*, in-fol., pp. 42.

1654. — Treaty Series. No. 19. — 1894. Convention between Great Britain and China, giving effect to Article III of the Convention of July 24, 1886, relative to Burmah and Thibet. Signed at London, March 1, 1894. [Ratifications exchanged at London, August 23, 1894.] Presented.... August 1894. London. [C. — 7547] Price 7*d.* in-8, pp. 9, carte.

Administration anglaise.

1655. — Commissioner's Report. Burma — its Trade. (*Siam Repository*, April 1870, Vol. 2, art. 46, pp. 210—214).

1656. — British Burma Its Trade and Customs for 1869—1870 Signed A. Fytche, Major Genl., C.S.I. Chief Commissioner British Burma, Agent to the Governor General. (*Ibid.*, Vol. 3, Jan. 1871, art. 47, pp. 126—142).

1657. — Report on the Trade and Customs of British Burma for 1870—71. (*Ibid.*, Vol. 4, July 1872, art. 60, pp. 369—370).

1658. — Burma. Abstracts from the British Burma Administration Report 1871—1872. (*Ibid.*, Vol. 5, Oct. 1873, art. 51, pp. 399—401, art. 70, pp. 488—491).

1659. — Burma. Abstracts from the British Burma Administration Report 1871—1872. Post office. (*Ibid.*, Vol. 6, Jan. 1874, art. 9, pp. 27—29).

1660. — Report on the Revenue Administration of British Burma for the year 1872—1873. (*Ibid.*, Vol. 6, April 1874, pp. 296—300).

1661. — Report on Public Instruction, British Burma, For the year 1872—73. (*Ibid.*, Vol. 6, April 1874, art. 49, pp. 203—5, 226—7).

.•.

1662. — Memorandum on the Comparative Progress of the Provinces now forming British Burma under British and Native Rule. By Colonel Albert Fytche. [Rangoon, 23rd August, 1867.] (*Proc. Roy. Geog. Soc.*, XII, 1868, pp. 198—201).

1663. — Burmans, Cambodians, and Peguans in Siam. (*The Phoenix*, III, Nº 25, July, 1872, pp. 2—3).

Du *Siam Weekly Advertiser.*

1664. — 'Paolo Chaix. — Notizie statistiche sull'alta e bassa Birmania secondo rapporti ufficiali inglesi. (*Cosmos*, Torino, X, I, pp. 1—7).

1665. — A University for Burma. By the Hen. Mr. Justice Jardine. First President of the Burma Board of Education. (*Imp. & As. Quart. Rev.*, N. S, VII, 1894, pp. 71—75).

1666. — In Burma with the Viceroy. By Mrs. Everard Cotes. (*Scribner's Mag.*, July 1902, pp. 58—72).

1667. — Burma. By Sir Frederic Fryer. (*Jour. Soc. of Arts*, Jan. 6, 1905, pp. 153—167).

.•.

1668. — In the Privy Council on appeal from the court of the recorder of Rangoon. — Between the Bombay Burmah trading corporation «limited» (Defendants).... Appellants and Mirza Mahomed Ally Sherazee, (Plaintiff).... The Burmah Company «limited» (co-Plaintiffs).... Respondents Date of Judgment of the Recorder of Rangoon 4th November 1876. Date of Application by Appellants for leave to Appeal to Her Majesty in Council 19th March 1877. Rangoon: British Burmah press. 1877, 2 parties in-4, pp. 28, 232—lxxxv.

1669. — The British Burma Manual; or, a Collection of Departmental Rules, Orders, and Notifications in force in the Province of British Burma; together with the Treaties concluded with the Kingdoms of Ava and Siam. Compiled and arranged by Captain C. B. Cooke, Madras Staff Corps; Political agent, Bhamo, Burma... Volume I. Corrected up to the 31st December, 1878... Calcutta: Thacker, Spink, and Co., MDCCCLXXIX, gr. in-8, pp. lxxviii—784.

1670. — Memorandum on the Forest Laws in force in Upper Burma by H. C. Hill, Conservator of Forests, Upper Burma Circle. Rangoon: Printed by the Supdt., Govt. Printing, Burma, 1889, in-8, pp. 12.

> Voir Nos. 1167—1170.

1671. — Report on the Frontier Affairs of Burma in 1889—90. — Rangoon: Printed by the Supdt., Government Printing, Burma. August 1890. in-fol., pp. 13—19—4—11—12—11—11, pl.

1672. — The Burma Forest Act, 1881, as amended by Act V of 1890 (An Act to amend the Indian Forest Act, 1878, and the Burma Forest Act, 1881) and Act XII of 1891 (An Act to repeal certain Obsolete Exactments and to amend certain other Enactments) with Notifications, Rules and Departmental Directions issued there under and Circulars and Instructions on Forest Matters. — Corrected up to 1st November 1893. — Rangoon: Printed by the Supdt., Govt. Printing, Burma. 1893, in-8, pp. ii—104.

— — Corrected up to the 7th December 1896. (Second Edition). Ibid., 1896, in-8, pp. ii—122.

1673. — The Opium Act, 1878, with Rules and Notifications thereunder in force in Burma. — Corrected up to the 1st January 1894. — Rangoon: Printed by the Supdt., Govt. Printing, Burma. 1894, in-8, pp. 53.

1674. — General Catalogue of All Publications of the Government of India and Local Governments and Administrations. Part I. All Publications, except Acts and Regulations and Publications which are not for sale. No. 5. Corrected up to June 30, 1902. Printed for the Government of India at the Government Central Printing Office, 8 Hastings Street, Calcutta, Dec. 1902, in-8, pp. 197.

> Burma, pp. 155—161. — Assam, pp. 169—179.

— General Catalogue.... Part I.... No. 9. Corrected up to 30th June 1904. Printed.... Calcutta, December 1904, in-8, pp. 252.

> Burma, pp. 183—194. — Assam, pp. 205.

— — Part 2. Acts and Regulations of the Imperial and Provincial Legislative Councils. No. 9... Printed... Calcutta, February 1905, in-8, pp. 89.

— — Part 3. Publications which are issued only under special orders and not for sale. Printed... Calcutta, March 1905, in-8, pp. 39.

> Burma, pp. 29—34. — Assam, pp. 37—8.

1675. — 'The Quarterly Civil List for Burma. List of Officers in Civil Employ in Burma with full particulars. Compiled by the Government of Burma. gr. in-8. Trimestriel.

Publications of the Government of Burma.

I ¹).

1676. —

Administration, Burma—

Annual Report on the Administration of —. Summary of the departmental reports; physical and political geography; administration of the land; protection; production and distribution; revenue and finance; vital statistics; and medical services; instruction; archæology, etc., with statistical returns. Compiled by the Government of Burma. For the years 1898—99 to 1900—01, Rs. 4-8, or 6*s.* 9*d.* (7*a.*) (each year); 1901—02, Re. 1-6, or 2*s.* 1*d.* (3*a.* 6*p.*); and 1902—03, Re. 1, or 1*s.* 6*d.* (2*a.* 6*p.*)

Allowance—

Burma Travelling — Manual. Compiled by the Accountant General, Burma. Super-royal, stiff board. As. 8, or 9*d.* (1*a.* 6*p.*)

Appointment—

Rules for the — of Subordinate Revenue and Land Records Officers in Burma. Anna 1, or 1*d.* (6*p.*)

Appointment and Allowances—

Manual of — of Officers in Burma. Compiled by the Accountant-General of Burma. Published 1900. Super-royal 8vo, stiff board, cloth back. As. 9. (2*a.*)

Archæology—

Archæological Work in Burma. Report on —. Compiled by Government Archæologist, Burma. Foolscap folio, paper cover. For the years 1901—02, As. 2, or 2*d.* (6*p.*); and 1902—03, As. 3, or 3*d.* (1*a.*)

List of Objects of Antiquarian and Archæological interest in Upper Burma. Compiled by the Government of Burma. Published 1901. Foolscap folio, paper cover. As. 8, or 9*d.* (1*a.*)

Publications of the Archæological Department, Burma, No. 2. — List of Pagodas at Pagan under the custody of Government. In English and Burmese. Compiled by the Government of Burma. Published 1901. Foolscap folio. Re. 1, or 1*s.* 6*d.* (2*a.* 6*p.*)

Arms—

Arms Manual, Burma. Containing the Indian Arms Act of 1878, together with Notifications and Rules and Circulars thereunder. Published 1902. Corrected up to 4th August 1902. Compiled by the Government of Burma. Super-royal 8vo, stiff board, cloth back. Re. 1-8, or 2*s.* 3*d.* (3*a.*)

Asylum, Lunatic—

Report on the — in Rangoon. Management of Lunatics in Burma. Compiled by the Government of Burma. Foolscap folio, stiff cover. For the years

---

1) D'après les pp. 188—194 du *General Catalogue*, Part 1, No. 9 (Voir supra, no. 1674).

—1899, As. 12, or 1s. 2d. (1a.); (triennium) 1900—2, As. 6, or 7d. (1a.); and 1903, As. 8, or 9d. (1a.)

Statements relating to Rangoon —, showing admissions, discharges, etc., of Lunatics. Compiled by the Government of Burma. Foolscap folio, paper cover. For the year 1901. As. 3, or 3½d. (6p.)

Boundaries—

Burma — Manual. Compiled by the Government of Burma. Super-royal, stiff board. As. 5, or 5½d. (1a.)

Catalogue—

1. General Department —. The Bernard Free Library. List of Books in the Library. Compiled by the Registrar, Educational Syndicate, Burma. Royal 8vo, stiff board, cloth back. Published 1903. Re. 1-7, or 2s. 2d. (1a. 6p.)

Census—

Census of India, 1901. — Volumes XII and XII-A, Burma. Compiled by Mr. C. C. Lewis, I.C.S., Superintendent, Census Operation of Burma. Published 1902. Foolscap folio, stiff board, cloth back, half bound. Part I — Report, Rs. 3-6 or 5s. (5a.); and Part II — Imperial Tables, Rs. 4, or 6s. (6a.)

Chin Hills—

Report on the Administration of the —. Administration of the Chin Hills, on the frontier affairs of the Upper Chindwin District, the Pakokku Chin Hills and Hill Tracts of Arakan. Compiled by the Government of Burma. For the years 1899—1900, Re. 1 (1a. 6p.); 1900—01, As. 10, or 11d. (1a.); 1901—02, As. 10, or 4d. (1a.); and 1902—03, As. 12, or 1s. 1½d. (1a.)

Circulars—

Burma Secretariat —, 1888—1901. A collection of Secretariat Circulars issued between 1888 and 1901. Compiled by the Government of Burma. Super-royal, stiff board, cloth back. In English, Rs. 2-8, or 3s. 9d. (5a. 6p.); and in Burmese, As. 14, or 1s. 4d. (2a. 6p.)

Index to Financial Commissioner's translated circulars for 1902. In Burmese. Royal 8vo, paper cover. As. 2, or 2d. (6p.)

Commerce—

Commercial Report on the trade of Yunnan with special reference to the Burma-Tengyueh trade, 1903. General description, trade routes, currency, banking of Yunnan. Compiled by the Government of Burma. Foolscap folio, paper cover. As. 12, or 1s. 1½d. (1a.)

Commissioner, Financial—

Circulars of the —, Burma. Compiled by the Government of Burma. Royal 8vo, stiff board, cloth back. For the years 1900, As. 8, or 9d. (1a. 6p.); and 1901, As. 10, or 9d. (2a. 6p.)

Courts—

Courts Manual. Circulars and Orders in force in Upper Burma. Compiled by the Judicial Commissioner, Upper Burma. Super-royal 8vo, stiff board, cloth back. In English, Rs. 3, or 4s. 6d. (4a. 6p.); in Burmese, Rs. 4-14, or 7s. 4d. (9a.)

Crop-Measurement—

Memorandum on — statistics in Burma. By the Director of the Department of Land Records and Agriculture, Burma. Foolscap folio, paper cover. Collected during the years 1898—99 and 1899—1900. Re. 1-12, or 2s. 8d. (1a.) (each year).

Customs—

Burma Sea — Manual. Compiled by the Chief Collector of Customs, containing rules, notifications, and orders applicable to Burma. Royal 8vo, stiff board, cloth back. Rs. 3, or 4s. 6d. (3a.)

Education—

Educational Code, Burma, 5th Edition. A guide to Civil Officers, Municipal Committees, Managers of Government and Aided Schools and others interested in education in the Province of Burma. Compiled by the Director of Public Instruction, Burma. Royal 8vo, stiff board, cloth back. In English, Re. 1, or 1s. 6d. (2a.); in Burmese, As. 5, or 6d. (1a. 6p.)

Educational Syndicate, Burma. Annual Report of the —. Compiled by the Registrar, Educational Syndicate, Burma. Foolscap folio, paper cover. For the years 1901—02 and 1902—03, As. 8, or 9d. (1a.) (each year).

Elephants—

A Treatise on —, their treatment in health and disease. By Veterinary Captain G. H. Evans, A.V.D. Published 1901. Super-royal, full leather, stiff board. Rs. 4-8, or 6s. 9d. (4a.) [*Out of print.*]

Examiner, Chemical—

Report of the —, Burma. Compiled by the Government of Burma. Foolscap folio, paper cover. For the years 1901 and 1901—02. As. 6, or 7d. (6p.) (each year); 1902—03, As. 8, or 9d. (6p.)

Excise—

Report on the Financial Result of the — Administration in Burma. Compiled by the Government of Burma. Foolscap folio, paper cover. For the years 1899—1900, Re. 1-12 (2a.); 1900—01, As. 10, or 11d. (1a); 1901—02, As. 9, or 10d. (1a.); and 1902—03, As. 8, or 9d. (1a. 6p.)

Explosives—

Explosives Manual, Burma. Corrected up to 1st June 1902. Containing the Indian Explosives Act 4 of 1884 as amended by Act 10 of 1889 and Act 12 of 1891, together with Notifications, Rules, and Circulars thereunder. Compiled by the Government of Burma. Published 1902. Super-royal, stiff board, cloth back. As. 9, or 10d. (2a.)

Factories—

Report on the Working of the Indian — Act in Lower Burma. Compiled by the Government of Burma. Published 1901. Foolscap folio, paper cover.

For the years 1900, As. 12, or 1s. 1½d. (1a.); 1901, As. 5, or 5½d. (1a.); and 1902, As. 5, or 5½d. (1a.)

Famine—

Famine in Burma. Analysis of Districts with reference to security against famine during 1901—02. Compiled by the Financial Commissioner. Foolscap, paper cover. Rs. 6-12, or 10s. or 1½d. (4a.)

Forest—

Report on — Administration of Burma. Resolution of the Government of Burma on the Forest Administration of Burma with a review of the various Circle Reports and accompanying statements, subjoined in detail. Compiled by the Government of Burma. For the years 1898—99 and 1899—1900, Rs. 4—12, or 7s. 1½d. (3a.) (each year); 1900—01, Rs. 2-8, or 3s. 9d. (1a. 6p.); 1901—02, Rs. 2-12, or 4s. 1½d. (2a. 6p.); and 1902—03, Rs. 3, or 4s. 6d. (2a. 6p.)

Forestry—

Forestry for Burmans. Manual of —. Compiled by the Conservator of Forests, Pegu Division. Super-royal, stiff board, cloth back.

    Volume II. Utilisation of Forest Produce. As. 15, or 1s. 5d. (1a. 6p.)
       » III. Protection of Forest and Forest Produce. As. 12, or 1s. 1½d. (1a. 6p.)
       » IV. Forest Engineering. As. 9, or 10d. (1a. 6p.)
       » V. Rudiments of Botany. As. 8, or 9d. (1a. 6p.)

Rudiments of — for Burmans. Compiled by the Director of Public Instruction. Burma. In Burmese. Published 1903. Super-royal, stiff board, cloth back. Rs. 2-6, or 3s. 7d. (4a.)

Frontier, North-Eastern—

Report on the administration of the North-Eastern Frontier. Compiled by the Government of Burma. Foolscap folio, paper cover. For the years 1899—1900. As. 10 (1a. 6p.); and 1901—02 and 1902—03, Re. 1, or 1s. 6d. (1a.) (each year).

Gazetteer—

Gazetteer of Upper Burma and Shan States. Physical geography of Upper Burma. History of the war, annexation, and final pacification. The Shan States and the Hill tribes; ethnology; religion; customs, etc., under Native rulers; archæology; geology; and economic mineralogy; vegetation; agriculture and arts and industries; different Departments of Administration, past and present; population and trade. With Glossary and Index; also with maps and 37 full-page illustrations. By J. G. Scott, Bar.-at-law, C.I.E., M.R.A.S., F.R.G.S. Published 1901. Royal 8vo, stiff board, cloth back. Part I, Volumes I and II, Rs. 12, or 18s. (Re. 1); Part II, Volumes I, II, and III, Rs. 12, or 18s. (Re. 1-4).

Glass-Mosaics—

Glass Mosaics of Burma, with Photographs. By H. L. Tilly. Published 1901. Rs. 9, or 13s. 6d. (5a.)

Hlutdaw—

Catalogue of the — Records. Volume I. Compiled by the Government of Burma. Published 1901. Royal 8vo, stiff board, cloth back. In Burmese. Rs. 8, or 12s. (5a. 6p.)

Hospitals and Dispensaries—

Notes and Statistics of the — in Burma. Notes and Statistics concerning the administration of the Civil, Railway, and Police Hospitals and Dispensaries in Burma. Compiled by the Government of Burma. Foolscap folio, paper cover. For the years 1899, Re. 1-4, or 1s. 10$\frac{1}{2}$d. (2a.); 1900, Re. 1, or 1s. 6d. (1a. 6p.); (triennium) 1899 to 1901, Re. 1-4, or 1s. 10$\frac{1}{2}$d. (1a. 6p.); and 1902, Re. 1-4, or 1s. 10$\frac{1}{2}$d. (1a. 6p.)

Income-tax—

Rules for the guidance of the — Office, Rangoon. Compiled by the Government of Burma. Published 1901. Foolscap folio, paper cover. As. 4, or 4$\frac{1}{2}$d. (6p.)

Working of the — Act, II of 1886, in Burma. Containing Revenue on Income-tax in Burma. Compiled by the Government of Burma. Foolscap folio, paper cover. For the years 1899—1900, As. 6, or 7d. (6p.); 1900—01, As. 7, or 8d. (1a.); triennium) 1899, 1900—02, As. 6, or 7d. (1a.); and 1902—03, As. 5, or 5$\frac{1}{2}$d. (1a.)

Inscriptions—

Inscriptions collected in Upper Burma, Vol. II. In Burmese. Compiled by the Government Archæologist, Burma. Published 1904. Super-royal 4to, stiff boards, paper cover, cloth back. Rs. 4-4, or 6s. 4$\frac{1}{2}$d. (7a.)

Instruction, Public—

Report on — in Burma. Controlling agencies; university education; secondary education; primary éducation; special instructions; female éducation; education of special classes; and general statistics. Compiled by the Director of Public Instruction. Foolscap folio, paper cover. For the years 1899—1900. Re. 1-4, or 1s. 10$\frac{1}{2}$d. (2a.); and 1900—01 and 1902—03, As. 10, or 11d. (1a. 6p.) (each year).

Second Quinquennial Report on — in Burma for the years 1897-98—1901-02. General statistics of institution and peoples, controlling agencies, collegiate education, secondary education, Upper and Lower female education, etc. Compiled by the Director of Public Instruction, Burma. Published 1902. Foolscap folio, paper cover. As. 10, or 11d. (2a.)

Irrigation—

Triennial Report of — Works, Burma, for the period ending the 31st March 1902. Compiled by the Government of Burma, Public Works Department. Published 1903. Foolscap folio, paper cover. Rs. 3-12, or 5s. 7$\frac{1}{2}$d. (1a. 6p.)

Ivory-Carving—

Monograph on — in Burma. By H. S. Pratt, I.C.S. Published 1901. Royal 8vo, stiff board, cloth back. As. 12, or 1s. 1½d. (1a.)

Justice—

CIVIL. Report on the Civil — Administration in Burma summarised. Compiled by the Government of Burma. Foolscap folio, paper cover. For the years 1899, Re. 1 (1a. 6p.): 1900, As. 14, or 1s. 4d. (1a.); 1901, As. 10, or 11d. (1a.); and 1902, As. 11, or 1s. (1a.)

CRIMINAL. Report on the Criminal — in Burma. Reported crime judicially dealt with in Burma summarised. Compiled by the Government of Burma. Foolscap folio, paper cover. For the years 1899, Re. 1-8 (2a.); 1900, As. 13, or 1s. 3d. (1a.); and 1901 and 1902, As. 12, or 1s. 1½d. (1a.) (each year).

Kachin or Chingpaw—

Kachin or Chingpaw language. A practical hand-book of the — containing the grammatical principles and peculiarities of the language, colloquial exercises, and a vocabulary. Compiled by H. F. Hertz, C.I.E. Published 1902. Super-royal, stiff board, cloth back. Re. 1-3, or 1s. 9d. (2a. 6p.)

Land Records—

Report on — administration. Compiled by the Government of Burma. Foolscap folio, paper cover. For the years ending 30th June 1902, As. 5, or 5½d. (1a.); and 1903, As. 8, or 9d. (1a.)

Land Records and Agriculture—

Report on the Department of —, Burma. Compiled by the Director, Department of Land Records and Agriculture. Foolscap folio, paper cover. For the years 1899—1900, Re. 1, or 1s. 6d. (2a. 6p.); and 1900—01, As. 7, or 8d. (1a.)

Land Revenue—

Land Revenue Manual, Lower Burma — Containing the (Lower Burma) Land and Revenue Act, 1876, the (Lower Burma) Fisheries Act, 1875, the Land Improvement Loans Act, 1883, the Agriculturists' Loans Act, 1884, the Revenue Recovery Act, 1890, and the Rules, Notifications and Orders thereunder in force in Lower Burma, in Burmese. Super-royal, Rs. 4-4, or 6s. 4½d. (6a. 6p.)

Land Revenue Manual, Upper Burma. Corrected up to 1st April 1902, in Burmese. Containing the Land Revenue Regulation, 1889, the Land Improvement Loans Act, 1883, the Agriculturists' Loans Act, 1884, and the Rules, Notifications, and Orders thereunder in force in Upper Burma. Compiled by the Government of Burma. Published 1902. Super-royal, stiff board, cloth back. Rs. 2-4, or 3s. 4½d. (5a.)

Land Revenue administration of Burma. Report on the —. Compiled by the Government of Burma. Foolscap folio, paper cover. During the fifteen months ended 30th June 1902. As. 11, or 1s. (1a. 6p.); and during the year ended 30th June 1903, As. 15, or 1s. 5d. (1a. 6p.)

Land Surveying—

Aid to —. Large edition. Compiled by the Assistant Director of Land Records and Agriculture. Containing Practical Geometry. Mensuration of Surfaces, Plane Trigonometry, Map Drawing, Chain Surveying, Theodolite Surveying, Levelling, Astronomy, etc., with illustrations and examples for practice. Foolscap folio, stiff board, cloth back. Rs. 6, or 8s. (7a.) Small edition. Rs. 2, or 2s. 8d. (3a.) In Burmese, Rs. 2, or 3s. (4a.)

Law, Burmese Buddhist—

Translation of a Digest of the —. Compiled by the Goverment of Burma. Published 1903. Super-royal, stiff board, cloth back. Rs. 3, or 4s. 6d. (6a.)

Leases -

Rules for — of Land in Towns other than Scheduled Towns for Building, Residential, and Industrial purposes. Compiled by the Government of Burma. Published 1901. Royal 8vo, paper cover. As. 2, or 2$^1/_2$d. (6p.)

Leather—

Tanning and Working in —. Compiled by E. J. Colstan, M.A., I.C.S., and published by the Government of Burma. Containing chapters on Trade Statistics, curing and tanning processes, sandals and shoes manufactured in Burma, hide drums, table of import and export, etc. Royal 8vo, stiff boards, paper cover, cloth back. Rs. 2-8, or 3s. 9d. (2a. 6p.)

Legislation—

Effect of — by the Lieutenant Governor of Burma in Council, 1903. Containing Table showing the Acts passed by the Government of Burma, the enactments affected and the extent of the repeal or amendment caused thereby. Compiled by the Government of Burma. Royal 8vo, paper cover. Anna 1, or 1d. (6p.)

Light-houses—

Thirty-fourth Annual Report on the — and Light Vessels off the coast of Burma for the year 1900—01. Compiled by the Government of Burma. Published 1901. Foolscap folio, paper cover. As. 3, or 3$^1/_2$d. (1a.)

List, Civil—

The Quarterly — for Burma. List of Officers in Civil employ in Burma, with full particulars. Compiled by the Government of Burma. Royal 8vo, paper cover. Issued quarterly. Corrected up to the 1st April 1904. Re. 1, or 1s. 6d. (2a. 6p.) (each quarter).

Manual—

Rules —. Vol. I — List of Local Rules and Orders made under General Statutes, Acts, Local Acts, Burma Acts, Regulation and Appendices. Compiled by the Government of Burma. Published 1903. Super-royal, stiff board, cloth back. Re. 1-9, or 2s. 4d. (4a.) Vol. II, As. 15, or 1s. 5d. (3a.)

Subdivisional and Township Office —. Departments of works, classes of documents, Register, Correspondence, etc., with appendices. Compiled by the Government of Burma. Second edition, 1904. Super-royal, stiff board, cloth back. As. 9, or 10d. (2a.); in Burmese, As. 12, or 1s. 1¹/₂d. (1a. 6p.)

Village Headman's —. Upper Burma. Compiled by the Government of Burma. Dealing with the appointment, privileges, powers, and duties of Village Headmen. Published 1904. Super-royal 8vo, paper cover. In English or Burmese. As. 4, or 4¹/₂d. (1a.) (each).

Mayo—

Report on the — Sailors' Home, Rangoon. Foolscap folio, paper cover. For the years 1901, As. 3, or 3¹/₂d. (6p.); 1902, As. 3, or 3d. (6p.), and 1903, As. 3, or 3¹/₂d. (1a.)

Municipalities—

Report on the working of the Rangoon Municipality for the year 1901—02. Compiled by the Government of Burma. Published 1902. Foolscap folio, paper cover. As. 12, or 1s. 1¹/₂d. (6p.)

Resolution reviewing the Reports on the Working of the — in Burma. Compiled by the Government of Burma. Foolscap folio, paper cover. For the year 1898—99, Re. 1-12, or 2s. 8d. (1a.); 1900—01, Re. 1, or 1s. 6d. (1a.); 1901—02, As. 10, or 11d. (1a.); and 1902—03, As. 15, or 1s. 7d. (1a.)

Names, Geographical—

List of — of which the Burmese Orthography has been authorized by the Text Book Committee. Compiled by the Director of Public Instruction in Burma. Royal 8vo, paper cover, As. 3, or 3¹/₂d. (1a.)

Office—

Office Manual containing a code of instructions for dealing with all correspondence, files, proceedings, and registers other than those appertaining to the Judicial Department, in the Offices of the Deputy Commissioners and their Subordinates. Compiled by the Government of Burma. Published 1901. Royal 8vo, stiff board, cloth back. As. 10, or 11d. (2a).

Plague—

The Burma — Manual, 1st Edition. Containing the Epidemic Diseases Act, 1897, and Rules, Orders, and Notifications issued thereunder. Compiled by the Government of Burma. Published 1901. Royal 8vo, stiff board, cloth back. As. 12, or 1s. 1¹/₂d. (2a.)

Pleaders—

Pleaders of the Chief Court and of the Subordinate Courts and Revenue Offices of Lower Burma. Rules for the qualification, admission, and certificates of —. Compiled by the Registrar, Chief Court, Lower Burma. Royal 8vo, paper cover. As. 5, or 5¹/₂d. (6p.)

Police—

Burma — Manual—

Volume I, Second Edition. — Containing orders and rules made for the Burma Police. By A. St. J. Ingle, Officiating District Superintendent of Police. Published 1900. Royal 8vo, full cloth. Rs. 3, or 4s. 6d. (6a. 6p.)

Volume II. — A Hand-book containing portions of Criminal Procedure and Penal Codes, of the Evidence Act, and of certain Special and Local Acts bearing on Police Action and Procedure. By the Inspector-General of Police, Burma. Published 1900. Super-royal 8vo, full cloth bound. Re. 1-8, or 2s. 3d. (4a.)

Military — Manual for Burma. Orders and Rules made for the Military Police of Burma by Lieut.-Colonel C. S. F. Peile, Inspector General of Police, Burma. By the Inspector General of Police, Burma. Published 1901. Super-royal, stiff board, full calico. Re. 1, or 1s. 6d. (2a. 6p.)

Rangoon — Manual. Containing Orders and Rules for the Rangoon Police. By R. G. P. P. McDonnell, Commissioner of Police. Published 1901. Super-royal, stiff board. Rs. 4-8, or 6s. 9d. (3a.)

Report on the — Administration of Burma. Strength, cost, efficiency of the Police in defecting the various kinds of crimes against the State and against property and person. Compiled by the Deputy Inspector-General of Civil Police. Foolscap folio, paper cover. For the years 1899, Rs. 2, or 3s. (2a. 6p.); 1900, Re. 1-8, or 2s. 3d. (2a.); 1901, Re. 1-2, or 1s. 8d. (1a. 6p.); and 1902, Re. 1-5, or 1s. 11½d. (2a.)

Report on the Rangoon Town — of Burma. Report on the working of Town Police as reorganised by the Rangoon Police Act, 1899. Compiled by the Commissioner of Police. Foolscap folio, paper cover. For the years 1899, As. 14, or 1s. 4d. (1a. 6p.); 1900, As. 12, or 1s. 1½d. (1a. 6p.); 1901, As. 10, or 11d. (1a. 6p.); 1902, Re. 1, or 1s. 6d. (1a.); and 1903, Re. 1, or 1s. 6d. (1a. 6p.)

Report on the — Supply and Clothing Department in Burma. Statistics regarding the Police Supply and Clothing. Compiled by the Deputy Inspector-General of Civil Police. Foolscap folio, paper cover. For the years 1899—1900, As. 6, or 7d. (1a.); 1900—01 and 1901—02, As. 2, or 2½d. (1a.) (each year); and 1902—03, As. 2, or 2d. (6p.)

Prison—

Prison Administration of Burma. Compiled by the Government of Burma. Foolscap folio, stiff cover. For the years 1899, Rs. 2, or 3s. (2a); and 1900, 1901, and 1902, Re. 1-8, or 2s. 3d. (1a. 6p.) (each year); and 1903, Re. 1-8, or 2s. 3d. (2a.)

Rainfall—

Report on the — in Burma for the year ending 31st March 1900. Compiled by the Director, Department of Land Records and Agriculture. Published 1900. Foolscap folio, paper cover. As. 8, or 9d. (1a.)

Red Karen—

Elementary Hand-book of — Language. By Captain R. J. R. Brown, I.S.C. Published 1900. Super-royal 8vo, stiff board, cloth back. Re. 1-8, or 2s. 3d. (2a.)

Reformatory—

Annual Report of the Insein —. Conduction of the Insein Reformatory. Compiled by the Government of Burma. Foolscap folio, paper cover. For the years 1900 and 1901, As. 3, or 3½d. (1a.) (each year); 1902, As. 3, or 3d. (6p.); and 1903, As. 3, or 3½d. (1a.)

Registration—

Notes on the — Department in Burma. Notes and Statistics concerning the work of Registration of Deeds Department. Compiled by the Government of Burma. Foolscap folio, paper cover. For the years 1899—1900, Re. 1-4, or 1s. 10½d. (1a. 6p.); 1900—01, As. 14, or 1s. 4d. (1a.); (triennium) 1899—1900—01—02, Re. 1-4, or 1s. 10½d. (1a. 6p.); 1902, As. 9, or 10d. (1a.); and 1903, As. 8, or 9d. (1a.)

Registration of Deeds Manual, Lower Burma, 1904. Compiled by the Financial Commissioner, Burma, Super-royal 8vo. Containing the Indian Registration Act, 1877, and rules and directions thereunder in force in Lower Burma. Re. 1, or 1s. 6d. (3a.)

Regulations, Civil Service—

Supplement to the —. Regulation for Officers of the Civil Service and others regarding pay, allowance, and leave, etc., with appendices. Compiled by the Accountant General, Burma. Published 1903. Super-royal, stiff board, cloth back. As. 14, or 1s. 4d. (1a. 6p.)

Revenue—

Report on the — Administration of Burma. Compiled by the Government of Burma. Foolscap folio, paper cover. For the years 1899—1900, Rs. 4-8, or 6s. 9d. (4a. 6p.); and 1900—01, Re. 1, or 1s. 6d. (2a.)

Revenue, Land—

Resolution of the Government of India, 1902. Compiled by the Government of Burma. In Burmese. Published 1903. Royal 8vo, stiff board, cloth back. As. 9, or 10d. (1a. 6p.)

Rulings—

Upper Burma —, 1892—1896. Volume I — Criminal. Rulings of the Judicial Commissioner, Upper Burma, during 1892—1896. Compiled by the Judicial Commissioner, Upper Burma. Published 1901. Super-royal 8vo, paper cover. Rs. 2-8, or 3s. 9d. (5a.)

Upper Burma —, 1892—1896. Volume II — Civil. Compiled by the Judicial Commissioner, Upper Burma. Published 1900. Super-royal 8vo, paper cover. Rs. 4, or 6s. (6a.)

Upper Burma —, 1897—1901. Volume I — Criminal. Compiled by the Judicial Commissioner, Upper Burma. Super-royal 8vo, stiff board, cloth back. Rs. 3-8, or 5s. 3d. (4a. 6p.)

Sales, Transfers etc.—

Notes on the statistics regarding sales, transfer, rents, and prices of produce collected by the Land Records Department in the Districts under Supplementary Survey in Lower and Upper Burma in 1898—99. By the Director of Department of Land Records and Agriculture. Published 1900. Foolscap folio, paper cover. Rs. 12, or 18s. (4a. 6p.)

Salt—

Report on the Administration of the — Revenue in Burma. Production and consumption, distribution, and prices of salt in Burma. Compiled by the Government of Burma. Foolscap folio, paper cover. For the years 1899, As. 6, or $6^{1}/_{2}d.$ (1a.); 1900, As. 6, or $6^{1}/_{2}d.$ (1a. 6p.); 1901, As. 4, or $4^{1}/_{2}d.$ (1a.); and 1902, As. 4, or $4^{1}/_{2}d.$ (6p.)

Sanitation—

Report on the Sanitary Administration of Burma. Vital Statistics; history of the chief diseases and of sanitary works in Burma. Compiled by the Government of Burma. Foolscap folio, paper cover. For the years 1899, Rs. 2, or 3s. (2a.); 1900, As. 10, or 11d. (1a. 6p.); 1901, As. 14, or 1s. 4d. (1a. 6p.); and 1902, As. 15, or 1s. 5d. (1a.)

Season and Crop—

Season and Crop Report of Burma. Rainfall and harvest agricultural stock, prices obtainable by cultivators, etc. Compiled by the Government of Burma. Foolscap folio, paper cover. For the years ending 30th June 1902, As. 5, or $5^{1}/_{2}d.$ (1a.); and 1903, As. 8, or 9d. (1a.)

Services, History of—

History of Services in Burma. Compiled by the Government of Burma. Royal 8vo, paper cover—

Volume I. — Services of Gazetted Officers. Corrected up to the 1st July of each of the years 1900 and 1901, Rs. 2-8, or 3s. 6d. (4a. 6p.) (each year); and 1902, and 1903, Rs. 2-12, or 4s. $1^{1}/_{2}d.$ (4a. 6p.) (each year).

Volume II. — Services of other Officers. Corrected up to the 1st July of each of the years 1900, 1901, 1902, and 1903, Re. 1-8, or 2s. 3d. (2a. 6p.) (each year).

Settlement—

BAWNI CIRCLE OF THE PEGU DISTRICT. Report on the settlement operations in the — Season 1900—01. Description of country, condition of people, past and proposed assessment with maps. Compiled by the Government of Burma. Published 1902. Foolscap folio, paper cover. Rs. 4-2, or 6s. 2d. (1a. 6p.)

HENZADA DISTRICT. Report on the settlement of certain areas in the — Season 1900—01. Compiled by the Government of Burma. Published 1902. Foolscap folio, paper cover. Rs. 4, or 6s. (1a. 6p.)

HENZADA DISTRICT. Report on the revision settlement operations in the — Season 1900—01. Description of country, condition of people, past and proposed assessment with maps. Compiled by the Government of Burma. Published in 1902. Foolscap folio, paper cover. Rs. 8, or 12s. (2a.)

INSTRUCTIONS TO REVISION OFFICERS. Supplementary instructions to the directions to Settlement Officers and to the directions to the Revenue Officers concerning supplementary survey. By the Director, Department of Land Records and Agriculture. Published 1900. Royal 8vo, stiff board, cloth back. As. 4, or 5d. (1a.)

PROME DISTRICT. Report on the revision settlement operations in the — Season 1900—01. Description and general changes of area, Revision proposals, garden and miscellaneous cultivation with map. Compiled by the Government of Burma. Published 1902. Foolscap folio, paper cover. Rs. 5, or 7s. 6a. (3a.)

SAGAING DISTRICT. Report on the settlement operations in the — Season 1893—1900. Compiled by the Government of Burma. Foolscap folio, paper cover. Rs. 17-12, or £ 1 5s. 7½d. (8a. 6p.)

THARRAWADDY DISTRICT. Report on the revision settlement operations in the — Season 1900—01. General changes in the Revision area, Economic changes, Revision proposals, with maps. Compiled by the Government of Burma. Published in 1902. Foolscap folio, paper cover. Rs. 2-12, or 4s. 1½d. (2a.)

THAYETMYO DISTRICT. Report on the Settlement Operations in the — Season 1900—01. Compiled by the Government of Burma. Published 1902. Foolscap folio, paper cover. Rs. 6, or 9s. (3a.)

Shan States—

Report on the Administration of the —. The administration of the Southern and Northern Shan States. Compiled by the Government of Burma. Foolscap folio, paper cover. For the years 1899—1900, Re. 1, or 1s. 6d. (2a.); 1900—01, Re. 1-8, or 2s. 3d. (2a.); 1901—02, Re. 1-3, or 1s. 9½d. (1a. 6p); and 1902—03, Re. 1-10, or 2s. 5d. (1a. 6p.)

Shan States Manual, 1901. Rules and Notifications affecting the Shan States. Compiled by the Government of Burma. Published 1901. Super-royal 8vo, stiff board, cloth back. Re. 1-4, or 1s. 10½d. (2a.)

Silk—

Monograph on — in Burma with litho plates. By J. P. Hardiman, I.C.S. Published 1901. Royal 8vo, stiff board, cloth back. Rs. 3, or 4s. 6d. (2a.)

Silver—

Silver work of Burma, with photographs. By H. L. Tilly, Chief Collector of Customs, and P. Kher. Super-royal, foolscap, stiff boards, cloth back. Rs. 10, or 15s. (5a. 6p.)

Stamp—

Note on the Administration of the — Revenue in Burma. Statistical information on the working of the Stamp Law. Compiled by the Government of Burma.

Foolscap folio, paper cover. For the years 1899—1900, Re. 1, or 1s. 6d. (1a.); 1900—01 and (triennium) 1899—1900—01—02, As. 7, or 8d. (1a.) (each); and 1902—03, As. 5, or 5½d. (1a.)

The Burma Stamp Manual, 1903, containing the Court Fees Act, 1870 (VII of 1870), the Indian Stamp Act, 1899 (II of 1899), and Rules and Directions thereunder in force in Burma. Compiled by the Government of Burma. Published 1903. Super-royal 8vo, stiff boards, cloth back. Re. 1-4, or 1s. 10½d. (3a. 6p.)

Steamers—

Report on the Government —, Vessels, and Launches in Burma. Compiled by the Government of Burma. Foolscap folio, paper cover. For the years 1899—1900, Re. 1-8, or 2s. 3d. (1a. 6p.); and 1900—01, 1901—02, and 1902—03, As. 10, or 11d. (1a.) (each year).

Survey—

Burma Revenue — Class Scheme, 1903. Rules regarding admission, course of study, fees payable, examinations, etc. Royal 8vo. As. 2, or 2½d. (6p.)

Supplementary — in Upper Burma. Directions to Revenue Officers concerning — in Burmese. Compiled by the Government of Burma. Super-royal 8vo, stiff boards, cloth back. As. 8, or 9d. (1a. 6p.)

Tables, Calculating—

Part I, revised and enlarged, containing tables of logarithms, traverse, levelling, interest, exchange, loans, advance, wages, etc. Compiled by the Assistant Director of Land Records and Agriculture. Foolscap, stiff board. Re. 1, or 1s. 4d. (4a.)

Parts I and II. Part I — Survey Section. Part II — General. In English and Burmese. Rs. 2, or 2s. 8d. (7a. 6p.)

Trade and Navigation—

Annual Statement of the Sea-borne — of Burma for the year ending 31st March 1900. By the Chief Collector of Customs, Burma. Published 1901. Royal folio, thin boards. Volume I — Foreign, Rs. 12, or 18s. (6a.); Volume II — Coasting, Rs. 5-8, or 8s. 3d. (3a. 6p.)

Annual Statement of the Sea-borne — of Burma. Part I — Foreign, Part II — Coasting. By the Chief Collector of Customs, Burma. Foolscap folio, stiff board, cloth back. For the years 1900—01, 1901—02, and 1902—03, Rs. 8, or 12s. (3a. 6p.) (each year).

Memorandum on the Trade between Burma and adjoining Foreign Countries, for the year ending 31st March 1900. Containing the exports and imports of trade between Burma and adjoining Foreign countries for the year 1899—1900. Compiled by the Government of Burma. Published 1900. Foolscap folio, paper cover. Re. 1-12, or 2s. or 7½d. (1a. 6p.)

Note on the Transfrontier Trade of Burma. Foolscap folio, paper cover. For the years 1900—01, Re. 1-6, or 2s. 1d. (1a.); and 1902—03, As. 12, or 1s. 1½d. (1a.)

Report on the — of Burma. Annual Review on the Trade of Burma. Compiled by the Government of Burma. Foolscap folio, paper cover. For the years 1899—1900, Re. 1, or 1s. 6d. (1a. 6p.); and 1900—01 and 1901—02, As. 8, or 9d. (1a.) (each year).

Report on the Maritime Trade of Burma, 1902—03. Compiled by the Chief Collector of Customs. Foolscap folio, paper cover. As. 10, or 11d. (1a.)

Report on the Trade between Burma and the Adjoining Foreign Countries during the year 1901—02 and the triennial period ending 31st March 1902. Foolscap folio, paper cover. Re. 1-12. (1a.)

Transliteration—

Tables for the — of Shan Names into English. Compiled by the Government of Burma. Published 1900. Royal 8vo, paper cover. As. 2, or 2d. (8p.)

Treasury—

Treasury Manual, Burma, 4th Edition. Published 1902. The Treasury Manual containing instructions to Officers generally in dealing with Treasuries. Compiled by the Accountant-General, Burma. Super-royal, stiff board, cloth back. Re. 1, or 1s. 6d. (3a. 6p.)

Vaccination—

Notes and Statistics on — in Burma. Compiled by the Government of Burma. Foolscap folio, paper cover. For the years 1899—1900, As. 8, or 9d. (1a.); 1900—01, As. 7, or 8d. (1a.); (triennium) 1899—1900—01—02, As. 9, or 10d. (1a.); and 1902—03, As. 5, or 5½d. (1a.)

Veterinary—

Annual Report of the Civil — Department, Burma. Work of the Veterinary Department during the year detailed. Compiled by the Government of Burma. Foolscap folio, paper cover. For the years ending 31st March 1900, As. 12, or 1s. 1½d. (1a. 6p.); 1901 and 1902, As. 4, or 4½d. (1a.) (each year); and 1903, As. 7, or 8d. (1a.)

Village—

Village administration in Burma. Resolution on —. Compiled by the Government of Burma. Foolscap folio, paper cover. For the years 1901, As. 6, or 6½d. (6p.); and 1902, As. 5, or 5½d. (1a. 6p.)

Wild-Animals—

Report on the Extermination of — and Snakes in Burma for the year 1900. Compiled by the Government of Burma. Published 1901. Foolscap folio, paper cover. As. 8, or 9d. (6p.)

Wood-Carving—

Wood Carving of Burma with Photographs. By H. L. Tilly, Chief Collector of Customs, and P. Klier. Super-royal, foolscap. Rs. 12, or 18s. (4a. 6p.)

Working-plan—

For the Pyu-Kun Working Circle of the Toungoo Forest Division to be known as Pyu-Chaung and Pyu-Kun Reserves. Published 1902. Compiled by the Conservator of Forests, Tenasserim Circle, Burma. Foolscap folio, paper cover. Rs. 8-8, or 12s. 9d. (2a. 6p.)

II [1]).

1677. —

Accountant General, Burma—

Gradation and Distribution List of Officers of the — Compiled by the Accountant General. Royal 8vo, stiff board, cloth back.

Report on the Balances on the Book of the — on the 31st March 1902 and 31st March 1903. — Report on the account of Government, unfunded debt, deposits, and advances not bearing interest; Provincial advance and loan accounts; Remittances; Cash Balances; Appendices; Report on the several funds- in the Province with statement of receipts and expenditure. Compiled by the Accountant General. Foolscap folio, paper cover.

Burma Famine Code, 1904 (Draft). — Standing preparations, Preliminary measures when serious scarcity is imminent, Declaration of Famine and commencement of famine relief, Relief Works, Public Works, Village Works, Wages and Rations, Orphans, Measures for the protection of Cattle, Accounts, Miscellaneous. Compiled by the Financial Commissioner. March and June 1904. Foolscap, folio, paper cover.

Burma Forest Act, 1902. — Rules and notifications under —. Revised rules and notifications under the Burma Forest Act, 1902. Compiled by the Government of Burma. Published 1903. Royal 8vo, paper cover.

Certificates—

Issued in Burma under the Indian Steam Ships Act VII and under the Inland Steam Vessels Act VI of 1884. Particulars of local —. Compiled by the Secretary to the Government. Published 1901. Foolscap folio, paper cover.

Issued in Burma under the Indian Steam Ships Act VII of 1884, and the Indian Steam Vessels Act VI of 1884 during 1903. Particulars of local —. Compiled by the Principal Port Officer, Rangoon. Published 1904. Foolscap folio, paper cover.

Particulars of Local — issued under Indian Steam Ships Act VII of 1884 during the year 1902. Particulars of certificates issued to 1st and 2nd class Engineers and Engine-drivers, 1st and 2nd class Masters and Serangs, etc. Compiled by the Principal Port Officer. Published 1903. Foolscap folio, paper cover.

Chemical Examiner, Burma. — Report of the — for 1900. Compiled by the Financial Commissioner. Published 1901. Foolscap folio, paper cover.

Chief Court Library Catalogue, 1903. — Index of Authors. Compiled by the Registrar, Chief Court. Published 1903. Royal 8vo, paper cover.

Circuit, Rest, and Shelter Houses and Inspection and Dâk Bungalows in Upper and Lower Burma, 1900. — List of —. Compiled by the Public Works Secretariat. Published 1901. Foolscap folio, paper cover.

---

1) D'après les pp. 29—34 du *General Catalogue* Part 8, No. 9 (Voir supra, no. 1676).

Classified List and Distribution Returns of the Public Works Department Establishment (corrected up to 31st December 1900, 30th June 1901, 31st December 1902, and 31st December 1903). Compiled by the Public Works Secretariat. Royal 8vo, stiff paper cover.

Dufferin Hospital, Rangoon. — Rules for the Management of —. Compiled by the Secretary, Countess of Dufferin's Fund, Burma Branch. Royal 8vo, paper cover.

Educational Syndicate, Burma. — Annual Report of the — for the year 1900—01. Compiled by the Registrar, Educational Syndicate. Published 1901. Foolscap folio, paper cover.

Education Code, Burma Revised Chapter V. — Indigenous Schools, Provincial Standards of ordinary instruction; outlines of Syllabus for indigenous Schools, Grants-in-aid to indigenous Schools, etc. Compiled by the Director of Public Instruction. Published May 1904. Royal 8vo, paper cover.

Embankment Report of the Bassein and Henzada Division for 1900—01, and from 1st April 1902 to 31st October 1902. Foolscap folio, paper cover.

**Extant Circulars and General Orders issued by the Deputy Postmaster General, Burma Circle, Volume II. Reprint of —. Compiled by the Deputy Postmaster General. Published 1901. Royal 8vo, stiff board, cloth back.

Forest School, Vernacular. — Rules to regulate the course of instruction at, admission to, and discipline at the —, Tharrawaddy, Burma. Containing rules as per title together with instructions for regulating the admission of officers of the Subordinate Forest Service in Burma as students of the School. Compiled by the Revenue Secretary. Published 1904. Foolscap folio, paper cover.

Hackney Carriages. — Rules for the regulation and control of — within the limits of the notified area of Maymyo. Compiled by the Government of Burma. Published 1903. Royal 8vo.

Military Accounts Department, Madras Command, Circle Pay Office, Rangoon. Instructions for the guidance of officers drawing pay through the Circle Pay Office, Rangoon, and for officers proceeding direct from Burma on furlough or on duty to England. Compiled by the Circle Pay Master. Published 1904. Royal 8vo, paper cover.

Mon Canals Project, 1900. — Note by the Superintending Engineer, Irrigation Circle, Public Works Department, Burma, giving location of proposed canals, preparation of project, Distribution of the Mon Valley proposed canals, etc. Compiled by the Government of Burma, Public Works Department. Published 1901. Foolscap folio, stiff board, cloth back.

Municipalities. — Report on the Working of — for the year 1900—01. Compiled by the President of the Municipality. For the Municipalities of — Allanymo, Mandalay, Myanaung, Myaungmya, Pakokku, Salin, Toungdwingyi, Zalun. And for the year 1902—03 for the Municipalities of Bhamo, Shwegyin and Pagan.

Plans. — Catalogue of — in the Pakokku Division, corrected up to 31st December 1903. Plans of roads, bridges, buildings, etc. Compiled by the Superintending Engineer, Chindwin Circle. Published 1904. Foolscap folio, paper cover.

Postal Officials of the Burma Circle drawing Rs. 30 and below. — Gradation List of —. Corrected up to 1st April 1903. List of Postal officials drawing Rs. 30 and below. Compiled by the Deputy Postmaster-General. Published 1903. Foolscap folio, paper cover.

Post Office Manual, Vol. II. — Rules for the guidance of Branch Postmasters, etc. Compiled by the Deputy Postmaster-General. Published 1903. Super-royal, stiff board, cloth back.

Previous Conviction Registers—

of Upper Burma for 1899. — Index to —. Compiled by the Judicial Commissioner, Upper Burma. Published 1903. Foolscap folio, half leather bound.

of Lower Burma for 1901. — Index to —. Compiled by the Chief Court, Lower Burma. Published 1904. Foolscap folio, half binding in leather.

of Upper Burma for 1902. — Index to —. Compiled by the Judicial Commissioner, Upper Burma. Published 1904. Foolscap folio, half binding in leather.

Public Works Department, Burma (Building and Roads Branch). — Administration Report of the — for 1900—01. Compiled by the Chief Engineer, Public Works Department. Published 1901. Foolscap folio, paper cover.

Public Works Department, Burma (Buildings and Roads Branch, excluding Irrigation). — Administration report of — for the year 1902—03. General, Military Works, Civil Works, Metalled roads, Unmetalled roads, etc. Compiled by the Public Works Secretary. Published 1903. Foolscap folio, paper cover.

Public Works Department, Burma (Irrigation). — Administrative Accounts for the triennium ending 1901—02. Administrative Accounts. Compiled by the Public Works Secretary. Published 1903. Foolscap folio.

Public Works Department, Burma (Irrigation Branch). — Irrigation Chapter, Administration Report, 1902—03. Report and Statistical Statement. Compiled by the Public Works Secretary. Published 1903. Foolscap folio, paper cover.

Public Works Department, Burma (Military Section). — Administration Reports for 1902—03. Compiled by the Public Works Secretary. Published 1903. Foolscap folio, paper cover.

Road Programme—

Akyab District. — Position and conditions of roads in the Akyab District. Compiled by the Superintending Engineer, Rangoon Circle. Foolscap folio, paper cover.

Arakan Hill Tracts. — Position, condition, and suggestions as to improvement or otherwise of roads in the Arakan Hill Tracts District. Compiled by the Superintending Engineer, Rangoon Circle. Published 1904. Foolscap folio, paper cover.

Hanthawaddy District. — Position and condition of roads in the Hanthawaddy District with map. Compiled by the Superintending Engineer, Rangoon Circle. Foolscap folio, paper cover.

Henzada District. — Position and condition of roads in the Henzada District with map. Compiled by the Commissioner, Irrawaddy division. Foolscap folio, paper cover.

Katha District. — Position and condition of roads in the Katha District with map. Compiled by the Superintending Engineer, Mandalay Circle. Foolscap folio, paper cover.

Kyaukpyu District. — Position, condition, and suggestions as to improvements or otherwise of roads in the Kyaukpyu District. Compiled by the Superintending Engineer, South-Western and Rangoon Circles. Foolscap folio, paper cover.

Magwe District, 1903. — Name and nature of roads, their cost for maintenance, and suggestion whether or not they should be improved. General remarks with a map. Compiled by the Superintending Engineer, Toungoo Circle. Published 1903. Foolscap folio, paper cover.

Mandalay District. — Position, condition, and suggestions as to improvements or otherwise of roads in the Mandalay District with map. Compiled by the Superintending Engineer, Mandalay Circle. Foolscap folio, paper cover.

Minbu District, 1903. — Name and nature of roads, their cost for maintenance, and suggestion whether or not they should be improved General remarks with a map. Compiled by the Superintending Engineer, Toungoo Circle. Published 1903. Foolscap folio, paper cover.

Myingyan District. — Position, condition, and suggestions as to improvements or otherwise of roads in the Myingyan District. Compiled by the Superintending Engineer, Chindwin Circle. Published 1904. Foolscap folio, paper cover.

Sagaing District. — Position and condition of roads in the Sagaing District. Compiled by the Superintending Engineer, Mandalay Circle. Foolscap folio, paper cover.

Salween District, 1903. — Name and nature of roads, their cost for maintenance, and suggestion whether or not they should be improved. General remarks with a map. Compiled by the Superintending Engineer, Toungoo Circle. Published 1903. Foolscap folio, paper cover.

Sandoway District. — Position, condition, and suggestions as to improvements or otherwise of roads in the Sandoway District. Compiled by the Superintending Engineer, Rangoon Circle. Published June 1904. Foolscap folio, paper cover.

Thatòn District, 1903. — Name and nature of roads, their cost for maintenance, and suggestion whether or not they should be improved. General remarks with a map. Compiled by the Superintending Engineer, Toungoo Circle. Published 1903. Foolscap folio, paper cover.

Roads, their construction and maintenance, Burma, Public Works Department. Materials, selecting and testing road materials, construction. Compiled by the Public Works Department Secretary. Published 1903. Royal 8vo, paper cover.

Schedule of Rates for Building Materials. — Compiled by the Super-intending Engineer of the Division or Circle. Foolscap folio, paper cover. In the—

Amherst Division.

Amherst Division in the Toungoo Circle of Superintendence, 1904.

Arakan Division in the South-Western Circle (corrected up to March 1901 and 1904).

Eastern Irrigation Division in the Irrigation Circle for 1901—02 and 1904—05.

Henzada Division.

Independent Irrigation Sub-Division for 1901—02. Published 1901.

Kengtung Division.

Mandalay Canal Division in the Irrigation Circle for 1901—02.

Mandalay Division in the Mandalay Circle of Superintendence, for 1903—04.

Mandalay Division in the North-Eastern Circle for 1901—02.

Martaban Division, 1900.

Meiktila Division in the Chindwin Circle of Superintendence.

Myitkyina Division.

Northern Shan States Division in the North-Eastern Circle for 1901—02.

Pegu Division.

Pegu Division, Toungoo Circle.

Rangoon Construction Division (corrected up to 31st March 1904).

Shwebo Canal Division in the Irrigation Circle of Superintendence for the year 1904—05.

Shwebo Division in the Mandalay Circle.

Southern Shan States.

Sea Transportation Operations at Durban, South Africa, during the Boer War, 1899 to April 1901. Report on the —. Compiled by Com-mander G. E. Holland. Foolscap folio, paper cover.

Southern Shan States Railway Project, 1901—1902, Report. — Preliminary Location Gradients and Curves, Construction, Engineering Labour, Materials, Arrangement of Staff, Traffic and Statistics, etc. Compiled by the Secretary, Public Works Department, Railway Branch. Published 1903. Foolscap folio, stiff board, cloth back.

Sorting Section, R. 7, Rangoon to Mandalay, Sorting List of the Railway Mail Service. — Railway Mail Service Sorting List, Rangoon to Mandalay. Compiled by the Deputy Postmaster General. Published 1903. Super-royal, full calico.

Specification and rates. — Instructions regarding the making of Specification for Public Works Department, Works. Compiled by the Public Works Secretary. Published 1903. Foolscap folio, paper cover.

Specifications and Rates, Public Works Department. — Specifications and Notes. Compiled for general use in the Province of Burma with a view to obtaining uniformity and a high standard of work from Contractors of the Public Works Department. Compiled by the Public Works Secretariat. Royal 8vo, foolscap, paper cover.

Standing Orders. — Rangoon Arsenal. Standing Orders of the Rangoon Arsenal, regarding general routine, establishment, office and clerks, receipts, issues, transport, etc. etc. Ordnance Officer, Rangoon. Published 1903. Royal 8vo, stiff board, cloth back.

Statement, Revised— Showing the comparison between village and the Government 9-gallon baskets. Compiled by the Commissioner, Tenasserim Division. Published June 1904. Foolscap folio, paper cover.

Statement— Showing the Comparison between village and 9-gallon basket in Thayetmyo District. Compiled by the Director, Land Records and Agriculture. Published June 1904. Foolscap folio, paper cover.

Sub-Treasury Officers. — Rules for the guidance of —. Compiled by the Accountant General. Royal 8vo, paper cover.

Table of Conversion— Village to Standard baskets. Compiled by the Director, Land Records and Agriculture. Published June 1904. Foolscap folio, paper cover. For the—

Magwe Township, Magwe District.
Myingun Township, Magwe District.
Myothit Township, Magwe District.
Natmauk Township, Magwe District.
Taungdwingyi Township, Magwe District.
Yenangyaung Township, Magwe District.

Tube Wells in Rangoon. — Report on —. The process by which the wells are bored; the Geological Condition of the Wells; the result of enquiry and investigation, etc., with plan of tube wells in Rangoon. Compiled by E. G. Foy, Sanitary Engineer, Burma. Published 1903. Foolscap folio, paper cover.

4) France.

1678. — A Mission in Burmah 1873—1874. By Count A. Marescalchi. (*The Journal of Eastern Asia.* Vol. I. No. I. July—1875, pp. 63—89).

Trad. de la *Revue des Deux Mondes*, Sept. 1874, par le lieut. W. B. Forbes, R N.

1679. — Une ambassade birmane. (*Ann. de l'Ext. Orient*, 1883—1884, VI, pp. 48—50).

Ambassade à Paris.

1680. — Le traité entre la France et la Birmanie. (*Ibid.*, 1884—1885, VII, pp. 262—264).

1681. — La convention franco-birmane. (*Ann. de l'Ext. Orient*, 1885—1886, VIII, pp. 94—95).

1682. — La France, la Haute-Birmanie, et le Tong-kin Par Fernand d'Avéra Membre et Délégué Général de la Société pour la Birmanie Britannique, Ancien Secrétaire de Commandements du feu roi de Birmanie. (*Bull. Soc. Acad. Indo-Chinoise*, 2° sér., III, 1890, pp. 191—204).

5) Questions contemporaines.

1683. — The Political Situation in Burmah. By Archibald Forbes. (*Nineteenth Century*, V, 1879, pp. 740—754).

1684. — Burma reformed. By A. C. Yate. (*Blackwood's Mag.*, CXLI, May 1887, pp. 711—718).

1685. — Effets of Civilization on the Burmese. By A. R. Macmahon. (*As. Quart. Review*, VI, July-Oct. 1888).

1686. — 'J. Chailley-Bert. Colonisation de l'Indo-Chine. L'expérience anglaise. Paris, 1892, in-12.

  B. M. 10058. cc. 82.

1687. — The Indo-Chinese Opium Question as it stands in 1893. By Robert Needham Cust. (*Calcutta Review*, XCVII, July 1893, pp. 119—136).

1688. — Ce qu'est devenue la Birmanie — Ce que peut devenir l'Indo-Chine française. Par Paul Macey. (*Bul. Soc. Géog. Est*, 1890, pp. 349—355).

1689. — 'Georges Burghard. — La Birmanie et la colonisation anglaise. Paris, Chevalier-Marescq, 1902, in-8, pp. 28.

  Ext. de la *Revue internat. de l'Enseignement*.

6) Chemins de fer.

1690. — 'Direct Commerce with the Shan States and West of China, by Railway from Rangoon to Kian-Hung, on the Upper Kamboja River, on the South West Frontier of China. Memorial from the Wakefield Chamber of Commerce to the Lords of Her Majesty's Treasury, 1869, in-8.

1691. — Exploration Survey for a Railway Connection between India, Siam, and China. By Holt S. Hallett, C.E. (*Proc. R. Geog. Soc.*, VIII, 1886, Jan., pp. 1—20; carte, p. 64).

1692. — Address of Mr. Holt S. Hallett, C.E., F.R.G.S., M.R.A.S., upon Burmah: our Gate to the Markets of Western and Central China; treating with the proposed connection of Burmah with China by railway. Delivered before the Birmingham Chamber of Commerce on the 26th May, 1887, Mr. Henry W. Elliott, President of the Chamber, in the Chair. London: P. S. King & Son, Parliamentary Agency. — 1887, in-8, pp. 20.

1693. — A. R. Colquhoun. — Report on Railway connexion of Burmah and China. London, 1888, in-fol., pp. 239.

  Voir Nos. 445—450.

1694. — *Indo—Burma—China. Railway connections a pressing necessity. London, 1888, in-8, pp. 75.

> B. M. 8235. f. 42 (5).

1695. — *H. S. Hallett. Address upon Eastern Markets for Lancashire. London, 1889, in-8, pp. 24.

> B. M. 08229. f. 3 (14).

1696. — The Burmah—Siam—China Railway. By Holt S. Hallett. (*Blackwood's Mag.*, CXLVI, Nov. 1889, pp. 647—659).

1697. — The Remedy for Lancashire. A Burma—China railway. By Holt S. Hallett. (*Ibid.*, CLII, Sept. 1892, pp. 348—363).

1698. — General Rules for open lines of Railway in British India administered by the Government. — Rangoon: Printed by the Supdt., Govt. Printing, Burma. August 1896, in-8, pp. 21.

1699. — *Notes on Railways in Ceylon and Burmah. By J. T. Lawrence (*map and ill.*). (*Railway Mag.*, V, Aug. 1899, p. 136).

1700. — Un nouveau chemin de fer en Birmanie. (*Bull. Com. Asie française*, Avril 1904, p. 213).

ASSAM.

I. — Ouvrages généraux.

1701. — A Description of Asàm by Mohammed Cazim, translated from the Persian by Henry Vansittart, Esq. (*Asiatick Researches*, Calcutta, II, 1790, pp. 171—185).

> «This account of *Asàm* was translated for the Society, but afterwards printed by the learned translator as an appendix to his *Aâlemgirnâmah*. It is reprinted here, because our government has an interest in being as well acquainted as possible with all the nations *bordering* on the *British* territories». Note, p. 171.

1702. — Description of the kingdom of Assam, taken from the Alemgeernameh of Mohammed Cazim, and translated by Henry Vansittart, Esq. (Extracted from Mr. Gladwine's *Asiatick Miscellany*, printed at Calcutta.) (*Asiatic Annual Register*, 1800, pp. 42—50, *Miscel. Tracts*).

1703. — A Description of Ásám: extent and boundaries of its three principal divisions; with Notices of the States and Tribes bordering on the north and south. By E. Stevens. (*Chin. Rep.*, V, 1836, pp. 49—55, 97—104).

1704. — 'Assam: Sketch of its History, Soil, and Productions, with the Discovery of the Tea-Plant, and of the Countries adjoining Assam, 1839, in-8. Maps.

1705. — A Descriptive Account of Asam: with a Sketch of the Local geography, and a concise History of The Tea-plant of Asam: to which is added, a short account of the neighbouring tribes, exhibiting their history, manners and customs. By William Robinson, Gowhatti Government Seminary. Illustrated with four maps, drawn expressly for the work. Calcutta: Ostell and Lepage, London: Thomas Ostell & Co. MDCCCXLI, in-8, pp. xv—421.

1706. — A Sketch of Assam: with some account of the Hill Tribes. By an Officer in the Hon. East India Company's Bengal Native Infantry in Civil Employ. With Illustrations from Sketches by the Author. London: Smith Elder & Co., 1847, in-8, pp. viii—220.

1707. — A Statistical Account of Assam. By W. W. Hunter, B.A., LL.D., C.I.E., Director-General of Statistics to the Government of India; Trübner & Co. London, 1879, 2 vol. in-8.

> Vol. I. Districts of Kamrup, Darrang, Nowgong, Sibsagar, and Lakhimpur. — Vol. II. Districts of Goalpara (including the Eastern Dwars), the Garo hills, the Naga hills, the Khasi and Jaintia hills, Sylhet, and Cachar.

1708. — A Glimpse of Assam. Edited & Published By Mrs. S. R. Ward. — Calcutta: Thomas S. Smith, 1884, in-12, pp. II—219.

1709. — Sketches in Assam. By S. O. Bishop, M.R.C.S., E. — Calcutta, «City Press», 1885, in-12, pp. IX—257.

1710. — Die britisch-indische Provinz Assam. Von Emil Jung. (*Mitt. k. u. k. geog. Ges. Wien*, 1888, pp. 1—14.)

1711. — *Physical and Political Geography of the Province of Assam. Physical features, area, climate, and chief staples; historical summary; form of administration; character of land tenures, and system of settlement and survey; Civil divisions of British territory; details of the last Census; and frontier relations and Feudatory States. Reprinted from the Report on the Administration of the Province of Assam for the year 1892—93. 1896, gr. in-8.

1712. — *Kurt Klemm. — Völkerbilder aus Asam. (*Beilage Allgemeine Zeitung*, CLXXVIII, pp. 1—5; CLXXIX, pp. 2—7).

1713. — *The Province of Assam. By Sir C. J. Lyall. (*Jour. Soc. Arts*, LI, 1903, pp. 612—636).

II. — Géographie.

Ouvrages divers.

> «L'Assam séparé du Bengale en 1874, publie un rapport depuis 1889 (*Report... for the year* 1888—1889). On trouvera les principaux traits de la géographie de l'Assam dans le *Report... for the year* 1892—1893 (Part IIA, Chapter I—VII); ces chapitres ont été publiés à part sous le titre de *Physical and Political Geography of Assam*». — Voir No. 1711.
>
> Raveneau, *Annales de Géographie*, pp. 184—5, Bibl. de 1897.

1714. — Memoir of a Survey of the Southern part of Silhet, made in the years 1821, 1822, by order of His Excellency the Most Noble the Marquis of Hastings, K.G., G.C.B., &c., &c., &c., Governor General of India. By Lieutenant Thomas Fisher, 24th Regiment N. I., Surveyor. Folio, on 45 pages.

> *Contents.* — Position and face of the country. Area. Boundaries, Rivers, Climate. Of the people. Education. Religion, Character, physical, moral and intellectual.
> *Section* 1. — Banks of the Sunná from Chhagáon in Silbet to Gobindpur in Cachar.
> *Section* 2. — From Bángá to Chargolá and Pratápgazh.
> *Section* 3. — From Latu to Pathariá, Langta and Adampur, including the Jorí and Manu Rivers.
> *Section* 4. — The country on the left bank of the Manu River from Sarkár Bázár, and Balasirá on the east to Lakshmí and Rosimnagar (?) on the west.
> Note. — The above sections are dealt with under the following heads: — Face of the country: lakes and rivers; mountains; roads; towns, &c.; woods and principal places from which supplies may be procured.

— Journal kept on a Survey up the Brahmaputra and Sukátu River to Brahmakunda. From March 3rd to April 11th, 1825 (?). On pages 1 to 59. By Captain James Bedford.

Also

— Extract from a Journal kept on the Dihang River by Captain James Bedford. From November 18th to November 25th, 1825 (?). On pages 1 to 17.

And

— Journal kept during a Survey up the Disang River, containing some account of the Mishmis, who inhabit the villages on its right bank. Also a short vocabulary of Mishmi words. From November 26th to December 31st, 18⬛⬛. On 57 pages.

> Note. — These three works are bound in one folio volume, and contain the results of an exploring trip in canoes up the rivers referred to, with marginal records of observations for altitude of the sun and of the polar star, and observations for temperature of air and water.
> Extrait: Analytical Catalogue to the Materials in the Geographical Department, India Office, for the Imperial Statistical Account of India. Calcutta: Office of the Superintendent of Government Printing, 1878, in-fol., pp. 10.

1715. — On the Geography and Population of Asam. — By Captain John Bryan Neufville, Deputy Assistant Quarter Master General. (*As. Researches*, XVI, 1828, pp. 331—352).

1716. — On the Identity of the Sanpu and Irawadi Rivers. (*Gleanings in Science*, 1830, II, Calcutta, pp. 66—7).

1717. — Topography of Asam, by John M'Cosh, Officiating Second Assistant Surgeon General Hospital, Officiating Lecturer in Clinical Medicine New Medical College, Calcutta. — Printed by Order of Government. Calcutta: G. H. Huttmann, 1837, in-8, pp. xii—166.

1718. — A peculiarity of the river names in Asam and some of the adjoining countries. By S. E. Peal, Sibsagar, Asam. (*Jour. As. Soc. Bengal*, Vol. 48, 1879, Pt. I, pp. 258—270).

1719. — On the Operations for obtaining the Discharges of the large Rivers in Upper Asam, during Season 1877—78. — By Lieut. H. J. Harman, R.E. — Communicated by Major-Gen. J. T. Walker. (*Ibid.*, Vol. 48, 1879, Pt. 2, pp. 4—36).

Cartes.

Maps, Plans, etc., published by the Government of India [1]).

Assam, Provincial Maps.

		Year of Survey	Date of last edition	Scale	Size	Price
364	Assam Province	—	1883	1″ = 24 M	27″ × 20″	1/6d
363	Assam Province	—	1877	1″ = 16 M	40″ × 27″	4/—
	Assam Province (without Hills)	—	1876	,,	,,	2/—
364A	Assam Province, 8 sheets	1878—81	1891—3	1″ = 8 M	30″ × 22″	16/—
101A	Assam Province Tea Districts (Skeleton), 5 sheets	—	1863	1″ = 4 M	40″ × 27″	12/—
	Assam Province. Part of North-Eastern Frontier in the Daphla Hills	1874—75	1875	,,	30″ × 22″	1/—
21	Assam Province. Part of the North-East Frontier in the Mishmi Hills	1877—78	1883	,,	34″ × 26″	1/—
762A	Assam Province. Part of the Lushai Hills, Cachar and Manipur, 2 sheets	1871—72	1881	,,	40″ × 27″	4/—
484	Miri Hills	1877—78	1879	,,	26″ × 17″	1/—
764	Hill Tipperah, Lushai Hills, and North Chittagong, Parts of	1872—73	1876	,,	34″ × 26″	1/—
	Daphla Hills, Portion of the (North-East) Frontier, Assam	1874—75	1875	1″ = 2 M	40″ × 25″	2/—
774	Assam Province	1877	1897	1″ = 16 M	40″ × 27″	3/—
774A	Assam Province	—	1895	1″ = 16 M	44″ × 31″	3/6
774A	Assam (without hills)	—	1902	1″ = 16 M	40″ × 25″	2/8
1018	Assam Province, 2 sheets	—	1899	1″ = 48 M	17″ × 13″	0/7
1	Index Map of the Assam Survey, showing scales of Publication	—		,,	,,	0/7
1020	Assam Province	—	1900	1″ = 32 M	22 × 17	0.9

Assam, District Maps.

737	Cachar	1865—74	1881 Corr. to 1890.	1″ = 4 M	38″ × 25″	2/—
549	Darrang	1871—74	1899	1″ = 4 M	40″ × 27″	1/6
	do (Skeleton)	—	1874	,,	,,	1/—
822	do	—	Corr. to 1883.			

---

1) Cette liste a été dressée à l'aide de: A Catalogue of Maps, Plans, &c., of India and Burma and other Parts of Asia. — Published by order of Her Majesty's Secretary of State for India in Council. — London: 1891, in-fol., pp. 154—7. — et les supp. sous forme d'App. Nos. I—XLIV (May 1903).

		Year of Survey	Date of last edition	Scale	Size	Price
659	Garo Hills, Lower Assam	1871—74	1886	1″ = 4 M	27″ × 26″	2/—
	Garo Hills, 4 sheets	1870—74	1874	1″ = 2 M	34″ × 26″	4/—
826	Garo Hills, Lower Assam, 4 sheets		1891	,,	,,	4/—
575	Goalpara	1855—75	1893	1″ = 4 M	34″ × 30″	3/—
574	Kamrup	1865—69	1893	,,	34″ × 25″	2/—
605	Lakhimpur	1866—73	1890	,,	40″ × 27″	2/—
598	Manipur and Eastern Naga Hills, 2 sheets	1872—82	1883	,,	34″ × 26″	4/—
614	Naga Hills	1866—76	1884	,,	38″ × 38″	4/—
	Naga Hills, Eastern Portion	1873—74	1875	,,	24″ × 26″	1/—
550	Nowgong	1869—72	1882	,,	40″ × 27″	2/—
			Corr. to May 1887.			
557	Sibsagar	1862—75	1882	,,	38″ × 25″	3/6
542	Sylhet	1860—66	1894	,,	35″ × 28″	2/—
58A	Cachar (South). Surveyed by N. T. Davey, Esq., Revenue Survey, 7 sheets	1864—68	1870	1″ = 1 M	40″ × 27″	21/—
	Sheet 1 Katigara, Chandpur, Gumra, Haritikar	1864—67	,,	,,		• 3/—
	Sheet 2 Udarband Haut	1865—68	,,	,,		,,
	Sheet 3 Silchar Station, Barbari, Hailakandi, Jafarband	1864—68	,,	,,		
	Sheet 4 Lakhipur, Sunamukhi	1865—68	,,	,,		
	Sheet 5 Aenakhall, Bahdram or Koya, Alexandrapur, Loharband	1867—68	,,	,,		
	Sheet 6 Monierkhal, Mainadahar Dubidhar	,,	,,	,,		
	Sheet 7 Jhalnachara	,,	,,	,,		
326	Lakhimpur. Surveyed by Captains J. H. Willoughby Osborne and E. W. Samuels, and Lieutenant E. W. Barron, Revenue Survey, 17 sheets	1866—73	1879	,,		51/—
	Sheet 1 Lanpati, Laina, Bhati Sadiya, Sadiya Cantonment, Ujan Sadiya	1867—70	1874	,,		3/—
	Sheet 2 Portions of Rivers Brahmaputra and Tengapani	1872—73	1879	,,		
	Sheet 3 Bardalani, Gaguldubi, Pothalipam	1869—71	1874	,,		
	Sheet 4 Dhomaji, Sisi	1869—70	,,	,,		
	Sheet 5 Dibrugarh Station, Lahoal	1867—70	,,	,,		
	Sheet 6 Siripuria, Dumdum, Rangagora	1867—73	,,	,,		
	Sheet 7 Jenthumukh, Dirak Halka	1872—73	1879	,,		
	Sheet 8 Lakhimpur Town, Kamlabari, Kuddum	1870—71	1874	,,		
	Sheet 9 Harhi, Gohaigaon, Dhukoa, Khana	1867—71	,,	,,		

	Year of Survey	Date of last edition	Scale	Size	Price
Sheet 10 Khowang, Tenga Khat, Jokai	1866—69	1874	1″ = 1 M	40″ × 27″	3/—
Sheet 11 Makum, Jaipur Cantonment, Chapatoli	1866—69	„	„		
Sheet 12 Narainpur	1870—71	„	„		
Sheet 13 Lalukdalani, Biteri, Khaora, Bangphang, Narainpur	„	„	„		
Sheet 14 Jhalbari, Dihingia	1867—71	„	„		
Sheet 15 Jaipur, Khowang	1866—70	„	„		
Sheet 16 Narainpur	1870—71	„	„		
Sheet 17 Bhangphang and Area Settlement	„	„	„		
102B Sibsagar. Surveyed by H. B. Talbot, Esq. (Revenue Survey), 11 sheets	1862—72	1873	„		33/—
Sheet 1 Salmara and Kamlabari, Banmukh, Kumar, Kharadhara, Kowarpur	1870—71	„	„		3/—
Sheet 2 Salmara and Kamlabari, Banmukh, Belabari, Bokota, Sibsagarnagar, Obhoypur, Shilakuti, Khalaighogora, Bhangsu	1866—68	„	„		
Sheet 3 Obhoypur, Khalaighogora, Barua Chali	1868—69	„	„		
Sheet 4 Batmara, Kukela, Dihingia-Nikri, Burgohi-Chapori	1869—70	„	„		
Sheet 5 Johrat Station, Garhamur, Karatigaon, Salmara and Kamlabari, Jakaichuk, Tulsijan, Gahkerkoa, Nalkota	1870—71	„	„		
Sheet 6 Sibsagar Town, Obhoypur, Gitaki, Dopdarcharlgaun, Jakaichuk, Silakuti, Ghergong, Nazira	1865—72	„	„		
Sheet 7 Obhoypur	1868—69	„	„		
Sheet 8 Bhugdour, Ramdiong, Kajiranga	1871—72	„	„		
Sheet 9 Ghologhat Station and Town, Kamargaon, Bhagdour, Burgohi-Chapori, Rangamati	1869—72	„	„		
Sheet 10 Sonari, Nakachari, Dhandu, Dakinhengra, Puranimati, Jorhat	1862—70	„	„		
Sheet 11 A'th Gaon, Elengial, Ghila-Dhari and Noagora, Tirnal, Morangi	1870—71	„	„		-
66 Sylhet. Surveyed by N. T. Davey Esq. (Revenue Survey), 11 sheets	1860—65	1868	„		33/—
Sheet 1 Sonamganj, Tahirpur, Katikapur, Haut, Shukhire, Rasulganj Haut, Bangsikura	1861—62	„	„		3/—
Sheet 2 Chhatak, Bholaganj, Gwinghat, Cheragong Tea Plantation, Chandipur	1838—61	„	„		

	Year of Survey	Date of last edition	Scale	Size	Price
Sheet 3 Jaintiapur, Molagul, Aratael	1838—66	1868	1″ = 1 M	40″ × 27″	3/—
Sheet 4 Dharampassa, Panchashal, Makhalkandi	1860—62	1867	„		
Sheet 5 Sylhet Station, Fenchuganj, Tajpur, Kubaspur	1860—64	1869	„		
Sheet 6 Latu, Bairagi, Azamganj, Kalyuri	1862—66	1869	„		
Sheet 7 Habiganj, Lakai, Azmiriganj	1860—61	1868	„		
Sheet 8 Moulvi-Bazar, Karimganj, Adampur, Motiganj, Kalighat, Lashkarpur	1860—64	1868	„		
Sheet 9 Manikgani, Chirapathar Hill, Rotauri Bazar	1863—64	1868	„		
Sheet 10 Bejura, Murakuri	1860—61	1868	„		
Sheet 11 Muchikandi, Ghazipur, Fuskuri Langlia Tea Estates	1863—64	1868	„		
Sylhet — South part of. Surveyed by Major W. F. Badgley, S.C., and Lieutenant Colonel R. G. Woodthorpe,R.E., Topographical Survey. (North-East Frontier Survey)	1877—83	1883—6	2″ = 1 M	„	30/—
Kedargal, Fukua, Chargola Bazar Singari	1877—79	1883	„		3/—
Medeli, Pinjora, Paila, Sora, Oslam, Lakhimamla, Tatar-Band, Nora-Cherra, Fanair-Band, Fanai-Cherra, and Gambhira-Cherra Tea Gardens	1877—81	1883	„		..
Pesarpar, Kesrigal Tea Garden, Adam Tila	1879—81	1884	„		2/—
Gambhira-Cherra, Tatar-Band	1878—81	1883	„		„
Garibpur, Silua, Sagarnal	1879—82	1883	„		
Haragaj Hill, Rajardor	1881—82	1883	„		
Shamshernagar, Kanihati, Dao Sora, Tilakpur, Satlapur, and Alinagar Tea Gardens,Chitalgaon, Sangaon	1881—83	1886	„		
Daluagaon, Vaipehi	1881—82	1883	„		
Indarnagar, Bhatra, Barmsal, Singur Ita, Luaioni, Rajnagar, Kijildara, Bingajia, Langla, Manir Tea Gardens	1881—83	1884	„		
Jagarnathpur, Naraincherra, Chaotali, and Balicherra, Mertinga Tea Gardens	1881—83	1886	„		
Lakai-Cherra,Fuskuri,Shinderkhan, Rajghat, Langlia-Cherra, and Barma-Cherra Tea Gardens	1881—83	1886	„		
Burinao, Baragaon, Amrail, Mirzapur, and Satgaon Tea Gardens, Raipuram	1882—83	1884	„		

	Year of Survey	Date of last edition	Scale	Size	Price
Chandpur and Amo Tea Gardens, Parkul, Gazinagar, Sonbari, Hugliagaon	1882—83	1884	2″ = 1 M	40″ × 27″	2/—
Lalchand, Panchasbari, Bhikamkhan, Chandpur, Chandi-Cherra Tea Gardens, Shimla and Shahazi Bazars, Musapara	1882—83	1884	„	„	2/—
986 Cachar District	—	1900	1″ = 8 M	17 × 13	0/7
1027 Lakhimpur District	—	1900	1″ = 12 M	13 × 9	0/5
	—	1902	„	15 × 10	0/7
898 Goalpara District	—	1901	1″ = 8 M	17 × 14	0/7
899 Sylhet District	—	1902	„	„	0/7

Station Plan.

	Year of Survey	Date of last edition	Scale	Size	Price
** Aijal Station, N. Lushai Hills, 2 sheets	1898—1900	1901	24″ = 1 M	40 × 30	4/6

Cantonment and City Maps.

Cachar District.

	Year of Survey	Date of last edition	Scale	Size	Price
580 Silchar (Cachar) Civil Station and Cantonment. — Surveyed by N. T. Davey, Esq. (Revenue Survey)	1867	1878	6″ = 1 M	25″ × 20	1/—

Darrang District.

	Year of Survey	Date of last edition	Scale	Size	Price
309 Tezpur Cantonment, Civil Station and Environs. — Surveyed by Captain J. H. W. Osborne (Revenue Survey)	1871—72	1873	6″ = 1 M	30″ × 22	2/—

Garo Hills District.

	Year of Survey	Date of last edition	Scale	Size	Price
Tura Civil Station. — Surveyed by Lieutenant R. G. Woodthorpe, R.E. (Topographical Survey)	1872—74	1874	24″ = 1 M	30″ × 22	0 6

Goalpara District.

	Year of Survey	Date of last edition	Scale	Size	Price
Dhubri and Kasba Jamira. — Surveyed by J. H. O'Donnel, Esq. (Revenue Survey)	1867—68	1875	8″ = 1 M	30″ × 22	1/—
398 Goalpara Civil Station. — Surveyed by Major D. Macdonald (Revenue Survey)	1874—75	1877	6″ = 1 M	40″ × 27	2/—

Kamrup District.

	Year of Survey	Date of last edition	Scale	Size	Price
103A Gauhati Civil Station and Environs. — Surveyed by Captain A. D. Butter. (Revenue Survey)	1868—69	1870	6″ = 1 M	30″ × 22	3/—

Khasi and Jaintia Hills.

	Year of Survey	Date of last edition	Scale	Size	Price
578 Shillong Sanitarium. — Surveyed by Lieutenant-Colonels W. F. Badgley, S.C., and R.G. Woodthorpe, R.E. (Topographical Survey)	1878—83	1884	24″ = 1 M	34″ × 26	24/—
Shillong Sanitarium— A reduction from the above	1878—83	1884	6″ = 1 M	40″ × 27	4/—

Lakhimpur District.

310 Dibrugarh Cantonment, Civil Station and Environs. — Surveyed by Lieutenant W. Barron (Revenue Survey)	1867—68	1873	6″ = 1 M	30″ × 22	2/—
Sadiya Cantonment. Surveyed by the Executive Engineer, Upper Assam Division		1882	12″ = 1 M	40″ × 27	1/—
102A Sadiya Cantonment and Environs. — Surveyed by Captain J. H.W. Osborne (Revenue Survey)	1869—70	1871	6″ = 1 M	34″ × 26	1/—

Naga Hills District.

Samaguting Civil Station. — Surveyed by Lieutenant R. G. Woodthorpe, R.E. (Topographical Survey)	1873	1874	12″ = 1 M	22″ × 15	0 6

Nowgong District.

401 Nowgong Civil Station and Environs. — Surveyed by Lieutenant D. C. Andrew (Revenue Survey)	1870—71	1875	12″ = 1 M	40″ × 27	4/—
400 Nowgong Civil Station and Environs. — Surveyed by Lieutenant D. C. Andrew (Revenue Survey)	1870—71	1875	6″ = 1 M	30″ × 22	2/—

Sibsagar District.

408 Sibsagar Civil Station. — Surveyed by H. B. Talbot, Esq. (Revenue Survey)	1866—67	1875	16″ = 1 M	34″ × 26	4/—
407 Sibsagar Civil Station. — Surveyed by H. B. Talbot, Esq. (Revenue Survey)	1866—67	1875	6″ = 1 M	22″ × 15	1/—

Sylhet District.

67A Sylhet Town. — Surveyed by N. T. Davey, Esq. (Revenue Survey)	1863	1870	12″ = 1 M	44″ × 28	2/—

Standard Sheets of the Province of Assam.

721 Comprising the District surveys, on a scale of one inch to the mile.

	Year of Survey	Date of last edition	Scale	Size	Price
Sheet 1 Goalpara. — Repu, Raimana	1867—68	1876	1″ = 1 M	40″ × 27″	3/—
2 Goalpara. — Ghurla, Guma, Parbatjuar, Repu	1867—75	„	„		3/—
3 Goalpara. — Ghurla, Agamani, Dimaguri, Kherbari, Jamira, Makrampur, Parbatjuar, Partabganj, Taria, Khagrabari	1874—75	„	„		3/—
4 Goalpara. — Aurangabad, Jamira, Patoamari, Kalumalupara	„	„	„		3/—
5 Goalpara. — Aurangabad, Singmari, Jamira, Kalumalupara, Karaibari, Manikarchar, Kakripara	„	„	„		3/—
6 Goalpara. — Karaibari	„	„	„		3/—
7 Goalpara. — Chirang	1867—68	„	„		3/—
8 Goalpara. — Chirang, Khuntaghat, Parbatjuar, Repu town, Ramana, Sidli town	„	„	„		3/—
	1895—98	1902	„		2/3
9 Goalpara. — Chapar town, Guma, Khuntaghat, Datma, Fakiragaon, Parbatjuar, Repu, Sidli	1867—75	1876	„		3/—
	1895—98	1901	„		2/3
10 Goalpara. — Chapar, Bilasupara, Gola, Alamganj, Jamira, Dhubri, Ganipur, Khuntaghat, Mechpara, Lakhipur, Parbatjuar, Bogribari, Noabad, Faltori	1873—75	1876	„		3/—
11 Goalpara. — Kalumalupara, Jamira, Mechpara	„	„	„		3/—
12 Goalpara. — Karaibari, Puthimari	1874—75	„	„		3/—
13 Not yet published.					
14 „ „ „					
15 Goalpara. — Bijni, Chirang	1867—69	„	„		3/—
Kamrup. — Bijni	1867—68	1872	„		3/—
16 Goalpara. — Bijni, Chirang, Sidli	1867—69	1876	„		3/—
Kamrup. — Chokabansi, Dumka, Bijni, Kamargaon, Chapakhamar	1866—68	1872	„		3/—
	1893—97	1901	„		2/3
17 Goalpara. — Bijni Town, Chapar, Salmara, Khuntaghat, Sidli, Tangaigaun	1868—75	1876	„		3/—
Kamrup. — Bansmura, Bhobanipur, Boguribari, Barpeta, Chokabausi, Ruposi, Roha, Dumka Town	1865—67	1872	„		3/—
18 Goalpara. — Town and Civil Station, Mechpara, Chapar, Habraghat, Khuntaghat	1873—74	1876	„		3/—

	Year of Survey	Date of last edition	Scale	Size	Price
Kamrup. — Bogribari, Barpeta, Konora, Kholabunda	1865—66	1872	1″ = 1 M	40″ × 27″	3/—
	1896—97	1902	„	„	2/3
Sheet 19 Goalpara. — Habraghat, Jira, Meohpara	1873—74	1876	„		3/—
20 to 23 Not yet published.					
24 Kamrup. — Baskah, Chapaguri, Bijni	1867—68	1872	„		
	1883—86				
25 Kamrup. — Chapaguri, Khagrabari, Bijni, Bojahti	1866—68	1890	„		
26 Kamrup. — Barpeta, Koital, Kochi, Bhobanipur	1865—67	„	„		
27 Kamrup. — Choygong, Soru, Bungsur, Kholabunda, Kharija, Barunti, Dheknaboi, Chamoria, Nagarberha	1865—69	„	„		„
Goalpara. — Habraghat	1873—74	1876	„		„
	1884—97	1902	„		2/3
28 Kamrup. — Kuliha, Dhopgori, Nalapara, Shamuka, Jaipur, Bandapara	1867—68	1874	„		3/—
Goalpara. — Habraghat	1873—74	1876	„		„
	1885—86	1901	„		2/3
29 Khasi Hills. — Nongstoin	1866—69	1882	„		3/—
Kamrup	„	„	„		„
30 Khasi Hills. — (Eastern half of the sheet)	1866—79	1881	„		
31 Khasi Hills	„	„	„		
32 to 36 For these sheets see Sylhet District.					
37 Kamrup. — Baskah, Gurkbulah, Dewangiri, Durunga	1867—68	1872	„		
Darrang. — Burigoma, Khaling	1872—73	1875	„		
38 Kamrup. — Baskah, Haolli, Gurkhula, Baroigaon	1866—68	1872	„		
Darrang. — Desh-Darrang, Khaling, Singribari, Nalbari	1872—75	1876	„		„
	1885—97	1902	„		2/3
39 Kumrup. — Nalbari, Rangiya, Kalag	1865—67	1872	„		3/—
Darrang. — Desh-Darrang	1872—74	1876	„		„
Nowgong. — Raha	1869—70	1875	„		
	1885—87	1890	„		
40 Kamrup. — Gauhati Civil Station and Environs, Hajo, Gandamal	1865—69	1874	„		
Darrang.— Desh-Darrang, Karwa	1872—74	1876	„		

	Year of Survey	Date of last edition	Scale	Size	Price
Sheet 41 Kamrup. — Bholagong, Kharija, Bardoa	1868—69	1874	1″ = 1 M	40″ × 27″	3/—
Khasi Hills. — Nongpoh, Jirang, Umlur, Umrau	1866—78	1882	″		
42 Khasi Hills. Shillong Sanitarium, Nunklow	1864—78	″	″		
43 Khasi Hills. — Cherra Ponjee, Surarim, Moflong, Lailangkot	1864—70	″	″		
44 Khasi Hills. — Chelapunji, Maosmai, Taria Ghat	1864—79	″	″		
45 to 48 For these sheets see Sylhet District.					
49 Darrang. — Burigoma, Khaling, Kuriapara, Odalguri	1872—73	1875	″		″
	1886—96	1902	″		2/3
50 Darrang. — Aurang, Dalgaon, Bengbari, Kaupati	1872—75	1877	″		3/—
Nowgong. — Chapuri	1869—70	1874	″		″
51 Darrang. — Desh-Darrang, Mangaldai, Rangamati, Chutia	1872—75	1877	″		
Nowgong. — Raha, Chapri	1869—70	1875	″		
52 Kamrup. — Panbari, Kharija, Dumoria, Sonapur	1865—69	1874	″		
Nowgong. — Datipar, Nokla, Raha, Jagi, Tatalia	1869—70	1875	″		″
	1886—99	1902	″		2/3
53, 54 Not yet published.					
55 Khasi Hills	1867—68	1875	″		3/—
Jaintia Hills. — Jowai	″	″	″		″
56 Not yet published.					
57 Cachar	1878—80	1887	″		
58, 59 For these sheets see Sylhet District.					
60 Darrang. — Tezpur, Charduar, Bokagaon, Nanduar	1871—72	1883	″		
61 Darrang. — Tezpur Cantonment Civil Station and Environs, Nanduar, Pasigaon, Charduar, Benuguri, Modopi	1871—72	1883	″		″
Nowgong	1870—71	1874	″		″
	1887—98	1902	″		2/3
62 Nowgong. — Nowgong Civil Station and Environs, Kakomari, Baropujia, Khatwalgaon	1869—72	1875	″		3/—
	1887—98	1902	″		2/3
63 Nowgong, Kothiatoli, Khaigar, Raha, Doboka	1869—72	1875	″		3/—
	1887—99	1901	″		2/3

	Year of Survey	Date of last edition	Scale	Size	Price
Sheet 64 Nowgong. — Jamuna Mukh, Datpar	1870—71	1875	1″ = 1 M	40″ × 27″	3/—
65, 66, 67 Not yet published.					
68 Cachar. — Silchar, Kategara	1878—82	1887	„		„
69 Cachar. — Halikandi	1880—83	1897	„		2/3
70 Cachar	1880—81	1887	„		3/—
71 Not yet published.					
72 Darrang. — Partabgarh, Pabha, Behali	1871—72	1874	„		
73 Darrang. — Tezpur, Bishnath, Sutia	1871—72	1883	„		
Nowgong. — Rangalugarh	1871—72	1875	„		
74 Not yet published.					
75 Nowgong. — Jamuna, — Mukh, Sonarigaon	1870—72	1875	„		
76 Nowgong. — Jamuna Mukh	1870—71	1875	„		
77 to 79 Not yet published.					
80 Cachar. — Lakhipur	1881—82	1887	„		
81 Cachar	1881—82	1883	„		
82, 83 Not yet published.					
84 Darrang	1871—72	1883	„		
85 Darrang. — Gohpur	„	„	„		
86 Darrang	„	„	„		
Nowgong. — Bagri	„	1875	„	„	
87 Nowgong	„	„	„	„	
98 District Lakhimpur	1867—71	1893	„	40 × 27	„
130 do	1867—73	„	„	„	
138 do	„	„	„		
140 do	„	„	„		
144 do	„	„	„		
114 Parts of Lakhimpur and Sibsagar	1866—73	„	„		„
129 Part of Lakhimpur	„	„	„		„
162 North Lushai Hills	1897—99	1900	„		2/3
163 „	1898—1900	1901	„		„
165 Lushai Hills	1899—1901	1902	„		

Standard Sheets of the Province of Assam.

627 Comprising the District and other Surveys, on the scale of 1″ = 2 M. Sheets published are shown by the Provincial Index Sheet Number.					
Sheet 13 Garo Hills	1870—74	1875	1″ = 2 M	22″ × 15″	0 9
14 Garo Hills, Dalu	„	„	„	„	0 9
21 Garo Hills, Kylas, Sumaseri River Khasi Hills	1869—71	1872	„		0 9

	Year of Survey	Date of last edition	Scale	Size	Price
Sheet 22 Garo Hills	1869—71	1872	1" = 2 M	22" × 15"	0 9
Khasi Hills					
28 Garo Hills	1866—69	1870	„		0 9
Khasi Hills					
29 Khasi Hills. — Nongstoin, Umsau	„	1873	„		0 9
30 Khasi Hills	1865—69	1885	„		0 9
31 Khasi Hills. — Rolang Bazar	1866—79	1881	„		0 9
40 Khasi Hills	1868—69	1870	„		0 9
41 Khasi Hills. — Umran, Umsau, Nongpho, Sparoi, Umlur, Umsao, Jirang, Kamrup	1866—78	1879	„		0 9
42 Khasi Hills. Mairang, Nongklau, Shillong, Moyong, Umsning Dâk Bungalow	1864—78	1882	„		0 9
43 Khasi Hills, Cherra Ponjee, Surarim, Moflong, Saigong, Lailangkot	1864—79	1881	„		0 9
44 Khasi Hills. — Tharia Ghât, Maosmai Falls	„	„	„		0 9
47 Hill Tipperah	1879—82	1883	„		3 0
52 Khasi Hills. — Nangklao Khalla	1867—69	1870	„		0 9
53 Khasi Hills	1867—68	1883	„		0 9
Jaintia Hills					
54 Khasi Hills	„	„	„		0 9
Jaintia Hills. — Nartiang Pamura Maodumang					
55 Khasi Hills	„	„	„		0 9
Jaintia Hills. — Dingling, Jowai, Jarain, Nongjurong					
56 Khasi Hills	„	„	„		0 9
Jaintia Hills. — Sankar	„	„	„		0 9
59 Hill Tipperah	1879—82	1883	„		3 0
63 Khasi Hills	1866—69	1870	„		0 9
64 Khasi Hills	1868—74	1876	„		0 9
Jaintia Hills					
65 Jaintia Hills	1867—74	1876	„		0 9
North Cachar					
66 Jaintia Hills	1867—69	1890	„		0 9
North Cachar. — Muthbir, Bilsazar					
67 Jaintia Hills	1867—79	1882	„		0 9
North Cachar					
68 North Cachar	„	„	„		0 9
74 Naga Hills. — (Rengma)	1872—73	1885	„		0 9
Mekir Hills					

		Year of Survey	Date of last edition	Scale	Size	Price
best 75	Naga Hills Mekir Hills	1872—74	1875	1″ = 2 M	22″ × 15″	0 9
76	Naga Hills Mekir Hills	1873—74	„	„		0 9
77	Naga Hills North Cachar	„	„	„		0 9
78	Naga Hills Manipur North Cachar	1868—69	1890	„		0 9
79	North Cachar. — Asalu Manipur	1868—74	1875	„		0 9
80	North Cachar Manipur	1869—74	„	„		0 9
86	Naga Hills	1873—74	1876	„		0 9
87	Naga Hills. — (Rengma) Mekir Hills	1872—74	1875	„		0 9
88	Naga Hills Mekir Hills	„	„	„		0 9
89	Naga Hills. — Dunapur, Sama- guting	1870—74		„		0 9
90	Naga Hills. — Kenoma or Pa- langmai Manipur	„	„	„		0 9
91	Naga Hills Manipur	„	„	„		0 9
92	Naga Hills Manipur. — Daibiram	1873—74	„	„		0 9
93	Manipur Town	„	„	„		0 9
101	Naga Hills Naga Tribes	1874—75	1878	„		0 9
102	Naga Hills. — Lakhuti Naga Tribes	„	„	„		0 9
103	Naga Hills. — Wokha, Nongse- chong Naga Tribes	1873—76		„		0 9
104	Naga Hills Naga Tribes	1870—75	1876	„		0 9
105	Naga Hills. — Kohima Naga Tribes Manipur ·	1870—74	1875	„		0 9
107	Manipur.—(Part surveyed only)	1881—82	1883	„		0 9
108	Manipur. — (Eastern half only)	„	„	„		0 9
109	Manipur. — (Eastern half only)	„	„	„		0 9

		Year of Survey	Date of last edition	Scale	Size	Price
Sheet 110	Manipur. — (Eastern half only)	1881—82	1883	1″ = 2 M	22″ × 15″	0 9
116	Naga Tribes	1874—75	1878	„	„	0 9
117	Naga Tribes	1874—76	1878	„		0 9
118	Naga Tribes. — Mobonchoki, Mongsembi	1874—76	1877	„		0 9
119	Naga Tribes. — Longsa. — (Part only)	1875—76	1880	„		0 9
120	Naga Tribes. — (Part only)	1874—76	1879	„		0 9
121	Naga Tribes	1873—74	1879	„		0 9
123	Manipur	1881—82	1883	„		0 9
124	Manipur	1881—82	1883	„		0 9
125	Manipur	1881—82	1883	„		0 9
126	Manipur	1881—82	1883	„		0 9
	Burma					
131	Naga Tribes	1874—75	1882	„		0 9
132	Naga Tribes. — Zil, Lakhma, Neaunu	1874—76	1884	„		0 9
133	Naga Tribes. — Chen or Than	1874—76	1879	„		0 9
134	Naga Tribes	1875—76	1879	„		0 9
139	Mishmi Hills	1876—77	1889	„		0 9
140	Naga Hills. — (Portion of Assam falling within the inner and outer lines of boundary)	1873—74	1878	„		0 9
141	Naga Tribes. — Namsung. — (Portions of Assam falling within inner and outer lines of boundary)	1873—74	1878	„		0 8
142	Naga Tribes. — Portions of Assam falling between the inner and outer lines of boundary)	1873—74	1878	„		0 9
145	Mishmi Hills	1876—77	1880	„		0 9
146	Naga Hills. — Portions of Assam falling between the outer and inner boundary)	1876—77	1878	„		0 9
147	Naga Hills. — (Portions of Assam falling between the outer and inner boundary)	1873—74	1878	„		0 9

Maps, Plans, etc., published by the Government of India, before 1891 [1]).

asam Province, Scale 16 miles to 1 inch. 1875. Without Hills.

ssam, 1878. To be completed in 9 sheets. Scale 8 miles to 1 inch.

    Sheet 1. Western Bhutan [Butan].

ower Provinces Revenue Survey. Civil Station and Cantonment of Silchar, District Cachar. 1867. Calcutta, 1878, 6″ = 1 M.

ssam, 1″ = 8 M.

    Sheet 4. Garo Hills, &c.

he Province of Assam under the Jurisdiction of the Chief Commissioner. 1875, 1″ = 24″.

ssam, 1879, 1″ = 8 M.

    Sheets 5, 6, containing parts of Districts Kamrup, Darrang, Nowgong, Sylhet, Cachar, Khasi, Jaintia and Naga Hills, and Manipur.

.hasi, Garo, and Naga Hills Topographical Survey. 1873—74. 1″ = 2 M.

    Sheets 107 third ed., 111, 125, 126, 129.

'orth Brahmaputra Exploration Survey. 1877—78. Part of the Miri Hills. 1″ = 4 M.

    Sheets 161, 162, 163, 164, 165, 168, 170, 171, all on 1 sheet.

art of the Mishmi Hills, North-East Frontier, Assam. Surveyed by Capt. R. G. Woodthorpe, R.E., and Mr. W. Robert, 1877—78. 1″ = 4 M.

    Degree Sheets 20, 21, 24, 25, all on 1 sheet.

ssam, 1880, 1″ = 8 M.

    Sheet 3. Parts of Lakhimpur and Sibsagar Districts.

ssam, 1880, 1″ = 8 M.

    Sheets 2, 7 and 8 in one, 9 containing only Title and Index. [Completing the Map of Assam in 9 sheets.]

.hasia [Khasi] and Garo Hills Topographical Survey. 1″ = 2 M. Seasons 1864—67 and 1876—78.

    Sheets 14, 15, second edition.

istrict Cachar. 1865—70 and 1873—74. Pub. April 1881. 1″ = 4 M.

ssam, Second ed., 1881. Sheet 5, and Sheets 7 and 8 on one sheet. 1″ = 8 M.

ssam, Second ed., 1881, Sheet No. 3.

.hasia and Garo Hills Topographical Survey. 1864—79. 1″ = 1 M. Part of Sheets 12 and 13, on one sheet, second ed. — Sheet 16, second ed. — Sheet 17, second ed.

- — 1″ = 2 M. Sheet 13, second ed. — Sheets 16 and 17, on one sheet, second ed.

reliminary Map. District Sylhet. 1860—66. 1″ = 4 M.

he Province of Assam under the jurisdiction of the Chief Commissioner. 1881. 1″ = 24 M.

---

1) Cette liste a été dressée à l'aide des listes publiées par le «Statistics and Commerce leographical) Department, India Office» depuis No. 1 of 1878, Feb. 7th 1878 jusqu'à lo. 55, 26th May 1891.

District Durrang, Assam. 1871—74. 1″ = 4 M.

District Nowgong, Assam. 1869—72. 1″ = 4 M.

District Sibsagar. Seasons 1862—75. Pub. 1882. 1″ = 4 M. — Size 25″ × 38.

District Sylhet. 1860—66. With addition to 1882. 1″ = 4 M. — Size 26″ × 34.

District Goalpara. 1855—75. 1″ = 4 M. — Size 35″ × 32.

District Kamrup. 1865—69. 1″ = 4 M. — Size 26″ × 34.

Shillong Sanatorium. Sheets 2, 3, 5, 6, 8, 9, 11, 12. — 24″ = 1 M.

North-East Frontier Topog. Survey. Part of South Sylhet. 1877—79. 1″ = 2 M.

Eastern Naga Hills and Manipur, with adjoining portions of Burmah. Surveyed during the years 1872—74 and 1881—82. 1″ = 4 M. — 2 sheets.

In connection with Khasia and Garo Hills Topog. Survey.

Khasi, Garo, and Naga Hills Topog. Survey. 1874—76. 1″ = 2 M. Sheet 107. — 4th ed.

District Lakhimpur, Assam, 1884. 1″ = 4 M. — Size 40″ × 27.

District Sylhet. 1860—66. Additions to 1883. 1″ = 4 M. — Size 27″ × 33.

Assam Survey. Part of Khasi Hills. Sheet 30. 1″ = 2 M. — 1885. — 1/3 d.

North-East Frontier Survey. Part of South Sylhet. Sheet 7. 1886. 2″ = 1 M.
— — Sheet 10. 1886. 2″ = 1 M.

North-East Trans-Frontier. Parts of Singpho and Naga Hills. 1″ = 4 M. 1886. — Sheet 22, N.W.

— — 1″ = 2 M. 1886. — Sheet 22, $\dfrac{\text{N.W.}}{1}$

— — 1″ = 2 M. 1886. — Sheet 22, $\dfrac{\text{N.W.}}{3}$

Province of Assam. 1886. 1″ = 24 M. — 2/—

Garo Hills (Lower Assam). 1886. 1″ = 4 M. — 2/6 d.

Assam. North-East Frontier Survey. Sheet No. 11. Part of South Sylhet. 2″ = 1 M. 1881—82—83. — 1886.

North-Eastern Trans-Frontier. Parts of Singpho and Naga Hills. — Sheet No. 22.

Burma and Assam Frontier (Skeleton Map). 1″ = 32 M. 1886.

Assam Survey. Sheets 57, 70, 80, and 81. District Cachar. (Preliminary Editions) 1″ = 1 M. — 3/6 d. per sheet, 1887.

Lushai and adjoining Hill Tracts. 1889. 1″ = 8 M. — 2/—

District Sibsagar. 1889. 1″ = 4 M. — 4/—

Parts of Lushai, Cachar and Manipur. 1889. 1″ = 8 M. — 1/—

Assam Survey (Naga Hills). Sheets 104, 105, 120, and 121 (in one). 1″ = 2 M. — 1889, 3/6 d.

Assam Survey. Sheet 39 (Prelim. Ed.). 1″ = 1 M. — 3/6 d. 1890.

Index to Sheets and Maps of Assam. 1889. 1″ = 48 M. — 6 d.

District Cachar. 1890. 1″ = 4 M. — 2/6 d.

Assam Survey. Sheet 25. 1″ = 1 M. — 1890. 3/6 d.

North-Eastern Frontier. Sheet 15. Manipur and surrounding Tracts. 1″ = 8 M. — 3/6 d. 1890.

Tribus de la Frontière indienne.

1720. — Customs common to the Hill Tribes bordering on Assam and those of the Indian Archipelago. By J. R. Logan. (*Jour. Ind. Archipelago*, II, 1848, pp. 229—236).

1721. — Notes on the Languages spoken by the various Tribes inhabiting the Valley of Asam and its Mountain Confines. By William Robinson, Inspector of Government Schools in Asam. (*Jour. As. Soc. Bengal*, XVIII, Pt. I, 1849, pp. 183—237; *ibid.*, XVIII, Pt. I, 1849, pp. 310—349).

1722. — On the Aborigines of Nor-Eastern India. By B. H. Hodgson, Esq. (*Ibid.*, XVIII, Pt. I, 1849, pp. 451—460).

1723. — On the Aborigines of the Eastern Frontier. By B. H. Hodgson, Esq. (*Ibid.*, XVIII, Pt. II, 1849, pp. 967—975).

1724. — Aborigines of the North-East Frontier. By B. H. Hodgson, Esq. (*Ibid.*, XIX, 1850, pp. 309—316).

1725. — On the Indo-Chinese Borderers and their connexion with the Himalayans and Tibetans. By B. H. Hodgson, Esq. (*Ibid.*, XXII, 1853, pp. 1—25).

1726. — The Hill Tribes of the Northern Frontier of Assam; by Rev. C. H. Hesselmeyer. (*Ibid.*, Vol. 37, Pt. 2, 1868, pp. 192—208).

Avec un alphabet Hrusso or Angka.

1727. — Selection of Papers regarding the Hill Tracts between Assam and Burmah, and on the Upper Brahmaputra. Printed at the Bengal Secretariat Press, 1873, gr. in-8, pp. 335.

Contents:

Vol. 1. — Memoir of a Survey of Assam and the Neighbouring Countries, executed in 1825—6—7—8. By Lieut. R. Wilcox.

Vol. 2. — Abstract of the Journal of a Route travelled by Capt. S. F. Hannay, in 1835—36, from the Capital of Ava to the Amber Mines of the Hookong Valley, on the South-East Frontier of Assam. By Capt. R. B. Pemberton.

Vol. 3. — Journal of a Trip to the Mishmi Mountains, from the Debouching of the Lohit to about Ten Miles East of the Ghalums. By W. Griffith.

Vol. 4. — Journey from Upper Assam towards Hookboom, Ava, and Rangoon. By W. Griffith.

Vol. 5. — Narrative of a Journey from Ava to the Frontiers of Assam, and back, performed between December 1836 and May 1837. By G. T. Bayfield.

Vol. 6. — Notes on a Trip across the Patkoi Range from Assam to the Hookoong Valley. By H. L. Jenkins, in 1869—70.

Vol. 7. — Notes on the Burmese Route from Assam to Hookoong Valley. By H. L. Jenkins. *Map*.

Vol. 8. — Report of a Visit by Capt. Vetch to the Singpho and Naga Frontier to Luckimpore, 1842.

Vol. 9. — Reports of Lieut. Brodie's Dealings with the Nagas on the Seebsaugor Frontier, 1841—46.

Vol. 10. — Notes on a Visit to the Tribes inhabiting the Hills South of Seebsaugor, Assam. By S. E. Peal.

Royal Geographical Society's Library.

1728. — Notes on the Locality and Population of the Tribes dwelling between the Brahmaputra and Ningthi Rivers. By the late G. H. Damant, M.A., M.R.A.S., Political Officer, Nága Hills. (*Journ. R. As. Soc.*, N. S., Vol. XII, Art. VIII, April 1880, pp. 228—258).

1729. — History of the Relations of the Government with the Hill Tribes of the North-East Frontier of Bengal: by Alexander Mackenzie, of the Bengal Civil Service... Calcutta: Home Department Press. 1884, in-8, pp. IV + XIV + pp. 586.

1730. — The Tribes of the Brahmaputra Valley: — A Contribution on their Physical Types and Affinities. — By L. A. Waddell... (*Jour. As. Soc. of Bengal*, Vol. 59, Pt. III, 1900, pp. 1—127, Planches).

1731. — Burmese Border Tribes and Trade Routes. By A. R. MacMahon, Major-general. (*Blackwood's Mag.*, CXL, Sept. 1886, pp. 394—407).

1732. — Note on the Languages spoken between the Assam Valley and Tibet. By Sten Konow, of the University of Christiania, Norway. (*Journ. R. A. S.*, Jan. 1902, pp. 127—137).

Akas.

1733. — Notes on Akas and Akaland. — By Major C. R. Macgregor. (Abstract.) (*Proc. As. Soc. Bengal*, No. XI, Dec. 1884, pp. 198—212).

1734. — *L. A. Waddell. — Note on the poisoned arrows of the Akas. (*Journ. Anthr. Instit. of Great Britain and Ireland*, XXIV, p. 57, 1 table).

1735. — A Short Vocabulary of the Aka Language. By J. D. Anderson, *I.C.S.*, Some time Deputy Commissioner of Darrang. — Compiled in 1893. — Shillong: Printed at the Assam Secretariat Printing Office, 1896, in-8, pp. IV—20.
    Préf. datée: Chittagong, 26th April 1895.

Daflas.

1736. — *Wm Robinson. — Notes on the Dophlás and the Peculiarities of their Language. (*Jour. As. Soc. Bengal*, XX, 1852, pp. 126 et seq.)

1737. — An Outline Grammar of the Dafla Language as spoken by the Tribes immediately south of the Apa Tanang Country by R. C. Hamilton, Esq. Indian Civil Service. Shillong: Printed at the Assam Secretariat Printing Office. 1900, in-8, pp. 127 + 2 ff. n. ch.

Abor-Mîris.

1738. — On the Meris and Abors of Assam. By Lieut. J. T. E. Dalton, Assistant Commissioner, Assam. In a letter to Major Jenkins. Communicated by the Government of India. (*Jour. As. Soc. Bengal*, XIV, pt. I, 1845, pp. 426—430).

1739. — Outline Grammar of the Shâi yâng Miri Language as spoken by the Miris of that Clan residing in the Neighbourhood of Sadiya. With illustrative sentences, phrase-book, and vocabulary. By J. F. Needham, Assistant political Officer, Sadiya. Shillong: Printed at the Assam Secretariat Press. 1886, in-8, pp. II—157.

1740. — Excursion in the Abor Hills; from Sadiya on the Upper Assam. By J. F. Needham, Assistant Political Officer, Sadiya. (*Proc. R. Geog. Soc.*, VIII, 1886, May, pp. 313—328).

Mishmi.

Chulikatā — Digāru — Mijū Mishmi.

1741. — Journal of a Visit to the Mishmee Hills in Assam. By Wm. Griffith, M.D. Madras Medical Establishment. (*Jour. As. Soc. Bengal*, VI, May 1837, pp. 325—341).

1742. — Visit to the Mishmee Hills in Assam, By Wᵐ Griffith, M.D. (*Asiatic Journal and Monthly Register*, XXV, 1838, pp. 233—244).

1743. — Report of an Expedition into the Mishmee Hills to the north-east of Sudyah. By Lieutenant E. A. Rowlait, 21st Regt. N. I. In a letter to Major F. Jenkins, Governor General's Agent, N. E. Frontier, dated Saikwah, 1st January 1845. Communicated by the Government of India. (*Jour. As. Soc. Bengal*, XIV, pt. II, 1845, pp. 477—495).

1744. — Notes on the Languages spoken by the Mi-Shmis, by W. Robinson, Esq. (Communicated by the Government of Bengal). (*Ibid.*, XXIV, 1855, pp. 307—324).

1745. — A few Digârô (Tàroàn), Mîjû (M'jû), and Thibetian [*sic*] words collected by J. F. Needham, Esq., Assistant Political Officer, Sadiya, during a trip from Sadiya to Rima and back in December 1885 and January 1886. Pièce in-8, pp. 29, s. l. n. d.

Voir T. T. Cooper, No. 879.

Lakhimpur et Sibsagar.

1746. — An Outline Grammar of the Deori Chutiya Language spoken in Upper Assam with an Introduction, Illustrative Sentences, and Short Vocabulary. By W. B. Brown, B.A., I.C.S., late Assistant Commissioner, North Lakhimpur. — Shillong: Printed at the Assam Secretariat Printing Office. 1895, in-8, pp. VIII—84 + 1 f. n. ch. à la fin.

«The Deori Chutiyas are a small and secluded tribe in the Lakhimpur and Sibsagar districts of Upper Assam. Their principal settlements are on the Majuli Island in Sibsagar, and on the Dikrang river in North Lakhimpur. They number less than four thousand in all.

«As the name implies, they are the representatives of the priestly or Levite class among the Chutiyas, who are one of the most numerous castes in these districts, numbering 87,691 at the census of 1891; and whom we know from history to have been the ruling race in Upper Assam before the Ahom invasion in the fifteenth Century. The other two divisions of the race, the Hindu Chutiyas and Ahom Chutiyas, have long lost all trace of their language and origin, and have become merged in the general mass of semi-Hinduised Assamese; but their original connection with the Deoris has never been disputed, and is freely acknowledged by themselves. The main interest attached to the Deoris is that they have preserved the language, religion, and customs which, we may presume, have descended to them with comparatively little change from a period anterior to the Ahom invasion. The Chutiya language, indeed, may fairly claim to be the original language of Upper Assam».

1747. — *G. A. Gammie. —· Report on a Botanical Tour in the Lakhimpur District Assam. (*Records of the Botanical Survey of India*, Calcutta, 1895, I, No. 5).

États Shans.

1748. — Alphabets of the Tai Language. By the Rev. N. Brown, Missionary in Assam. (*Jour. As. Soc. Bengal*, VI, Jan. 1837, pp. 17—21).

1749. — A Comparative Vocabulary of Shan, Ka-kying and Pa-laong. By the Right Rev. P. A. Bigandet. (*Jour. Ind. Arch.*, N. S., Vol. II, 1858, pp. 221—9).

1750. — Route from Toangoo to the Shan States. By Edward O'Reily, Esq. (*Proc. Roy. Geog. Soc.*, VI, 1862, p. 83).

1751. — The Shan and Burmese war. (*Siam Repository*, Jan. 1869, Vol. I, Art. XXII, pp. 47—48).

    (Extrait du *Rangoon Times*).

1752. — The Laos or Shans, as the Burmese call them. (*Siam Repository*, April or July?, 1869, Vol. I, Art. LXXIV, pp. 141—143).

1753. — Shans. (*Ibid.*, July 1869, Vol. I, Art. XCV, pp. 184—186).

    Abstracts from the *Missionary Magazine*.

1754. — Shan land-sketches. (*Ibid.*, July 1869, Vol. I, Art. CXVIII, pp. 231—33).

1755. — Introductory Sketch of the History of the Shans in Upper Burma and Western Yunnan. By Ney Elias, attaché, Foreign Department... Calcutta: Printed at the Foreign Department Press. 1876, in-8, pp. 63.

1756. — *J. N. Cushing. — Grammar of the Shan Language. 1871, in-8, pp. XII—60.

1757. — *J. N. Cushing. — Grammar of the Shan Language. 2nd Edition, thoroughly revised and enlarged. 1887, in-8, pp. 118.

1758. — *J. N. Cushing. — Elementary Handbook of the Shan Language. 1880, pet. in-4, pp. 121.

1759. — *J. N. Cushing. — Elementary Handbook of the Shan Language. New Edition, revised and enlarged, with an English-Shan Vocabulary. 1888, in-8, pp. 272.

1760. — *J. N. Cushing. — Shan-English Dictionary. 1881, in-8, pp. VI—600.

1761. — Amongst the Shans, by Archibald Ross Colquhoun, A.M.I.C.E., F.R.G.S. Author of «Across Chrysê», etc. With upwards of Fifty whole-page Illustrations and an historical sketch of the Shans, by Holt S. Hallett, M.T.C.E., F.R.G.S. Preceded by an introduction on the Cradle of the Shan Race, by Terrien de Lacouperie, Professor of Indo-Chinese Philology, University Coll. Lond., ... London: Field & Tuer, ... 1885, in-8, pp. IV—392.

    Notices: *Spectator*, LVIII, 551. — *Athenaeum*, 1885, I, 273. — *Literary World*, Boston, XVI, 95. — *Saturday Review*, LIX, 797.

1762. — The Cradle of the Shan Race. — By Terrien de Lacouperie, br. in-8, s. d., pp. 35.

1763. — The Shan States. By A. C. Yate. (*As. Quart. Review*, VI, July-Oct. 1888, pp. 309—236).

1764. — Eighteen hundred miles on a Burmese Tat through Burmah, Siam, and the Eastern Shan State... By G. J. Younghusband, 1888. (Voir No. 1457).

1765. — *A Thousand Miles on an Elephant in the Shan States. By Holt S. Hallett. London and Edinburgh: William Blackwood and Sons, 1889, in-8.
> Notice: *Nature*, XLI, 1889—90, pp. 265—268.

1766. — The ancient Shan Kingdom of Pong. By A. R. Macmahon. (*As. Quart. Review*, X, July-Oct. 1890, pp. 18—35).

1767. — Far Cathay ... by Major-General A. Ruxton Mac Mahon. 1893. (Voir No. 37).

1768. — Les Etats Shans birmans. Par Jos. Pina, Vice-Consul de France. (*Rev. Indo-chinoise illust.*, Mai 1894, pp. 32—48).

1769. — *G. C. Rigby. — Report on a tour through the Northern Shan States. Season 1894—95. Rangoon, 1895, in-8, pp. 26—LXII, illustrations, carte.

1770. — The Country of the Shans. By Colonel R. G. Woodthorpe, C.B., R.E. (*The Geog. Jour.*, VII, June 1896, pp. 577—602).

1771. — *R. G. Woodthorpe. — The Shan Hills: their People and Products. (*Jour. Soc. Arts*, 1896, XLIV, pp. 197—210).

1772. — Shan States. By Colonel Woodthorpe. Read before the Indian Section of the Society of Arts.
> Réimp. de la *Rangoon Gazette*, de 1896, dans G. W. Bird's *Wanderings in Burma*, pp. 10—35.

1773. — Some Account of the Shans and Hill Tribes of the States on the Mekong. By Col. R. G. Woodthorpe, C.B., R.E. (*Journ. Anthrop. Inst. of Gt. Brit. and Ireland*, Vol. XXVI, 1896—97, pp. 13—28).
> With plate.

1774. — Shan and Siam. By Capt. G. E. Gerini. (*Imp. & As. Quart. Rev.*, 3rd Ser., V, 1898, pp. 145—163).

1775. — Shan and Siam. (A Reply and Discussion). By E. H. Parker. (*Ibid.*, 3rd Ser., V, 1898, pp. 401—405).

1776. — Shan and Siam. By R. F. St. Andrew St. John, M.R.A.S. (*Ibid.*, 3rd Ser., V, 1898, pp. 423—424).

1777. — Along a Shan Road. Southern Shan States, Upper Burma. By Wm. Sutherland, Assistant Superintendent of Telegraphs, Lower Burma. (*Scottish Geog. Jour.*, XIV, 1898, pp. 188—198).

1778. — La Birmanie et les Etats Shans par Madame Massieu. (*Bul. Soc. Géog. Toulouse*, 1898, pp. 321—9).

1779. — Les États Shans du Sud. Traduit du *Rangoon Gazette* par Jules Dutertre. (*Revue Indo-Chinoise*, 1904, pp. 95—106).
> Entre Thasi et Taungyi, viâ Yawnghwe et le lac Inle.

Ahom.

1780. — Interpretation of the Ahom Extract, published as Plate IV of the January number of the present volume. By Major F. Jenkins, Commissioner in Assam. (See page 18). (*Jour. As. Soc. Bengal*, VI, Nov. 1837, pp. 980—4).

1781. — Note on Ghargáon, Asám. By J. M. Foster. (*Ibid.*, Vol. 41, 1872, Pt. 1, pp. 32—41).

    Ghargáon, pendant de nombreuses années, capitale des rois Ahom d'Assam.

1782. — Abstract of the Contents of one of the Āhŏm Puthis. By E. A. Gait. (*Ibid.*, Vol. 63, 1894, Pt. 1, pp. 108—111).

1783. — Notes on some Āhŏm Coins. — By E. A. Gait. (*Ibid.*, Vol. 64, 1895, Pt. 1, pp. 286—289).

1784. — Notes on Āhŏm. By G. A. Grierson. (*Zeit. D. Morg. Ges.*, Bd. 56, 1902, pp. 1—59).

    «Āhŏm belongs to the same sub-group of the Tai languages as Khāmti and Shān».

1785. — An Ahom Cosmogony, with a Translation and a Vocabulary of the Ahom Language. By G. A. Grierson. (*Jour. R. As. Soc.*, April 1904, pp. 181—232).

    «The Ahoms are a tribe of the Tai branch of the Indo-Chinese. They conquered Assam early in the thirteenth century A.D., and held it, as the ruling nation, for many centuries. Their language, which is now extinct, was an old form of the Tai language from which Siamese and Shan have sprung. It is now known by tradition to a few priests of the old Ahom religion. It had a considerable literature (including several valuable historical works), manuscripts of which are still extant. Some years ago the Assamese Government deputed a native official, Babu Golap Chandra Baruā, to learn the language and translate such documents are were of value and had survived. He is, I believe, the only person who knows both Ahom and English. Through his assistance I was enabled to publish a short grammar of Ahom (with selections and a vocabulary) in vol. LVI of the *Zeitschrift der Deutschen Morgenländischen Gesellschaft*. Since then I have received from him a short Ahom *kŏṣa*, or dictionary, and also the text and translation of the cosmogony printed below». P. 181. Notice: *Deutsche Literaturzeitung*, No. 27, 1904.

Kakhyen ou Singpho. — Khamti.

1786. — Sketch of the Singphos, or the Kakhyens of Burmah: the position of This Tribe as regards Baumo, and the Inland Trade of the Valley of the Irrawaddy with Yuman [*sic*] and their connection with the north-eastern Frontier of Assam. — Calcutta: W. Ridsdale, 1847, in-8, pp. 77.

1787. — Grammatical Sketch of the Kakhyen Language. By the Rev. J. N. Cushing, of the American Baptist Mission, Rangoon, Burma. (*Jour. R. A. S.*, N. S., Vol. XII, Art. XVI, July 1880, pp. 395—416).

    «The Kakhyen or Singpho are the most numerous people occupying the mountainous region stretching from Upper Assam across Northern Burma beyond the Chinese boundary into Yunan. In Burma they extend as far south as Momeit and Theinni. During the last forty years, at different times, more or less attention has been called to this interesting people. On the Assam side, Hannay, Robinson, Bronson, Brown and Dalton, and on the Burman side, Anderson, Bowers, and Roman Catholic and Protestant missionaries have published sketches of their language and mode of life».

1788. — The Kunnungs. By S. E. Peal. (*Nature*, XXV, 1881—2, p. 529).

Sibsagar, Asam.

1789. — Notes sur la contrée des Singphos Kampti Frontière Nord-est. Par Chas. H. Lepper. — Traduit de l'anglais, par M. C.-H. Desgodins. Ext. des *Proc. de la Soc. As. de Bengale*, de mars 1882. (*Bul. Soc. Géog. Rochefort*, VII, 1885—6, pp. 47—54).

1790. — Outline Singpho Grammar. Pièce in-8, pp. 24, s. d.

Au bas de la dernière page: C. R. Macgregor, Major, 44th Regiment, S L.I. Contient 700 mots Singpho et 500 Khámti. — Privately Printed.

1791. — Rough Notes on Traditions, Customs, &c. of the Singphos and Khámptis. Pièce in-fol. pp. 5.

Signée: C. R. Macgregor, Major, 44th L.I., Dibrugarh: 22nd March 1886.

1792. — 'C. R. Mac Gregor. — Rough Notes on the Traditions, Customs &c. of the Singphos and Khåmptis. (*Babylonian and Oriental Record*, VII, pp. 172—76).

1793. — Outline Grammar of the Singpho Language as spoken by the Singphos, Dowanniyas, and others, residing in the neighbourhood of Sadiya, with Illustrative Sentences, Phrase-Book, and Vocabulary By J. F. Needham, Assistant Political Officer, Sadiya. Shillong: Printed at the Assam Secretariat Press. 1889, in-8, 2 ff. prél. n. ch. + pp. 119.

1794. — Outline Grammar of the ∞' (Khåmti) Language as spoken by the Khåmtis residing in the neighbourhood of Sadiya, with Illustrative Sentences, Phrase-Book and Vocabulary by J. F. Needham, Assistant Political Officer, Sadiya. — Rangoon: Printed by the Superintendent, Government Printing, Burma. — 1894, in-8, pp. III—201.

«The Khåmtis residing within British territory (chiefly up the Tengapani) on our north-east frontier are a small, well-behaved, and industrious community, numbering about 2 000 souls.

«They call themselves ∞' (Tai), and their forefathers came to Assam over 100 years ago from the country known to us as Bôr or great Khåmti, a valley of considerable extent lying high up the Irrawaddy, in latitude 27° and 28° north (eastward of Sadiya)». *Preface.*

1795. — On the Khámtis. By P. R. Gurdon. (*Jour. Roy. As. Soc.*, Jan. 1895, pp. 157—164).

«The habitat of the Bor Khåmtis, who are said to number 20,000, is in a valley high up the Irrawaddy, in latitude 27° and 28° east of Sadiya. The Khåmtis that we know in Assam are those that have emigrated from «Bor Khåmti» and have settled in Assam after the breaking up of the kingdom of Pong by Alomphra These settlers established themselves early in this century on the «Tenga Pani» (a river in the vicinity of Sadiya), with the permission of the Ahom Kings. Before proceeding further, it will be interesting to note that this Khåmti movement is the second instance of Tai emigration that we have on record. Some considerable time previously the Ahoms, who spoke a language much akin to the Khåmti tongue, and who are also of the Tai race, made an irruption over the Pátkoi range and invaded and conquered Assam».

1796. — 'Edward Harper Parker. — The Burmo-Chinese Frontier and the Ka-khyen Tribes. (*The Fortnight. Rev.*, Lond., 1897, N. S., LXII, pp. 86—104).

1797. — Ernst Kuhn. — Die Sprache der Singpho oder Ka-khyen: *Festschrift Bastian*, pp. 355—60.

Lushai.

(Voir Nos. 808—836.)

1798. — Notes on the Looshais. By Archibald Campbell, M.D. (*British Ass.*, Brighton, 1872, p. 176).

1799. — The Lushais. From a Narrative Report by Capt. W. F. Badgley, B.S.C. Topographical Survey. (*Indian Antiquary*, II, 1873, pp. 363—66, d'après le *Report of the Topograph. Survey of India*, 1871—72).

1800. — The Lushai Expedition. From Reports of the Surveyors. (*Proc. Roy. Geog. Soc.*, XVII, 1873, pp. 42—55).

1801. — Progressive Colloquial Exercises in the Lushai Dialect of the 'Dzo' or Kúki Language, with Vocabularies and Popular Tales (notated). By Capt. Thomas Herbert Lewin, B.S.C., Deputy Commissioner, Chittagong Hills. Calcutta: Calcutta Central Press Company, 1874, in-4, pp. 90—xxx.

> On lit dans l'introd : «The 'Dzo' tribes inhabit the hilly country to the east of the Chittagong district in Lower Bengal; their habitat may be roughly stated as comprised within the parallels of Latitude 22'45 N. and 25'20 N, and between the Meridians of Longitude 92'30 and 93'45....................... I would invite attention, nevertheless, to the subjoined comparative list of words, which would seem to give strength to the theory above propounded; it at least, I think, gives reasonable grounds for considering the Lushai tribes, including the inhabitants of Munipoor, to have sprung from the same stock as the Ghúrkas and other Himalayan tribes (Mongoloid of Huxley)».

1802. — 'B. N. Shaha. — A Grammar of the Lúsháï Language, to which are appended a few illustrations of the Zau of Lúsháï Popular Songs, and Translations from Æsop's Fables. 1884, gr. in-8, pp. VIII—94.

1803. — A Short List of Words of the Hill Tippera Language, with their English Equivalents. Also of Words of the Language spoken by Lushais of the Sylhet Frontier. Collected by J. D. Anderson, Esq., C.S., Subdivisional Officer, South Sylhet, during the cold season of 1883—84. To which have been added, for comparison, the Bodo (Kachari) equivalents taken from Mr. Brian Hodgson's Essay on the Koch, Bodo, and Dhimal tribes, Calcutta, 1847; and from the Revd. Mr. Endle's Kachari Grammar, Shillong, 1884; also Lushai equivalents from the dialect spoken by the Lushais of the Chittagong Frontier: these latter are taken from Captain Lewin's Exercises in the Lushai Language, and are marked C. Shillong: Printed at the Assam Secretariat Press. — 1885, br. in-8, pp. 13.

1804. — A Short Account of the Kuki-Lushai Tribes on the North-East Frontier (Districts Cachar, Sylhet, Nága Hills, etc., and the North Cachar Hills), with an Outline Grammar of the Rangkhol-Lushai Language and A Comparison of Lushai and other Dialects. By C. A. Soppitt, Assistant-Commissioner, Burma, late sub-divisional Officer, North Cachar Hills, Assam. — Shillong: Printed at the Assam Secretariat Press. 1887, in-8, pp. IX—88.

> De la préface datée: «Bhamo, Burma: The 17th April 1887» j'extrais les passages suivants:

«In this short history of the people, commonly grouped under the head of «Kuki», the writer has classified the different sects under two main heads, though four tribes are named:—
(a) Rângkhôl, co-tribe Bâtê, sub-tribes Sakajaib, Langrong, &c.
(b) Jansen, co-tribe Tâdôi, sub-tribes Kôtâng, Slûk, &c »

. . . .

«The Burma frontier north of Bhamo, bordering China eastwards and the Patkoi range and Singpho country north, is a most interesting field for ethnological research. The Kachyens bordering the plains to the west of the Irrawaddy bear a great resemblance in many ways to the Nágas, Lushais (Kukis), &c. Their worship is much the same and general mode of life quite in keeping with what is seen on the Assam frontier.
«They are not Buddhists like most of the Shans and some Singphos and Kamptis.
«This term «Singpho», or «Singphaw», it is stated, is used by some of the Kachyens as their tribal designation, and it is therefore likely that the people commonly spoken of by that name should be mentioned by some other term.
«Another tribe living in the plain north of Bhamo may be said to have been more or less recently formed. These people, called «Shans», and so calling themselves, though they occasionally use the term «Phoong», have a different language from the Shans proper and the Burmese, though in manners, dress, and belief they are nearly allied to the latter. They might be described as Shan-Burmese They occupy a number of the villages about the great plains, thirty miles north of Bhamo, near Megaong and the Endawgjee, or Big Lake.
«All these tribes, in common with the Burmese themselves, are of Mongolian origin. . . . . »

1805. — ʼMizo leh vai thon thu (folk tales), pp. 32. Price one rupee (1s. 4d.)
1898. Mizo zir tir bu (grammar, etc.) pp. 26. Price two annas, 1889. Printed at the Assam Secretariat Printing Office. in-8.

By Major J. Shakespear, C.I.E., D.S.O., I.S.C. Réunis par l'employé lushai Suaka. — J. M. L[yres] (*Journal Anthropological Institute of Great Britain*, XXX, p. 69.

1806. — ʼLushai Primer (Mi-Zo Leh Vai Thon Thu) — A Primer, containing 10 reading lessons in Lushai in Roman character without any English translation. By Major Shakespear, C.I.E., D.S.O., I.S.C. 1898, gr. in-8, pp. 32.

1807. — ʼJ. Shakespear. — The Lushais and the land they live in. (*Journ. Soc. of Arts*, XLIII, pp. 167—188, 1 carte).

1808. — Note on some Tribal and Family Names employed in speaking of the Inhabitants of the Lushai Hills. — By Major John Shakespear. (*Jour. As. Soc. Bengal*, Vol. 67, 1898, Pt. 3, pp. 116—117).

1809. — Chin-Lushai Land... By A. S. Reid, 1893. Voir No. 315.

1810. — A Folktale of the Lushais. By Bernard Houghton. (*Ind. Antiq.*, XXII, 1893, pp. 78—80).

From Major T. H. Lewin's *Progressive Lessons in the Lushai Dialect*, Calcutta, 1891.

1811. — Vocabulary of the Lushai Language, by R. H. Sneyd Hutchinson, Superintendent, South Lushai Hills. Calcutta: Bengal Secretariat Press. 1897. in-4, pp. II—22.

1812. — A Grammar and Dictionary of the Lushai Language (Dulien Dialect). Part I — Grammar. Part II — Useful Sentences. Part III — Dictionary from Lushai to English. Part IV — Dictionary from English to Lushai. By Revd. J. Herbert Lorrain and Revd. Fred. W. Savidge. 1898, gr. in-8, pp. 346.

1813. — ʼAmong the Head-Hunters of Lushai. By J. H. Lorrain and F. W. Savidge (*ill.*). (*Wide World Mag.*, IV, Dec. 1899, p. 375).

1814. — *J. H. Lorrain und F. W. Savidge bei den Luschais in Assam. (*Globus*, LXXVII, pp. 163—167). Illustrations.

1815. — *Mi-zo. — Zir Tir Na Bu. A Lushai Primer. In the Lushai Dialect. (Shillong), 1899, in-4, pp. 10, 6d.

> The Looshai are Indian Tribes inhabiting the Hills of Cachar and Chittagong, Bengal.

1816. — Lushai Primer (Mi-Zo Zir Tir Bu). [2nd edition]. — A Lushai Primer written in Roman character. Alphabet, spelling lessons, easy reading lessons (without English version), and arithmetical tables of calculation. 1901, gr. in-8. — 3rd ed. — 1903, gr. in-8.

1817. — Lushai-English Primer. (Mizo Leh Sâp Tawng Hma-bu). A Primer containing 271 lessons in Lushai in Roman character with English translation. Part I by Edwin Rowlands. Part II by David E. Jones, Welsh Presbyterian Mission, North Lushai Hills. 1903, gr. in-8.

1818. — Tod und Jenseits bei den Luschais. (*Mitth. Geogr. Gesellsch. Iena*, XIII, pp. 30 et seq.)

> D'après G. O. Newport dans le journal des Missions indiennes «*The Harvest Field*».

Khasi et Jaintia Hills.

1819. — On the Climate of the Jyntea Hills. By Hy. L. Beadon, Esq. M.D. (*Trans. Medical and Phys. Soc. Calcutta*, IV, 1829, pp. 315—9).

1820. — Some Account of the Cásiah Hills. (*Gleanings in Science*, Jan. to Dec. Vol. I, Calcutta, 1829, pp. 252—5).

1821. — Jasper from the Cásia Hills. (*Ibid.*, Jan. to Dec. Vol. I, Calcutta, 1829, pp. 374—5).

1822. — Climate of the Cásia Hills. (*Ibid.*, 1830, II, Calcutta, pp. 290—291). By W. P.

1823. — *New Testament, translated into the Khassee Language. Serampore, 1831. In-8.

1824. — Account of the Cossyahs, and of a Convalescent Depot established in their Country, 280 miles N.E. from Calcutta. Extracted from the private Letters of an Officer quartered there; and communicated by Lieut. Murphy, R.E. Read 9th Jan., 1832. (*Journ. Roy. Geogr. Soc.*, II, 1832, pp. 93—98).

> 25° 12′ 30″ lat. N. — 91° 35′ long. E., 30 milles au N.O. de Sylhet.

1825. — *Die Cassia-Sprache im nordöstlichen Indien, nebst Bemerkungen über das Tai, oder Siamesische, von W. Schott. Berlin 1839. In-4.

1826. — *Grammatik und Wörterbuch der Kassia-Sprache, von H. C. von der Gabelentz. Leipzig 1858. In-8.

1827. — *Report on the Administration of the Cossyah and Jynteah Hills Territory, 1858. Report and Appendices. By W. J. Allen, Esq., Member of the Board of Revenue (on deputation). 1858, in-fol.

> Rep. at the Assam Secretariat Press in 1900.

1828. — *H. Roberts. — A Grammar of the Khassi Language. London, Paul, 1891, in-8.

1829. — *Hit-Upodesa translation into Khasia by Jeebon Roy. Shillong, Ri Khasi Press, 1898—99, 4 Parties, pp. 70, 57, 42, 40.

1830. — *F. R. Bohnheim. — Bible history in Khasi. Shillong, Ri Khasi Press, 1900, pp. 88.

1831. — *Basanta Kumar Roy. — A Khasi word book. Shillong, Ri Khasi Press, 1900, pp. 24.

1832. — *Jeebon Roy. — History of India (in Khasi). Mawkhar, Shillong, Ri Khasi Press, 1900, pp. 146.

1833. — *Nissor Singh. — Hints on the study of Khasi language. Shillong, Ri Khasi Press, 1900, pp. 58.

1834. — *Note on the Khasis, Syntengs, and allied Tribes, inhabiting the Khasi and Jaintia Hills district in Assam. By Major P. R. T. Gurdon. With Plates. (*Journ. As. Soc. Bengal*, LXXIII, Pt. 3, 1904, pp. 57—74).

1835. — Khasi Customs. (*Calcutta Review*, April 1905, pp. 261—9).

Naga.

1836. — On the Poison of the Nagas. By P. Breton. (*Trans. Medical and Phys. Soc. Calcutta*, IV, 1829, pp. 235—240).

1837. — Extracts from the Narrative of an Expedition into the Naga territory of Assam. By E. R. Grange, Esq. Sub-Assistant to the Commissioner, Assam. (*Jour. As. Soc. Bengal*, VIII, June 1839, pp. 445—470).

1838. — *M. Bronson. — Phrases in English and Na'ga. 1840, pet. in-12, pp. 32.

1839. — Extracts from the Journal of an Expedition into the Naga Hills on the Assam Frontier. By Lieut. Grange, Assistant Political Agent, undertaken by order of Government in the Beginning of 1840, (taken by permission from the records of the Political Secretariat under the Government of India. (*Jour. As. Soc. Bengal*, IX, Pt. II, 1840, pp. 947—966).

1840. — Despatch from Lieut. H. Bigge, Assistant Agent, detached to the Naga Hills, to Capt. Jenkins, Agent Governor General, N. E. Frontier, communicated from the Political Secretariat of India to the Secretary to the Asiatic Society. (*Ibid.*, X, Pt. I, 1841, pp. 129—136).

1841. — Extracts from a report of a journey into the Naga Hills in 1844. By Mr. Browne Wood, Sub-Assistant Commissioner, in a letter to Captain A. Sturt, Principal Assistant Commissioner, Nowgong, dated 14th April, 1844, Golaghat. (*Ibid.*, XIII, Pt. II, N° 154, 1844, pp. 771—785).

1842. — Narrative of a Tour over that part of the Naga Hills lying between the Diko and Dyang river, in a Letter from Capt. Brodie, P.A. Commissioner to Major Jenkins, Commissioner of Assam. Communicated from the Foreign Department. (*Ibid.*, XIV, Pt. II, 1845, pp. 828—844).

1843. — Extract from a Memoir of some of the Natural Productions of the Angami Naga Hills, and other parts of Upper Assam, by J. W. Masters, Esq. (Communicated by G. A. Bushby, Esq. Secretary to the Government of India). (*Jour. As. Soc. Bengal*, XVII, Pt. I, 1848, pp. 57—59).

1844. — Notes on a Visit to the Tribes inhabiting the Hills south of Sibságar, Asám. By S. E. Peal. (*Ibid.*, Vol. 41, 1872, Pt. 1, pp. 9—31).
  Voir p. 29: *Specimen of a Naga Vocabulary*.

1845. — Vocabulary of the Banpará Nágás. By S. E. Peal, Sibságar, Asám. (*Ibid.*, Vol. 42, 1873, Pt. I, pp. xxx—xxxvi).

1846. — Eastern Nagas of the Tirap and Namtsik. By S. E. Peal. (*Ibid.*, Vol. 65, Pt. 3, 1896, pp. 9—17).

1847. — On some traces of the Kol-Mon-Anam in the Eastern Naga Hills. By S. E. Peal. (*Ibid.*, Vol. 65, Pt. 3, 1896, pp. 20—24).

1848. — A Rough Comparative Vocabulary of some of the Dialects spoken in the «Nágá Hills», District. — Compiled by Capt. John Butler, Officiating Political Agent. (*Ibid.*, Vol. 42, 1873, Pt. I, App., pp. ii—xxix).
  English. — Assamese. — Kachári. — Mikir. — Kúki. — Angámi Nágá. — Rengmá Nágá. — Kutchá Nágá.

1849. — A Rough Comparative Vocabulary of two more of the Dialects spoken in the «Nágá Hills». — Compiled by Capt. John Butler, Political Agent, Nágá Hills. (*Ibid.*, Vol. 44, 1875, Pt. 1, pp. 216—227).
  English. — Lhotá Nágá. — Jaipuriá Nágá.

1850. — Rough Notes on the Angámi Nágás and their Language. — By Capt. John-Butler... (*Ibid.*, Vol. 44, 1875, Pt. 1, pp. 307—346).

1851. — The Naga Hills. (Surveying Work of Major Godwin Austen, 1872—73). (*Ocean Highways*, N. S., Vol. I, May 1873, pp. 65—66).

1852. — A Specimen of the Zoongee (or Zurngee) Dialect of a Tribe of Nagas, bordering on the Valley of Assam, between the Dikho and Desoi Rivers, embracing over Forty Villages. By the Rev. Mr. Clark, Missionary at Sibsagar. (*Journ. R. As. Soc.*, N. S., Vol. XI, Art. XI, April 1879, pp. 278—86).

1853. — Naga Customs. (*Ind. Antiq.*, VIII, 1879, pp. 88, 206).

1854. — Notes on the Wild Tribes inhabiting the so-called Naga Hills, on our North East Frontier of India. Part I & II. By Lieut. Col. R. G. Woodthorpe, R.E. (*Jour. Anth. Inst.*, XI, Lond. 1882, pp. 56—73, 196—214).

1855. — On some Naga Skulls. By George D. Thane, Prof. of Anatomy in University College, London. (*Ibid*, XI, Lond. 1882, pp. 215—219).

1856. — A Short Account of the Kachcha Nága (Empèo) Tribe in the North Cachar Hills, with an Outline Grammar, Vocabulary, & illustrative Sentences. By C. A. Soppitt, Sub-divisional Officer, North Cachar Hills. — Shillong: Printed at the Assam Secretariat Press. 1885, in-8, 3 ff. prél. n. ch. + pp. 47.
  Préface datée de: Gunjong, North Cachar Hills. The 26th January 1885.

857. — Outline Grammar of the Angāmi Nāgā Language, with a Vocabulary and Illustrative Sentences. By R. B. Mc Cabe, C.S., Deputy Commissioner of the Naga Hills District, Assam. Calcutta: Printed by the Superintendent of Government Printing, India, 1887. in-8, pp. 95.

858. — The Angami Nagas by David Prain. Reprinted from the *Revue Coloniale Internationale*, Vol. V, pt. 6, pp. 472—494, December, 1887. (*Revised*, September 1890). s. l. [Calcutta, Printed by Umbica Charan Shome...] in-8, pp. 24.

1859. — *David Prain. — Memoirs and Memoranda, chiefly botanical. Reprints from Periodicals, 1887—1893. Calcutta, printed at the Baptist Mission Press, 1894, in-8, pp. 419.

> Pages 1—24: The Angami Nagas. Reprinted from the *Revue Coloniale Internationale*, V. Revised, September 1890.

1860. — The Ao Naga Language of Southern Assam, br. in-8, pp. 23.

> By John Avery. Reprinted from *American Journal of Philology*, Vol. VII, No. 3.

1861. — Outline Grammar of the Lhōtā Nāgā Language; with a Vocabulary and Illustrative Sentences. By Rev. W. E. Witter, M.A., Wokha, Naga Hills, Assam. Calcutta: Printed by the Superintendent of Government Printing, India. 1888, in-8, pp. 161.

> «With the exception of a few words collected by Captain John Butler, B.S.C., the following Outline Grammar, with a vocabulary and illustrative sentences, is the first presentation of the speech of the Lhōtā Nāgās». *Preface.*

1862. — Naga ornaments. By R. G. Woodthorpe. (*Journ. Anthrop. Inst. of Gt. Brit. and Ireland*, Vol. XIX, 1890—91, p. 252).

1863. — Naga Ornaments. By Charles H. Read. (*Ibid.*, XIX, 1890—91, p. 441).

1864. — *S. W. Rivenburg. — Yohán Kethu Die Kevi. Calcutta, American Baptist Mission Union, 1891. In-8, pp. 84.

> Traduction de l'Evangile de St. Jean en Angámi-Naga.

1865. — *Ketse Keshu Mha Kechuka. The Acts of the Apostles, translated into Angami Naga by S. W. Rivenburg. Kohima (Assam), American Baptist Miss. Union, 1892. In-8, pp. 82.

1866. — Ketse Keshu Mha Kechuka. Acts of the Apostles in Angami Naga translated from the Greek with the Revisers' Readings. By Rev. S. W. Rivenburg, M.A., M.D. 1904, gr. in-8.

1867. — A Primer containing 30 lessons in Angami Naga in Roman character without any English translation. By S. W. Rivenburg. 1903, in-12.

1868. — *S. W. Rivenburg. — Angami Naga Spelling-Book. In Angami Naga. Calcutta, 1904, in-8, pp. 16.

1869. — *S. W. Rivenburg. — Ao Ken Temeshi. Sacred hymns in Ao-Naga. Assam, published by the Author. 1900, pp. 90.

1870. — Ao Naga Grammar with Illustrative Phrases and Vocabulary, by Mrs. E. W. Clark, Molung, Naga Hills, Assam. Shillong: Printed at the Assam Secretariat Printing Office. 1893, in-8, 3 ff. prél. n. ch. + pp. 181.

> «By a tradition, more or less supported by present facts, the Naga tribe known as the Ao have from very early times had two dialects, — the Zungi and Mungsen. The legend is, that a colony of Zungi and friendly Ahoms migrated to these parts hundreds of years ago. The Zungis stopped for years at Zungi Imti, a place just behind the upper villages of the tribe, and the Ahoms resided awhile at a place now occupied by one of the upper villages called Longmisa or Tzümar Menden. Tzüma is what the Aos call the valley of Assam, and Tzümar Menden means the seat or abode of Assamese, or Ahoms, as they were called before the English occupation of the valley...»
>
> L'auteur dit dans la préface: «In the preparation of this work, I have had access to my husband's *Ao Naga-English Manuscript Dictionary*...»

1871. — A Collection of a few Moshang Naga Words. By F. J. Needham, Esq., Assistant Political Officer, Sadiya. Shillong: Printed at the Assam Secretariat Printing Office. 1897, br. in-8, pp. 11.

> «Môshang is the name of one of the tribal subdivisions of the Nágas inhabiting the country south of the Patkoi».

1872. — Nágá and other Frontier Tribes of North-East India. By Gertrude M. Godden. (*Journ. Anthrop. Inst. of Gt. Brit. and Ireland*, Vol. XXVI, 1896—97, pp. 161—201; ibid., Vol. XXVII, 1897—98, pp. 2—51).

> With plates. — Notice: *L'Anthropologie*, VIII, pp. 716 et seq., par Th. Volkov.

1873. — *The Story of Jesus translated into Tángkhul Nágá by W. Pettigrew. Tángkhul Nágá Hill, Manipur, published by the Translator (printed by C. W. Thomas, Calcutta), 1899, pp. 88.

1874. — *The Story of Jesus translated into Tangkhul Naga by W. Pettigrew. Manipur, published by the translator, 1900, pp. 138.

1875. — *Our Raid in Nagaland. By Rev. E. M. Hadow. (*Ill.*) (*Wide World Mag.*, IV, Feb. 1900, p. 561).

Cachari.

1876. — On the Origin, Location, Numbers, Creed, Customs, Character and Condition of the Kócch, Bodo and Dhimàl people, with a general description of the climate they dwell in. By B. H. Hodgson, Esq. (*Jour. As. Soc. Bengal*, XVIII, Pt. II, 1849, pp. 702—747).

1877. — The Hill Tribes of the North-East Frontier. (*Indian Antiquary*. I, 1872, pp. 62—3; d'après le *Bengal Times*, Dec. 30, 1871).

> North Kachar. — Manipur.

1878. — Sword Worship in Kâchâr. By G. H. Damant. (*Ibid.*, IV, 1875, pp 114—115).

1879. — Outline Grammar of the Kachári (Bårå) Language as spoken in District Darrang, Assam; With Illustrative Sentences, Notes, Reading Lessons, and a short Vocabulary. By Rev. S. Endle, S.P.G. Assam Church Mission, Late Student, St. Augustine's College, Canterbury. Shillong: Printed at the Assam Secretariat Press. 1884, in-8, pp. xii + v + xiv + 2 ff. n. ch. + pp. 99.

> Voir au commencement: Note on the relation of the Kachári (Bårå) Language to that of Hill Tipperá. — Hills Kachári compared with that spoken in the plains.

1880. — An Historical and Descriptive Account of the Kachari Tribe in the North Cachar Hills, with Specimens of Tales and Folk-lore. By C. A. Soppitt, Esq. 1885, gr. in-8.

> Reprinted with an introduction by B. C. Stuart Baker, Esq., 1901.

1881. — 'John Avery. — On the relationship of the Kachari and Garo Languages of Assam. (*Proceedings American Oriental Society*, May 1887, pp. viii—xi).

1882. — A Collection of Kachári Folk-Tales and Rhymes, intended as a Supplement to Reverend S. Endle's Kachári Grammar. By J. D. Anderson, Indian Civil Service. Shillong: Printed at the Assam Secretariat Printing Office. 1895, in-8, pp. v—61.

> «These stories were collected during a tour of only six weeks' duration in the Kachári mauzas of Mangaldai, and cost only the effort of taking down the tales as they were dictated».

1883. — 'J. D. Anderson. — Kāchāri Folk-Tales. (*Journ. Buddh. Text Society*, IV, I, Appendix, pp. 17—36).

1884. — M. J. Wright. — Three Years in Cachar.

> Voir Manipour.

1885. — The Morāns. — By Major P. R. T. Gurdon, Superintendent of Ethnography in Assam. (*Jour. As. Soc. Bengal*, LXXIII, Pt. I, No. 1, 1904, pp. 36—48).

Mikir.

1886. — 'R. C. Neighbor. — Vocabulary in English and Mikir, with sentences illustrating the use of words. Calcutta, 1878, in-8, pp. 84.

1887. — 'Mikir Primary Arithmetic. By Rev. P. E. Moore and Rev. J. M. Carwell. 1904, gr. in-8.

1888. — 'An English-Mikir Vocabulary with Assamese Equivalents, to which have been added a few Mikir Phrases. By S. P. Kay. 1904, gr. in-8.

Garo.

1889. — On the Gāro Hills. By Major H. H. Godwin-Austen, F.R.G.S., Deputy Superintendent, Topographical Survey of India. [Read, November 25th, 1872]. (*Journ. Roy. Geog. Soc.*, XLIII, 1873, pp. 1—46).

1890. — On the Garo Hills. By Major H. H. Godwin-Austen, F.R.G.S. (*Proc. Roy. Geog. Soc.*, XVII, 1873, pp. 36—42).

1891. — The Garos. By the Rev. W Ayerst. (*Ind. Antiq.*, IX, 1880, pp. 103—6).

1892. — Bengali-Garo Dictionary. By Rev. M. Ramkhe. — Tura, Assam. Published by the Garo Mission, American Baptist Missionary Union. 1887, in-8, à 2 col.

> On lit au bas de la dernière page: «Calcutta: Printed by J. W. Thomas, Baptist Mission Press. 1887».
> La préface est signée: «M. C. Mason. Tura, Garo Hills, Assam, September, 1887». Elle commence ainsi: «In opening schools among the Garos, who had no written language, the supply of text-books was one of the first problems. A few books in Garo for beginners have been prepared by American Baptist Missionaries, and are mostly in use. An Arithmetic thus prepared was destroyed by fire, and has not yet been replaced.... [Rev. Ramkhe] began in 1877, and he had the present work completed in 1881».

1893. — 'M. C. Mason. — Markani Seya Námá Kháthá. The Gospel of Mark. Tura (Assam) 1893, in-8, pp. 76.

1894. — 'M. C. Mason. — Mathini Seya Námá Kháthá. The Gospel of Matthew. Tura (Assam) 1893, in-8, pp. 116).

1895. — 'M. C. Mason. — Ambáchen. A Adita Tikámu. Genesis translated into Garo, with explanatory notes. Tura (Assam). 1893, in-8, pp. 258.

Manipour.

1896. — 'Report on the Eastern Frontier of British India. By Captain R. Boileau Pemberton. Calcutta, 1835.

> Voir pp. 19—58.

1897. — Report on the Eastern Frontiers of British India; Manipúr, Assam, Arracan, &c. By Captain R. Boileau Pemberton, 44th N. I. Calcutta, 1836. (*Journ. Roy. Geog. Soc.*, VIII, 1838, pp. 391—397).

1898. — Description of Manipúr: its situation, productions, government, language, and religion; with some account of the adjoining tribes. By E. Stevens. (*Chin. Rep.*, V, 1836, pp. 212—218).

1899. — 'Gordon's Dictionary in English, Bangali and Manipuri. Calcutta, 1837, in-8.

1900. — Notes on Pa-laong. By J. R. Logan. (*Jour. Ind. Archip.*, N. S., Vol. II, 1858, pp. 233—6).

1901. — 'W. Mc Culloch. — Account of the Valley of Munnipore and of the Hill Tribes, with a comparative Vocabulary of the Munnipore and other Languages; printed in Roman characters. 1859, in-8, pp. XLIV—75.

1902. — Manipur. By Major M'Culloch.

> Vol. imp. en 1859 dans la collection «Selections from the Records of the Government of India (Foreign Department, No. XXVII)».

1903. — 'Statistical Account of Manipur and the Hill Territory under its Rule. By Dr. R. Brown. Calcutta, 1874.

1904. — Notes on Manipuri Grammar. By G. H. Damant, Cachar. (*Jour. As. Soc. Bengal*, Vol. 44, 1875, Pt. 1, pp. 173—181).

1905. — The Two Brothers: A Manipuri Story. By G. H. Damant. (*Indian Antiquary*, IV, 1875, pp. 260—4).

1906. — The Story of Khamba and Thoibí: A Manipuri Tale. Translated by G. H. Damant. (*Ibid.*, IV, 1877, pp. 219—226).

1907. — Note on the old Manipuri Character. By G. H. Damant. (*Jour. As. Soc. Bengal*, Vol. 46, 1877, Pt. 1, pp. 36—38).

1908. — A Manipuri Grammar, Vocabulary, and Phrase Book to which are added some Manipuri Proverbs and Specimens of Manipuri Correspondence. By A. J. Primrose, c.s., Officiating Political Agent, Manipur. — Shillong: Printed at the Assam Secretariat Press. — 1888, in-8, 4 ff. prél. n. ch. p. l. tit. etc. + pp. 100.

> On lit à la fin de la préface datée: «Manipur: August 1887»: «In the preparation of this book I have been assisted by my head-clerk, Russic Laul Coondoo, and by my Burmese Interpreter, Purander Sing, who both deserve my best thanks».

1909. — *George Watt. — The aboriginal tribes of Manipur. (*Journ. Anthrop. Inst.*, XVI, pp. 346—368). (2 Plates).

> Extrait dans le *Globus*, LII, No. 10, pp. 156—159.

1910. — *v. L. — Manipur. (*Globus*, LIX, 303).

1911. — History of the Relations of the Government with the Hill Tribes of the North-East Frontier of Bengal. By Alexander Mackenzie, of the Bengal Civil Service... — Calcutta, Home Department Press, 1884, in-8, pp. xiv—586.

> «The following are the chief sources of information regarding Manipur:
> «Capt. R. Boileau Pemberton's 'Report on the Eastern Frontier of British India' pp. 19 to 58 (Calcutta, 1835) contains a fair amount of information; while a good account of Manipur, by Major M'Culloch, who was for many years political agent there, was printed in 1859, as a vol. of the Selections from the Records of the Government of India». (Foreign Department, No. XXVII).
> «The most complete monograph, however, on the country will be found in Dr. R. Brown's 'Statistical Account of Manipur and the Hill Territory under its Rule' (Calcutta, 1874). Dr Brown was political agent in Manipur in 1873.
> «Sir A. Mackenzie's 'History of the Relations of the Government with the Hill Tribes of the North-East Frontier of Bengal' (Calcutta, 1884), contains in chapter XVI, some geographical information about Manipur; but the greater part of the chapter is taken up with a long résumé of the political events of the State since 1828, when the action taken by the British Government to restore Gumbheer Sing, one of the members of the deposed Manipur family, may be said to mark the beginning of the period of British Supremacy».
> — Hunter's Imp. Gas. of India.
> — Assam Administration Reports.

1912. — Manipur. (*Proc. Roy. Geog. Soc.*, 2° Sér., XIII, 1891, pp. 291—3).

1913. — Le Manipour. Par G. M. (*La Nature*, 9 mai 1891, pp. 355—6).

1914. — *Ethel St. Clair Grimwood, My Three Years in Manipur, and Escape from the Recent Mutiny, with portraits, illustrations and plan. 1891, in-8.

1915. — Manipur. Von Emil Schlagintweit. (*Deutsche Rund. f. Geog. u. Stat.*, XIV, 1891—2, pp. 97—103, 171—176).

1916. — *Lairel Sing. — Hindi Lal Tamannabá. A Hindi-Manipuri Vocabulary. Calcutta, Ganesh Chandra Dás, 1892. In-8, pp. 80.

1917. — Three Years in Cachar with a short Account of the Manipur Massacre by M. J. Wright Edited by James H. Hartley. London, S. W. Partridge & Co., s. d. [1896], pet. in-8, pp. 188.

1918. — My Experiences in Manipur and the Naga Hills by the late Major-General Sir James Johnstone K.C.S.I. With an introductory Memoir. Illustrated. London, Sampson Low... 1896, in-8, pp. XXVII—286.

1919. — *A Translation of the Gospel of St. Luke into Manipuri by W. Pettigrew. Calcutta, British and Foreign Bible Society, 1899, pp. 102.

1920. — *W. Pettigrew. — T'anglen Láirik. A Christian Pamphlet in Manipuri. Manipur, published by the Author, 1900, pp. 44.

1921. — *Manipour. (Tijds. Ned. Ind., XX, II, pp. 9—17).

1922. — *Mundu [Wergeld in Manipur]. (Beil. Allgemeine Zeitung, XLVI, p. 8).

1923. — Manipur and its Tribes. By T. C. Hodson. (Jour. Soc. of Arts, April 7, 1905, pp. 545—563).

Tsang-la — Bhutan.

1924. — Some Tsangla-Bhutanese Sentences. By E. Stack. — Part III. — Shillong: Printed at the Assam Secretariat Printing Office, 1897, in-8, 2 ff. n. ch. + pp. 91.

> La préf. signée E A. Gait, Shillong, The 11th November 1896 indique que la mort prématurée en 1887 de M. Stack a interrompu ses travaux sur l'Assam et que seule cette partie III d'une grammaire a été revue par l'auteur.

III. — Ethnographie et Anthropologie.

1925. — Notice of the Deo Monnees, or sacred beads of Assam, by H. Piddington, Curator Museum Economic Geology. (Jour. As. Soc. Bengal, XVI, pt. II, 1847, pp. 713—715).

1926. — Note on Platform-Dwellings in Assam. By S. E. Peal, Esq. (Jour. Anth. Inst., XI, Lond., 1882, pp. 53—6).

1927. — On the 'Morong' and other Customs of the Natives of Assam. By S. E. Peal. (Brit. Ass. Adv. Science, Cardiff, 1891, pp. 801—2).

1928. — On the «Morong», as possibly a relic of Pre-Marriage Communism. By S. E. Peal. (Jour. Anth. Inst., XXII, 1893, pp. 244—261).

1929. — Identical Customs of Dyaks and of Races around Assam. By S. E. Peal. (Nature, LVI, 1897, pp. 53—54).

1930. — *R. C. Temple. — Chained Images. (Folk-lore, IV, p. 249).

1931. — *Th. Bloch. — On an Assamese drum or «doba» forwarded by F. J. Needham. (Proc. As. Soc. of Bengal, 1898, pp. 186).

> Avec une inscription en sanscrit.

1932. — *[Bericht über einen Vortrag von K. Hagen: Ethnographie von Assam] (*Correspondenz Blätter der Deutschen Gesellschaft für Anthropologie*, etc., XXIX, pp. 56.)

IV. — Climat et Météorologie.

1933. — Report on the progress of the Magnetic Survey and the researches connected with it in Sikkim, the Khosia Hills and Assam, April to December, 1855. By Hermann Schlagintweit, Esq. (*Jour. As. Soc. Bengal*, XXV, 1856, pp. 1—30).

V. — Histoire naturelle.

Zoologie.

1934. — A List of Mammalia and Birds collected in Assam by John Mc Clelland... (*Proc. Zool. Soc.*, VII, 1839, pp. 146—167).

1935. — A List of Mammalia and Birds collected in Assam by John Mc Clelland, Esq., Assistant Surgeon in the service of the East-India Company, Bengal Establishment: revised by T, Horsfield, M.D... (*Annals Nat. Hist.*, VI, 1841, pp. 366—374, 450—461).

1936. — A Decade, or Description of ten new Species of Coleoptera, from the Kasya Hills, near the boundary of the Assam District. By F. Parry. (*Trans. Entom. Soc.*, IV, 1845—47, pp. 84—7).

1937. — Descriptions of new Species of Coleoptera, from the Kasyah Hills, near the boundary of Assam, in the East Indies, lately received from Dr. Cantor. By the Rev. F. W. Hope. (*Ibid.*, IV, 1845—47, pp. 73—7).

1938. — Descriptions of some undescribed species of Reptiles collected by Dr. Joseph Hooker in the Khassia Mountains, East Bengal, and Sikkim Himalaya. By J. E. Gray. (*Annals Nat. Hist.*, XII, 2d Ser., 1853, pp. 386—92).

1939. — Notes on the mode of Capture of Elephants in Assam. By Dr. A. Campbell, late Superintendent of Darjeuling. (*Proc. Zool. Soc.*, 1869, pp. 136—140).

1940. — Descriptions of new Land and Freshwater Molluscan Species collected by Dr. John Anderson in Upper Burma and Yunan. By W. T. Blanford. (*Ibid.*, 1869, pp. 444—50).

1941. — On three new Species of Squirrels from Upper Burmah and the Kakhyen Hills, between Burmah and Yunan. By John Anderson. (*Ibid.*, 1871, pp. 139—42).

1942. — On *Manouria* and *Scapia*, two Genera of Land Tortoises. By John Anderson. (*Ibid.*, 1872, pp. 132—44).

1943. — Further Remarks on the External Characters and Anatomy of *Macacus brunneus*. By John Anderson, M.D. (*Proc. Zool. Soc.*, 1872, pp. 203—12).

1944. — Descriptions of new Land and Freshwater Shells from the Khási, North Cachar, and Nágá Hills, N. E. Bengal. By Major H. H. Godwin-Austen. (*Ibid.*, 1872, pp. 514—518).

1945. — Descriptions of Ten new Birds from the Nágá Hills and Munipúr Valley, N. E. Frontier of Bengal. By Major H. H. Godwin-Austen. (*Ibid.*, 1874, pp. 43—8).

1946. — Descriptions of five new Species of *Helicidae* of the Subgenus *Plectopylis*, with remarks on all the other known forms. By Major H. H. Godwin-Austen. (*Ibid.*, 1874, pp. 608—613).

1947. — Description of a new *Sibia* from the Nágá Hills, North-east Frontier, Bengal. By Major H. H. Godwin-Austen. (*Annals Nat. History*, 4 S., XIII, 1874, pp. 160—1).

1948. — Descriptions of nine species of Alycaeinae from Assam and the Naga Hills. By Major H. H. Godwin-Austen. (*Jour. As. Soc. Bengal*, Vol. 43, 1874, Pt. 2, pp. 145—150).

1949. — Fourth list of Birds principally from the Naga Hills and Munipur, including others from the Khasi, Garo, and Tipperah Hills. By Major H. H. Godwin-Austen... (*Ibid.*, Vol. 43, 1874, Pt. 2, pp. 151—180).

1950. — Descriptions of New Species of Mollusca of the genera *Helix* and *Glessula* from the Khasi Hills and Munipur. By Major H. H. Godwin-Austen. (*Ibid.*, Vol. 44, 1875, Pt. 2, pp. 1—4).

1951. — Descriptions of four New Species of Mollusca belonging to the family *Zonitidae* from the N. E. Frontier of Bengal, with drawings of *Helicarion gigas*, Benson and of a variety of the same. By Major H. H. Godwin-Austen. (*Ibid.*, Vol. 44, 1875, Pt. 2, pp. 4—7).

1952. — Descriptions of New Operculated Landshells belonging to the genera *Craspedotropis*, *Alycaeus*, and *Diplommatina*, from the Nágá Hills and Assam. By Major H. H. Godwin-Austen. (*Ibid.*, Vol. 44, 1875, Pt. 2, pp. 7—10).

1953. — Fifth List of Birds from the Hill Ranges of the North-East Frontier of India. By Major H. H. Godwin-Austen. (*Ibid.*, Vol. 45, 1875, Pt. 2, pp. 191—204).

1954. — On the *Helicidae* collected during the Expedition into the Dafla Hills, Assam. By Major H. H. Godwin-Austen. (*Ibid.*, Vol. 45, 1875, Pt. 2, pp. 311—318).

1955. — Description of a supposed new *Actinura* [*A. daflaensis*] from the Dafla Hills. By Major H. H. Godwin-Austen. (*Annals Nat. History*, 4 S., XVI, 1875, pp. 339—340).

1956. — Description of a supposed new *Suthora* [*S. daflaensis*, n. sp.] from the Dafla Hills, and a *Minla* [*M. Mandellii*] from the Nágá Hills, with Remarks on *Pictorhis* (*Chrysomma*) *altirostre*, Jerdon. By Major H. H. Godwin-Austen. (*Annals Nat. History*, 4 S., XVII, 1876, pp. 32—4).

1957. — List of the Birds collected on the Expedition into the Dafla Hills, Assam, together with those obtained in the adjacent Darrang Terai. — By Major H. H. Godwin-Austen... (*Jour. As. Soc. Bengal*, Vol. 45, 1876, Pt. 2, pp. 64—85).

1958. — On the Cyclostomacea of the Dafla Hills, Assam. By Major H. H. Godwin-Austen. (*Ibid.*, Vol. 45, 1876, Pt. 2, pp. 171—184).

1959. — Descriptions of supposed new Birds [*Turdinus nagaënsis*, *Staphida plumbeiceps*] from the Naga Hills and Eastern Assam. By Lieut.-Col. H. H. Godwin-Austen. (*Annals Nat. History*, 4 S., XX, 1877, pp. 519—520).

1960. — Descriptions of three new Species of Birds of the Genera *Pellorneum*, *Actinura*, and *Pomatorhinus*; lately collected in the neighbourhood of Saddya, Assam, by Mr. M. J. Ogle of the Topographical Survey. By Major H. H. Godwin-Austen. (*Jour. As. Soc. Bengal*, Vol. 46, 1877, Pt. 2, pp. 41—44).

1961. — Notes on and Description of the Female of *Ceriornis blythii*, Jerdon. By Lieut.-Col. H. H. Godwin-Austen. (*Proc. Zool. Soc.*, 1879, pp. 457—9).

1962. — Note on the Female of *Lophophorus sclateri*, Jerdon, from Eastern Assam. By Lieut.-Col. H. H. Godwin-Austen. (*Ibid.*, 1879, p. 681).

1963. — On Specimens of the Male and Female of *Phasianus humiae*, from Munipur, with a Description of the latter. By Lieut.-Col. H. H. Godwin-Austen. (*Ibid.*, 1882, pp. 715—8).

1964. — On new Species and Varieties of the Land-Molluscan Genus *Diplommatina* from the Garo, Naga, and Munipur Hill-ranges, Assam. By Lieut.-Col. H. H. Godwin-Austen. (*Ibid.*, 1892, pp. 509—520).

1965. — Description of a new Species of *Helix* of the Subgenus *Plectopylis*. By Lieut.-Col. H. H. Godwin-Austen. (*Annals Nat. History*, 6 S., X, 1892, pp. 300—1).

1966. — On some new Species of the Land-Molluscan Genus *Alycaeus* from the Khasi and Naga Hill Country, Assam, Munipur, and the Ruby Mine District, Upper Burmah; and on one Species from the Nicobars. By Lt.-Col. H. H. Godwin-Austen. (*Proc. Zool. Soc.*, 1893, pp. 592—5).

1967. — Hawk Moth Larva. By E. R. Johnson, Surgeon Major, Bengal Medical Department. (*Nature*, XXVII, 1882—3, pp. 126—7).
> Shillong, October 16.
> [Found in the Khasi Hills, Assam.]

1968. — A new Species of *Simulium* from Assam. — By Dr. Edward Becher, Vienna. Communicated and translated by the Natural History Secretary. (*Jour. As. Soc. Bengal*, Vol. 53, 1884, Pt. 2, pp. 199—200).

1969. — On a Collection of Lepidoptera made at Manipur and on the Borders of Assam by Dr. George Watt. By Arthur G. Butler. (*Annals Nat. History*, 5 S., XVI, 1885, pp. 298—310, 334—347).

1970. — The Mithun. By S. E. Peal. (*Nature*, XXXIII, 1885—6, p. 7).
Sibsagar, Assam, September 26.

1971. — Sailing Flight of Large Birds over Land. By S. E. Peal. (*Ibid.*, XL, 1889, pp. 518—519).
Sibsagar, Assam, August 8.

1972. — Notes on Assam Butterflies. By William Doherty, Cincinnati, U.S.A. (*Jour. As. Soc. Bengal*, Vol. 58, 1889, Pt. 2, pp. 118—134).

1973. — Description of a new Genus of the Homopterous Family *Cicadidae* [*Angamiana oetherea*, n. sp.]. By W. L. Distant. (*Annals Nat. History*, 6 S., V, 1890, pp. 234—5). .

1974. — On Butterflies collected by Mr. W. Doherty in the Naga and Karen Hills and in Perak. — Part I. By H. J. Elwes. (*Proc. Zool. Soc.*, 1891, pp. 249—289).
Part II. (*Ibid.*, 1892, pp. 617—664).

1975. — *Some Observations on the Life-history of *Sclerostomum tetracanthum*. Dieting in connection with a so-called Outbreak of «Surra» at Shillong. By Surgeon G. M. J. Giles, M.B., F.R.C.S. — On a new Sclerostome from the large Intestine of Mules (a postcript to the preceding paper). By Surgeon G. M. J. Giles. (*Scientific Memoirs*, Part VII, 1892).

1976. — List of the Fishes collected by Mr. E. W. Oates in the Southern Shan States, and presented by him to the British Museum. By G. A. Boulenger. (*Annals Nat. History*, 6 S., XII, 1893, pp. 198—203).

1977. — New Species of Geometers and Pyrales from the Khasia Hills. By Col. C. Swinhoe. (*Ibid.*, 6 S., XIV, 1894, pp. 135—149, 197—210).

1978. — New Species of Lepidoptera from the Khasia Hills. By Col. C. Swinhoe. (*Ibid.*, 6 S., XVII, 1896, pp. 357—363).

1979. — On a new species of Flying Lizard from Assam. By A. Alcock. (*Jour. As. Soc. Bengal*, Vol. 64, 1895, Pt. 2, pp. 14—15).

1980. — On a new Species of Babbler (*Turdinulus guttaticollis*) from the Miri Hills to the North of Assam. By W. R. Ogilvie Grant. (*Ibis*, 7 Ser., I, 1895, pp. 432—3).
— On the Species of the Genus *Turdinulus*. By W. R. Ogilvie Grant. (*Ibis*, 7 Ser., II, 1896, pp. 55—61).

1981. — On a new Species of Tit-Babbler from the Naga and Manipur Hills. By W. R. Ogilvie Grant. (*Ibis*, 7 Ser., II, 1896, pp. 61—2).

1982. — New Species of *Pyralidae* from the Khasia Hills. By W. Warren. (*Annals Nat. History*, 6 S., XVII, 1896, pp. 452—466; XVIII, 1896, pp. 107—119, 163—177, 214—232).

1983. — Notes on some Birds obtained at Kalaw, in the Southern Shan States. By Major G. Rippon. ((*Ibis*, 7 Ser., II, 1896, pp. 357—362).

1984. — An additional List of Birds obtained at Kalaw, Southern Shan States, during April and May, 1896. By Major G. Rippon, 7th Burma Infantry. (*Ibis*, 7 Ser., III, 1897, pp. 1—5).

1985. — On the Birds of the Southern Shan States, Burma. By Lieut.-Col. G. Rippon, 7th Burma Battalion. (*Ibis*, 8 Ser., I, 1901, pp. 525—561).

1986. — On a Collection of Birds from Manipur. By Lieut. H. H. Turner. (*Jour. As. Soc. Bengal*, Vol. 68, 1899, Pt. II, pp. 235—245).

1987. — Descriptions of new Species of Fossorial Hymenoptera from the Khasia Hills, Assam. By P. Cameron. (*Ann. Nat. Hist.*, 7 S., X, 1902, pp. 54—69, 77—89).

1988. — On some new Genera and Species of Parasitic and Fossorial Hymenoptera from the Khasia Hills, Assam. By P. Cameron. (*Ibid.*, 7 S., XI, 1903, pp. 173—185, 313—331).

1989. — On some new Genera and Species of Parasitic Hymenoptera from the Khasia Hills, Assam. By P. Cameron. (*Ibid.*, 7 S., XII, 1903, pp. 266—273...).

Botanique.

1990. — Remarks on a Collection of Plants, made at Sadiyá, Upper Assam, from April to September, 1836. By William Griffith, Assistant Surgeon, Madras Establishment, on duty in Upper Assam. (*Jour. As. Soc. Bengal*, V, Dec. 1836, pp. 806—813).

1991. — Report on the Caoutchouc Tree of Assam made at the request of Captain Jenkins, Agent to the Governor General. By William Griffith, Assistant Surgeon on deputation with the Bhotan Mission. (*Ibid.*, VII, Feb. 1838, pp. 132—142).

1992. — Observations on the Flora of the Naga Hills, by Mr. J. W. Masters, Communicated by the Government of India. To Captain T. Brodie, Principal Assistant Commissioner of Assam. (*Journ. of the As. Soc. of Bengal*, Vol. XIII, Pt. II, No. 153, 1844, pp. 707—734).

> Botanical Observations made in Upper Assam, during the month of February 1844, while passing over that portion of the first ranges of the Naga Hills, lying between the Dikho and Dhunsiri Rivers.

1993. — Botanical Observations made in a Journey to the Naga Hills (between Assam and Muneypore), in a Letter addressed to Sir J. D. Hooker... by C. B. Clarke, Esq., F.R.S. (*Jour. Linn. Soc., Bot.*, XXII, 1887, pp. 128—36).

1994. — On the Plants of Kohima and Muneypore. By Charles Baron Clarke, M.A. (*Ibid.*, XXV, 1890, pp. 1—107).

1995. — Lichenes Manipurenses, a cl. Dr. G. Watt circa Manipur, ad limites orientales Indiae Orientalis 1881—1882, lecti, auctore Dr. J. Müller. (*Jour. Linn. Soc., Bot.*, XXIX, 1893, pp. 217—231).

1996. — Noviciae Indicaae XXII. An undescribed *Aralaceous* Genus from Upper Burma. — By D. Prain. (*Jour. As. Soc. Bengal*, LXXIII, Pt. II, No. 1, 1904, pp. 23—4, 1 pl.).
Woodburnia Prain.

Thé.

Voir Nos. 1704, 1705.

1997. — Discovery of the Genuine Tea Plant in Upper Assam. (*Jour. As. Soc. of Bengal*, IV, Jan. 1835, pp. 42—49).

1998. — Report on the Manufacture of Tea, and on the Extent and Produce of the Tea Plantations in Assam. By C. A. Bruce, Superintendent of Tea Culture. (*Jour. As. Soc. Bengal*, VIII, June 1839, pp. 497—526).

1999. — *Tea Company. Report of the Provincial Committee of the Assam Company, made on the 31st January 1840, with an Abstract of the Deed of Settlement of the Company. 1840. In-8.
Report of the Directors and Auditors, made... 7th May 1841, with Appendix. 1841. In-8.
The same, 6th May 1842, with Appendix. 1842. In-8.
The same, 5th May 1843, with Appendix. 1843. In-8.
The same (Circular Report &c. 1844).
The same, 2nd May 1845. 1845. In-8. Map.
The same, 11th November 1845. 1845. In-8.

2000. — Notes on the Production of Tea in Assam, and in India generally. — By J. C. Marshman, Esq. (*Journ. Roy. As. Soc.*, XIX, M.DCCC.LXII, Art. XII, pp. 315—320).

2001. — *A Run through the Assam Tea Gardens. By J. W. Masters. Golaghat, 1863, pp. 30, in-fol.
Notice: *Jour. of Botany*, II, 1864, pp. 57—60.

2002. — A Visit to the Tea Gardens of Assam. (*Siam Repository*, Jan. 1870, Vol. 2, art. 71, pp. 150—153; art. 78, pp. 163—166).

2003. — L'Assam et ses plantations de thé. (Notes de voyage). par A. D. (*Bul. Soc. Géog. Com.*, IV, 1881—2, pp. 177—182).

2004. — *J. W. Mason. — Report on the Tea-mite of Assam. London, 1884, in-8, pp. 20.
B. M. 7296. g. 5.

2005. — A Tea Planter's Life in Assam. By George M. Barker. With seventy-five illustrations by the Author. Calcutta: Thacker, Spink & Co., 1884, pet. in-8, pp. VIII—247.

2006. — *F. Deas. — Tea Planter's Companion. London, 1886, in-8, pp. 100.
B. M. 7074. f. 10.

2007. — *Tea-Garden Sanitation, being a few remarks on the construction of coolie lines and the sanitary management of coolies, with special reference to the prevention of the disease known as anaemia of coolies, *Beri-beri*, and Anchylostomiasis. By Dr. Geo. M. Giles, M.B., F.R.C.S., San. Sci. Cert. Univ., Lond., Surgeon, I. M. S. 1891, gr. in-8.

2008. — *J. Buckingham. — Tea-Garden Coolies in Assam. Calcutta, 1894, in-4, pp. 76.
B. M. 8285. cc. 48.

2009. — *Charles Dowding. — Tea-Garden Coolies in Assam. Calcutta, Thacker Spink & Co., 1894, in-8, pp. 102.

2010. — *Report on Tea Culture in Assam for 1889, 1891, 1892, and 1893. Shillong, 1890—94. In-folio.

2011. — *Report on Tea-Culture in Assam. Report and Statements. Compiled in the Office of the Secretary to the Chief Commissioner of Assam. in-fol.
For the years 1899 and 1900.

2012. — *Geo. Watt. — The Pests and Blights of the Tea Plant. Being a Report of Investigations conducted in Assam, and to some extent also in Kangra. Calcutta, 1898, gr. in-8, 5/—

2013. — The Assam Tea Garden Labour Question. By A. Logsdail. (*Calcutta Review*, April 1903, pp. 155—259).

2014. — *The Tea of Assam. s. l. n. d. in-8.

Géologie et Minéralogie.

2015. — Notes relative to the collection of some Geological Specimens in the Kásia Hills between Assam and Nunklow. By W. Cracroft, Esq. C. S. (*Jour. As. Soc. of Bengal*, III, 1834, pp. 293—296).

2016. — Native Account of Washing for Gold in Assam. By Moneeram, Revenue Sheristadar, Bur Bundaree. (*Jour. As. Soc. Bengal*, VII, July 1838, pp. 621—625).

2017. — Further information on the Gold Washings of Assam, extracted from Capt. Hannay's communications to Capt. Jenkins, Agent to the Governor General in Assam. (*Ibid.*, VII, July 1838, pp. 625—628).

2018. — Account of a Visit to the Jugloo and Seesee Rivers in Upper Assam, by Capt. E. T. Dalton, together with a note on the Gold Fields of that Province, by Major Hannay. (*Ibid.*, XXII, 1853, pp. 511—521).

2019. — Notes on the Iron Ore Statistics and Economic Geology of Upper Assam. By Lieut.-Col. S. F. Hannay, communicated by the Government of Bengal. (*Jour. As. Soc. Bengal*, XXV, 1856, pp. 330—344).

2020. — Note on recent investigations regarding the extent and value of the auriferous deposits of Assam, being abstracts of Reports by Captain E. T. Dalton and Lieut.-Colonel S. F. Hannay, dated October 1855. (*Mem. Geolog. Survey India*, I, 1859, pp. 90—3).

2021. — On the Geological Structure of a portion of the Khasi Hills, Bengal. By Thomas Oldham. (*Ibid.*, I, 1859, pp. 99—210).

2022. — Geological Sketch of the Shillong Plateau: by H. B. Medlicott, F.G.S., Geol. Survey of India. (*Records Geolog. Survey of India*, Vol. II, Pt. I, 1869, pp. 10—11).

2023. — Geological Sketch of the Shillong Plateau in North-Eastern Bengal, by Henry B. Medlicott. (*Mem. Geolog. Survey India*, VI, 1869, pp. 57).

2024. — Geological Sketch of the Shillong Plateau in North-Eastern Bengal, by Henry B. Medlicott. (*Ibid.*, VII, 1871, pp. 151—207).

2025. — Notes on the Geology of part of the Dafla Hills, Assam; lately visited by the Force under Brigadier-General Stafford, C.B. — By Major H. H. Godwin-Austen. (*Journ. As. Soc. Bengal*, Vol. 44, 1875, Pt. 2, pp. 35—41).

2026. — The Evidence of past Glacial Action in the Nágá Hills, Assam. By Major H. H. Godwin-Austen. (*Ibid.*, Vol. 44, 1875, Pt. 2, pp. 209—213).

2027. — On Iridosmine from the Noa-Dihing River, Upper Assam, and on Platinum from Chutia Nágpur, by F. R. Mallet, F.G.S., Geological Survey of India. (*Records Geol. Survey of India*, XV, Pt. 1, 1882, pp. 53—55).

2028. — Report on the Geology of parts of Manipur and the Naga Hills, by R. D. Oldham. (*Mem. Geolog. Survey India*, XIX, 1883, pp. 26).

2029. — Note on a Traverse through the Eastern Khasia, Jaintia, and North Cachar Hills by Tom D. La Touche, B.A., Geological Survey of India. (*Records Geol. Survey of India*, XVI, Pt. 4, 1883, pp. 198—203).

2030. — Notes on the Geology of the Aka Hills, Assam, by Tom D. La Touche, B.A., Geological Survey of India. (With a Map). (*Ibid.*, XVIII, Pt. 2, 1885, pp. 121—124).

2031. — Geology of the Upper Dehing basin in the Singpho Hills, by Tom D. La Touche, B.A., Geological Survey of India. (With a Map). (*Ibid.*, XIX, Pt. 2, 1886, pp. 111—115).

2032. — Notes on the Geology of the Garo Hills, by T. D. La Touche, B.A., Geological Survey of India. (*Ibid.*, XX, Pt. 1, 1887, pp. 40—43).

2033. — Note on the Geology of the Lushai Hills, by Tom D. La Touche. (*Records Geolog. Survey India*, XXIV, 1891, pp. 98—9).

2034. — The Fossil Vertebrata of India, by R. Lydekker, B.A., F.G.S. (*Rec. Geol. Survey of India*, XX, Pt. 2, 1887, pp. 51—80).

2035. — Notes on Tin Smelting in the Malay Peninsula, by T. W. Hughes Hughes. (*Records Geol. Survey India*, XXII, 1889, pp. 235—6).

2036. — Field Notes from the Shan Hills (Upper Burma), by Fritz Noetling. (*Ibid.*, XXIII, 1890, pp. 78—9).

2037. — The Geology of the Mikir Hills in Assam, by F. H. Smith. (*Mem. Geol. Survey India*, XXVIII, Pt. 1, 1898, pp. 71—95).

Pétrole.

2038. — On the Assam Petroleum Beds (in a letter to Major Jenkins, communicated by him). By Captain P. S. Hannay. (*Jour. As. Soc. Bengal*, XIV, Pt. II, 1845, pp. 817—821).

2039. — Petroleum in Assam, by Theodore W. H. Hughes, A.R.S.M., F.G.S., Geological Survey of India. (*Records Geol. Survey of India*, Vol. VII, Pt. 2, 1874, pp. 55—57).

Charbon.

2040. — Report upon the Coal Beds of Assam. (Submitted to Government by the Committee appointed to investigate the Coal and Iron resources of the Bengal Presidency, as a supplement to their first printed report). (*Jour. As. Soc. Bengal*, VII, Nov. 1838, pp. 948—965).

2041. — Further Discovery of Coal Beds in Assam. By Captain F. Jenkins. (*Ibid.*, IV, Dec. 1835, pp. 704—705).

2042. — The Coal of Assam; results of a brief visit to the Coal-Fields of that Province in 1865; with Geological Notes on Assam and the hills to the south of it, by H. B. Medlicott, A.B., F.G.S., Deputy Superintendent, Geological Survey of India. (*Mem. Geolog. Survey India*, IV, 1865, pp. 56).

2043. — 'On the prospects of useful coal being found in the Garrow Hills. (*Records Geolog. Survey India*, I, 1868).

2044. — On the Coal-Fields of the Nágá Hills bordering the Lakhimpur and Sibságar Districts, Assam, by F. R. Mallet. (*Mem. Geol. Survey India*, XII, 1876, pp. 95).

2045. — Report on the Cherra Poonjee Coal-Field, in the Khasia Hills; by Tom. D. La Touche. (With a plan). (*Records Geol. Survey India*, XXII, 1889, pp. 167—171).

2046. — Report on the Lakadong Coal-Fields, Jaintia Hills; by Tom D. La Touche. (With 2 plans). (*Ibid.*, XXIII, 1890, pp. 14—17).

2047. — Report on the Coal-fields of Lairungao, Maosandram, and Mao-be-lar-kar, in the Khasi Hills, by Tom D. La Touche. (*Ibid.*, XXIII, 1890, pp. 120—4).

2048. — Report on the Coal-fields in the Northern Shan States, by Fritz Noetling. (*Ibid.*, XXIV, 1891, pp. 99—119).

Tremblements de Terre.

2049. — Memoranda of Earthquakes and other remarkable occurrences in Upper Assam, from January 1839 to September 1843. By Capt. Hannay, B.N.I. (*Jour. As. Soc. Bengal*, XII, Pt. II, 1843, pp. 907—909).

2050. — Earthquakes in Assam. Communicated by Major Jenkins, Agent to the Governor General. By J. Butler. (*Ibid.*, XVIII, pt. I, 1849, pp. 172—3).

2051. — Earthquakes experienced in Assam in the latter end of January, 1849. (*Ibid.*, XVIII, pt. I, 1849, pp. 173—4).

2052. — Memorandum on earthquakes in January, 1849, at Burpetah, Assam. (*Ibid.*, XVIII, pt. I, 1849, pp. 174—5).

2053. — Record of the Occurrence of Earthquakes in Assam during the years 1874, 1875, 1876. Communicated by Col. R. H. Keatinge... Chief Commissioner. (*Ibid.*, Vol. 46, 1877, Pt. 2, pp. 294—309).

— during 1877. (*Ibid.*, Vol. 47, 1878, Pt. 2, pp. 4—11).

— during 1878. (*Ibid.*, Vol. 48, 1879, Pt. 2, pp. 48—55).

2054. — List of Earthquakes recorded in Assam during the years 1879 and 1880. — By the Government of Assam. (Communicated by the Meteorological Reporter to the Government of Bengal). (*Ibid.*, Vol. 50, Pt. 2, 1881, pp. 61).

2055. — The Cachar Earthquake of 10th January 1869, by the late Thomas Oldham..., Superintendent of the Geological Survey of India, edited by R. D. Oldham... (*Mem. Geol. Survey India*, XIX, 1883, pp. 98).

2056. — R. D. Oldham. — Report on the Great Earthquake of 12th June 1897. (*Ibid.*, XXIX, Calcutta, 1899, in-8, pp. xxx + 379 + xviii, 44 fig., 45 pl., 3 cartes).

2057. — List of Aftershocks of the Great Earthquake of 12th June 1897, compiled by R. D. Oldham. (*Memoirs Geol. Survey India*, XXX, 1900, pp. 1—102).

2058. — R. D. Oldham. — On Tidal Periodicity of the Earthquakes of Assam. (*Jour. As. Soc. Bengal*, LXXI, Pt. II, No. 3, p. 139, 1902).

2059. — 'On Tidal Periodicity in the Earthquakes of Assam. By R. D. Oldham. (Extract from the *Journal of the Asiatic Society of Bengal*, vol. LXXI, pp. 139—153, 1902). Calcutta, 1902, in-8.

2060. — Tidal Periodicity of Earthquakes in Assam. (*Geog. Jour.*, April 1903, pp. 451—2).

D'après R. D. Oldham, *Jour. As. Soc. Bengal*, vol. LXXI, 1902, pp. 139—153.

2061. — Périodicité des tremblements de terre en Assam. Par le Dr. L. Laloy. (*La Géographie*, 15 sept. 1903, pp. 153—4).

2062. — Preliminary Notice of the Bengal Earthquake of 14th July 1885, by H. B. Medlicott, M.A., Geological Survey of India. (*Records Geol. Survey of India*, XVIII, Pt. 3, 1885, pp. 156—158).

Affecting Upper Assam.

2063. — Report on the Bengal Earthquake of July 14th, 1885, by C. S. Middlemiss, B.A., Geological Survey of India. (*Records Geol. Survey of India*, XVIII, Pt. 4, 1885, pp. 200—221).

> Affecting Assam and Burmah.

2064. — *Report on the Earthquake of the 12th June 1897, so far as it affected the Province of Assam. Contains official correspondence showing the extent and effect of the disaster. Compiled in the Office of the Secretary to the Chief Commissioner of Assam. 1897, in-fol.

2065. — *The Great Indian Earthquake of 1897. By Dr. Charles Davison (map). (*Knowledge*, XXIII, July 1900, p. 147).

2066. — *The Assam Earthquake of June 12, 1897 — A Request for Data. (*Terrestrial Magnetism*, Cincinnati, 1897, II, p. 156).

2067. — Der amtliche Bericht über das Erdbeben in Assam am 12. Juni 1897. (*Globus*, Braunschweig, 1897, LXXII, pp. 236—7).

2068. — *The Earthquake in Assam. By H. Luttman-Johnson. (*J. S. Arts*, 46, 1898, pp. 473—495).

2069. — *Ernst Hanmer. — Das Indische Erdbeben vom 12. July 1897. (*Zeits. Vermessungswesen*, Stuttgart, XXX, 1901, pp. 304—7).

2070. — *Johannes Walther. — Die geologischen Wirkungen des indischen Erdbebens vom Jahre 1897. (*Naturwiss. Wocheschft.*, Jena, XVII, 1901, pp. 2—4).

VI. — Population.

2071. — *Census of India, 1891, ASSAM. By E. A. Gait, Esq. Volume I. — Report. Volume II. — Imperial Tables. — Volume III. — Provincial Tables. 1892, in-fol.

2072. — Census of India, Assam, 1891. (*Calcutta Review*, XCVI, Jan. 1893, pp. 220/229).

2073. — *Census of India, 1901, ASSAM. By B. C. Allen, Esq. Part I, Report; Part II, Tables: 1902, in-fol.

VII. — Gouvernement. [1])

VIII. — Jurisprudence.

2074. — *Assam Code. Edition 1897, — Containing the Bengal Regulations, Local Acts of the Governor General in Council, Regulations made under the Government of India Act, 1870 (33 Vict., Chap. 3), and Acts of the Lieutenant-Governor of Bengal in Council in force in Assam; with Chronological Tables and Index, gr. in-8.

----

1) Voir le chapitre consacré à l'Administration anglaise.

IX. — Histoire.

Divers.

2075. — History of Cooch Behár, being an extract of a passage from Dr. Buchanan's Account of Rungpur (Rangapura). [Revised and communicated by Major F. Jenkins]. (*Jour. As. Soc. Bengal*, VII, Jan. 1838, p. 1/19).

2076. — *Tarikh — 1 Asham* — Récit de l'expédition de Mir-Djumlah au pays d'Assam traduit sur la version hindoustani de Mir-Huçaini par Théodore Pavie. Paris, Benjamin Duprat. MDCCCXLV, in-8, pp. xxxi—316.

2077. — Koch Bihár, Koch Hájo, and Ásám, in the 16th and 17th centuries, according to the Akbarnámah, the Pádisháhnámah, and the Fathiyah i 'Ibriyah. By H. Blochmann. (*Jour. As. Soc. Bengal*, Vol. 41, 1872, Pt. 1, pp. 49/101).

2078. — *Assam Buranji* or the History of Assam. Including the history of the ancient Kingdom of Kamrup. From the earliest times to the end of 1875 and containing a brief notice of the castes, language, religion, commerce, agriculture, arts and social customs of the people and the internal government of the Province. By Goonabhiram Borooah, Author of the Ramnavami Natak etc. etc. Calcutta: Printed by Babooram Sircar, at the Roy Press, 17, Bhowani Churn Dutt's Lane and Published by the author, 1876, pet. in-8.

2079. — An Account of Asam at the time of its Conquest by Mir Jumla in A. D. 1663. By Kaviraj Syamal Das... (Translated by Bábu Ráma Prasáda...) (*Ind. Antiq.*, XVI, 1887, pp. 222/6).

2080. — 'Historical Research in Assam. Circular N° 40 G. Shillong, Government Printing Office, 1894, in-folio, pp. I, II.

    Contient en outre de deux écrits officiels de P. G. Melitus et C. J. Lyall, un rapport de E. A. Gait sur les sources de l'histoire d'Assam, principalement pendant la domination des Áhóm, avec une liste de 28 hóm-Puthis.

2081. — 'The Koch Kings of Kámrupa. An historical Sketch of the Koch dynasty of Kamrup. [A Reprint from the *Journal Asiatic Society of Bengal*, Vol. LXII, Part I, N° 4, 1893]. By E. A. Gait, Esq., I. C. S. gr. in-8, 1895.

2082. — Report on the Progress of Historical Research in Assam. Deals with coins, inscriptions on rocks, temples, cannon, etc., copper plates, Ahom *buranjis*, other historical writings, quasi-historical writings, religious works, folk-lore and mythology. The Appendices contain, among other things, a list of archaeological remains in Assam and an account of the rise and progress of journalism in the Assam Valley. By E. A. Gait, Esq. I.C.S. 1897, in-fol.

    Page 80—86: Liste des écrits relatifs à l'Assam.

2083. — A History of Assam by E. A. Gait of the Indian Civil Service. Calcutta: Thacker, Spink & Co., 1906, in-8, pp. vii + 1 f. n. ch. + pp. 383, carte, grav.

> «The only attempt at a connected history in English is the brief account given by Robinson — some 43 pages in all — in his *Descriptive Account of Assam*, published in 1841. Two histories have been published in the vernacular, one by Kāsinath Tāmuli Phukan in 1844, and the other by the late Rai Ganābhirām Barua Bahadur in 1884. The former deals only with the Ahoms». (Int., p. III.)
> Notice: *Journ. Roy. As. Soc*, July 1906, pp. 733—736. Par Vincent A. Smith.

2084. — 'K. Tamuli Phukan. — *Asám Buranji Puthi*. The Book on the History of Assam. In Assamese. Reprint. Calcutta, 1907. In-8, pp. 136.

Antiquités.

2085. — Description of Ancient Temples and Ruins at Chárdwâr in Assam. By Captain G. E. Westmacott, Assistant, Governor General's Agent, N. E. Frontier. (*Jour. As. Soc. of Bengal*, IV, April 1835, pp. 185/195).

2086. — Paper on Ancient Land Grants on Copper, discovered in Assam. Communicated by Major F. Jenkins. Governor General's Agent N. E. Frontier. (*Jour. As. Soc. Bengal*, IX, Pt II, 1840, pp. 766/782).

2087. — Notes on Ancient Temples and other remains in the vicinity of Sudyah, Upper Assam. — By Major S. F. Hannay, Communicated by W. Seton Karr, Esq., Under-Secretary to the Government of Bengal. (*Jour. As. Soc. Bengal*, XVII, pt. I, 1848, pp. 459/472).

2088. — Notes on Assam Temple Ruins, by Capt. E. Taite Dalton, Principal Assistant of the Commissioner of Assam. (*Jour. As. Soc. Bengal*, XXIV, 1855, pp. 1/24).

2089. — The Temple of Jayságar, Upper Ásám. By J. M. Foster, Názirah, Ásám. (*Jour. As. Soc. Bengal*, Vol. 43, 1874, Pt. I, pp. 311/318).

2090. — Old Relics in Kamrup. By Jogesh Chunder Dutt. — Calcutta: Printed by Nundo Mohun Banerjee & Co., s. d. [1891], in-12, 2ff. n. ch. + pp. 27.

> Avait d'abord paru dans le journal the *Indian Nation.*

2091. — The Gauhati Copper-plate Grant of Indrapāla of Prāgjyōtiṣa in Asām. By Dr. A. F. Rudolf Hoernle. (*Jour. As. Soc. Bengal*, Vol. 66, 1897, Pt. 1, pp. 113/132).

2092. — The Nowgong Copper-plate Grant of Balavarman of Prāgjyōtiṣa in Āsām. By Dr. A. F. R. Hoernle. (*Jour. As. Soc. Bengal*, Vol. 66, 1897, Pt. 1, pp. 285/297).

2093. — Two Copper-plate Grants of Ratnapāla of Prāgjyōtiṣa in Āsām. By Dr. A. F. Rudolf Hoernle. (*Jour. As. Soc. Bengal*, Vol. 67, 1898, Pt. 1, pp. 99/125).

2094. — Dr. T. Bloch's Archaeological Report for 1902—1903.

Dímápúr.

2095. — On the Ruins of Dímápúr on the Dunsiri River, Asám. By Major H. H. Godwin—Austen, ... Deputy Superintendent, Topographical Survey of India. (*Jour. As. Soc. Bengal*, Vol. 43, 1874, Pt. I, pp. 1/6).

2096. — Dimāpūr. By R. F. St. Andrew St. John. (*Jour. R. As. Soc.*, April 1897, pp. 423/7).

2097. — Dr. F. H. Burton—Brown. Ruins of Dimūpūr in Assam. (*Journ. Roy. As. Soc.*, April 1897, pp. 439/440).

2098. — W. F. Sinclair (late I. C. S.) Dimāpur. (*Journ. Roy. As. Soc.*, July 1897, pp. 623/4).

Numismatique.

2099. — Ueber die Nepalischen, Assamischen und Ceylonischen Münzen des Asiatischen Museum; von A. Schiefner. (*Bul. Cl. hist.-phil. Ac. Imp. Sc. St. Pét.*, XII, 1855, col. 150—4).

2100. — *Catalogue of the Coins in the Indian Museum, Calcutta. By Vincent A. Smith, Vol. I, Oxford. 1906.

Notice: *Journ. Roy. As. Soc.*, April, 1907, pp. 472—475. By O. C.

X. — Religion.

Divers.

2101. — A short account of the Moa Morah sect, and of the country at present occupied by the Bor Senaputtee. By S. O. Hannay, Capt. 40th Regt. N. I. Asst. to the Commissioner in Assam. (*Jour. As. Soc. Bengal*, VII, Aug. 1838, pp. 671—679).

2102. — Notes on the «Mahápurushyas», a Sect of Vaishnavas in Asám. — By Capt. E. T. Dalton, Political Assistant Commissioner Assam, in charge of Kámrup. (*Jour. As. Soc. Bengal*, XX, 1851, pp. 455—469).

2103. — Notes on the Worship of Hayagriba Madhava by the Hindus and the Buddhists, etc., — By Kaviratna Gaurinath Chakravarti. (*Journ. Buddhist Text Soc.*, II, Pt. II, 1894, App. II, pp. VI—XI).

«The Temple of Hayagriba Mādhava, is situated on the summit of a hill at Hajo, a village in Assam».

2104. — A Brief Sketch of the Religious Beliefs of the Assamese People. By M. N. Ghoshi, M. A. (Bachelor in Law) of the Provincial Civil Service, Assam. — Methodist Publishing House, Culcutta, 1896, pet. in-8, pp. II—61, 1 tab.

2105. — The Mahāpuruṣ Sect of Assam. By Çrī Gouri Nātha Çakravartti. (*Journ. Buddhist Text*, Vol. V, 1897, Pt. I, pp. 37—40).

Missions catholiques.

2106. — ʼM. M. Dombrowski. Trzęsienie ziemi w Assamie. (*Missye Katolickie*, Krakau, 1897, XVI, pp. 276—8).

Abele.

2107. — Let. du R. P. Gebhard Abele, de la Soc. du Divin Sauveur, Assam. (*Ann. Prop. Foi*, Sept. 1902, pp. 324—342).

>Trad. de l'Allemand.

Bohnheim, Corbinien, de la Congrégation du Divin Sauveur.

2108. — Lettre. [Voyage de Trieste à Shillong. — Détails sur la mission d'Assam]. (*Miss. Cath.*, XXVII, 30 Août 1895, pp. 409—410).

Muenzloher, R. P. Ange-Marie, de la Société du Divin Sauveur, préfet apostolique de l'Assam.

2109. — Rapport, de Shillong. (*Miss. Cath.*, XXX, 22 Avril 1898, p. 183).

2110. — Let. du R. P. Ange-Marie Muenzloher, de la Soc. du Divin Sauveur, préf. apost. de l'Assam. Shillong, 2 juillet 1898. (*Ann. Prop. Foi*, Janv. 1899, pp. 24).

>Trad. de l'allemand.
>La préfecture apostolique de l'Assam a été fondée le 13 déc. 1889; elle appartient à la Société du Divin Sauveur, dont la Maison-Mère est à Rome: Via Borgo Vecchio, 165.

Missions protestantes.

2111. — ʼThe Holy Bible, containing the old and New Testaments. Translated from the originals into the Assam language, by the Serampore missionaries. Serampore, miss. pr. 1820. In-8, 5 vols. ibid. 1833. In-8.

>Caractères Nagaris.

2112. — ʼThe New Testament. Translated into the Asamese Language, by Nathan Brown, Baptist Missionary. (2ᵉ édition) Sibsagor. Assam 1849. In-8.

2113. — The New Testament of our Lord and Savior Jesus Chist [sic]: translated into the Asamese Language, from the combined Text of Griesbach, Knapp, and Scholz. By Nathan Brown, American Baptist Missionary. — Third Edition. — Sibsagor, Asam: Printed at the American Baptist Mission Press, for the American and Foreign Bible Society, 1850, in-8.

2114. — ʼThe Old Testament, in Asamese, by Babu Nidhi Levi Farwell. Sibsagor, 1859—60, 3 part. en un vol. in-4.

XI. — Sciences et Arts.

2115. — Extract from a Letter from D. Scott, Esq. to Mr. G. Swinton, dated Assam, 28 July, 1826. (*Trans. Medical and Phys. Soc. Calcutta*, III, 1827, pp. 430—1).

>Substitute for quinine = *chutwun.*

2116. — Extract of a Letter from R. Mac Isaac, Esq. describing a medicinal Root, in use among the Natives of Assam, dated May 6th, 1827. (*Trans. Medical and Phys. Soc. Calcutta*, III, 1827, p. 432).

　　Misimee Teeta.

2117. — Report of the Society of Arts on Specimens of Rice, Wool &c. from Nepál and Assam. (*Jour. As. Soc. Bengal*, V, June 1836, pp. 365—371).

2118. — Remarks on the Silk Worms and Silks of Assam. By Mr. Thomas Hugon, Sub. Asst. Nowgong. (*Jour. As. Soc. Bengal*, VI, Jan. 1837, pp. 21—38).

2119. — India-rubber. (*Ocean Highways*, N. S., Vol. I, May 1873, p. 67). Cartes.

　　A propos de: *Report on the Caoutchouc of Commerce; being Information on the Plants yielding it, their Geographical Distribution, Climatic conditions, and the possibility of their Cultivation and Acclimatization in India. By James Collins, F.B.S., Edin., &c., &c.; with a Memorandum on the same subject, by Dr. Brandis, Inspector-General of Forests to the Government of India. (Allen & Co., ...Stanford... King & Co... and Trübner, 1873).

2120. — *G. Mann. — Progress Reports, Forest Administration Province of Assam. 1874—75. Shillong, 1875, in-fol.

—— Id. 1875—76. Shillong, 1876, in-fol.

—— Id. 1876—77. Shillong, 1877, in-fol.

—— Id. 1877—78. Shillong, 1878, in-fol.

2121. — Assam Rubber for West-Africa. [*Ficus elastica*, Bl.]. (*Kew Bull.*, 1891, pp. 97—102).

2122. — *Monograph on Dyes and Dyeing in Assam. Details of the dyes, and of the methods of their preparation and use, and a few paragraphs containing general information on the subject, with a glossary of the Vernacular names of dyes. By W. A. M. Duncan, Esq. I.C.S. 1896, in-fol.

2123. — Note on an Inspection of Certain Forests in Assam. By H. C. Hill, Officiating Inspector-General of Forests. Dated 31st March 1896. Calcutta: Office of the Superintendent of Government Printing, India. 1896, in-fol., pp. II—24.

2124. — *Notes on some Industries of Assam, from 1884 to 1895. This is a Reprint of (1) Silk in Assam. By E. Stack, Esq., I.C.S., 1884. (2) Cotton in Assam. By H. Z. Darrah, Esq., I.C.S., 1885. (3) Three Manufactures of Assam — (a) the Brass-Work of the Morias, (b) the Gold enamelling of Jorhat, and (c) Iron-smelting in the Khasi Hills. By H. Z. Darrah, Esq., I.C.S., 1885. (4) The *Eri* Silk of Assam. By H. Z. Darrah Esq., I.C.S., 1890. (5) Brass and Copper Wares in Assam. By E. A. Gait, Esq., I.C.S., 1894. (6) Pottery in Assam. By E. A. Gait, Esq., I.C.S. Compiled in the Office of the Secretary to the Chief Commissioner of Assam, 1896, gr. in-8.

2125 — *Monograph on the Cotton-Fabrics of Assam. Deals with the cotton spinning and weaving industry; the manner in which this industry has been affected by imports from abroad; trade in home-made-fabrics; materials used in manufacture of fabrics; process of manufacture, and the fabrics themselves. By H. F. Samman, Esq. I.C.S. 1897, in-fol.

2126. — 'Monograph on the Silk—Cloths of Assam. History of the industry, the *Eri* worm and silk and the *Muga* worm and silk. By B. C. Allen, Esq., B. A., I.C.S. Shillong, 1899, gr. in-8, pp. 24.

2127. — The Lac Industry of Assam. (*The Times Weekly Edition*, Sept. 28, 1900, p. 622).

    From a report of the Assistant-Director of Agriculture in Assam.

2128. — 'Monograph on Ivory—Carving in Assam. Deals with historical aspect of the industry, causes of its decline, class and number of persons now acquainted with ivory carving in Assam; value of articles terned out, industry on the verge of extinction, and a list of articles made of ivory with their usual prices. By James Donald, Esq., M.A., I.C.S. 1900, gr. in-8.

2129. — 'Note on the Lac Industry of Assam. Bulletin N° 6 (Agricultural Department, Assam), Industrial Series N° 1. Production of lac in Assam; exports of lac from Assam; trees on which lac is found or reared; method of rearing lac; munufactured lac; lac-dye; composition of lac-made colours; lac-wares; how lac is applied to wood; woods used in making lac-toys, etc., and miscellaneous uses of lac. By B. C. Basu, Esq., B.A., M.R.A.C., M.R.A.S. (Eng.) 1900, gr. in-8.

2130. — Pani ghao-Water-Sore-commonly called "sore feet" of Assam Coolies. (*Journ. of Tropical Medicine*, Dec. 1900, pp. 103—110).

2131. — 'Way to Health. (A Sanitary Primer in Assamese); — Introductory; pure air; pure water; wholesome food; light; clothes; gymnastic; sleeping; comfortable house; protection of towns and villages; diseases; vital statistics; necessity of practice. By H. C. Baura, in-16, 1901.

2132. — Cholera on Assam Tea Gardens. By William E. Lloyd Elliot, M. D. (*Journ. of Tropical Medicine*, Jan. 1, 1904, pp. 4—6).

2133. — P. N. Gagai. — *Asamiyá Larár Ganarara Adi Puthi*. The First Book on Arithmetical Tables for Assamese Boys. In Assamese. Assam, 1906. in-12, pp. II, 46. 6*d*.

2134. — 'S. Bhattachariyya. — Padhásúlir Asamiyá Pátiganit. Assamese Arithmetic for Pathásálá Boys. Eighth Edition, Assam, 1907, in-12, pp. 189.

2135. — 'Sakhayat Ali. — Serájal Echhlám. Light of Islam. In Arabic and Asamese. Calcutta, 1907, gr. in-8, pp. 68.

XII. — Langue.

2136. — A Grammar of the Asamese Language. By W. Robinson. Government Seminary, Gowhatti. Serampore Press, 1839, in-8, pp. ii—78.

2137. — 'Vocabulary and Phrases in English and Asamese, by Mrs. H. B. C. Cutter. Jaipur, Printed at the American Baptist Mission press. 1840. In-12, pp. 251.

2138. — Grammatical Notices of the Asamese Language. By N. Brown. —

Sibsagor: Printed at the American Baptist Mission Press. 1848, in-8, pp. xxvi—80.

2139. — 'N. Brown. Grammatical Notices of the Assamese Language. Sibsagor, 1862, in-8.
     Second Edition.

2140. — Grammatical Notes on the Assamese Language. By N. Brown. — Third Edition. — American Baptist Missionary Union, Nowgong, Assam, 1893, in-8, pp. xii + 1 f. n. ch. + pp. 95.

2141. — English and Assamese Phrases, s. l. n. d., pet. in-8, pp. 98.

2142. — Brief Vocabulary in English and Assamese with Rudimentary Exercises. By Mrs. S. R. Ward. Sibsaugor, Assam: American Baptist Mission Press. 1864, pet. in-8, pp. xii—104.

2143. — 'M. Bronson. — Assamese—English Dictionary, 1867, in-8, pp. 609.

2144. — 'H. B. L. Cutter. — Phrases in English and Assamese. Revised by E. W. Clark, 1877, in-8, pp. 98.

2145. — 'Glossary of Vernacular Terms, ordinarily used in official correspondence in the Province of Assam. Contains technical terms generally adopted in official use. Compiled in the Assam Secretariat Office, 1879, gr. in-8.

2146. — 'G. F. Nicholl. — Manual of the Bengali language, comprising a Bengali Grammar and Lessons, specimens of current handwriting and various other appendices, including an Assamese Grammar. 1894, in-12, pp. xxiv—359.

2147. — 'S. E. Peal. — Table of comparison of selected words and numerals in several Assam languages. (*Proc. As. Soc. of Bengal*, 1895, pp. 170—175).

2148. — Hema Kosha or an Etymological Dictionary of the Assamese Language by Hemchandra Barua. — Edited by Capt. P. R. Gurdon, I.S.C., Deputy Commissioner, and Srijut Hemchandra Gosain, Sub-Deputy Collector. Published under the Authority of the Assam Administration, 1900, gr. in-8 à 2 col.

2149. — Hema Kosha. Hem Chandra Barua. By R. N. C.[ust]. (*Jour. R. As. Soc.*, Oct. 1901, pp. 911—913).

2150. — Linguistic Survey of India. — Vol. II. Mōn-Khmēr and Siamese-Chinese Families (including Khassi and Tai). Compiled and edited by G. A. Grierson, C.I.E., ... Calcutta: Office of the Superintendent of Government Printing, India. 1904, gr. in-4, pp. ii—233.

2151. — Linguistic Survey of India. — Vol. III. Tibeto-Burman Family. Part III. Specimens of the Kuki-Chin and Burma Groups. Compiled and edited by G. A. Grierson, C.I.E., ... Calcutta: Office of the Superintendent, Government Printing, India, 1904, gr. in-4, pp. viii—403.

2152. — 'S. Ch. Chaudhuri. — *A'khara Chináki. A'gchhová.* An Assamese First Book of Reading. Calcutta, 1904, pet. in-8, pp. 26.

2153. — 'S. Chaudhuri. — Akhara Chináki Agchhová. An Assamese First Book of Reading. Part 1. Sixth Edition. Calcutta, 1907, pet. in-8, pp. 26.

2154. — *L. Hazarika. — A Complete Key to First Book of Reading. In Assamese and English. Assam, 1905. in-8, pp. 64. 9d.

2155. — *P. N. Gagai. — *Lara Sikshá «Scha-Chhová.* Instruction for Children. Last Part (Part III). In Assamese. Assam, 1906. in-12, pp. II—44. 6d.

2156. — *B. C. Sarma. — An Elementary Book on English Composition. In Assamese and English. Second Edition. Calcutta, 1906. ln-12, pp. 126.

2157. — *Ch. K. Gosvami. — A Key to First Book of Reading. In Assamese and English. Calcutta, 1907. In-16, pp. 82.

2158. — *D. K. Dev Gosvami. — Sachitra Asamíyá Hitachintá. Good Thoughts in Assamese. Kamrup, 1907. Part 1, in-12, pp. 52.

XIII. — Littérature.

2159. — Some Assamese Proverbs. — Compiled and Annotated by Captain P. R. Gurdon, I.S.C., Deputy Commissioner, Goalpara. Shillong: Printed at the Assam Secretariat Printing Office, 1896, in-8, pp. XXIV—98.

> Notice: *J. R. As. Soc.,* Oct 1896, pp. 807—9, par R. N. Cust.

2160. — Some Assamese Proverbs. (Second edition). Compiled and annotated by Major P. R. T. Gurdon, I.A., Deputy Commissioner, and Superintendent of Ethnography in Assam. Shillong: Assam Secretariat Printing Office, 1903, in-8, pp. III—118.

2161. — Assamese Literature. Communicated by Geo. A. Grierson. (*Ind. Antiq.,* XXV, 1896, pp. 57—61).

2162. — Index-Catalogue of Indian Official Publications in the Library, British Museum. Compiled by Frank Campbell (Late of the Library, British Museum). [London: Printed by William Clowes] s. d., gr. in-4.

2163. — Catalogue of Assamese Books. [in the British Museum], in-4, pp. 34 à 2 col.

2164. — *Professor J. F. Blumhardt. — Catalogue of the Library of the India Office. Vol. II, pt. 4. Bengali, Oriya, and Assamese Books. London, 1905, in-8.

XIV. — Mœurs et Coutumes.

2165. — Notes on the Marriage Systems of the Peoples of Assam. — By a Native Assamese. Calcutta: K. C. Datta, 1892, in-12, pp. 56.

2166. — *T. Kinney. — Old times in Assam. Calcutta, Pritchard, 1896, in-8, pp. 189.

2167. — Human Sacrifices in Ancient Assam. By E. A. Gait. (*Jour. As. Soc. Bengal,* Vol. 67, 1898, Pt. 3, pp. 56—65.)

2168. — *Mrs. P. H. Moore. — Twenty years in Assam. Calcutta, printed by J. W. Thomas, 1901, pp. 238.

XV. — Voyages.

2169. — Memoir of a Survey of Asam and the neighbouring Countries, executed in 1825—6—7—8. — By Lieutenant R. Wilcox. (*As. Researches*, **XVII**, 1832, pp. 314—469.)

2170. — William Griffith, 1847. — Voir No. 1419.

2171. — Notes on a Trip across the Patkoi Range, from Assam to the Hookoong Valley. By II. L. Jenkins. [Communicated by Robert C. Noble, Esq., Calcutta.] (*Journ. Roy. Geog. Soc.*, XLI, 1871, pp. 342—348).

2172. — The Mishmee Hills: an account of a journey made in an attempt to penetrate Thibet to Assam to open new routes for commerce... Illustrated. London, 1873, in-8.

> By T. T. Cooper.

2173. — Notes of a trip up the Dihing basin to Dapha Pani, &c., January and February, 1882. — By S. E. Peal. (*Jour. As. Soc. Bengal*, Vol. 52, 1883, Pt. 2, pp. 7—53.)

> Voir p. 53: Some words in Kunung.

2174. — Exploration of route between Assam and Upper Burma. (*Proc. R. Geog. Soc.*, **X**, 1888, June, pp. 377—378).

2175. — Ernst Hartert. — Schilderungen aus Ober-Assam und über Assam im allgemeinen. (*Verhand. Ges. Erdk. Berlin*, XVI, 1889, pp. 192—205.)

2176. — 'J. F. Needham. — Journey along the Lohit Brahmaputra between Sadiya in Upper Assam and Lima in South Eastern Tibet. (*Supplementary Papers R. Geog. Soc.*, II, pp. 487—555, carte). London, 1889, in-8.

2177. — Direct Communication between Upper Assam and Northern Burma. (*Proc. R. Geog. Soc.*, XIV, 1892, June, pp. 404—407).

2178. — 'Diary of a Journey to the Bor Khamti country, and sources of the Irrawaddy, made by Mr. J. Errol Gray, season 1892—93, from Assam, 1893, br. in-fol.

2179. — Mr. Errol Gray's Journey from Assam to the Sources of the Irawadi. (*Geographical Journal*, III, March 1894, pp. 221—228).

> D'après l'exemplaire transmis à la R. Geog. Soc. par le Secretary of State for India de la «Diary of a Journey to the Bor Khamti country and sources of the Irawadi, made by Mr. I. Errol Gray, season 1892—93, from Assam».
> «Mr. Errol Gray is a tea-planter, who has long resided in Assam, and interested himself in the development of the trade of that country with the adjoining regions beyond the British frontier. His object in making the present journey was to travel from Assam into Western China, through the country which had been first explored by Lieut. Wilcox in 1827, and afterwards by Col. Woodthorpe and Major Macgregor in 1884—85, until he reached the Nam-kiu river, the western source of the Irawadi, which was the extreme limit of their explorations».

2180. — From Yun-nan to British India. By Prince Henry of Orleans. (*Ibid.*, March 1896, pp. 300—309).

> Traduit du *Bul. de la Soc. de Géog.*, de Paris.

2181. — Société de Géographie de Lille-Conférence par le Prince Henri d'Orléans 12 Mai 1896. Lille, Imprimerie L. Danel, pet. in-8, pp. 63. Portrait.

Sur papier du Japon.

2182. — Henri d'Orléans. — Du Tonkin aux Indes, 1898. — Voir No. 455.

2183. — Henri d'Orléans. — From Tonkin to India, 1898. — Voir No. 465.

2184. — Wild Sports of Burma and Assam by Colonel Pollok late Staff Corps, and W. S. Thom Assistant District Superintendent of Police, Burma. With Illustrations and Maps. London: Hurst and Blackett, 1900, in-8, pp. xx—507.

2185. — A Geographical Account of Countries round the Bay of Bengal, 1669 to 1679 by Thomas Bowrey Edited by Lt.-Col. Sir Richard Carnac Temple, Bart., C.I.E. Cambridge: Printed for the Hakluyt Society MDCCCCV, in-8, pp. lvi—387.

Forme le No. XII Second Series of Works issued by The Hakluyt Society — Issued for 1903.

2186. — A Handbook for Travellers in India Burma and Ceylon including the Provinces of Bengal, Bombay, Madras, the United Provinces of Agra and Lucknow, the Panjab, the North-West Frontier Province, Beluchistan, Assam, and the Central Provinces, and the Native States of Rajputana, Central India, Kashmir, Hyderabad, Mysore, etc. Fifth Edition with seventy-eight Maps. London, John Murray, 1905, in-8, pp. cxv—524.

2187. — 'W. Del Mar. The Romantic East: Burma, Assam and Kashmir. With 64 illustrations from Photographs. London, A. and C. Black, in-8, pp. xv—211.

Notice: *Lond. & China Express*, Oct. 12, 1906.

XVI. — Commerce.

2188. — 'Report on Trade between Assam and the adjoining Foreign Countries for the periods of three years ending 31st March 1890 and 1893. By H. Z. Darrah. Shillong, 1890—93. In-folio.

2189. — 'Report on the River-borne Trade of the Province of Assam for the year 1896—97. By F. J. Monahan. Calcutta, 1897, pp. iv—16—lx, Carte.

2190. — 'Report on the Foreign Trade of Assam. Statistical tables showing the trade between Assam and the adjoining foreign countries. By the Director, Department of Land Records and Agriculture, Assam, 1899, in-fol.

For the three years ending the 31st March 1899.

2191. — 'Report on the Rail and River-borne Trade of the Province of Assam. Report and appendices. By the Director, Department of Land Records and Agriculture, Assam, in-fol.

For the years 1899—1900 and 1900—1901.
Publication trimestrielle.

2192. — 'Report on the Trade between Assam and the adjoining Foreign Tribes and Countries for the Three Years ending March 31, 1905. By A. C. Barnes. Shillong, 1905, pp. 20.

XVII. Administration Anglaise.

2193. — *The Assam Association. Memorial to the Right Hon. Viscount Cran-
brook and Report of the Deputation to his Lordship, 31st July 1878. 1878.
In-8.

2194. — *Budget (Imperial) Estimate of Military Works for the year 1893—94
in the Assam Province, in-fol.

2195. — Assam. By H. Luttman—Johnson (Late Indian Civil Service). (Pages
134—172 de *The British Empire Series*, Vol. I, London, 1899, in-8).

2196. — *Classified List and Distribution Return of Establishment, Public Works
Department, Assam. List of officers and subordinates under the Public Works
Department in Assam. Compiled in Office of the Secretary to the Chief
Commissioner of Assam in the Public Works Department, gr. in-8.

> Publié tous les trois mois. — Depuis le 31 déc. 1899.

2197. — *Assam. The Colonization of Waste Lands, being a Reprint of the
official Correspondence between the Governm. of India and the Chief Commissioner of Assam. Calcutta, Indian Daily News, 1899, in-8, pp. 131.

2198. — *A Report of an Investigation into the causes of the Diseases known
in Assam as *Kala-azar* and Beri-Beri. Introductory remarks; general course
and result of investigation; prevalence of *Kala-azar* as judged by available
statistics; facts relating to spread of *Kala-azar*; symptoms of *Kala-azar*
illustrated by cases; life-history of parasite; effects of various conditions on
life of the free stage; method of infection by parasite; remarks on pathology, diagnosis, and treatment, etc., of Anchylostomiasis in tea gardens. By
Dr. Geo. M. Giles, M.B.... Surgeon, I.M.S. 1900, gr. in-8.

2199. — *Report on the North-Eastern Frontier for the year 1899—1900.
Report on the administration of the North-Eastern Frontier. Compiled by
the Government of Burma, 1900, in-fol.

2200. — *Catalogue of books and publications of the Assam Administration
which are intended for sale for the half year ending 30th June 1900. Shillong, Assam Secretariat Printing Office, 1900, in-folio oblong.

2201. — *Further Papers on Reconstitution of the Provinces Bengal and Assam,
1905, in-8.

2202. — Reconstitution of the Provinces of Bengal and Assam. (*Imp. & Asiat.
Quart. Rev.*, Oct. 1905, pp. 384—392).

> Text, Resolution of the Government, Simla, July 1905.

2203. — *Sir J. Bampfylde. — His Resignation of the Lieut.-Governorship of
Eastern Bengal and Assam, 1906.

2204. — *Observations on the Administration of the Province of Assam. By
Anandiram Dhekiāl Phukan.

> Printed in Mill's Report.

2205. — *Emil Jung. — Die britisch-indische Provinz Assam. (*Mitt. Geog. Ges.*, Wien, XXXI, 1, pp. 1—14).

Publications of the Government of Assam.

I ¹).

2206. —

Account—

An Account of the Province of Assam and its Administration. An Account of the Province of Assam and its Administration (reprinted from the Report on the Administration of the Province of Assam for the year 1901—1902). Compiled in the office of the Secretary to the Chief Commissioner of Assam. Published 1903. Demy 8vo, flush bound. Re. 1, or 1s. 6d.

Addresses—

Addresses presented to His Excellency the Right Hon'ble Lord Curzon of Kedleston, P.C., G.M.S.I., G.M.I.E., Viceroy and Governor General of India, and His Excellency's replies thereto, on the occasion of his visit to Assam, March 1900. Contains addresses presented at Dibrugarh, Tezpur, and Gauhati, and the Viceroy's replies thereto. Compiled in the Office of the Secretary to the Chief Commissioner of Assam. Published 1900. Superroyal 8vo, stitched, with cover. As. 2, or 2d.

Administration, Assam—

Report on the Administration of the Province of Assam. Part I—General Summary; Part II—Statistical Tables. Compiled in the Office of the Secretary to the Chief Commissioner of Assam. Foolscap, flush bound. For the years—1898-99 to 1900-01, Rs. 2-8, or 3s. 9d. (each year); and 1901-02 and 1902-03, Rs. 2, or 3s.

Aka—

A Short Vocabulary of the — Language. Contains words from English into Aka with short illustrative sentences. By J. D. Anderson, I.C.S. Published 1896. Royal 8vo, flush bound. As. 8, or 9d.

Angami Naga—

Outline Grammar of the — Language with a Vocabulary and illustrative sentences. Philology of the language; grammar, dealing with orthography, etymology, and syntax; short English sentences rendered into Angami; and an English-Angami Vocabulary. By R. B. McCabe, I.C.S. Published 1887. Royal 8vo, flush bound. Rs. 2, or 3s.

Primer. A Primer, containing 30 lessons in Angami Naga in Roman character without any English translation. By S. W. Rivenburg. Published 1903. Foolscap 12mo, stitched, with cover. Anna 1, or 1d.

1) D'après les pages 205—217 du *General Catalogue*, Part I, No. 9 (voir supra, no. 1674).

Ao Naga—

Ao Naga Grammar, with illustrative phrases and Vocabulary. The Grammar is preceded by a short traditional account of the tribe and their dialect. The Vocabulary is from English into Ao. By Mrs. E. W. Clark. Published 1893. Royal 8vo, flush bound. Rs. 2, or 3s.

Assam Gazette—(Published every Saturday.)

The —. Part I—Appointments, Postings, Transfers, Powers, Leave, and other Personal Matters relating to the Officers serving in Assam. Part IA—Orders of Commandants of Volunteer Corps; Part II—Regulations, Orders, Notifications, Rules, etc., issued by the Chief Commissioner and Heads of Departments; Part IIA—Orders, Notifications, and Rules of the Government of India, of the Government of Bengal, and of the Calcutta High Court, and other papers extracted from the *Gazette of India* and the Provincial Gazettes; Part III—Acts of the Governor General's Council assented to by the Governor General; Part IV—Bills introduced into the Council of the Governor General for making Laws and Regulations or published under Rule 23; Part V—Advertisements and notices, etc.; Supplement—Such official papers as may be deemed to be of interest to the public and as may usefully be made known; Vernacu'ar Part—Notifications, Notices, and Advertisements. Published under the authority of the Chief Commissioner of A-sam. Foolscap. Parts I, IA, II, IIA, and V—Single copy (without postage) 4 annas, or 5d., postage according to weight: annual subscription Rs. 7-4, or 10s. 11d., without postage, and Rs. 9, or 13s. 6d., with postage; Parts III and IV are not issued to private subscribers; Supplement—Single copy (without postage) 4 annas, or 5d., postage according to weight; annual ubscription Rs. 3-8, or 3s. 9d., without postage, and Rs. 4-4, or 6s. 5d., with postage; Vernacular Part—Same as Supplement.

Assamese—

Hemkosha, or an Etymological Dictionary of the — Language. By Babu Hem Chandra Barua (edited by Captain P. R. T. Gurdon, I.S.C.). Published 1900. Super-royal 8vo, leather, half bound. Rs. 5, or 7s. 6d. (10a.)

Some — Proverbs. Deals with proverbs current in the Sibsagar, Nowgong, and Gauhati districts. Transliterated and translated into English with Explanatory notes. By Captain P. R. T. Gurdon, I.S.C. Published 1896. Royal 8vo, flush bound. Rs. 2, or 3s. 2nd edition. Published 1903. Re. 1, or 1s. 6d.

Assistants, Hospital—

The Quarterly List of Civil — serving in Assam. Compiled in the Office of the Principal Medical Officer and Sanitary Commissioner, Assam. Royal 8vo, stitched, with cover. Issued quarterly. From 1st January 1901 to 1st April 1904. As. 8, or 9d. (per quarter).

Asylums, Lunatic—

Report on the — at Tezpur. The Report is preceded by the remarks made by the Principal Medical Officer and Sanitary Commissioner, Assam, on the Asylum, and followed by the Chief Commissioner's Resolution on the Report. By the Superintendent, Tezpur Lunatic Asylum. Foolscap, stitched, with cover. For the years—1899, 1900, 1901, (triennium) 1900-1901-1902, and 1903. Re. 1, or 1s. 6d. (each).

Report (Statistical Returns) on the Tezpur —, 1901. By the Principal Medical Officer and Sanitary Commissioner, Assam. Published 1902. Foolscap, stitched, with cover. Re. 1, or 1s. 6d.

Bengali-Garo—

The — Dictionary. From Bengali to Garo, written in Bengali character. By Rev. M. Ramkhee. Published 1887. Demy 8vo, flush bound. Rs. 7-10, or 11s. 5d.

Beri-Beri—

A Report of an Investigation into the causes of the Diseases known in Assam as *kala-azar* and —. Introductory remarks; general course and result of investigation; prevalence of *kala-azar* as judged by available statistics; facts relating to spread of *kala-azar*; symptoms of *kala-azar* illustrated by cases; life-history of parasite; effect of various conditions on life of the free stage; method of infection by parasite; remarks on pathology, diagnosis, and treatment, etc., of anchylostomiasis; preventive and remedial measures, and Anchylostomiasis in tea gardens. By Dr. Geo. M. Giles, M.B., F.R.C S., SAN.SCI.CERT.UNIV., LON., Surgeon, I.M.S. Published 1890. Royal 8vo, stitched, with cover. Re. 1, or 1s. 6d. (1a., or 1d.)

Boards, Local—

Assam — Budgets. Annual Budgets of the Silchar, Hailakandi, North Sylhet, Habiganj, Sunamganj, South Sylhet, Karimganj, Dhubri, Goalpara, Gauhati, Barpeta, Tezpur, Mangaldai, Nowgong, Sibsagar, Jorhat, Golaghat, Dibrugarh, and North Lakhimpur Local Boards preceded by an abstract of the above Local Boards' Budget Estimate of Receipts and Disbursements. Compiled in the Office of the Secretary to the Chief Commissioner of Assam in the Public Works Department. Foolscap, stitched, with cover. For the years — 1900-01, 1901-02, 1902-03, and 1903-04, Re. 1, or 1s. 6d. (each year).

Resolution by the Chief Commissioner on the Working of — in Assam. Report, Statements, and Appendices. Compiled in the Office of the Secretary to the Chief Commissioner of Assam. Foolscap, stitched, with cover. For the years — 1899-1900, 1900-01, 1901-02, and 1902-03, Re. 1, or 1s. 6d. (each year).

Books—

Catalogue of — in the Shillong Government Library. By A. G. Bell, Librarian. Published 1904. Super-royal 8vo, stitched, with cover. As. 4, or 5d.

Buildings and Roads—

Report on the Finance Accounts of the — Branch of the Public Works Department, Assam. Report, Statements, and Accounts. By the Examiner of Public Works Accounts, Assam. Foolscap, stitched, with cover. For the years — 1900-01 to 1902-03, Re. 1, or 1s. 6d. (each year).

Bulletin—

Bulletin N°. 7 (Cultivation of Plantain in the Assam Valley). By B. C. Basu. Published 1901. Royal 8vo, stitched, with cover. As. 2, or 2d.

Bulletin N°. 8 (Agricultural). By B. C. Basu. Published 1902. Foolscap, stitched, with cover. As. 2, or 2d.

Bulletin N° 9 (Agricultural Series N°. 5). The Cultivation of Pulse Crops, in the Assam Valley. By B. C. Basu. Published 1902. Royal 8vo, stitched, with cover. As. 2, or 2d.

Census—

Census of India, 1891, Assam. By E. A. Gait, I.C.S. Published 1892. Foolscap, flush bound —

Volume I.—Report   Rs. 3, or 4s. 6d. (7a., or 8d.)
Volume II.—Imperial Tables.   Rs. 3, or 4s. 6d. (7a., or 8d.)
Volume III.—Provincial Tables. Rs. 2, or 3s.   (4a. 6p., or 6d.)

Census of India, 1901, Assam. By B. C. Allen, B.A., I.C.S. Published 1902. Part I, Report; Part II, Tables. Foolscap, flush bound. Rs. 2, or 2s. 8d. (per part).

Cossyah and Jynteah—

Report on the Administration of the — Hill Territory. Method of administering the Civil, Criminal, Revenue, and General affairs of the Cossyah and Jynteah Hill Territory. By W. J. Allen, Member of the Board of Revenue (on deputation). Published 1904. Foolscap, flush bound. Re. 1, or 1s. 6d.

Cotton-Fabrics—

Monograph on the — of Assam. Deals with the cotton spinning and weaving industry; the manner in which this industry has been affected by imports from abroad; trade in home-made fabrics; materials used in manufacture of fabrics; process of manufacture, and the fabrics themselves. By H. F. Samman, I.C.S. Published 1897. Foolscap, stitched, with cover. Rs. 3-4, or 4s. 11d.

Crop-Experiments—

Annual Note on — in Assam. Section I deals with the nature, number, and results of experiments on rice, sugarcane, miscellaneous crops, and mustard; and Section II with experiments by supervisor kanungos and mandals under the mauza-book rules on rice, mustard, and rape-seed, *matikalai*, and sugarcane. By the Director, Department of Land Records and Agriculture, Assam. Foolscap, stitched, with cover. For the years — 1899-1900, 1900—01, and 1901-02, As. 8, or 9d. (each year).

Dafla—

An Outline Grammar of the — Language as spoken by the Tribes immediately south of the Apa Tanang country. Orthography, accidence, syntax, illustrative phrases, short stories and a vocabulary from Dafla into English and *vice versâ*; and a note on the language of the Western Daflas. By R. C. Hamilton, I.C.S. Published 1900. Super-royal 8vo, flush bound. Re. 1, or 1*s*. 6*d*.

Deori-Chutiya—

An Outline Grammar of the — Language spoken in Upper Assam, with an introduction, illustrative sentences, and short vocabulary. The introduction contains a historical sketch of the Deori-Chutiya Tribe. The grammar opens with a note on the connection between the Chutiya and Káchári Languages and then deals with the grammar proper. The vocabulary is from English to Chutiya and treats of nouns, adjectives, and verbs only. There is an appendix, which contains «Notes on the Chutiyas of Upper Assam by Lieutenant E. T. Dalton», with Mr. H. J. Kellner's and the Author's remarks thereon. By W. B. Brown, B.A., I.C.S. Published 1895. Royal 8vo, flush bound. Re. 1-8, or 2*s*. 3*d*.

Digaro—

A few — (Taroan, Miju, Mju) and Thibetan Words with their English Synonyms. By F. J. Needham, C.I.E. Royal 8vo, tacked. Re. 1, or 1*s*. 6*d*.

Dispensaries—

Report on — in Assam. Report, Statements, and Resolution of the Chief Commissioner at the end. By the Principal Medical Officer and Sanitary Commissioner, Assam. Foolscap, stitched, with cover. For the years — 1899 and 1900, (triennium) 1899 to 1901, 1902, and 1903, Re. 1, or 1*s*. 6*d*. (each).

Dyes and Dyeing—

Monograph on — in Assam. Details of the dyes, and of the methods of their preparation and use, and a few paragraphs containing general information on the subject, with a glossary of the Vernacular names of dyes. By W. A. M. Duncan, I.C.S. Published 1896. Foolscap, stitched, with cover. Rs. 2, or 3*s*.

Earthquake—

Report on the — of the 12th June 1897, so far as it affected the Province of Assam. Contains official correspondence showing the extent and effect of the disaster. Compiled in the Office of the Secretary to the Chief Commissioner of Assam. Published 1897. Foolscap, stitched, with cover. Re. 1, or 1*s*. 6*d*.

Education—

Report on the Progress of — in Assam during the years 1897-98 to 1901-02. By M. Prothero, M.A., Officiating Director of Public Instruction, Assam. Published 1902. Foolscap, stitched, with cover. Re. 1, or 1*s*. 6*d*.

Excise—

Report on the Administration of the — Department in Assam. Report, Appendices, and Resolution of the Chief Commissioner at the end. By the Commissioner of Excise, Assam. Foolscap, stitched, with cover. For the years—1899-1900, Re. 1, or 1s. 6d.; 1900-01, As. 11, or 1s.; 1901-02, Re. 1, or 1s. 6d.; and 1902-03, Re. 1, or 1s. 6d.

Forest—

The Assam — Regulation, VII of 1891. Published under the authority of the Chief Commissioner of Assam. Published 1892. Royal 8vo, stitched. As. 12, or 1s. 2d. In Bengali. As. 8, or 9d.

Report on the Administration of the — Department in Assam. Report, Forms and Appendices, and Resolution of the Chief Commissioner at the end. By the Conservator of Forests, Assam. Foolscap, stitched, with cover. For the years—1898-99 to 1902-03, Re. 1, or 1s. 6d. (each year).

Geography—

Physical and Political — of the Province of Assam. Physical features, area, climate, and chief staples; historical summary; form of administration; character of land tenures, and system of settlement and survey; Civil divisions of British territory; details of the last Census; and frontier relations and Feudatory States. Reprinted from the Report on the Administration of the Province of Assam for the year 1892-93. Published 1896. Super-royal 8vo, flush bound. Re. 1, or 1s. 6d.

Health—

Way to —(A Sanitary Primer in Assamese):—Introductory; pure air; pure water; wholesome food; light; clothes; gymnastic; sleeping; comfortable house; protection of towns and villages; diseases; vital statistics; necessity of practice. By H. C. Barua. Published 1901. Foolscap, 16mo, stitched, with cover. As. 2, or 2d.

Immigration, Labour—

Report on — into Assam. Report and Statements. Compiled in the office of the Secretary to the Chief Commissioner of Assam. Foolscap, stitched, with cover. For the years 1899 and 1901. Re. 1, or 1s. 6d.

Resolution on Labour Immigration into Assam for the year 1902-03. Compiled in the office of the Secretary to the Chief Commissioner of Assam. Published 1903. Foolscap, stitched, with cover. Re. 1, or 1s. 6d.

Income-tax—

Report on the Working of the — Act, II of 1886, in Assam. Report and Appendices. Compiled in the office of the Secretary to the Chief Commissioner of Assam. Foolscap, stitched, with cover. For the years—1899-1900, Re. 1, or 1s. 6d.; 1900-01, As. 8, or 9d.; (triennium) 1899—1900 to 1901-02, Re. 1, or 1s. 6d.

Returns of Income Tax of the Province of Assam for the year 1902-03

Compiled in the office of the Secretary to the Chief Commissioner of Assam. Published 1903. Foolscap, stitched, with cover. As. 8, or 9d.

Industries—

Notes on some — of Assam, from 1884 to 1895. This is a Reprint of— (1) Silk in Assam. By E. Stack, I.C.S., 1884. (2) Cotton in Assam. By H. Z. Darrah, I.C.S., 1885. (3) Three Manufactures of Assam—(a) the Brass-Work of the Morias, (b) the Gold enamelling of Jorhat, and (c) Iron-smelting in the Khasi Hills. By H. Z. Darrah, I.C.S., 1885. (4) The *Eri* Silk of Assam. By H. Z. Darrah, I.C.S., 1890. (5) Brass and Copper Wares in Assam. By E. A. Gait, I.C.S., 1894. (6) Pottery in Assam. By E. A. Gait, I.C.S., 1895. Compiled in the office of the Secretary to the Chief Commissioner of Assam. Published 1896. Royal 8vo, flush bound. Re. 1, or 1s. 6d.

Instruction, Public—

Report on — in Assam. Report, Statements, Appendices, and Resolution of the Chief Commissioner at the end. By the Director of Public Instruction, Assam. Foolscap, stitched, with cover. For the years—1899-1900, 1900-01, and 1902-03, Re. 1, or 1s. 6d. (each year).

Ivory-Carving—

Monograph on — in Assam. Deals with historical aspect of the industry, causes of its decline, class and number of persons now acquainted with ivory-carving in Assam; value of articles turned out, industry on the verge of extinction, and a list of articles made of ivory with their usual prices. By James Donald, M.A., I.C.S. Published 1900. Royal 8vo. As. 2, or 2d.

Jail—

Report on the Administration of the — Department in Assam. Report, Imperial Statements, Provincial Statements, and Resolution of the Chief Commissioner at the end. By the Inspector General of Jails, Assam. Foolscap, stitched, with cover. For the years—1899, 1900, 1901, 1902, and 1903, Re. 1, or 1s. 6d. (each year).

Kachari—

An Historical and Descriptive Account of the — Tribe in the North Cachar Hills, with specimens of tales and folk-lore. By C. A. Soppitt. (Reprinted with an introduction by B. C. Stuart Baker, 1901.) Published 1885. Super-royal 8vo, flush bound. Re. 1, or 1s. 6d.

Outline Grammar of the — (Bara) Language, as spoken in the Darrang District, Assam, with illustrative sentences, notes, reading lessons, and a short vocabulary. The grammar proper is preceded by a philological and historical sketch of the language. The reading lessons are given in Kachari, written in Roman character; and the vocabulary, which is from Kachari into Assamese and English, contains most of the words used in the reading lessons. By Rev. S. Endle. Published 1884. Royal 8vo, stitched, with cover. Rs. 2, or 3s.

A Collection of — Folk-Tales and Rhymes. Contains a few Kachari Folk-Tales and Rhymes. (This is intended to serve as a supplement to the Rev. S. Endle's Kachari Grammar and as a reading-book for those who have acquired an elementary knowledge of the Kachari Language.) By J. D. Anderson, I.C.S. Published 1895. Royal 8vo, flush bound. Re. 1, or 1s. 6d.

Kachcha Naga (Empeo)—

A Short Account of the — Tribe in the North Cachar Hills, with an outline grammar, vocabulary, and illustrative sentences. Ethnographical and historical account; social and religious condition of tribe; outline grammar of tribal language dealing with orthography, etymology and syntax, with exercises on translation; vocabulary from English to Kachcha Naga, containing most of the words in every-day use and used in the reading lessons and exercises given in the book. By C. A. Soppitt. Published 1885. Royal 8vo, stitched, with cover. Rs. 2, or 3s.

Kala-azar—

Report of an investigation of the epidemic in Assam of —. History of *kala-azar*; clinical description of *kala-azar*, with illustrative cases and treatment; blood changes in *kala-azar* and Anchylostomiasis; pathology and nature of *kala-azar*; general course and distribution of epidemic; communicability of *kala-azar*; origin of disease and its resemblance to the «Burdwan Fever»; conclusion as to nature of epidemic and method of infection; recommendations; two Appendices on anæmia of coolies and on spread of *kala-azar* and how to check it, and a glossary of medical and scientific terms used. By Captain L. Rogers, M.B., B.S., F.R.C.S., I.M.S. Published 1897. Royal 8vo, cloth, full bound. Rs. 3, or 4s. 6d. (3a. or 3d.)

Ketse Keshu Mha Kechuka—

Acts of the Apostles in Angami Naga translated from the Greek with the Revisers' Reading. By Rev. S. W. Rivenburg, M.A., M.D. Published 1904. Royal 8vo, stitched, with cover. As. 4, or 5d.

Khamti—

Outline Grammar of the — Language, as spoken by the Khamtis residing in the neighbourhood of Sadiya, with illustrative sentences, phrase-book, and vocabulary. The preface gives a short historical account of the people and the language. Exercises in the Khâmti character transliterated and translated into English. The Vocabulary is from English into Khamti with English transliteration. By F. J. Needham, C.I.E. Published 1894. Royal 8vo, flush bound. Re. 1, or 1s. 6d.

Khasi and Jaintia Hills—

Report on the —, 1853. Report on the Khasi and Jaintia Hills; sanitary condition of the Cherra station and jail; history of the Political Agency and its resources; Khasi chiefs; treaties with Khasi chieftains; account of Khasi courts of judicature and of the Khasi form of Government; explanation regarding the proceedings in certain cases; missionary enterprise, educational and evangelical; and minute by the Most Hon'ble the Governor of Bengal and Resolution of the Government of Bengal on Mr. Mills' Report. By A. J. M. Mills, Officiating Judge, Sudder Court (on deputation). Published 1901. Foolscap, stitched, with cover. Re. 1, or 1s. 6d.

Koch—

The — Kings of Kámrupa. An historical sketch of the Koch dynasty of Kamrup. [A Reprint from the Journal, Asiatic Society of Bengal, Volume LXII, Part I, N°. 4, 1893.] By E. A. Gait, I.C.S. Published 1895. Royal 8vo, stitched, with cover. Re. 1, or 1s. 6d.

Kuki-Lushai—

A Short Account of the — Tribes on the North-East Frontier (Districts Cachar, Sylhet, Naga Hills, etc., and the North Cachar Hills), with an outline grammar of the Rangkhol-Lushai language and a comparison of Lushai with other dialects. Ethnographical and historical account; social and religious condition of tribes; outline grammar of tribal language dealing with orthography, etymology, and syntax, with exercises on translation; vocabulary from English to the tribal dialect containing most of the words in every-day use and used in the reading lessons and exercises given in the book. By C. A. Soppitt. Published 1887. Royal 8vo, stitched, with cover. Rs. 2, or 3s.

Labour and Emigration—

Rules under the Assam — Act, VI of 1901, made by the Chief Commissioner of Assam. Published 1902. Foolscap, stitched, with cover. As. 8, or 9d.

Lac—

Note on the — Industry of Assam. Bulletin N°. 6 (Agricultural Department, Assam), Industrial Series N°. 1. Production of lac in Assam; exports of lac from Assam; trees on which lac is found or reared; method of rearing lac; manufactured lac; lac-dye; composition of lac-made colours; lac-wares; how lac is applied to wood; woods used in making lac-toys, etc., and miscellaneous uses of lac. By B. C. Basu, B.A., M.R A.C., M.R.A.S. (Eng.). Published 1900. Royal 8vo, stitched, with cover. As. 2, or 2d.

Land and Revenue—

Assam — Regulation, I of 1886, as amended by Regulation II of 1889. This is an enactment of the Legislative Council of the Governor-General for regulating the assessment of land revenue in Assam. Published under the authority of the Chief Commissioner of Assam. Published 1894. Foolscap, stitched. As. 15, or 1s. 5d. [Reprinted at the Assam Secretariat Press.] In Bengali. Published 1900. Foolscap, tacked. As. 15, or 1s. 5d.

Land Records and Agriculture—

Report of the Department of —, Assam. Report, Appendices, and Resolution of the Chief Commissioner at the end. By the Director, Department of

Land Records and Agriculture, Assam. Foolscap, stitched with cover. For the years — 1899-1900 to 1901-02 and 1902-03, Re. 1 or 1s. (each year).

Land Revenue—

Report on the Administration of the — in Assam. Report and Statements. Compiled in the office of the Secretary to the Chief Commissioner of Assam. Foolscap, stitched, with cover. For the years — 1899-1900 and 1900-01, Re. 1, or 1s. 6d. (each year).

Report on the Administration of the — in the Assam Valley Districts. Report, Statement, Appendices, and Resolution of the Chief Commissioner at the end. By the Commissioner, Assam Valley Districts. Foolscap, stitched, with cover. For the years — 1899-1900, 1900-01, 1901-02, and 1902-03, Re. 1, or 1s. 6d. (each year).

Resolution on the Land Revenue Administration of Assam. Compiled in the office of the Secretary to the Chief Commissioner of Assam. Foolscap, stitched, with cover. For the years — 1901-02 and 1902-03, As. 8, or 9d.

Lhota Naga—

Outline Grammar of the — Language, with a vocabulary and illustrative sentences. A short philological sketch of the language, grammar, and illustrative sentences from English into Lhota. The vocabulary is from English to Lhota. By Rev. W. E. Witter, M.A. Published 1888. Royal 8vo, flush bound. Rs. 2, or 3s.

List, Civil—

The Quarterly — for the Province of Assam. List of Officers in Civil employ in Assam. Compiled in the office of the Secretary to the Chief Commissioner of Assam. Royal 8vo, stitched, with cover. Issued quarterly. From 1st January 1900 to 1st April 1904. As. 11, or 1s. (per quarter).

List, Classified—

and Distribution Return of Establishment, Public Works Department, Assam. List of officers and subordinates under the Public Works Department in Assam. Compiled in the office of the Secretary to the Chief Commissioner of Assam in the Public Works Department. Royal 8vo, stitched, with cover. Issued quarterly. From 31st December 1899 to 31st March 1904. As. 2, or 2d. (per quarter).

Lushai—

A Grammar and Dictionary of the — Language (Dulien Dialect). Part I— Grammar, Part II—Useful Sentences, Part III—Dictionary from Lushai to English, Part IV—Dictionary from English to Lushai. By Rev. J. Herbert Lorrain and Rev. Fred. W. Savidge. Published 1898. Super-royal 8vo, flush bound. Rs. 3, or 4s. 6d.

Lushai-English Primer (Mizo Leh Sâp Tawng Hma-bu). A Primer, containing 271 lessons in Lushai in Roman character with English translation. Part I by Edwin Rowlands, Part II by David E. Jones, Welsh Presbyterian Mission,

North Lushai Hills. Published 1903. Super-royal 8vo, flush bound. As. 12, or 1s. 1d.

Lushai Primer (Mi-Zo Leh Vai Thon Thu)—A Primer, containing 10 reading lessons in Lushai in Roman character without any English translation. By Major Shakespear, C.I.E., D.S.O., I.S.C. Published 1898. Super-royal 8vo, stitched, with cover. Re. 1, or 1s. 6d.

Lushai Primer (Mi-Zo Zir Tir Bu). [2nd edition.]—A Lushai Primer written in Roman character. Alphabet, spelling lessons, easy reading lessons (without English version), and arithmetical tables of calculation. Published 1901. Super-royal 8vo, stitched, with cover. As. 2, or 2d. (6p., or 1d.) 3rd edition. Published 1903. Royal 8vo, stitched, with cover. As. 2, or 2d. (6p. or 1d.)

Manipuri—

Manipuri Grammar, Vocabulary, and Phrase-Book, to which are added some Manipuri proverbs and specimens of Manipuri correspondence. Grammar, vocabulary, phrase-book, specimens of Manipuri correspondence (Manipuri words and sentences have been written in Bengali character and then transliterated into Roman character). By A. J. Primrose, I.C.S. Published 1888. Royal 8vo, stitched, with cover. Rs. 2, or 3s.

Mensuration and Surveying—

Manual of — for Mandals and Patwaris in Assam. Part I—Mensuration; Part II—Surveying. By F. J. Monahan, I.C.S., and Babu Giris Chandra Datta. Published 1900. Super-royal 8vo, cloth, half-bound. Re. 1, or 1s. 6d. In Bengali. As. 11, or 1s. In Assamese. As. 8, or 9d.

Mikir—

Mikir Primary Arithmetic. By Rev. P. E. Moore and Rev. J. M. Carvell. Published 1904. Super-royal 8vo, flush bound. As. 4, or 5d.

Moshang Naga—

A Collection of a few — words. A few Moshang Naga words with their English synonyms; instructions to determine the parts of speech of the words in the language. By F. J. Needham, C.I.E. Published 1897. Royal 8vo, stitched, with cover. As. 4, or 5d.

Municipalities—

Report on — in Assam. Report, Appendix, and Statements. Compiled in the office of the Secretary to the Chief Commissioner of Assam. Foolscap, stitched, with cover. For the years—1899-1900 and 1900—01. Re. 1, or 1s. 6d. (each year).

Resolution by the Chief Commissioner on the Working of — in Assam. Compiled in the office of the Secretary to the Chief Commissioner of Assam. Foolscap, stitched, with cover. During—1901-02 and 1902-03. Re. 1, or 1s. 6d. (each year).

Pharmacopœia—

The Assam — and Prescriber's Companion for use in all Civil Dispensaries. Contains instructions regarding dispensing and care of drugs, and the preservation of surgical instruments and appliances; also some general prescriptions. By Colonel C. W. Carr-Calthrop, M.D., CH.D., I.M.S. Published 1900. Demy 8vo, flush bound. As. 12, or 1s. 2d. 2nd edition. Published 1903. Re. 1, or 1s. 4d.

Police—

Assam — Manual, in Bengali. Deals with police stations, outposts, pounds, etc. Compiled in the office of the Inspector-General of Police, Assam. Published 1900. Super-royal 8vo, flush bound. Re. 1, or 1s. 6d.

Report on the Administration of the — Department in Assam. Report, appendices, and resolution of the Chief Commissioner at the end. By the Inspector-General of Police, Assam. Foolscap, stitched, with cover. For the years—1899, 1900, 1901, 1902, and 1903, Re. 1, or 1s. 6d. (each year).

Public Works—

Report on the Administration of the — Department. Part I deals with Imperial and Provincial public works and railways; and Part II deals with local public works. Compiled in the office of the Secretary to the Chief Commissioner of Assam in the Public Works Department. Foolscap, stitched, with cover. For the years—1898-99, 1899-1900, and 1902-03, Re. 1, or 1s. 6d. (each year).

Registration—

Report on the Administration of the — Department in Assam. Report, forms, and resolution of the Chief Commissioner at the end. By the Inspector-General of Registration, Assam. Foolscap, stitched, with cover. For the years—1899-1900, Re. 1, or 1s. 6d.; 1900-01, As. 11, or 1s.; (triennium) 1899-1900 to 1901-02, Re. 1, or 1s. 6d.

Statistics of the — Department in Assam, with brief explanatory notes. By A. W. Davis, I.C.S., Inspector General of Registration, Assam. Foolscap, stitched, with cover. For the years—1902 and 1903, As. 8, or 9d. (each year).

Research, Historical—

Report on the Progress of — in Assam. Deals with coins, inscriptions on rocks, temples, cannon, etc., copper plates, Ahom *buranjis*, other historical writings, quasi-historical writings, religious works, folk-lore and mythology. The Appendices contain, among other things, a list of archæological remains in Assam and an account of the rise and progress of journalism in the Assam Valley. By E. A. Gait, I.C.S. Published 1897. Foolscap, stitched, with cover. Re. 1, or 1s. 6d.

Rules and Orders—

Supplement to the Manual of Local — made under enactments applying to Assam, to the 31st March 1902. Compiled in the office of the Secretary to the Chief Commissioner of Assam, Published 1902. Super-royal 8vo, flush bound. Re. 1, or 1s. 6d.

Sanitation—

Report on — in Assam. Report, appendices, and resolution of the Chief Commissioner at the end. By the Principal Medical Officer and Sanitary Commissioner, Assam. Foolscap, stitched, with cover. For the years — 1899, Re. 1, or 1s. 6d.; and 1900 to 1903. As. 11, or 1s. (each year).

Tea-Garden —, being a few remarks on the construction of coolie lines and the sanitary management of coolies, with special reference to the prevention of the disease known as anæmia of coolies, *Beri-beri*, and Anchylostomiasis. By Dr. Geo. M. Giles, M.B., F.R.C.S., SAN.SCI. CERT.UNIV., Lond., Surgeon, I.M.S. Published 1891. Royal 8vo, stitched, with cover. As. 8, or 9d. (6p., or 1d.)

School-Management—

A Treatise on — and Methods of Teaching. Mechanical arrangement of schools (house, furniture, apparatus, etc.) and methods of teaching. By Dvijendra Nath Neogi, B.A. Published 1900. Royal 8vo, flush bound. Re. 1, or 1s. 6d. (2a., or 2d.)

Season and Crops—

Report on the Season and Crops of Assam. Foolscap, stitched, with cover. For the years — 1901-02, 1902-03 and 1903-04, As. 8, or 9d. (each year).

Silk-Cloths—

Monograph on the — of Assam. History of the industry, the *Eri* worm and silk and the *Muga* worm and silk. By B. C. Allen, B.A., I.C.S. Published 1899. Super-royal 8vo, stitched, with cover. As. 4, or 5d.

Singpho—

Outline Grammar of the — Language as spoken by the Singphos, Dowanniyas, and others residing in the neighbourhood of Sadiya, with illustrative sentences, phrase book, and vocabulary. The preface gives a brief account of the philology of the tribal language. The grammar proper is followed by exercises and a vocabulary. The exercises are given in Singpho written in Roman character and then rendered into English. The vocabulary is from English into Singpho. By F. J. Needham, C.I.E. Published 1889. Royal 8vo, stitched with cover. Rs. 2, or 3s.

Stamp—

Report on the Administration of the — Department in Assam. Report and statements. By the Superintendent of Stamps, Assam. Foolscap, stitched, with cover. For the years — 1899-1900, 1900-01, and (triennium) 1899-1900 to 1901-02, As. 8, or 9d. (each).

Statistics of the Stamp Department in Assam for the year 1902-03, with brief explanatory notes. By A. W. Davis, I.C.S., Superintendent of Stamps, Assam. Published 1903. Foolscap, stitched, with cover. As. 8, or 9d.

Survey and Settlement—

Report on — Operations in Assam. Traverse survey, cadastral survey, record of rights, revision of survey and classification, demarcation of special estates, results, tours, inspections, and case-work. Resolution of Chief Commissioner at the end. By the Director, Department of Land Records and Agriculture, Assam. Foolscap, stitched, with cover. For the years ending 30th September—1899, 1900, and 1901, Re. 1, or 1s. 6d. (each year).

Tea-Culture—

Report on — in Assam. Report and Statements. Compiled in the office of the Secretary to the Chief Commissioner of Assam. Foolscap, stitched, with cover. For the years — 1899, 1900, and 1901, Re. 1, or 1s. 6d. (each year); and 1902 and 1903. As. 8, or 9d.

Terms, Vernacular—

Glossary of — ordinarily used in official correspondence in the Province of Assam. Contains technical terms generally adopted in official use. Compiled in the Assam Secretariat Office. Published 1879. Royal 8vo, stitched, with cover. As. 8, or 9d. (1a, or 1d.)

Tombs or Monuments—

List of Inscriptions on — in Assam. Compiled in the office of the Chief Commissioner of Assam. Published 1902. Foolscap, stitched, with cover. Re. 1-4, or 1s. 10d.

Trade—

Foreign. — Report on the Foreign — of Assam. Statistical tables showing the trade between Assam and the adjoining foreign countries. By the Director, Department of Land Records and Agriculture, Assam. Published 1899. Foolscap, stitched, with cover. Triennial. For the three years ending the 31st March — 1899 and 1902. Re. 1, or 1s. 6d. (each year).

Rail and River-borne. — Report on the Rail and River-borne — of the Province of Assam. Report and appendices. By the Director, Department of Land Records and Agriculture, Assam. Foolscap, stitched, with cover. For the years — 1899-1900, 1900-01, 1901-02, and 1902-03, Re. 1, or 1s. 6d. (each year).

Rail and River-borne. — Returns of the Rail and River-borne — of the Province of Assam. Statistical tables of trade. Compiled in the office of the Director, Department of Land Records and Agriculture. Assam. Foolscap, stitched, with cover. Issued quarterly. Re. 1, or 1s. 6d. (per quarter).

Report on the Trade between Assam and the adjoining Foreign Tribes and Countries. By F. C. Henniker, I.C.S., Director, Department of Land Records and Agriculture, Assam. Foolscap, stitched, with cover. For the years — 1902-03 and 1903-04, Re. 1, or 1s. 6d. (each year).

Tsangla-Bhutanese—

Some — Sentences, Part III. The sentences are rendered from English into Tsangla-Bhutanese, written in Roman character, and they were designed to form Part III of a Tsangla-Bhutanese Grammar, on which the late Mr. E. Stack was engaged, at the time of his death in 1887. By E. Stack, I.C.S. Published 1897. Royal 8vo, flush bound. Re. 1, or 1s. 6d.

Vaccination—

Report on — in Assam. Report, annual forms and appendices, and Resolution of the Chief Commissioner at the end. Compiled by Principal Medical Officer and Sanitary Commissioner, Assam. Foolscap, stitched, with cover. For the years — 1899-1900, Re. 1, or 1s. 6d.; 1900-01 and (triennium) 1899-1900 to 1901-02, As. 11, or 1s (each year).

Vaccination Returns of the Province of Assam, with brief explanatory notes. Foolscap, stitched, with cover. For the season — 1902-1903 and 1903-04, As. 11, or 1s. (each).

Vocabulary—

An English-Mikir — with Assamese Equivalents, to which have been added a few Mikir phrases. By S. P. Kay. Published 1904. Superroyal 8vo. flush bound. Re. 1-8, or 2s. 3d.

Wood-Carving—

Monograph on — in Assam. Carving by the Hindus for religious purposes; carved furniture, implements, conveyances, etc.; woods selected for carving; implements for carving; carving among the hill tribes; carvers; present state of the industry and its prospects. A. Majid, B.A., LL.B., Assistant Commissioner, Habiganj, Sylhet. Published 1903. Royal 8vo, stitched, with cover. As. 12, or 1s. 2d.

II [1]).

2207. —

Bulletin No. 10 (Agricultural Series No. 6).—The Shillong Government Farm Bulletin No. 1. Compiled by the Department of Land Records and Agriculture, Assam. Published 1904. Royal 8vo, stitched, with cover.

Corps Rules of the Assam Valley Light Horse.—Assam Valley, Light Horse Corps Rules as approved by the Hon'ble Mr. J. B. Fuller, C.S.I., C.I.E., I.C.S., Chief Commissioner of Assam, and Honorary Colonel, Assam Valley Light Horse, Surma Valley Light Horse, and Shillong Volunteer Rifles, on 4th September 1902, and Regulations for enrolment, duties, competitions, etc. By Lieutenant-Colonel C. T. Jessop, Commandant, Assam Valley Light Horse. Published 1903. Royal 8vo, flush bound.

Ka Kitab Jingkoit.—Khasi translation of Way to Health. By Rev. E. Williams. Published 1903. Foolscap 8vo, stitched, with cover.

---

1) D'après les pages 87—88 du *General Catalogue*, Part 3, No. 9 (voir supra, no. 1674).

Report—

(Administrative) on the Census of Assam, 1901.—Enumeration; Slip copying; Slip sorting and Compilation; Extracts from District Reports; Selections from Circulars issued to District Officers; Rules for Slip copying and Slip sorting with comments. By B. C. Allen, B.A., I.C.S., Superintendent of Census Operations, Assam. Published 1902. Foolscap, flush bound.

on the Administration of the Lushai Hills for 1899-1900, 1900-01, 1901-02, and 1902-03.—District Administration, Political, Revenue and impressed labour, Inspections and tours, Civil Police, Civil and Criminal Justice, Military Police, Medical, Transport and Supplies, Public Works, Telegraph and Postal arrangements, Education, Weather and Crops, Health and Material Condition of the People, Trade, and Summary and Conclusion, Foolscap folio, stitched, with cover.

on the Administration of the Political Agency, Manipur, for 1899-1900, 1900-01, 1901-02, 1902-03, and 1903-04.—General observations; Part I, Land Revenue; Part II, Case Work; and Part III, Survey and Settlement. By Lieutenant-Colonel H. St. P. Maxwell, C.S.I., I.S.C., Political Agent in Manipur and Superintendent of the State. Foolscap folio, stitched, with cover.

of the Assam Valley Light Horse for 1899-1900, 1900-01, 1901-02, and 1902-03.—Introductory remarks by Commandant; Roll of Officers and Staff, Government of India letters; Extracts from Regimental Orders; Roll of members entitled to Capitation Allowance; Certificate from Deputy Assistant Adjutant-General for Musketry; Civil Chief Master Armourer's Report; Rolls of Marksmen, of Members in possession of Proficiency Certificates, of Honorary Members, and of Winners, Prize shooting; Capitation grant account for the year; Statement of Assets and Liabilities; Abstract of Capitation grant claim; Act No. X of 1896; Rules and Regulations of the Corps; Orders of Dress; Orders for wearing Distinguishing Badges and Chevrons; Signals; Points to be specially noted in reconnaissance of a country; Hints on the Care of Arms, Accoutrements, Saddlery, etc.; Mobilization Rules; Defence of Positions, etc.; Rules for the grant of "The Volunteer Officers' Decoration" and of "The Volunteer Long Service Medal"; Rules for the Issue and Custody of Ammunition; Tables of Musketry Course; Short History of the Corps; Diagrams from the Manual of Elementary and Field Engineering. Super-royal 8vo, stitched, with cover.

on the Native States and Frontier Tribes of Assam for 1899-1900, 1900-01, 1901-02, 1902-03, and 1903-04.—Contains the annual accounts of the Manipur Native State and the Frontier tribes of the Naga Hills, Khasi and Jaintia Hills, Garo Hills, Lushai Hills, Kamrup, Darrang, Sibsagar, and Lakhimpur district. Compiled in the Assam Secretariat. Foolscap, stitched, with cover.

on the Re-assessment of *Ilam*, Pratabgarh, *Raiyatwari* and other temporarily-settled estates in the district of Sylhet.—Report of the *Ilam* Settlement Officer under rule 7 of the Rules for the Re-settlement of those estates, containing the results of his classification of villages and lands. The report is preceded by a Note by the Director, Department of Land Records and Agriculture, Assam, on the Re-assessment of *Ilam* Estates in Sylhet, and a Note by the Deputy Commissioner, Sylhet, on the proposals of the *Ilam* Settlement Officer. By Babu Giris Chandra Das, Settlement Officer, with a Note by D. H. Lees, I.C.S., Officiating Director, Department of Land Records and Agriculture, Assam. Published 1900. Foolscap, tacked.

(final) on the Re-settlement of the Cachar-district for 1894-99.—Introductory; History of the Survey and Preparation of Record of Rights; Demarcation; Re-assessment; Results; Receipt and Expenditure; Agency for the Maintenance of Settlement Records; Miscellaneous; Appendices A to L; Conclusion. The Report is preceded by the Remarks of the Director, Department of Land Records and Agriculture, Assam, and followed by the Resolution of the Chief Commissioner. By Rai Sarat Chandra Banarji, Bahadur, M.A., B.L., Settlement Officer, Cachar. Published 1901. Foolscap, stitched, with cover.

on Successions to Siemships in the Khasi States.—Captain Herbert's forwarding letter; abstract of the systems of succession; reports on the systems of succession prevailing in the Khasi States; appendices containing the proceedings of the Deputy Commissioner and statements of Siems, Lyngdops, mantris, lyngskors, etc., regarding the systems of succession. By Captain D. Herbert, I.A., Deputy Commissioner, Khasi and Jaintia Hills. Published 1903. Foolscap, half bound.

Rules of Business in the Assam Secretariat.—Constitution of the office, New receipts, Referencing, Noting, Drafting, Copying and Issuing, Branch Diaries, Recording and Compilation of Proceedings, Record Branch, Library, Accounts and Statistics, Returns, Reports, Manuals, compiled and issued by the Assam Secretariat, Arrear Lists, Treatment of confidential cases, General Appendices. Compiled in the Assam Secretariat. Published 1901. Demy 8vo, stitched, with cover.

Additions.

2208 [25*bis*]. — Birma und seine Zustände, von Ferdinand Hué. (*Das Ausland*, LVIII, 1885, pp. 949—953, 967—970.)

2209 [57]. — *‘Burma: a Handbook of Practical, Commercial, and Political Information’. By Sir George Scott, K.C.I.E., with special articles by recognized authorities on Burma. London: The De La More Press. 1906.

　　Notice: *Geogr. Journal*, October 1907, pp. 431—433. By J. R. Hobday.

2210 [57]. — The Province of Burma. A Report Prepared on Behalf of the University of Chicago. By Alleyne Ireland, F.R.G.S. (Colonial Administration in the Far East, Vols. I and II). Boston, U.S.A., Houghton Mifflin. pp. XXI + 1,023.

> [These are the first two volumes of a comprehensive work on Comparative Colo-
> nization in 12 volumes by the «Colonial Commissioner of the University of
> Chicago», covering British, French, Dutch, and American colonial methods, and
> including Burma, British North Borneo, Sarawak, Hong-kong, the Straits
> Settlements, the Federated Malay States, Tonkin, Annam, Cochin China, Cam-
> bodia, Laos, Java, and the Philippines.]
> Notice: *Times Weekly Ed. Lit. Sup.*, 8 Nov. 1907—Dec. 13, 1907.

2211 [93]. — The Course of the Upper Irawadi. By Malcolm Maclaren, D.Sc., F.G.S. (*Geogr. Journal*, Nov. 1907, pp. 507—511).

2212. — The Life and Adventures of John Christopher Wolf, late Principal Secretary of State at Jaffanapatnam, in Ceylon; together with a Description of that Island, its Natural Productions, and the Manners and Customs of its Inhabitants. Translated from the Original German. To the Whole is added, a short, but comprehensive Description of the same Island. By Mr. Eschels-kroon. — London, Printed for G. G. J. and J. Robinson, in Pater-noster-Row, MDCCLXXXV, in-8, pp. VIII—344.

> Bib. nat. O² l 23. — Voir No. 176.

2213 [191]. — Général de Beylié. — Fouilles à Prome (Birmanie). Paris, Ernest Leroux, 1907, in-8, pp. 33, 4 pl.

> Ext. de la *Revue archéologique*, 1907, II, pp. 193—235.

2214 [191]. — Publications de la Société française des fouilles archéologiques — I — Prome et Samara — Voyage archéologique en Birmanie et en Mésopotamie par le Général L. de Beylié. Paris, Ernest Leroux, 1907, gr. in-8, pp. 146.

2215 [264bis]. — The Holy Bible containing the Old and New Testaments, in Sgau Karen. — Translated by Francis Mason. Second Edition, ... 5000. Rangon: American Mission Press. Published by the American and Foreign Bible Society, the Burmah Bible and Tract Society, and by the American Baptist Missionary Union. C. Bennett. 1867, gr. in-8, à 2 col.

2216 [511bis]. — Prehistoric Man in Burma. By Rodway C. J. Swinhoe. (*The Zoologist*, Sept. 1902, pp. 321—336, 1 pl.)

— Some further Notes on chipped Flints at Yenangyoung, Upper Burma. By Rodway C. J. Swinhoe. (*Ibid.*, 1903, pp. 254—9).

2217 [661bis]. — A Contribution to our knowledge of the Birds occurring in the Southern Shan States, Upper Burma. By Lt. Col. C. T. Bingham. (*The Ibis*, 1903, 8 Ser., III, pp. 584—606).

2218 [665]. — On some new Species of Silver-Pheasants from Burma. By Eugene W. Oates. (*Annals and Mag. Nat. Hist.*, 7th Ser., XIV, 1904, pp. 283—7).

2219 [665bis]. — Descriptions of Indian and Burmese Land-Shells referred to the Genera *Macrochlamys*, Bensonia, Taphrospira (gen. nov.), Microcystina, Euplecta, and Polita. By W. T. Blanford. (*Proc. Zool. Soc. Lond.*, 1904, Vol. II, pp. 441—7, 1 pl.)

2220 [665bis]. — Notes on the Goral found in Burma. By Major G. H. Evans. (*Ibid.*, 1905, Vol. II, Pt. II, pp. 311—314).

2221 [665]. — Descriptions of new Species of *Sphegidae* and *Ceropalidae* from the Khasia Hills, Assam. By P. Cameron. (*Ann. and Mag. Nat. Hist.*, 7th Ser., XV, 1905, pp. 218—229; 415—424, 467—477).

2222 [665]. — On a new Race of *Sciurus lokriodes* from Burma. By J. Lewis Bonhote. (*Ibid.*, 7th Ser., XVIII, 1906, pp. 338—9).

2223 [809 *bis*]. — The Fauna of the Miocene Beds of Burma, by Fritz Noetling. (*Palaeontologia Indica*, N. S., Vol. I, N°. 3, 1901, pp. 378, 25 pl.).

2224 [809 *bis*]. On recent Changes in the Course of the Nam-tu River, Northern Shan States. By T. D. La Touche. (*Records Geolog. Survey India*, XXXIII, Pt. I, 1906, pp. 46—8, 1 pl.).

2225 [809 *bis*]. — Note on the Natural Bridge in the Gokteik Gorge. By T. D. La Touche. (*Ibid.*, XXXIII, Pt. I, 1906, pp. 49—54, 4 pl.).

Entre Maymyo et Lashio, États Shan nord.

2226 [809 *bis*] — On Explosion Craters in the Lower Chindwin District, Burma. By R. D. Oldham. (*Ibid.*, XXXIV, Pt. 2, 1906, pp. 137—147, 2 pl.).

2227 [809 *bis*]. — The Kabat Anticline, near Seiktein, Myingyan District, Upper Burma. By E. H. Pascoe. (*Ibid.*, XXXIV, Pt. 4, 1906, pp. 242—252, 4 pl.

— The Asymmetry of the Yenangyat-Singu Anticline, Upper Burma. By E. H. Pascoe. (*Ibid.*, pp. 253—260, 1 pl.).

— The Northern Part of the Gwegyo Anticline, Mingyan District, Upper Burma. By E. H. Pascoe. (*Ibid.*, pp. 261—265, 2 pl.).

2228 [809 *bis*]. — Note on the Brine-Well at Bawgyo, Northern Shan States. By T. D. La Touche. (*Ibid.*, XXXV, Pt. 2, 1907, pp. 97—101).

2229 [809 *bis*]. — Report on the Gold-bearing Deposits of Loi Twang, Shan States, Burma. By T. D. La Touche. (*Ibid.*, XXXV, Pt. 2, 1907, pp. 102—113).

2230 [809 *bis*]. — [G. H. Tipper]. Further Note on the Trias of Lower Burma and on the occurence of Cardita Beaumonti d'Arch. in Lower Burma. (*Ibid.*, XXXV, Pt. 2, 1907, p. 119).

2231 [809 *bis*]. — [E. H. Pascoe]. — Fossils in the Upper Miocene of the Yenangyaung Oil-field, Upper Burma. (*Ibid.*, XXXV, Pt. 2, 1907, p. 120).

2232 [859 *bis*]. — The Lashio Coal-Field, Northern Shan States. By T. D. La Touche and R. R. Simpson. (*Ibid.*, XXXIII, Pt. 2, 1906, pp. 117—124, 2 pl.).

2233 [859 *bis*]. — The Namma, Man-sang and Man-se-le Coal-Fieds, Northern Shan States, Burma. By R. R. Simpson. (*Ibid.*, XXXIII, Pt. 2, 1906, pp. 125—156, 2 pl.).

2234 [809 *bis*]. — [Guy E. Pilgrim]. — Fossils of the Irrawaddy series from Rangoon. (*Ibid.*, XXXIII, Pt. 2, 1906, pp. 157—8).

2235 [809 *bis*]. — The Lower Palæozoic Fossils of the Northern Shan States, Burma. By F. R. Cowper Reed. (*Palaeontologia Indica*, N. S., II, N°. 3, 1906, in-4, pp. 154 + 1 f. n. ch., 8 pl.).

2236 [1022]. — The S. S. Howland Collection of Buddhist Religious Art in the National Museum by Immanuel M. Casanowicz, Aid, Division of Historic

Archeology — N°. 136. — From the Report of the United States National
Museum for 1904, pages 735—744, with 17 plates. Washington, Government
Printing Office, 1906, in-8.

2237 [1022]. — 'Buddho's Gotamo. — Reden aus der längeren Sammlung
Dīghanikāyo des Pāli-Kanons übersetzt von K. E. Neumann. Vol. I. Munich,
1907. Gr. in-8, pp. x—346.

2238 [1023 bis]. — Pegu, voir p. 296 de la Relation... de Malabar... par le
P. François Barretto, Paris, 1645.

2239 [1191]. — Birmanisches Kunstgewerbe (Globus, Bd. LXIII, 1893, pp.
270—3).

2240 [1259]. — 'Nyein Tun. — Students English-Burmese Dictionary. Rangoon,
1906, in-8.

2241 [1261]. — 'A. Ali. — The Burmese—Hindustani Conversation Manual.
Part. I. In Burmese, Mandalay, 1907, in-16, pp. X, 100.

2242 [1261 bis]. — 'U. Thakeinda. — Heindu Wazana Lingaya Kyan. Hindustani Speaker, in Burmese, Rangoon, 1907. In-12, pp. III—179.

2243 [1305 bis]. — The New Testament of Our Lord and Saviour Jesus Christ
translated into the Burmese from the Original Greek by Rev. A. Judson,
D. D. — Boston: Published by the American Baptist Missionary Union. —
1891, pet. in-8 à 2 col.

2244 [1323 bis]. — 'Ch. Duroiselle. — A Practical Grammar of the Pali
Language. Rangoon, 1906, in-8, pp. 346.

2245 [1323]. — 'Lèdi Sayadaw. — Thátda Thankeik Letswè. Manual of Pâli
Grammar. In Pâli-Burmese. In-16, pp. IV, 255. Rangoon, 1907.

2246 [1323]. — 'Lèdi Sayadaw. — Thátda Thankeik Tiga Kyan. Key to the
Manual of Pâli-Grammar. In Pâli-Burmese. In-8, pp. II—440, Rangoon, 1907.

2247 [1375 bis]. — Birmanische Städte-Legenden. Von Dr. Adolf Bastian.
(Das Ausland, XXXVI, 1863, pp. 641—4).

2248 [1505 bis]. — 'Mandalay and Other Cities of the Past in Burma. By
V. C. Scott O'Connor. Hutchinson, pp. XX—435.
    Notice: Times Lit. Sup., Dec. 18, 1907.

2249 [1401]. — Handbook for Travellers in India, Burma and Ceylon. Sixth
Edition, 1907, in-8.

2250 [1482]. — 'E. Gallois. — En Birmanie. (Revue générale internationale
1898, pp. 35—123). Illustrations.

2251. — Poselstwo do Krolestwa Awy, w roku 1795 na rozkaz wielkiego Rzadty
Jndyiskiego przez Majora Symsa odprawione. Z Wstępem do Historyi Awy,
Pegu, i Arrakanu; z opisaniem tych Kraiow. i Uwagami nad Obyczaiami,
Rządem. i Językiem Birmánskim. z Angielskiego, z przedmowę i uwagami na
Polskie przelozone przez F. T. R. Z Mappę i pięcią Kopersztychami. — W
Krakowie 1807 w Drukarni Tekli Gröblowey, 3 vol. in-12, 8 ff. n. ch. +
pp. 186, 196 + 2 ff. n. ch. tab., 242 + 2 ff. tab.

    Bib. nat. $\frac{O^31}{200}$. — Voir No. 1583.

2252 [1586]. — Tracts, political, geographical, and commercial; on the Dominions of Ava, and the North Western Parts of Hindostaun. — By William Francklin, Major in the Service of the Hon. East India Company, and Author of a Tour to Persia... &c... — London: Printed for T. Cadell and W. Davies, 1811, in-8, pp. x + 1 f. n. ch. tab. + pp. 281.

> Observations on the Embassy to Ava. — On the Commerce of Ava. — Topography and Population of Ava. — Sketch of Rajepootaneh. — Operations of an Army in the West of India. — Plan for the extension and future security of the British Possessions in the East.
>
> «The Documents relating to Ava in the present volume, were procured chiefly from the papers of the late Captain Hiram Cox, whilst deputed on a mission to that court by the government of Bengal». (Pref.)
>
> J. M'Creery, Printer, Black-Horse Court, London.
>
> Bib. nat. $\frac{O^2 1}{22}$.

2252*bis* [1642]. — Reminiscences of the Court of Mandalay Extracts from the Diary of General Horace A. Browne, 1859—1879. Woking, The Oriental Institute, 1907, in-8, pp. 196.

2253 [1719]. — °S. Chatterji. — Purva Vanga. O Asámer Mánachitra. Map of Eastern Bengal and Assam. 1 Sheet. Lithographed. Calcutta, 1907.

2254 [1719]. — °N. Sarma. — Asamíyá Bhúgolsár. Essence of Geography. In Assamese. Eight Edition. Assam, 1907, in-12, pp. ii—120.

2255 [1779*bis*]. — °A Few Notes on Wa. By Captain G. Drage. Rangoon: Superintendent, Government Printing, Burma, 1907.

> «The Was are an uncivilised race of head-hunting hill men who inhabit portions of the Burmese Shan States. Linguistically they are of considerable interest because their dialects, together with those of the Palaung and Riang tribes, occupy a middle place between the Khasi language of Assam and the great Mon-Khmer family of speech».
>
> Notice by C. O. Blagden, *Journ. Roy. As. Soc.*, Jan. 1908, pp. 250—2.

2256 [1785*bis*]. — °Major P. R. T. Gurdon. A short Note on the Āhoms. (Report from the forthcoming *Encyclopaedia of Religion and Ethics*.) Edinburgh, 1907, pet. in-8.

2257 [1886—1888]. — °A Mikir Catechism in the Assamese character. Sibsagar, 1875.

2258 [1886—1888]. — °Sir C. J. Lyall, K.C.S.I. — Note on the geographical distribution and ethnological affinities of the Mikirs. (*Census Report of Assam for* 1881, Calcutta, 1883, pp. 78 et seq.)

> Revu et réimp. dans le *Census* de 1891.

2259 [1886—1888]. — A Grammar and Specimens of the Mikir Language. By Sir C. J. Lyall. (*Indian Antiq.*, XXXII, 1903, pp. 101—111, 205—212).

> According to the Census of 1901 Mikir is spoken in the following Assam Districts:—

District	Number of Speakers
Nowgong	34.275
Sibsagar	22.803
Khasi and Jaintia Hills	13.142
Kamrup	8.026
Darrang	8.106
Elsewhere	931
Total number	82.283

2260 [1886—1888]. — *Miss Pursell. — Arleng Alam. A Mikir Primer. Assam. 1891.

2261 [1886—1888]. — *Note by A. W. Davies on the Relations of the principal Languages of the Nāgā Group. (*Census Report of Assam for* 1891 by E. A. Gait, Shillong, 1892, pp. 163 et seq.)

Compare le Mikir avec les langues des groupes Nāgā et Bodo.

— *E. C. S. Baker. — Account of the Mikirs. (*Ibid.*, p. 254).

2262 [1890*bis*]. — Die Garo=, Khassia= und Naga=Völker an der indisch-birmanischen Grenze. Von Emil Schlagintweit. (*Globus*, XXXIV, 1878, pp. 262—265, 279—282, 295—7).

2263 [2048*bis*]. — Report on the Um-Rileng Coal-beds, Assam, by P. N. Bose. (*Records Geolog. Survey India*, XXXI, Pt. 1, 1904, pp. 35—7, 1 pl.)

HENRI CORDIER.

TABLE.

Birmanie.